AF806590

ISLANDS AND INTERNATIONAL LAW

Islands and their status in international law have become one of the more contentious issues in public international law. However, despite this, there is no contemporary book-length study on the question. This book fills that gap. Written by one of the world's leading public international lawyers, it offers an authoritative overview of how public international law operates in relation to islands. Key issues such as artificial islands, archipelagos, sovereignty, territorial rights, maritime entitlements, and governance are explored in depth. This will become a classic text in the field of international law.

Islands and International Law

Donald R Rothwell

•HART•
OXFORD • LONDON • NEW YORK • NEW DELHI • SYDNEY

HART PUBLISHING

Bloomsbury Publishing Plc

Kemp House, Chawley Park, Cumnor Hill, Oxford, OX2 9PH, UK

1385 Broadway, New York, NY 10018, USA

29 Earlsfort Terrace, Dublin 2, Ireland

HART PUBLISHING, the Hart/Stag logo, BLOOMSBURY and the Diana logo are trademarks of Bloomsbury Publishing Plc

First published in Great Britain 2022

Copyright © Donald R Rothwell, 2022

Donald R Rothwell has asserted his right under the Copyright, Designs and Patents Act 1988 to be identified as Author of this work.

All rights reserved. No part of this publication may be reproduced or transmitted in any form or by any means, electronic or mechanical, including photocopying, recording, or any information storage or retrieval system, without prior permission in writing from the publishers.

While every care has been taken to ensure the accuracy of this work, no responsibility for loss or damage occasioned to any person acting or refraining from action as a result of any statement in it can be accepted by the authors, editors or publishers.

All UK Government legislation and other public sector information used in the work is Crown Copyright ©. All House of Lords and House of Commons information used in the work is Parliamentary Copyright ©. This information is reused under the terms of the Open Government Licence v3.0 (http://www.nationalarchives.gov.uk/doc/open-government-licence/version/3) except where otherwise stated.

All Eur-lex material used in the work is © European Union, http://eur-lex.europa.eu/, 1998–2022.

A catalogue record for this book is available from the British Library.

A catalogue record for this book is available from the Library of Congress.

Library of Congress Control Number: 2022933883

ISBN: HB: 978-1-50995-542-8
ePDF: 978-1-50995-544-2
ePub: 978-1-50995-543-5

Typeset by Compuscript Ltd, Shannon

To find out more about our authors and books visit www.hartpublishing.co.uk. Here you will find extracts, author information, details of forthcoming events and the option to sign up for our newsletters.

PREFACE

This work most probably had its foundations laid during a childhood in which I awoke each day to see Cook Island from my home in Tweed Heads. Cook Island is just one kilometre off the northern New South Wales coast and is named after Captain James Cook, who was the first European to sail along the east coast of Australia. Cook's various voyages of discovery were influential in my early travels that eventually came to encompass the Whitsunday Islands of the Great Barrier Reef, New Zealand, the Hawaiian Islands, and Vancouver Island. Formal studies in law, with an eventual focus on the law of the sea and law of the polar regions, contained an islands dimension. When island-related international law issues arose in those contexts they were always investigated with delight.

The opportunity to undertake a detailed study on islands and international law arose following the completion of a number of senior leadership roles at the Australian National University College of Law. My former Dean, Professor Stephen Bottomley, provided encouragement for me to undertake this research when I departed those posts and I remain grateful for his support. Research and writing on this topic has been inevitably delayed by the COVID-19 pandemic. During periods of lockdown it was reassuring to have this project to work on so as to maintain a steady course. The team at Hart have been of great assistance and I extend my appreciation to Joanne Choulerton, Sasha Jawed, and Sinead Moloney for their contribution to the finalisation of the book.

My research has been immeasurably enhanced by a number of skilled research assistants over the course of the project, and especially Siena Hopkinson and Sam Saunders who proved pivotal at the early and latter stages of the project. A number of colleagues also kindly read drafts of various chapters and provided feedback. I extend many thanks and appreciation to Bill Campbell, Natalie Klein, David Letts, Joanna Mossop, Ash Roach, Imogen Saunders, Karen Scott, Tim Stephens, and Matthew Zagor for their critical insights. Others have also contributed in a number of ways, including Bob Beckman, Sarah Heathcote, Bill Mansfield, Ted McDorman, Erik Molenaar, Alex Oude Elferink, Clive Schofield, and Davor Vidas. It was a singular privilege to have had Judge James Crawford as my doctoral supervisor at the University of Sydney. While that polar law work did not have an islands focus, Judge Crawford's seminal work on *The Creation of States and International Law*, and ongoing editions of *Brownlie's Principles of International Law*, were all very influential at various stages of this project. I remain much indebted to him for his guidance, scholarship, and wisdom over many decades. His untimely death in 2021 was a great loss for the international law community.

My family have been very supportive of this project. Long-haul air travel from Australia to attend conferences, meetings and workshops over a number of decades is exhausting for the whole family and not only the traveller. I extend my thanks to Beth and Jennifer for their support and love throughout all of those years, and for Beth's particular support as copy editor during 2021 COVID lockdowns.

The law is stated as at 2021. Efforts have been made to take into account important legal and political events that have occurred throughout the year. All Internet references are correct as at this year. Place names of islands are given in English throughout. When there are non-English names for certain well known islands, they have been acknowledged.

Donald R Rothwell
Canberra, December 2021

CONTENTS

Preface ... v
List of Abbreviations ... xi
Table of Cases ... xiii
Table of National Laws and Statutes ... xvii
Table of Treaties and Other Instruments ... xxiii

Introduction ... **1**

1. Islands: Geography and Law ... **5**
I. Introduction ... 5
II. Islands and Geography ... 6
III. Islands and Juridical Classification ... 9
IV. Conclusions ... 18

2. Artificial Islands ... **19**
I. Introduction ... 19
II. Scope and Location of Artificial Islands ... 20
III. Historical Legal Framework ... 21
IV. Early State Practice ... 22
V. LOSC ... 23
VI. Contemporary State Practice ... 29
VII. Artificial Islands, Rocks and Land Reclamation ... 33
VIII. Conclusions ... 35

3. Islands and Territoriality ... **38**
I. Introduction ... 38
II. International Law and Territoriality ... 40
III. Islands and Territoriality ... 44
IV. Current State of the Law ... 54
V. Contemporary Island Territorial Disputes ... 65
VI. Conclusions ... 74

4. Islands, Status and Statehood ... **76**
I. Introduction ... 76
II. Islands and the International System ... 77
III. Chapter XI Non-Self-Governing Territories and Chapter XII Trust Territories ... 79

IV. Current Status of Islands 85
V. Special Regimes 98
VI. Conclusions 100

5. Archipelagic States 101
I. Archipelagos and International Law 101
II. Early Legal Developments 103
III. UNCLOS I 104
IV. The Indonesian and Philippines Claims 105
V. UNCLOS III 110
VI. The LOSC and Archipelagic States 112
VII. Archipelagic State Entitlements 120
VIII. Conclusions 140

6. Dependent Archipelagos 142
I. Introduction 142
II. Characterisation 143
III. Baselines 146
IV. Maritime Entitlements 153
V. State Practice 154
VI. Conclusions 160

7. Islands and Maritime Entitlements 162
I. Introduction 162
II. Baselines 163
III. Historic Waters 170
IV. Bays 174
V. Internal Waters 178
VI. Territorial Sea and Contiguous Zone 178
VII. Continental Shelf 180
VIII. Exclusive Economic Zone 183
IX. Conclusions 186

8. Islands and Maritime Boundaries 188
I. Introduction 188
II. Overview of Maritime Boundary Delimitation 190
III. Decisions of International Courts and Tribunals 195
IV. State Practice 204
V. Impact of Islands on Maritime Boundary Delimitation 213
VI. Conclusions 216

9. Islands and Human Rights 217
I. Introduction 217
II. Human Rights Treaties and Islands 218
III. Human Rights Issues and Islands 222
IV. Self-Determination 225
V. Small Island Developing States 234
VI. Conclusions 237

10. Islands and Sea-Level Rise 239
I. Introduction 239
II. Climate Science 240
III. Islands and Artificial Islands 242
IV. Status and Territoriality 243
V. Archipelagic States 245
VI. Maritime Entitlements and Maritime Boundaries 246
VII. Human Rights 249
VIII. Conclusions 250

11. A Regime of Islands? 253
I. Introduction 253
II. Regimes, Islands and International Law 255
III. Fragments of a Regime of Islands 257
IV. A Future Regime of Islands 260

Appendix 1 .... *262*
Bibliography *268*
Index *287*

LIST OF ABBREVIATIONS

ABG	Autonomous Bougainville Government
art(s)	article(s)
ASLP	Archipelagic Sea Lanes Passage
ATS	Australian Treaty Series
BIOT	British Indian Ocean Territory
CARICOM	Caribbean Community
CLCS	Commission on the Limits of the Continental Shelf
CRC	Convention on the Rights of the Child
CTS	Consolidated Treaty Series
EEZ	exclusive economic zone
FSM	Federated States of Micronesia
GPASL	General Provisions on the Adoption, Designation and Substitution of Archipelagic Sea Lanes
Ha	hectare
ICAO	International Civil Aviation Organization
ICCPR	International Covenant on Civil and Political Rights
ICERD	International Convention on the Elimination of all Forms of Racial Discrimination
ICESCR	International Covenant on Economic, Social and Cultural Rights
ICJ	International Court of Justice
ICJ Reps	ICJ Reports
ILA	International Law Association
ILC	International Law Commission
ILR	International Law Reports
IMB	International Maritime Boundaries
IMO	International Maritime Organization
IPCC	Intergovernmental Panel on Climate Change
ITLOS	International Tribunal for the Law of the Sea
km	kilometre
LOSC	Law of the Sea Convention (United Nations Convention on the Law of the Sea)
LTE	low-tide elevation
m	metre
nm	nautical miles
NSGT	non-self-governing territory
NZ	New Zealand

PCA	Permanent Court of Arbitration
PCIJ	Permanent Court of International Justice
PIF	Pacific Islands Forum
PNG	Papua New Guinea
PRC	People's Republic of China
ROC	Republic of China
ROK	Republic of Korea
SAMOA	SIDS Accelerated Modalities of Action
SIDS	Small Island Developing States
SLR	sea-level rise
TAAF	Territory of the French Southern and Antarctic Lands
TRNC	Turkish Republic of Northern Cyprus
UAE	United Arab Emirates
UNGA	United Nations General Assembly
UDHR	Universal Declaration of Human Rights
UK	United Kingdom
UKTS	United Kingdom Treaty Series
UN	United Nations
UNCED	United Nations Conference on Environment and Development
UNCLOS I	First United Nations Conference on the Law of the Sea
UNCLOS II	Second United Nations Conference on the Law of the Sea
UNCLOS III	Third United Nations Conference on the Law of the Sea
UNFCCC	United Nations Framework Convention on Climate Change
UN-OHRLLS	UN Secretary-General's High Representative for the Least Developed Countries, Landlocked Developing Countries and Small Island Developing States
UNSC	United Nations Security Council
UNTAET	United Nations Transitional Administration in East Timor
UNTS	United Nations Treaty Series
US	United States of America
USSR	Union of the Soviet Socialist Republics
USTIA	United States Treaties and Other International Acts
VCLT	Vienna Convention on the Law of Treaties
VOC	Dutch East India Company

TABLE OF CASES

Accordance with International Law of the Unilateral Declaration of Independence in Respect of Kosovo (Advisory Opinion) [2010] ICJ Reps 403 83
Advisory Opinion Concerning the Legality of the Use by a State of Nuclear Weapons in Armed Conflict [1996] ICJ Reps 66 17
Aegean Sea Continental Shelf (Greece v Turkey) (Judgment) [1978] ICJ Reps 3 .... 65–66, 249
Arbitration between Barbados and Trinidad and Tobago (Award) (11 April 2006) PCA Case No 2004-02 .... 190, 193, 195, 200–01
Award of the Arbitral Tribunal in the first stage of the proceedings between Eritrea and Yemen (Territorial Sovereignty and Scope of the Dispute) (*Eritrea v Yemen*) (1998) 22 RIAA 209 .... 49–50, 55, 63, 65
Award of the Arbitral Tribunal in the second stage of the proceedings between Eritrea and Yemen (Maritime Delimitation) (*Eritrea v Yemen*) (1999) 22 RIAA 335 .... 168, 193, 198–99
Case Concerning Delimitation of the Continental Shelf Between the United Kingdom and the French Republic (1979) 18 ILM 397 .... 196, 200, 214–15
Case Concerning East Timor (Portugal v Australia) (Judgment) [1995] ICJ Reps 90 .... 83, 226
Case Concerning Land Reclamation by Singapore in and around the Straits of Johor (*Malaysia v Singapore*) (Provisional Measures) (8 October 2003) ITLOS Reports 2003 33
Case Concerning the Delimitation of Maritime Areas between Canada and the French Republic (10 June 1992) 21 RIAA 265 .... 196–97, 215
Case of the S.S. 'Wimbledon' (1923) PCIJ Rep Series A No 1 .... 256–57, 260
Chagos Marine Protected Area Arbitration (Mauritius v United Kingdom) (Award) (18 March 2015) PCA Case No 011-03 .... 64, 229
Clipperton Island (France v Mexico) (1931) 2 RIAA 1105 .... 1, 45–46, 57, 64, 78
Continental Shelf (Libyan Arab Jamahiriya v Malta) (Judgment) [1985] ICJ Reps 13 .... 162, 189
Continental Shelf (Tunisia v Libya Arab Jamahiriya) (Judgment) [1982] ICJ Reps 18 .... 193, 253
Delimitation of the Maritime Boundary in the Atlantic Ocean (*Ghana v Côte d'Ivoire*) (Judgment) [2017] ITLOS Rep 4 192
Delimitation of the Maritime Boundary in the Bay of Bengal (*Bangladesh v Myanmar*) (Judgment) [2012] ITLOS Rep 4 .... 192, 203–04

Delimitation of the Maritime Boundary in the Gulf of Maine Area (Canada v United States) (Judgment) [1984] ICJ Rep 246..............................193
Dispute Concerning Delimitation of the Maritime Boundary between Mauritius and Maldives in the Indian Ocean (Mauritius v Maldives) (Preliminary Objections Judgment) (28 January 2021) ITLOS Case No 28 ....67, 119, 229
Fisheries Case (United Kingdom v Norway) (Judgment) [1951] ICJ Reps 116..........8, 12, 104, 106, 111, 114, 121, 147–50, 154, 160, 164–67, 171–72
Fisheries Jurisdiction (United Kingdom v Iceland) (Merits) [1974] ICJ Reps 3..........183–84
Frontier Dispute (*Burkina Faso/Republic of Mali)* (Merits) [1986] ICJ Reps 554..........55, 59
Fur Seals Arbitration (*Great Britain v USA*) [1893] in JB Moore, *History and Digest of the International Arbitrations to Which the United States Has Been a Party*, vol 1 (Government Printing Office 1898) 755..........21
Grisbådarna Arbitration (Norway v Sweden) (1910) 4 *American Journal of International Law* 226..........188, 194
Guyana and Suriname (Award) (17 September 2007) PCA Case No 2004-04..........194
In Re Duchy of Sealand (1989) 80 ILR 683..........25
In the Matter of the Arbitration before an Arbitral Tribunal constituted under Annex VII of the 1982 United Nations Convention on the Law of the Sea (Philippines v China) (Award on Jurisdiction and Admissibility) (29 October 2015) PCA Case No 2013-19..........73
In the Matter of the Bay of Bengal Maritime Boundary Arbitration (Bangladesh v India) (Award) (7 July 2014) PCA Case No 2010-16..........204–05, 249
In the Matter of the Maritime Boundary between Timor-Leste and Australia (Award) (9 May 2018) PCA Case No 2016-10..........195
In the Matter of the South China Sea Arbitration before an Arbitral Tribunal constituted under Annex VII of the 1982 United Nations Convention on the Law of the Sea (Philippines v China) (Merits) (12 July 2016) PCA Case No 2013-19..........2–3, 6–7, 12, 15–19, 27–37, 56–57, 73, 120–21, 129, 141, 143, 152, 169, 171–74, 176–77, 243, 246, 253–54, 257–58
Island of Palmas Case (United States of America v The Netherlands) (1928) 2 RIAA 829...........1, 40, 44–46, 55–58, 61–62, 74, 78
Kasikili/Sedudu Island (Botswana v Namibia) (Judgment) [1999] ICJ Reps 1045..........17

Land and Maritime Boundary between Cameroon and Nigeria (Cameroon v Nigeria: Equatorial Guinea intervening) (Judgment) [2002] ICJ Reps 303 .... 194–95, 200
Land, Island and Maritime Frontier Dispute (El Salvador v Honduras; Nicaragua intervening) (Judgment) [1992] ICJ Reps 351 .... 48, 59, 176
Legal Consequences for States of the Continued Presence of South Africa in Namibia (South West Africa) notwithstanding Security Council Resolution 276 (1970) (Advisory Opinion) [1971] ICJ Reps 16........226
Legal Consequences of the Construction of a Wall in the Occupied Palestinian Territory (Advisory Opinion) [2004] ICJ Reps 136........83
Legal Consequences of the Separation of the Chagos Archipelago from Mauritius in 1965 (Advisory Opinion) (25 February 2019) [2019] ICJ Reps 95 .... 2, 39, 66–67, 94, 226–29, 259
Legal Status of Eastern Greenland (Denmark v Norway) [1933] PCIJ Rep Series A/B No 53 .... 1, 46–47, 51–52, 55–58, 62–65, 70, 74, 78, 232
Maritime Delimitation and Territorial Questions between Qatar and Bahrain (Qatar v Bahrain) (Merits) [2001] ICJ Reps 40 .... 7, 11, 13, 50, 58, 63, 102, 119–20, 141, 148, 150–52, 168–69, 191, 193, 199, 215, 258
Maritime Delimitation in the Area between Greenland and Jan Mayen (Denmark v Norway) (Judgment) [1993] ICJ Reps 38........ 12–13, 194, 197–98, 215
Maritime Delimitation in the Black Sea (Romania v Ukraine) (Judgment) [2009] ICJ Reps 61 .... 1, 167, 192–95, 201–02, 215
Maritime Delimitation in the Caribbean Sea and the Pacific Ocean (Costa Rica v Nicaragua) and Land Boundary in the Northern Part of Isla Portillos (Costa Rica v Nicaragua) (Merits) [2018] ICJ Reps 139. 14
Maritime Dispute (Peru v Chile) (Judgment) [2014] ICJ Reps 3........194
Minquiers and Ecrehos Case (France v United Kingdom) (Judgment) [1953] ICJ Reps 47 .... 1, 12, 47–48, 56, 58, 62, 97
Monte Confurco (Seychelles v France) (Prompt Release Judgment) ITLOS Reports 2000, 86........14
Namibia (Advisory Opinion) [1971] ICJ Reps 16........83
North Sea Continental Shelf (Federal Republic of Germany v Denmark; Federal Republic of Germany v Netherlands) (Judgment) [1969] ICJ Rep 3 43
Obligations concerning Negotiations relating to Cessation of the Nuclear Arms Race and to Nuclear Disarmament (Marshall Islands v UK) (Preliminary Objections Judgment) [2016] ICJ Reps 833. 90
Pulp Mills on the River Uruguay (Argentina v Uruguay) [2010] ICJ Reps 14 36
Sovereignty over Pedra Branca/Pulau Betu Puteh, Middle Rocks and South Ledge Case (Malaysia v Singapore) (Merits) [2008] ICJ Reps 12........ 9, 13, 52–53, 56, 58–59, 62, 190

Sovereignty over Pulau Ligitan and Pulau Sipadan (Indonesia v Malaysia) (Merits) [2002] ICJ Reps 625 .... 50–52, 56, 64–65, 107, 109, 113, 122,
Territorial and Maritime Dispute (Nicaragua v Colombia) (Merits) [2012] ICJ Reps 624 .... 7, 13, 18, 53–54, 58–59, 63–65, 195, 202–03, 215
Territorial and Maritime Dispute between Nicaragua and Honduras in the Caribbean Sea (Nicaragua v Honduras) (Merits) [2007] ICJ Reps 659 .... 13, 17, 51, 56, 59, 65, 191–92, 195, 201, 215, 255
United States Diplomatic and Consular Staff in Tehran (United States of America v Iran) (Judgment) [1980] ICJ Reps 3 255
Volga Case (Russian Federation v Australia) (Prompt Release Judgment) (23 December 2002) ITLOS Reports 2002, 10 14
Western Sahara (Advisory Opinion) [1975] ICJ Reps 12 .... 83, 227

TABLE OF NATIONAL LAWS AND STATUTES

Antigua and Barbuda

Maritime Areas Act 1982 (Act No 18).. 116, 132–33, 140

Australia

Constitution Act 1934 (Tasmania)..87

Bahamas

An Act Respecting the Territorial Sea, Archipelagic Waters, Internal Waters and the Exclusive Economic Zone 1993 (Act No 37)................ 132, 140

Canada

Arctic Waters Pollution Prevention Act 1970..173

Cape Verde

Decree-Law No 126/77 delimiting the territorial sea of the Republic of Cape Verde 1977..115

Law No 60/IV/92 (1992)..132

Chile

Decree No 416 of 14 July 1977..155

Comoros

Law No 82-005 relating to the delimitation of the maritime zones of the Islamic Federal Republic of the Comoros of 6 May 1982................ 116, 132

Denmark

Act on Greenland Self-Government 2009 (Act No 473)..91
Faroe Islands Act 2005 (Act No 80)..90
Faroes Home Rule Act 1948 (Act No 137)..90
Foreign Policy Act of the Faroe Islands 2005.. 90, 233
Greenland Home Rule Act 1978 (Act No 577)..91
Ordinance No 598..157
Ordinance No 599..157
Takeover Act of the Faroe Islands 2005 (Act No 578).. 90, 233

Dominican Republic

Law No 66-07 (2007)..116, 128, 132

Ecuador

Supreme Decree No 959-A prescribing straight baselines for the measurement of the Territorial Sea (1971)..157

Fiji

Marine Spaces Act 1977..115

Grenada

Territorial Sea and Maritime Boundaries Act 1989 (Act No 25)........116, 132, 140

Indonesia

Act Concerning Indonesia Waters (Act No 4 of 1960)..107

Act of the Republic Regarding Indonesian Waters (Act No 6 of 1996) 125, 132, 140
Government Regulation No 37 on the Rights and Obligations of Foreign Ships and Aircraft Exercising the Right of Archipelagic Sea Lanes Passage through Designated Sea Lanes (28 June 2002) 131, 136–37, 140

Kiribati

Marine Zones (Declaration) Act 2011 .... 132, 140

Mauritius

Maritime Zones Act 2005 .... 117, 132, 140, 175

Myanmar

Territorial Sea and Maritime Zones Law 1977 158

New Zealand

Cook Islands Constitution Act 1964 88
Niue Constitution Act 1974 89

Papua New Guinea

Constitution of the Independent State of Papua New Guinea (1975) 231
National Seas Act 1977 115

Philippines

Presidential Decree No 1596 (1978) 73
Republic Act No 9522 (2009) 117, 127

Sao Tome and Principe

Decree-Law No 14/78 (1978) 115

Seychelles

Maritime Zones Act 1999 (Act No 2 of 1999) 118, 132–33, 140

Solomon Islands

Delimitation of Marine Waters Act 1978 (No 32) 118, 132, 140

Spain

Royal Decree No 2510/1977 159

Sri Lanka

Presidential Proclamation of 15 January 1977 in pursuance of Maritime Zones Law No 22 of 1 September 1976 184

Trinidad and Tobago

Archipelagic Waters and Exclusive Economic Zone Act 1986 (Act No 24) 118, 132, 140

Tuvalu

Maritime Zones Act 2012 .... 132, 140

United Kingdom

British Indian Ocean Territory Order 1965 (SI 1965/1920) 228
Territorial Sea (Baselines) Order 2014 (Order No 1353) 175

United States of America

Constitution of the State of Hawaii 1959 87
Covenant to Establish a Commonwealth of the Northern Mariana Islands in Political Union with the United States of America 1976 (48 USC §1801) 95
Puerto Rico Self-Determination Act 2021 95

Vanuatu

Maritime Zones Act 1982 (Act No 23) 115
Maritime Zones Act 2010 (Act No 6) 118, 132–33, 177

TABLE OF TREATIES AND OTHER INSTRUMENTS

Accord between the Government of the French Republic and the Government of the Republic of Madagascar dealing with the delimitation of maritime spaces situated between Reunion and Madagascar (adopted 14 April 2005, entered into force 18 June 2007) 2624 UNTS 46736. 211

Agreement (with Annex) concerning West New Guinea (West Irian) (Indonesia–Netherlands) (adopted 15 August 1962, entered into force 21 September 1962) 437 UNTS 273 61

Agreement between Finland and Sweden Concerning the Delimitation of the Continental Shelf in the Gulf of Bothnia, The Åland Sea and the Northernmost Part of the Baltic Sea (adopted 29 September 1972, entered into force 15 January 1973), in Department of State, (US), *Limits in the Seas No 71* (16 June 1976). 208

Agreement between Finland and Sweden Concerning the Delimitation in the Åland Sea and the Northern Part of the Baltic Sea of the Finnish Continental Shelf and Fishing Zone and the Swedish Economic Zone (adopted 2 June 1994, entered into force 30 July 1995) 1887 UNTS 32126. 208

Agreement Between Finland and the Soviet Union Concerning the Aaland Islands (adopted 11 October 1940, entered into force 13 March 1948) 67 UNTS 139. 99

Agreement between the Government of Jamaica and the Government of the Republic of Cuba on the Delimitation of the Maritime Boundary between the two States (adopted 18 February 1994, entered into force 18 July 1995). 209

Agreement between the Government of Malaysia and the Government of the Republic of Singapore to Delimit precisely the Territorial Waters Boundary in Accordance with the Straits Settlement and Johor Territorial Waters Agreement (adopted 7 August 1995, entered into force 7 August 1995). 205

Agreement between the Government of the French Republic and the Government of the Republic of Seychelles Concerning the Delimitation of the Maritime Boundary of the Exclusive Economic Zone and the Continental Shelf of France and Seychelles (adopted 19 February 2001, entered into force 19 February 2001) 2162 UNTS 28. 211

Agreement between the Government of the Kingdom of Denmark along with the Local Government of Greenland on the one hand and the Government of the Republic of Iceland on the other hand on the Delimitation of the Continental Shelf and Fishery Zone in the Area between Greenland and Iceland (adopted 11 November 1997, entered into force 27 May 1998)....206

Agreement between the Government of the Kingdom of Denmark and the Government of Canada relating to the Delimitation of the Continental Shelf between Greenland and Canada (adopted 17 December 1973, entered into force 13 March 1974) 950 UNTS 147....206

Agreement between the Government of the Kingdom of Denmark together with the Home Government of the Faroe Islands on the one hand and the Government of the United Kingdom of Great Britain and Northern Ireland on the other hand relating to the Maritime Delimitation in the area between the Faroe Islands and the United Kingdom (adopted 18 May 1999, entered into force 21 July 1999) (1999) UKTS No 76....208

Agreement between the Government of the Kingdom of Norway on the one hand, and the Government of the Kingdom of Denmark together with the Home Rule Government of Greenland on the other hand, concerning the Delimitation of the Continental Shelf and the Fisheries Zone in the Area between Greenland and Svalbard (adopted 20 February 2006, in force 2 June 2006) 2738 UNTS No I-42887....206

Agreement between the Government of the Kingdom of Sweden and the Government of the Union of Soviet Socialist Republics on the Delimitation of the Continental Shelf and the Swedish Fishing Zone and the Soviet Economic Zone in the Baltic Sea (adopted 18 April 1988, entered in force 22 June 1988) (1988) 27 ILM 295....208

Agreement between the Government of the Republic of Estonia and the Government of the Republic of Latvia on the Maritime Delimitation in the Gulf of Riga, the Strait of Irbe and the Baltic Sea (adopted 12 July 1996, entered into force 10 October 1996)....207

Agreement between the Government of the Republic of Estonia and the Government of the Kingdom of Sweden on the delimitation of the maritime zones in the Baltic Sea (adopted 2 November 1998, entered in force 26 July 2000) 2474 UNTS 55....208

Agreement between the Government of the Republic of Estonia, the Government of the Republic of Latvia and the government of the Kingdom of Sweden on the common maritime boundary point in the Baltic Sea (adopted 30 April 1997, entered into force 20 February 1998)....207–08

Agreement between the Government of the Republic of Mauritius and the Government of the Republic of Seychelles On the Delimitation of the Exclusive Economic Zone between the Two States (adopted 29 July 2008, entered into force 19 November 2008)....211

Agreement between the Republic of Estonia and the Republic of Finland on the boundaries of the maritime zones in the Gulf of Finland and the Northern Baltic Sea (adopted 18 October 1996, in force 7 January 1997). 208
Agreement between the United States of America and the Union of the Soviet Socialist Republics on the Maritime Boundary, with Annex (adopted 1 June 1990, in force provisionally) 29 ILM 941. 206
Agreement on Maritime Delimitation between the Government of Australia and the Government of the French Republic (adopted 4 January 1982, entered into force 10 January 1983) [1983] ATS 3.................... 18, 205
Agreement on the Delimitation of the Maritime Border between The Gabonese Republic and the Democratic Republic of Sao Tome and Principe (adopted 26 April 2001)....................210
Charter of the United Nations (adopted 26 June 1945, entered into force 24 October 1945) 1 UNTS XV.................... 60, 76–77, 79–81, 83, 90–91, 96, 113, 217–18, 225–26, 228, 237, 258
Convention between the Government of the French Republic and the Government of Mauritius on the Delimitation of the French and Mauritian Economic Zones between the Islands of Réunion and Mauritius (adopted 2 April 1980, entered into force 2 April 1980)....................211
Convention between the United States and Denmark (United States–Denmark) (adopted 4 August 1916, entered into force 17 January 1917) 7 USTIA 56....................61
Convention for the Protection of the Natural Resources and Environment of the South Pacific Region (adopted 24 November 1986, entered into force 22 August 1990) [1990] ATS 31....................185
Convention on the Conservation of Antarctic Marine Living Resources (adopted 20 May 1980, entered into force 7 April 1982) 1329 UNTS 47. 219
Convention on the Continental Shelf (adopted 29 April 1958, entered into force 10 June 1964) 499 UNTS 311....................22–23, 180–81, 183, 189
Convention on the Elimination of All Forms of Discrimination against Women (adopted 18 December 1979, entered into force 3 September 1981) 1239 UNTS 13. 221
Convention on the High Seas (adopted 29 April 1958, entered into force 30 September 1962) 450 UNTS 11....................107
Convention on the Rights of the Child (adopted 20 November 1989, entered into force 2 September 1990) 1577 UNTS 3. 220
Convention on the Territorial Sea and Contiguous Zone (adopted 29 April 1958, entered into force 10 September 1964) 516 UNTS 206....................10, 22, 105, 108, 121, 147, 164, 189
Convention regarding the Boundary between the Philippine Archipelago and the State of North Borneo (adopted 2 January 1930, entered into force 13 December 1932) 137 LNTS 297. 109

Convention relating to the Status of Refugees (adopted 28 July 1951, entered into force 22 April 1954) 189 UNTS 150. 250
Convention relating to the Status of Stateless Persons (adopted 28 September 1954, entered into force 6 June 1960) 360 UNTS 117. 250
Convention Respecting the Non-Fortification and Neutralisation of the Aaland Islands (adopted 20 October 1921, entered into force 6 April 1922) 9 LNTS 213. 99
Denarau Declaration on Human Rights and Good Governance (adopted 30 January 2015)....237
European Convention for the Protection of Human Rights and Fundamental Freedoms (as amended) (adopted 4 November 1950, entered into force 3 September 1953) 213 UNTS 221....222
International Convention on the Elimination of All Forms of Racial Discrimination (adopted 21 December 1965, entered into force 4 January 1969) 660 UNTS 1. ....217, 220, 238
International Covenant on Civil and Political Rights (adopted 19 December 1966, entered into force 23 March 1976) 999 UNTS 172....217, 219–20, 237, 249
International Covenant on Economic Social and Cultural Rights (adopted 16 December 1966, entered into force 3 January 1976) 999 UNTS 3....217, 238, 249
Kyoto Protocol to the United Nations Framework Convention on Climate Change (adopted 11 December 1997, entered into force 16 February 2005) 2303 UNTS 214. 239
Montevideo Convention on the Rights and Duties of State (adopted 26 December 1933, entered into force 26 December 1934) 165 LNTS 19. ....40, 86, 244, 258
Optional Protocol to the Convention against Torture and Other Cruel, Inhuman or Degrading Treatment or Punishment (signed 18 December 2002, entered into force 22 June 2006) 2375 UNTS 237. 220
Optional Protocol to the Convention on the Rights of Persons with Disabilities (adopted 13 December 2006, entered into force 3 May 2008) 2518 UNTS 283....221
Optional Protocol to the Convention on the Rights of the Child on the involvement of children in armed conflict (adopted 25 May 2000, entered into force 12 February 2002) 2173 UNTS 222. 221
Optional Protocol to the Convention on the Rights of the Child on the sale of children, child prostitution and child pornography (adopted 25 May 2000, entered into force 18 January 2002) 2171 UNTS 227. 221
Optional Protocol to the Convention on the Rights of the Child on a communications procedure, (adopted 19 December 2011, entered into force 14 April 2014) UNTS No. 2753. 221
Pacific Agreement on Closer Economic Relations Plus (PACER Plus) (adopted 14 June 2017, entered into force 13 December 2020) [2020] ATS 12. 90

Paris Agreement, (adopted 12 December 2015, entered into force 4 November 2016) UN Reg No 54113. 239, 241
Paris Convention between France and Great Britain and Russia respecting the Aaland Islands (adopted 30 March 1856, entered into force 27 April 1856) 114 CTS 405. 99
South Pacific Nuclear Free Zone Treaty (adopted 6 August 1985, entered into force 11 December 1986) [1986] ATS 32. 90
The Treaty of Peace Between the Allied and Associated Powers and Germany (adopted 28 June 1919, entered into force 10 January 1920) 225 CTS 188. 78–79
Treaty between Australia and the Democratic Republic of Timor-Leste Establishing Their Maritime Boundaries in the Timor Sea (adopted 6 March 2018, entry into force 30 August 2019) [2019] ATS 2019. 195
Treaty between Australia and the Independent State of Papua New Guinea concerning Sovereignty and Maritime Boundaries in the area between the two Countries, including the area known as Torres Strait and Related Matters (Australia–Papua New Guinea) (adopted 18 December 1978, entered into force 15 February 1985) [1985] ATS 4. 43, 179, 181, 186, 213–14
Treaty between Australia and the Republic of Indonesia on the Zone of Cooperation in an Area between the Indonesian Province of East Timor and Northern Australia (Australia–Indonesia) (adopted 11 December 1989, entered into force 9 February 1991) [1991] ATS 9. 60
Treaty between Malaysia and the Republic of Indonesia relating to the Legal Regime of Archipelagic State and the Rights of Malaysia in the Territorial Sea and Archipelagic Waters as well as in the Airspace above the Territorial Sea, Archipelagic Waters and the Territory of the Republic of Indonesia lying between East and West Malaysia (Jakarta Treaty) (adopted 25 February 1982, entered into force 25 May 1984). 126
Treaty between the Federal Republic of Nigeria and the Democratic Republic of São Tomé and Principe on the Joint Development of Petroleum and other Resources in Respect of Areas of the Exclusive Economic Zone of the Two States (adopted 21 February 2001, entered into force 2003). 211
Treaty between the Federated States of Micronesia and the Republic of the Marshall Islands Concerning Maritime Boundaries and Cooperation on Related Matters (adopted 5 July 2006, entered in force 24 July 2015) UN Registration No 54649. 212
Treaty between the Government of Australia and the Government of the Republic of Indonesia establishing an Exclusive Economic Zone Boundary and Certain Seabed Boundaries (adopted 14 March 1997, not in force) [1997] ATNIF 4. 211
Treaty between the Government of Australia and the Government of New Zealand Establishing Certain Exclusive Economic Zone Boundaries and Continental Shelf Boundaries (adopted 25 July 2004, entry into force 25 January 2006) [2006] ATS 4. 194, 213

Treaty between the Government of the United Kingdom of Great Britain and Northern Ireland and the Government of the Republic of Honduras concerning the Delimitation of the Maritime Areas between the Cayman Islands and the Republic of Honduras (adopted 4 December 2001, entered into force 1 March 2002) (2002) UKTS No 25. 209
Treaty Between the Government of the United States of America and the Government of Great Britain and Northern Ireland on the Delimitation in the Caribbean of a Maritime Boundary Relating to Puerto Rico/US Virgin Islands and the British Virgin Islands (adopted 5 November 1993, entered into force 1 June 1995) (1995) UKTS No 77. 209
Treaty Between the Government of the United States of America and the Government of Great Britain and Northern Ireland on the Delimitation in the Caribbean of a Maritime Boundary Relating to the US Virgin Islands and Anguilla (adopted 5 November 1993, entered 1 June 1995) (1995) UKTS No 71. 209
Treaty Concerning the Archipelago of Spitsbergen (adopted 9 February 1920, entered into force 14 August 1925) [1925] ATS 10. .... 98, 101
Treaty of Peace between Spain and the United States (Treaty of Paris) (adopted 10 December 1898, entered into force 11 April 1899) 187 CTS 100. .... 44, 61, 108
Treaty of Peace with Japan (adopted 8 September 1951, entered into force 28 April 1952) 136 UNTS 45. 61
Treaty Regarding Delimitation of the Maritime Boundary between the Federal Republic of Nigeria and the Republic of Equatorial Guinea Concerning Their Maritime Boundary (adopted 23 September 2000, entered into force 3 April 2002). 210
Treaty Regarding Delimitation of the Maritime Boundary between the Republic of Equatorial Guinea and the Democratic Republic of São Tomé and Principe (adopted 26 June 1999, in force provisionally). 210
Treaty Regarding Delimitation of the Maritime Boundary between the Federal Republic of Nigeria and the Republic of Equatorial Guinea Concerning Their Maritime Boundary (adopted 23 September 2000, entered into force 3 April 2002). 210
Treaty Regarding Delimitation of the Maritime Boundary between the Republic of Equatorial Guinea and the Democratic Republic of Sao Tome and Principe (adopted 26 June 1999, in force provisionally). 210
United Nations Conference on Environment and Development, 'Agenda 21, Rio Declaration' (United Nations 1992) 234–35
United Nations Convention on the Law of the Sea (adopted 10 December 1982, entered into force 16 November 1994) 1833 UNTS 397 .... 2–5, 8, 10–21, 23–29, 33–38, 71, 74, 85, 93, 99, 100, 103, 106, 112–22, 124–55, 158–64, 166, 168–76, 180–83, 186, 189–91, 193–95, 197–201, 204, 207, 211, 213–14, 216, 228, 240, 242, 245–47, 249, 251, 253–55, 257–58, 260–61

United Nations Declaration on the Rights of Indigenous Peoples (adopted 13 September 2007) UN Doc. A/RES/61/295....................................249
United Nations Framework Convention on Climate Change (adopted 9 May 1992, entered into force 21 March 1994) 1771 UNTS 107...................239
Universal Declaration of Human Rights (adopted 10 December 1948) UNGA Res 217 A(III)... 217, 237
Vienna Convention on the Law of Treaties (adopted 23 May 1969, entered into force 27 January 1980) 1155 UNTS 331.................17, 219–20, 248

Introduction

Islands and international law have a long standing association. In some instances they are connected with the names of distinctive islands that have made their way into the fabric of international law such as Clipperton Island,[1] Minquiers and Ecrehos,[2] and Serpents' Island.[3] Throughout the history of the development of international law in the twentieth century islands have held a significant place both in the case law and state practice. Seminal early decisions such as *Island of Palmas*[4] and *Eastern Greenland*[5] established important principles with respect to territoriality. Likewise, the 1920 Aaland Islands Commission of Jurists report[6] established some of the initial principles associated with self-determination and the rights of island peoples. The first contentious case before the International Court of Justice (ICJ) – *Corfu Channel*[7] – arose out of an incident in which the island of Corfu was prominent.

It is possible to identify numerous instances where international courts and tribunals have had occasion to consider the role and impact of islands. The aim of this study, however, is to consider those areas of international law where islands are the dominant object and where distinctive legal principles, doctrine and practices regarding islands have developed. The status of islands for the purposes of the law of the sea is a key dimension of the study, but critical issues with respect to status, statehood, and territoriality are also considered, in addition to the human rights of island peoples.

This study builds upon previous work by Bowett,[8] Jayaraman,[9] Jayewardene,[10] and Murphy[11] who all considered the status of islands in international law, albeit from a number of perspectives which also reflected the development and evolution of international law over 40 years. There have also been specialist studies on islands and international law, with a strong focus on the law of the sea by Papadakis,[12]

[1] *Clipperton Island (France v Mexico)* (1931) 2 RIAA 1105.

[2] *Minquiers and Ecrehos Case (France v United Kingdom)* (Judgment) [1953] ICJ Reps 47.

[3] *Maritime Delimitation in the Black Sea (Romania v Ukraine)* (Judgment) [2009] ICJ Reps 61.

[4] *Island of Palmas Case (United States of America v The Netherlands)* (1928) 2 RIAA 829.

[5] *Legal Status of Eastern Greenland (Denmark v Norway)* [1933] PCIJ Rep Ser A/B No 53.

[6] Report of the International Committee of Jurists entrusted by the Council of the League of Nations with the task of giving an advisory opinion upon the legal aspects of the Aaland Islands question (October 1920) *League of Nations Official Journal* 3.

[7] *Corfu Channel (United Kingdom v Albania)* [1949] ICJ Reps 4.

[8] D Bowett, *The Legal Regime of Islands in International Law* (Oceana/Sijhoff & Noordhoff 1978).

[9] K Jayaraman, *Legal Regime of Islands* (Marwah Publications 1982).

[10] HW Jayewardene, *The Regime of Islands in International Law* (Martinis Nijhoff 1990).

[11] SD Murphy, *International Law Relating to Islands* (Brill/Nijhoff 2017).

[12] N Papadakis, *The International Legal Regime of Artificial Islands* (Sijthoff 1977).

Symmons,[13] Munavvar,[14] and Kopela.[15] All of these works provided a foundation for various aspects of this study.

What becomes evident from a modern study of islands and international law is that not only is it a rich field, but increasingly vibrant as multiple island-related issues are considered by international courts and tribunals and state practice continues to evolve. The 2016 decision of the United Nations Convention on the Law of the Sea (LOSC)[16] Annex VII Arbitral Tribunal in the *South China Sea* arbitration[17] is one of the most prominent recent decisions of any international court or tribunal. That decision is of particular significance for this study because of the interpretation of LOSC Article 121 regarding islands, and its discussion of artificial islands. While *South China Sea* had a law of the sea focus, the ICJ in the 2019 *Chagos Archipelago* Advisory Opinion[18] considered issues associated with self-determination and territoriality. More recently, in 2021 the ICJ considered the impact of islands on the direction of a maritime boundary in the *Somalia v Kenya* boundary delimitation case.[19]

This study seeks to discuss the questions and issues raised by these and other cases in a contemporary context. Prominent current issues regarding islands and international law are given particular attention. In addition to reviewing relevant aspects of the legal issues associated with the status of the Chagos Archipelago, attention is also given to a number of prominent island territories engaged in self-determination processes, including the status of certain United Nations recognised non-self-governing territories such as New Caledonia which in 2021 voted against becoming independent from France. Another prominent 2021 issue that gained global attention during the Glasgow COP26 Climate Conference was sea-level rise (SLR) and the impacts this was having on islands, and island communities. Both the Pacific Islands Forum and the Association of Small Island States sought to highlight these issues in 2021 and put forward important proposals referencing the LOSC and law of the sea more generally that sought to provide certainty for maritime boundaries and maritime entitlements of island States.

This study does not attempt to assess all of the rich array of international law issues that have arisen with respect to islands. International straits between two adjacent islands, or an island and a continent, are not considered as such an analysis sits within the general law of the sea. Likewise, the very distinctive issues

[13] CR Symmons, *The Maritime Zones of Islands in International Law* (Martinus Nijhoff 1979).

[14] M Munavvar, *Ocean States: Archipelagic Regimes in the Law of the Sea* (Martinus Nijhoff 1995).

[15] S Kopela, *Dependent Archipelagos in the Law of the Sea* (Martinus Nijhoff 2013).

[16] United Nations Convention on the Law of the Sea (adopted 10 December 1982, entered into force 16 November 1994) 1833 UNTS 397 (LOSC).

[17] *In the Matter of the South China Sea Arbitration before an Arbitral Tribunal constituted under Annex VII of the 1982 United Nations Convention on the Law of the Sea (Philippines v China)* (Merits Award, 12 July 2016) PCA Case 2013-19.

[18] *Legal Consequences of the Separation of the Chagos Archipelago from Mauritius in 1965* (Advisory Opinion) (25 February 2019) [2019] ICJ Reps 95.

[19] *Maritime Delimitation in the Indian Ocean (Somalia v Kenya)* (Judgment) (12 October 2021) [2021] ICJ Reps.

arising with respect to islands and international watercourses are not considered. The studies noted above consider some of these issues in more detail.[20] Neither is an attempt made to consider every possible territorial dispute with respect to islands, which on its own would require a separate and very detailed consideration. Rather, the focus of this study is where islands are the subjects of international law. A feature of international law over the centuries is that its subjects have increasingly expanded. While the discipline remains very much State-centric, the developments that have taken place in international law during the post-1945 United Nations era have seen a broader scope develop in its subjects.

The study intentionally distinguishes between islands as the objects and subjects of international law. Very few areas of international law do not have some implications for islands as objects of a legal regime. The breadth and scope of the discipline – having expanded to encompass the land, air, sea, space and now cyber domain – leave very few, if any island activities, untouched. Islands being the objects of international law is not exceptional. Any general work on international law will have an island dimension – bearing in in mind that islands take multiple forms and include States such as Japan, Indonesia, New Zealand, and the United Kingdom, while prominent continental States such as China, France, the Russian Federation, and the United States also possess large islands. The central focus of this work is where islands are particular subjects of international law, whether that can be seen to be reflected in a *lex specialis* or in a distinctive aspect of the law and practice of general international law.

To begin, attention is given to the definition of islands in international law. The *South China Sea* arbitration is particularly helpful in that respect, especially given the Tribunal's interpretation of LOSC Article 121, which until 2016 had not been considered in detail by any international court or tribunal. *South China Sea* also highlighted the important distinction between a juridical island, a juridical rock, and an artificial island. The elements associated with each of these are discussed in detail, and relevant state practice is considered. This analysis combines law with geography, and is one of the bedrocks of any study of islands and international law. However, the status of islands in international law involves a consideration of more general international law and also the political status of islands and island territories. This discussion encompasses issues associated with the legal and constitutional status of islands not only as States, but also as sub-units within certain constitutional structures, as dependencies and as non-self-governing territories. The study also seeks to encompass the entitlements of islands under international law. This is most prominently demonstrated in the instance of archipelagic States which, under LOSC Part IV, gained a distinctive status both in international law and the law of the sea. More generally, the law of the sea and the LOSC especially has provided significant entitlements for islands since the 1970s. This is reflected

[20] See Bowett (n 8) 61–72 (Islands and their relation to Boundaries in Navigable Rivers); Jayewardene (n 10) 193–258 (Islands in Inter-State Boundary Rivers, Islands in International Lakes); Murphy (n 11) 113–23 (Islands within boundary rivers or lakes) 220–47 (Pacific settlement of island disputes).

in the range of maritime zones that islands can assert, creating an impetus for the resolution of maritime boundaries. The LOSC entitlements of islands in some instances have been a catalyst for conflict over the status of certain islands. This is particularly the case throughout East Asia and South East Asia, and this study seeks to highlight those issues which in turn give prominence to the intersection of history and international law. A prominent aspect of some elements of this study is not only change and evolution of international law, but also how certain islands and territories such as the Chagos Archipelago, the Falkland (Malvinas) Islands, Greenland, and Taiwan are part of that narrative.

This research has also highlighted how islands are at the forefront of some of the most contentious issues and significant developments in international law. Events in the South China Sea both prior to and since the 2016 award have drawn particular attention to artificial island building and the status of artificial islands in international law. This is a modern phenomenon that will continue to gain momentum throughout this century. One of the drivers for this development may prove to be SLR. There is compelling evidence of SLR and projections of its impact throughout the twenty-first century are significant. The legal consequences extend from maritime entitlements and boundaries, territoriality and statehood, to the human rights of islanders. Increased artificial island construction may be one response to SLR and can potentially be utilised in multiple settings ranging from archipelagic States, to island States, and even continental States who may seek to provide a place of refuge for people forced to relocate from islands. The human rights of islanders – encompassing general international law concepts such as territoriality, statehood, and self-determination – are increasingly intertwined in any assessment of these issues. It therefore needs to be borne in mind that while islands have occupied an increasingly distinctive place in international law for a century, islands and islanders are coming more to the forefront of international law and raising unique and novel issues. The study that follows outlines, assesses and considers those issues and concludes with an analysis as to whether there is an international legal regime of islands.

1

Islands: Geography and Law

I. Introduction

A discussion of islands and international law brings about consideration of two distinctive dimensions: the physical and the juridical. Assessing and characterising islands and their physical properties involves a study of their geography and associated characteristics and understanding these relationships involves an appreciation of the interaction between geography and law. There are multiple areas of municipal law where such a relationship exists, especially in agricultural law, environmental law, and land/property law.[1] The relationship between geography and international law is critical to some aspects of international law also, especially international law and territoriality, law of the sea, and international environmental law. The law of the sea, as reflected especially in the 1982 United Nations Convention on the Law of the Sea (LOSC),[2] highlights this relationship with the emphasis that it places on critical concepts such as atolls, bays, coastlines, continental margins, continental shelves, deltas, low-tide elevations, ocean-floors, reefs, rocks, sea-beds, and submarine areas. Remarkably not all of these terms are clearly defined in the LOSC, which has in turn resulted in debate over their juridical meaning.[3]

Islands are defined in LOSC Article 121, which is the sole provision in Part VIII dedicated to the 'Regime of Islands'. This allows for a study to be undertaken as to the juridical status of islands in international law and the relationship between islands and geography.[4] The approach taken in this chapter will be to first assess islands and geography, considering the types of islands and associated features. Next, consideration will be given to islands and their juridical characterisation with a particular focus on the LOSC, the decisions of courts and tribunals, and state practice. This will allow for some preliminary observations to be made as to

[1] See generally T O'Donnell, D Robinson and J Gillespie (eds), *Legal Geography: Perspectives and Methods* (Routledge 2020); J Holder and C Harrison (eds), *Law and Geography* (Oxford University Press 2003).

[2] United Nations Convention on the Law of the Sea (adopted 10 December 1982, entered into force 16 November 1994) 1833 UNTS 397 (LOSC).

[3] For attempts to define some of these terms see GK Walker (ed), *Definitions for the Law of the Sea: Terms Not Defined by the 1982 Convention* (Martinus Nijhoff 2012).

[4] Generally see K Purcell, *Geographical Change and the Law of the Sea* (Oxford University Press 2019) ch 1; for interdisciplinary research on this topic see E Stratford (ed), *Island Geographies: Essays and Conversations* (Routledge 2017).

the juridical status of islands in international law before more detailed assessment is undertaken in later chapters.

II. Islands and Geography[5]

The starting point for this assessment is that islands are naturally formed areas of land that are surrounded by water and are permanently above sea level.[6] Given increasing technological capabilities, emphasis needs to be given to an island comprising naturally formed land. Artificial islands are therefore to be distinguished from the islands that are the principal focus of the analysis that follows. They fall into a distinctive category and are separately considered in Chapter two. Another threshold issue that arises is the capacity of a naturally formed island to be subject to land reclamation. This is not an exceptional activity, and is also discussed in Chapter two. However, as became evident in the 2016 *South China Sea* arbitration,[7] there is a tipping point where land reclamation will convert a naturally formed feature into an artificial island.

Islands can be found within the territory of a State – such as in lakes and rivers. They can also be co-located adjacent to seas and oceans and found in deltas, estuaries, bays, and gulfs, some of which may comprise internal waters of a State. Principally, however, islands are located within oceans and it is those islands that are the core focus of this study. A naturally formed island can comprise many different geological substances such as coral, gravel, lava, rock, sand, and silt. Much will depend upon where the island is located within an ocean, and its proximity to a continental or other landmass, with which it will have a geological connection. Volcanic islands formed as a result of undersea volcanic activity are distinctive because of their particular geological history, and ongoing capacity to be formed as a result of new volcanic activity.[8] Some islands are more permanent than others. Issues may arise with respect to newly created islands as a result of earthquakes, erosion, or volcanic activity.[9] As islands are part of a dynamic maritime domain their geophysical volatility needs to be appreciated. This has especially been

[5] See generally H Jayewardene, *The Regime of Islands in International Law* (Martinus Nijhoff 1990) 3–9; K Jayaraman, *Legal Regime of Islands* (Marwah Publications 1982) 6–16.

[6] See definitions of 'island' at J Evers (ed), 'Island', *National Geographic Resource Library* (2012) www.nationalgeographic.org/encyclopedia/island/; S Royle and L Brinklow, 'Definitions and Typologies' in G Baldacchino (ed), *The Routledge International Handbook of Island Studies: A World of Islands* (Routledge 2018) 3–4.

[7] *In the Matter of the South China Sea Arbitration before an Arbitral Tribunal constituted under Annex VII of the 1982 United Nations Convention on the Law of the Sea (Philippines v China)* (Merits Award, 12 July 2016) PCA Case 2013-19, 345 [873] – Gavan Reef (North), 346 [877] – Johnson Reef (*South China Sea*).

[8] See eg S Plank et al, 'The Short Life of the Volcanic Island New Late'iki (Tonga) Analyzed by Multi-sensor Remote Sensing Data' (2020) 10 *Scientific Reports* 22293.

[9] ibid; P Nunn, *Vanished Islands and Hidden Continents of the Pacific* (University of Hawaii Press 2008) ch 9 references so-called 'vanished islands' in the Pacific in the Cook Islands, Fiji, Kiribati, Papua New Guinea, Solomon Islands, Vanuatu and elsewhere in the Pacific Ocean.

highlighted by the impacts of climate change, resulting in erosion, sea-level rise and shifting coastlines.[10]

A. Types of Islands

From both a juridical and scientific classification perspective, islands can be characterised in different ways. *National Geographic* identifies six types of islands: continental, tidal, barrier, oceanic, coral, and artificial.[11] The location of an island and its proximity to another landmass often determines how the island is generally characterised. An important starting point is that islands can be proximate to a continental or mainland coast, to an island coast, or be solitary. Coastal islands can also be characterised as constituting a 'barrier', 'fringe' or a 'shield', which references their proximity to a coastline. Islands can also be characterised as mid-ocean or solitary and not immediately proximate to other land. Groups of islands are archipelagos and they may be coastal, also referred to as 'dependent archipelagos', or mid-ocean and distant from another significant landmass. Importantly, as with much of how international law interacts with geography, the name given to a feature is not determinative.[12] As such an island can also be referred to as an atoll, cay, isle, islet, key, land, or rock.[13] Some of the titles conferred upon an area of land that is an island may reflect upon its size, or composition. An 'islet', for example, is often associated with a very small island.[14] The plural 'islands' can also be used to refer to an archipelago. Both the literature and case law suggest that care needs to be taken when considering the name given to a feature in multiple languages.[15] In *Nicaragua v Colombia*, the International Court of Justice (ICJ) observed with respect to some of these features as follows:

> Cays are small, low islands composed largely of sand derived from the physical breakdown of coral reefs by wave action and subsequent reworking by wind. Larger cays can accumulate enough sediment to allow for colonization and fixation by vegetation. … An atoll is a coral reef enclosing a lagoon. A bank is a rocky or sandy submerged elevation of the sea floor with a summit less than 200 metres below the surface. Banks whose tops rise close enough to the sea surface (conventionally taken to be less than 10 metres below water level at low tide) are called shoals. Maritime features which qualify as islands or low-tide elevations may be located on a bank or shoal.[16]

[10] These issues are discussed in more detail in Chapter 10 of this volume.

[11] *National Geographic Resource Library* (n 6); see also P Nunn et al, 'Classifying Pacific Islands' (2016) 3 *Geoscience Letters* 7.

[12] *South China Sea* (n 7) 206 [482].

[13] Royle and Brinklow, (n 6) 4.

[14] The National Geographic observes that 'Many islands are quite small, covering less than half a hectare (one acre). These tiny islands are often called islets.': *National Geographic Resource Library* (n 6).

[15] Royle and Brinklow (n 6) 3–4; this was an issue the Tribunal was aware of in *South China Sea*: *South China Sea* (n 7) xix–xx 'Glossary of Geographic Names mentioned in this Award'.

[16] *Territorial and Maritime Dispute (Nicaragua v Colombia)* (Merits) [2012] ICJ Reps 624, 637–38 [20] (*Nicaragua v Colombia*); see also *Maritime Delimitation and Territorial Questions between Qatar and Bahrain* (Merits) (Joint Dissenting Opinion of Judges Bedjaoui, Ranjeva and Koroma) [2001] ICJ Reps 40, 209 [198] (*Qatar v Bahrain*).

Islands can also vary considerably in size. Greenland is considered to be the largest island at 2,166,086 km^2 and the thirteenth-largest landmass, while Nauru is 21 km^2 and is the smallest recognised island State.[17] This in turn raises issues with respect to the distinction between an island and a rock.

B. Rocks

Rocks are commonplace throughout the ocean and a ubiquitous maritime feature. They may be in close proximity to an adjacent landmass, or may be isolated and solitary features. Rocks may be permanently above water, only above water at low-tide, or permanently below the surface. Rocks are often associated with being hazards to navigation. Like islands, the composition and size of rocks can vary considerably. From a legal perspective the most challenging aspect of characterising the status of a rock relates to its size. Prominent features that rise up from the sea-floor may be referred to as 'rock pinnacles'.[18] This critical aspect is considered in more detail below, but a useful benchmark is Rockall, a 'granite oceanic crag' located 461 km west off Scotland and 754 m^2 in size. Rockall was considered by the United Kingdom (UK) to be an island until 1997 when it was conceded to be a rock for the purposes of the LOSC.[19] The status of Rockall illustrates the issues associated with the characterisation and naming of features as either islands or rocks. In the *Fisheries* case the ICJ encountered this issue when it sought to characterise the combination of islands, islets, rocks, and reefs along the Norwegian coastline, which it described as the '"skjærgaard" (literally, rock rampart)'.[20] Distinguishing between a rock and an island based on practice, geography, science and the law can therefore be challenging. In some locations, certain features are even known as 'rock islands'.[21]

C. Associated Maritime Features

Associated maritime features can include many different categories ranging from very small areas of 'land' such as sandbars, to living organisms such as coral. They can be identified and characterised in many different ways, including as banks, ledges, reefs, sandbanks, sandbars, and shoals. They may also be very small or very

[17] Central Intelligence Agency (USA), 'Greenland' (*The World Factbook*) www.cia.gov/the-world-factbook/countries/greenland/; Central Intelligence Agency (USA), 'Nauru' (*The World Factbook*) www.cia.gov/the-world-factbook/countries/nauru/; see comment in Royle and Brinklow (n 6) 8.

[18] See the analysis and characterisation of these features in the world's ocean in V Prescott and C Schofield, *The Maritime Political Boundaries of the World* (2nd edn, Martinus Nijhoff 2005) 82–88.

[19] Royle and Brinklow (n 6) 6–7; Prescott and Schofield (n 18) 375.

[20] *Fisheries Case (United Kingdom v Norway)* (Judgment) [1951] ICJ Reps 116, 127.

[21] See eg the World Heritage List inscribed property of 'Rock Islands Southern Lagoon' (Palau): UNESCO, 'Rock Islands Southern Lagoon' (*World Heritage List*), https://whc.unesco.org/en/list/1386/.

large. The Great Barrier Reef (Australia) is the world's largest coral reef encompassing 344,400 km^2, 3000 coral reefs, 600 continental islands, 300 coral cays, and about 150 inshore mangrove islands.[22] A common general characteristic of associated maritime features is that they are organic and have a dynamic aspect to them. Their size may vary on a seasonal basis due to climate, and they can be prone to significant impact arising from environmental factors and weather conditions. These features are often closely associated with islands, but may also be solitary maritime features in their own right. Like rocks, they are often associated with being navigational hazards, and historically have been a location for lighthouses and other navigational aids.[23] That care needs to be taken in giving too much prominence to what the feature is called was illustrated in *Pedra Branca*, where the ICJ observed that 'South Ledge, at 2.2 nautical miles to the south-south-west of Pedra Branca/Pulau Batu Puteh, is a rock formation only visible at low-tide'.[24]

III. Islands and Juridical Classification

A. Diplomatic History[25]

Modern diplomatic history regarding islands commences with the 1930 Hague Conference for the Codification of International Law, where attention was given to the development of a multilateral instrument concerning the territorial sea. While the Hague Conference did not result in any substantive treaty, the initial discussions were of significance and provided an indicator as to how the maritime entitlements of islands would be viewed and how an island would be defined. The Hague Conference was of the view that: 'An island is an area of land, surrounded by water, which is permanently above high-water mark.'[26] The International Law Commission (ILC) in its work on the law of the sea considered these issues from 1952–1956 and proposed a draft article on islands providing that: 'Every island has its own territorial sea. An island is an area of land, surrounded by water, which in normal circumstances is permanently above high-water mark.'[27]

[22] Australian Government Great Barrier Reef Marine Park Authority, 'Reef Facts', www.gbrmpa.gov.au/the-reef/reef-facts.

[23] Some aspects of these features were considered by the ICJ in *Sovereignty over Pedra Branca/Pulau Batu Puteh, Middle Rocks and South Ledge (Malaysia v Singapore)* (Merits) [2008] ICJ Reps 12 (*Pedra Branca*).

[24] ibid 22 [18].

[25] See the general discussion in C Schofield, 'The Regime of Islands Reframed: Developments in the Definition of Islands under the International Law of the Sea' (2019) 3 *The Law of the Sea* 1, 3–8; D Bowett, *The Legal Regime of Islands in International Law* (Oceana Publications 1978) 1–44.

[26] 'Report of the Second Committee: Territorial Sea' (Hague Conference, 10 April 1930) reproduced in S Nandan and S Rosenne (eds), *United Nations Convention on the Law of the Sea: A Commentary*, vol III (Martinus Nijhoff 1995) 461, 479.

[27] International Law Commission, 'Report of the International Law Commission covering the work of the eighth session (23 April–4 July 1956)' in *Yearbook of the International Law Commission*, vol 2 (1956) UN Doc A/3159, 253, 270, art 10.

The ILC made clear in its accompanying commentary that the following were not to be considered islands:

> (i) Elevations which are above water at low tide only. Even if an installation is built on such an elevation and is itself permanently above water – a lighthouse, for example – the elevation is not an 'island' as understood in this article;
> (ii) Technical installations built on the sea-bed, such as installations used for the exploitation of the continental shelf.[28]

An allowance was made by the ILC for 'drying rocks and drying shoals' where those features were located within the territorial sea, with a recommendation that they could be relied upon for the purposes of determining the 'extension of the territorial sea.'[29] However, there was otherwise no specific distinction drawn between the entitlements of islands and rocks. The relevant parts of the ILC draft text eventually became Article 10 of the Convention on the Territorial Sea and Contiguous Zone,[30] which provides: '1. An island is a naturally-formed area of land, surrounded by water, which is above water at high-tide.' The inclusion of the words 'naturally-formed', proposed by the United States (US), was designed to ensure that artificial islands did not enjoy an entitlement to a territorial sea.[31] Article 10(1) became the basis of the current LOSC Article 121 definition of an island and repeats the Convention on the Territorial Sea and Contiguous Zone definition.

B. LOSC: Article 121

Article 121 was the subject of significant debate during the negotiations at the Third United Nations Conference on the Law of the Sea (UNCLOS III) and island States and those with significant island interests, such as Greece, Ireland, Malta, New Zealand, Trinidad and Tobago, actively contributed.[32] Three critical dimensions are established in Article 121 with respect to islands and the law of the sea. The first is what constitutes an island. The second is clarification as to the maritime entitlements enjoyed by an island. The third is the distinction between an island and a rock. These distinctions are critical with respect to the maritime entitlements of these geographic features and have been described as being at the 'core' of Article 121.[33] The effect is that the LOSC creates a distinction between a juridical island and a juridical rock.

[28] ibid.
[29] ibid.
[30] Convention on the Territorial Sea and Contiguous Zone (adopted 29 April 1958, entered into force 10 September 1964) 516 UNTS 206.
[31] See discussion in Nandan and Rosenne (n 26) 327.
[32] Nandan and Rosenne (n 26) 327–38; Prescott and Schofield (n 18) 58–81.
[33] ibid 338.

Article 121 provides as follows:

Article 121

Regime of Islands

1. An island is a naturally formed area of land, surrounded by water, which is above water at high tide.
2. Except as provided for in paragraph 3, the territorial sea, contiguous zone, the exclusive economic zone and the continental shelf of an island are determined in accordance with the provisions of this Convention applicable to other land territory.
3. Rocks which cannot sustain human habitation or economic life of their own shall have no exclusive economic zone or continental shelf.

A number of observations can be made regarding the core definitional elements of Article 121. First, the island is to be naturally formed. This suggests that either the island has existed in some form or another for time immemorial, or it may have been recently formed as a result of the forces of nature. An artificially constructed island therefore does not fall within the remit of Article 121(1). Second, the island must comprise an 'area of land'.[34] No clarity is given as to dimensions of this area, which suggests that it may be very small. The other criterion is that the area comprises 'land'. This is suggestive of the land being composed of a variety of natural material, as opposed to an artificially constructed island. An island which has been reinforced or enlarged by reclamation through gravel, rocks, and sand from the adjacent sea-bed or relocated from an island quarry would still constitute land for these purposes. Third, the island is to be surrounded by water. No distinction is made as to whether the island is surrounded by fresh water or salt water; however, given the LOSC focus on the sea, a natural interpretation of the words would indicate salt water. That the island may be connected to another area of land, such as a mainland or another island, by a bridge would not be a disqualifier. In this respect an island can be distinguished from a feature that has island-like characteristics but is connected to a mainland by a *land* bridge as in the case of a peninsula.[35] Fourth, the island is to be 'above water at high tide'. This is critical and goes to the distinction between an island and a LOSC Article 13 low-tide elevation. The island must therefore be permanently above water at all times irrespective of tidal variations.[36] The size of the island may vary depending on tidal dynamics; however, providing that an area of the island is permanently above water at high tide, this critical

[34] See comment on this criterion in *Qatar v Bahrain* (n 16) (Joint Dissenting Opinion of Judges Bedjaoui, Ranjeva and Koroma) 208–9 [198].

[35] Whether the Hawar Islands were a distinctive island, or connected to another island by way of a peninsula, was the subject of comment by the ICJ in *Qatar v Bahrain* (n 16) (Joint Dissenting Opinion of Judges Bedjaoui, Ranjeva and Koroma) 173 [87], where it was observed that 'The Hawar "Islands" are not actually islands but an indivisible part of the land mass of Qatar, cut off by the sea when the tide comes in and joined to the land again when the tide goes out.'

[36] On this point see the observations by Judge Vereshcetin in *Qatar v Bahrain* (n 16) (Declaration of Judge Vereshchetin) 220–21 [13].

dimension is met. This does, however, clearly raise issues with respect to the characterisation of an island when taking into account the effects of climate change and sea-level rise. These first four elements constitute a juridical island which has the same maritime entitlements as any other area of land. Fifth, a distinction is drawn between a juridical island and a juridical rock, which is a 'category' of island.[37] The LOSC significance arising from this distinction is that a juridical rock does not generate an entitlement to a continental shelf or exclusive economic zone (EEZ). The key Article 121(3) elements are that the rock 'cannot sustain human habitation', or that rocks do not have an 'economic life of their own'. No clear guidance is given in the LOSC as to how these terms are defined. Likewise, no reference is made as to the size of a rock being determinative, though clearly some rocks will be so small that they are unable to sustain human habitation.

C. Decisions of Courts and Tribunals

There are only a small number of decided cases in which LOSC Article 121 has been considered. The most recent of these, the 2016 *South China Sea* arbitration, is the most prominent. The characterisation of islands for the purposes of the LOSC, and more generally international law, is the focus of the analysis that follows. Broader discussion of how international courts and tribunals have considered islands in multiple international law contexts occurs in other chapters.

(i) International Court of Justice

Remarkably, the ICJ considered the distinctive issue of islands and rocks as early as the 1951 *Fisheries* case.[38] The Court assessed the features of the Norwegian 'skjærgaard', which are the combination of islands and rocks that shield the Norwegian mainland coast from the Atlantic Ocean, and referred to these features along the Norwegian coast as 'literally [a] rock rampart'.[39] However, no attention was given to whether these features met any distinctive criteria regarding islands and rocks, and the ICJ focussed on Norway's ability to draw straight baselines along its coast from which its maritime entitlements could be proclaimed. Likewise, in the 1953 *Minquiers and Ecrehos* case the ICJ was principally considering matters associated with sovereignty and territoriality rather than the juridical status of the islands, islets, rocks, and associated maritime features in dispute.[40]

Of the more recent cases focussing on the LOSC, in the 1993 *Greenland/Jan Mayen* case the Court accepted that Jan Mayen was a juridical island for the purposes of maritime boundary delimitation, notwithstanding the sparse

[37] *South China Sea* (n 7) 206 [481].
[38] *Fisheries Case* (n 20) 116.
[39] ibid 127.
[40] *Minquiers and Ecrehos Case (France v United Kingdom)* (Judgment) [1953] ICJ Reps 47.

settlement of the island and its inhospitable climate.[41] In 2001 the Court in *Qatar v Bahrain* considered Article 121 to be reflective of customary international law.[42] The status of Oit'at Jaradah in the Persian Gulf and whether it was an island or a low-tide elevation was under review. The Court assessed the feature to be an Article 121 island,[43] but did not elaborate on its reasoning. Questions arose as to whether other maritime features were properly characterised as a low-tide elevation or an extension of an island, but no clear determinations were made in the context of Article 121.[44] In the 2007 *Nicaragua v Honduras* case, the ICJ referenced Article 121 in the context of a number of Nicaraguan and Honduran cays in the relevant maritime area, but as their status as islands was not in dispute and neither party sought to assert an EEZ or continental shelf entitlement there was no occasion to give further consideration to the Article 121(3) island/rock distinction.[45] Soon after, in the 2008 *Pedra Branca* case the Court principally considered questions associated with sovereignty over an island, rock, and a low-tide elevation.[46] While particular attention was given to LOSC Article 13 and whether a low-tide elevation was capable of appropriation, there was no consideration of Article 121 and the island/rock distinction.[47]

The 2012 *Nicaragua v Colombia* case is the most comprehensive ICJ decision to date concerning Article 121. The Court reaffirmed the customary international law status of Article 121,[48] and effectively accepted that a rock is a sub-category of an island, stating that 'even an island which falls within the exception stated in Article 121, paragraph 3, of UNCLOS is entitled to a territorial sea.'[49] Little precise guidance was given by the Court on the island/rock distinction and interpretation of Article 121(3) in particular. A number of very small islands were the subject of close consideration by the Court, but other than assessing that they were entitled at a minimum to a 12 nm territorial sea, no determination was made as to whether they were Article 121(3) rocks.[50] The maritime feature known as Quitasueño best highlighted the island/rock distinction for the Court,[51] and whether any of the

[41] *Maritime Delimitation in the Area between Greenland and Jan Mayen (Denmark v Norway)* (Judgment) [1993] ICJ Reps 38, 73 [80]; also at 46 [15] where the Court noted that Jan Mayen had no settled population and was a base for 25 technical and other staff.

[42] *Qatar v Bahrain* (n 16) 91 [167], 99 [195]; cf *Qatar v Bahrain* (n 16) (Separate Opinion of Judge Oda) 125 [8].

[43] *Qatar v Bahrain* (n 16) 99 [195], where on the basis of the Court's observations the island was very small: 'at high tide its length and breadth are about 12 by 4 metres, whereas at low tide they are 600 and 75 metres. At high tide, its altitude is approximately 0.4 metres.'

[44] ibid (n 16) 104–9 [216]–[220], discussing the status of Fasht al Azm.

[45] *Territorial and Maritime Dispute between Nicaragua and Honduras in the Caribbean Sea (Nicaragua v Honduras)* (Judgment) [2007] ICJ Reps 659, 702 [137], 703–4 [144], 738–39 [262] (*Nicaragua v Honduras*).

[46] *Pedra Branca* (n 23).

[47] ibid 99–101 [288]–[299].

[48] *Nicaragua v Colombia* (n 16) 674 [139].

[49] ibid 690 [176].

[50] ibid 691–92 [180] considering the status of Roncador, Serrana, the Alburquerque Cays and EastSoutheast Cays.

[51] Described by the Court as 'a large bank approximately 57 km long and 20 km wide' at ibid 640 [24].

54 identified features on this bank were islands, rocks, or low-tide elevations. Relying on contemporary evidence,[52] the Court concluded that the largest feature on Quitasueño – referred to as QS32 – was an island, as it was naturally formed and above water at high tide.[53] That QS32 was composed of coral was considered 'irrelevant' and the 'fact that QS 32 is very small does not make any difference, since international law does not prescribe any minimum size which a feature must possess in order to be considered an island.'[54] The Court accepted the view of both parties that QS32 was an Article 121(3) rock and did not elaborate on the island/rock distinction.[55] All other features on Quitasueño were assessed as low-tide elevations.[56] More recently the ICJ briefly referenced Article 121 when characterising the status of the Corn Islands in the 2018 *Costa Rica v Nicaragua* case.[57] The islands, described as having a 'significant number of inhabitants and [able to] sustain economic life', were granted their full Article 121(2) LOSC entitlements.[58]

(ii) International Tribunal for the Law of the Sea

The International Tribunal for the Law of the Sea (ITLOS) has not given detailed consideration to Article 121. It did, however, arise in the context of two cases in which the entitlements of islands to an EEZ were under consideration. In *Monte Confurco* the EEZ adjacent to the French Southern Ocean island territory of Kerguelen was considered following arrest of a vessel. Judge Vukas in a Declaration expressed a view that it was 'highly questionable' whether the establishment of an EEZ off Kerguelen was in accordance with the LOSC deliberations at UNCLOS III.[59] These views were expanded upon in the subsequent *Volga* case which related to the enforcement of fisheries laws in the EEZ adjacent to the Australian Southern Ocean territories of Heard and McDonald Islands.[60] Judge Vukas again focussed on concerns that the establishment of an EEZ adjacent to these islands was inconsistent with the 'letter and spirit' of the LOSC.[61] Direct reference was made to Article 121(3) where it was observed 'we find many of the elements obviously present in this group of Australian islands/isles/islets/rocks'.[62] Commenting that the terminology in Article 121(3) was 'vague, and the relationships between the

[52] ibid 644 [36].

[53] ibid 645 [37].

[54] ibid 645 [37]; the Court also considered QS32 capable of appropriation.

[55] ibid 693 [183].

[56] ibid 692 [181].

[57] *Maritime Delimitation in the Caribbean Sea and the Pacific Ocean (Costa Rica v Nicaragua) and Land Boundary in the Northern Part of Isla Portillos (Costa Rica v Nicaragua)* (Merits) [2018] ICJ Reps 139 (*Costa Rica v Nicaragua*).

[58] ibid 191 [140]; the islands were described as having a population of 7,400 persons (at 159 [49]).

[59] *Monte Confurco (Seychelles v France)* (Prompt Release Judgment) (Declaration of Judge Vukas) (18 December 2000) ITLOS Reports 2000, 86, 122.

[60] *Volga Case (Russian Federation v Australia)* (Prompt Release Judgment) (23 December 2002) ITLOS Reports 2002, 10 (*Volga*).

[61] ibid (Declaration of Vice-President Vukas) 42 [2].

[62] ibid 44 [6].

components of this rule are rather unclear', Judge Vukas was of the view that these islands were effectively rocks and not islands entitled to an EEZ. Significance was given to the absence of permanent habitation on the islands and their geographical and climatic characteristics.[63] Judge Anderson, in dissent on other grounds, made clear that Heard Island was an island and not a rock.[64] Otherwise, ITLOS did not make any specific observations on this issue. No subsequent ITLOS decisions have considered Article 121.

(iii) Annex VII Arbitral Tribunals

In the 2016 *South China Sea* arbitration between the Philippines and China the Tribunal principally considered eight features in the South China Sea and their status vis-à-vis the parties as islands, rocks, or low-tide elevations.[65] In doing so a number of important observations were made regarding the island/rock distinction as the Tribunal sought to identify what it referred to as a 'fully entitled island'[66] capable of generating the full suite of LOSC maritime entitlements. In reaching its conclusions the Tribunal referenced the context of Article 121 within the historical development of the law of the sea and LOSC,[67] and relevant LOSC *travaux préparatoires*.[68]

With respect to the interpretation of Article 121(3), the following conclusions were drawn:[69]

1. An Article 121(3) 'rock' is not limited to a feature composed of solid rock and its geological and geomorphological characteristics are not relevant;
2. A maritime feature's status is to be determined on the basis of its 'natural capacity' without additions or modifications to sustain human habitation or economic life of its own;
3. The term 'human habitation' involves inhabitation by an indigenous or non-indigenous population encompassing a 'stable community of people' for which the island is a home on which they can remain, and includes small groups of peoples, family groups, and periodic or habitual residence by nomadic peoples;

[63] ibid 44–45 [6]–[7].

[64] *Volga* (n 60) (Dissenting Opinion of Judge Anderson) 57 [2]; for analysis see C Schofield, 'The Trouble with Islands: The Definition and Role of Islands and Rocks in Maritime Boundary Delimitation' in JM Van Dyke and S-Y Hong (eds), *Maritime boundary disputes, settlement processes, and the law of the sea* (Martinus Nijhoff 2009) 19, 29–30.

[65] The features were Cuarteron Reef, Fiery Cross Reef, Gavan Reef (North), Johnson Reef, McKennan Reef, Mischief Reef, Scarborough Shoal, Second Thomas Shoal; consideration was also given to Itu Aba (Republic of China/Taiwan) and some other associated high-tide features generally in the Spratly Islands.

[66] *South China Sea* (n 7) 119 [280].

[67] ibid 213–18 [507]–[520].

[68] See ibid 218–26 [521]–[538].

[69] ibid 227–31 [540]–[551].

4. The term 'economic life of their own' is linked to human habitation and the island sustaining an economic life associated with its human habitation oriented around the island itself and not focussed solely on the surrounding waters;
5. The text of Article 121(3) is disjunctive and the ability of an island to sustain either human habitation, *or* have an economic life of its own, is sufficient for the feature to have an EEZ and continental shelf, though ordinarily a feature would need to have a stable human community to possess an economic life;
6. The island must have an objective capacity to sustain human habitation or have an economic life of its own, which is not determined on the basis of past or present activity;
7. Each feature will be assessed on a case-by-case basis in which a number of principal factors can be taken into account including the presence of water, food and shelter to enable persons to live on the feature;
8. The capacity of a feature should be assessed with due regard to the potential for a group of islands to 'collectively sustain human habitation and economic life';
9. The objective physical conditions of a particular feature will not be determinative in all instances and insufficient for 'features that fall close to the line'. Historical usage of the feature will be the 'most reliable evidence of the capacity of a feature'. Particular reference was made to size not being 'dispositive of a feature's status as a fully entitled island or rock, and is not, on its own, a relevant factor.'[70]

The Tribunal concluded that all of the eight maritime features were either Article 121(3) rocks or Article 13 low-tide elevations, and as such none were juridical islands.

D. State Practice

Any assessment of the island/rock distinction, and interpretation of Article 121(3) in particular, needs to take account of state practice; both pre-1994, and post-1994. Pre-1994 state practice relates to how States viewed the entitlements of islands prior to the entry into force of the LOSC. This is reflected in the delineation of island EEZ and continental shelf claims, and how States agreed upon maritime boundaries and whether islands were granted their full maritime entitlements. Post-1994 state practice relates to the period since entry into force of the LOSC. This latter state practice was under consideration in *South China Sea*, as the dispute arose at a time when both China and the Philippines had ratified the LOSC and the convention had been in force for 22 years by the time of the 2016 award. The Annex VII Arbitral Tribunal noted the importance of taking into account state

[70] ibid 227 [538].

practice, especially in the context of interpreting Article 121(3) and considering the role of 'subsequent practice' in the application of a treaty.[71] However, it was concluded that as far as the case before it was concerned there was 'no evidence for an agreement based on State practice' that differed from the Tribunal's interpretation.[72]

There are some prominent examples in state practice, including that concerning the status of Rockall. The UK persisted in its view that Rockall was a juridical island until 1997, after which it conceded it was a juridical rock and no longer pressed its claims to a continental shelf and EEZ in maritime boundary negotiations with Denmark and Ireland.[73] Mexico has taken the view that the Alijos Rocks in the Pacific Ocean are also juridical rocks.[74] Other examples of where States have conceded that certain islands were juridical rocks can be found in maritime boundary cases before the ICJ where the Court has observed that the parties have not sought to claim that relevant features under consideration generated a maritime entitlement other than a territorial sea.[75]

Protest is another relevant form of state practice in this area. Aves Island (Bird Island) in the Caribbean was given full effect in separate maritime boundary agreements between Venezuela and France (1980), the Netherlands (1978), and the US (1978). However, in 1997 Venezuela's claim was contested on the grounds that Aves Island was claimed as a juridical rock by other Caribbean neighbours including Antigua and Barbuda, St Kitts and Nevis, Saint Lucia, and St Vincent and the Grenadines.[76] Japan in 2008 made a LOSC Article 76 submission to the Commission on the Limits of the Continental Shelf with respect to an extended continental shelf claim, which included the feature known as Okinotorishima. This resulted in diplomatic exchanges with the Commission via the UN Secretary-General from China and the Republic of Korea, asserting that Okinotorishima was a juridical rock,[77] and some inconclusive deliberations at the Meeting of State Parties to the LOSC.[78] Instances of where islands were granted their full maritime entitlements, albeit modified to reflect the final settlement of the maritime boundary, can be found with respect to Kerguelan (France) and Heard and McDonald

[71] ibid 231 [552]; referencing the Vienna Convention on the Law of Treaties (adopted 23 May 1969, entered into force 27 January 1980) 1155 UNTS 331 and decisions of the ICJ in *Advisory Opinion Concerning the Legality of the Use by a State of Nuclear Weapons in Armed Conflict* (Advisory Opinion) [1996] ICJ Reps 66, 75 [19], 81–82 [27]; *Kasikili/Sedudu Island (Botswana v Namibia)* (Judgment) [1999] ICJ Reps 1045, 1075–87 [48]–[63].

[72] *South China Sea* (n 7) 232 [553].

[73] C Symmons, 'Ireland and the Rockall Dispute: An Analysis of Recent Developments' (Spring 1998) *IBRU Boundary and Security Bulletin* 78; Prescott and Schofield (n 18) 375–76, 613.

[74] JA Roach and R Smith, *Excessive Maritime Claims* (3rd edn, Martinus Nijhoff 2012) 197.

[75] *Nicaragua v Honduras* (n 45) 738 [262], 749–51 [299]–[303].

[76] Roach and Smith (n 74) 178; Prescott and Schofield (n 18) 72–74.

[77] Commission on the Limits of the Continental Shelf (CLCS), 'Outer limits of the continental shelf beyond 200 nautical miles from the baselines: Submissions to the Commission: Submission by Japan' (United Nations Oceans and Law of the Sea, 27 December 2013) www.un.org/Depts/los/clcs_new/submissions_files/submission_jpn.htm.

[78] Roach and Smith (n 74) 198–200.

Islands (Australia), and in the Coral Sea in the maritime delimitation between Australia and France (with respect to New Caledonia).[79] Finally, following the *South China Sea* arbitration there is ongoing regional state practice arising from EEZ or continental shelf claims being challenged. This is reflected in diplomatic exchanges in the public domain, including via the Commission on the Limits of the Continental Shelf.[80]

IV. Conclusions

In this study, islands encapsulate a unique combination of geography, geology, geomorphology and the law. The definition of an island as land surrounded by water at high tide contains essential elements, but, as this analysis has shown, can under some circumstances be challenging. The status of Rockall and features in the South China Sea, however, has been both legally and politically significant. This is one of the consequences of the LOSC and the distinction it makes between the maritime entitlements of a juridical island and a juridical rock. A juridical island is part of the land territory of a coastal State for the purposes of the LOSC. While a juridical rock may be part of the territory of a coastal State, it is clearly distinguishable from a juridical island in terms of its maritime entitlements. As Prescott and Schofield have observed, a juridical island with no maritime neighbours has the potential to generate 125,644 nm^2 of territorial sea, EEZ and continental shelf, while a juridical rock is only entitled to a territorial sea of 452 nm^2.[81] The decisions of international courts and tribunals over the past two decades have given some greater clarity to the interpretation of Article 121 in particular. The ICJ's judicial method in *Nicaragua v Colombia* is a helpful frame. First a determination was made whether a feature was an island or a low-tide elevation, after which the Article 121(3) island/rock distinction was considered. With this basic framework for analysis outlined, it is now possible to proceed to consider the various other dimensions of islands and their interaction with international law.

[79] Agreement on Maritime Delimitation between the Government of Australia and the Government of the French Republic (adopted 4 January 1982, entered into force 10 January 1983) [1983] ATS 3.

[80] See eg Commission on the Limits of the Continental Shelf (CLCS), 'Outer limits of the continental shelf beyond 200 nautical miles from the baselines: Submissions to the Commission: Partial Submission by Malaysia in the South China' (United Nations Oceans and Law of the Sea, 18 August 2021) www.un.org/Depts/los/clcs_new/submissions_files/submission_mys_12_12_2019.html, and communications from Australia, France, Germany, New Zealand, UK; see also Commission on the Limits of the Continental Shelf (CLCS), 'Outer limits of the continental shelf beyond 200 nautical miles from the baselines: Submissions to the Commission: Submission by the Kingdom of Tonga' (United Nations Oceans and Law of the Sea, 7 November 2019) www.un.org/Depts/los/clcs_new/submissions_files/submission_ton_73_2014.htm, and communications from Fiji.

[81] Prescott and Schofield (n 18) 249; Schofield (n 25) 9.

2

Artificial Islands

I. Introduction

Artificial islands have existed since ancient times[1] and have been a legal and political curiosity in the modern law of the sea.[2] For much of the twentieth century efforts were made to address the phenomena of artificial islands. The outcome was the establishment of a basic legal framework under the LOSC[3] which sought to distinguish artificial islands[4] from natural islands, which in turn had implications for the regime of islands.[5] However, with increased technological capability, artificial island building has become more significant in the twenty-first century. The result has been much greater attention being given to international law and artificial islands, and the distinctions and parallels that exist with the general international legal regime of islands. A particular focus has been the analysis that occurred in *South China Sea*, where the Annex VII Arbitral Tribunal considered China's artificial island-building and land reclamation activities.[6] That attention has continued since the 2016 Award as a result of China's ongoing artificial island-building activities in the South China Sea.[7]

[1] SR Fischer, *Islands: From Atlantis to Zanzibar* (Reaktion Books 2012) 36–37.

[2] For some of the discussion in the early literature see AMJ Heijmans, 'Artificial Islands and the law of Nations' (1974) 21 *Netherlands International Law Review* 139; AHA Soons, 'Artificial Islands and Installations in International Law' (Occasional Paper No 22, Law of the Sea Institute, University of Rhode Island 1974); DHN Johnson, 'Artificial Islands' (1951) 4(2) *International and Comparative Law Quarterly* 203.

[3] United Nations Convention on the Law of the Sea (adopted 10 December 1982, entered into force 16 November 1994) 1833 UNTS 397 (LOSC).

[4] ibid art 60.

[5] ibid art 121 and pt VIII.

[6] *In the Matter of the South China Sea Arbitration before an Arbitral Tribunal constituted under Annex VII of the 1982 United Nations Convention on the Law of the Sea (Philippines v China)* (Merits) (12 July 2016) PCA Case 2013-19, 399–415 [994]–[1043] (*South China Sea*), and the discussion below.

[7] See in particular Asia Maritime Transparency Initiative, 'Occupation and Island Building' (2021) https://amti.csis.org/island-tracker/; and analysis in T Davenport, 'Island-Building in the South China Sea: Legality and Limits' (2018) 8 *Asian Journal of International Law* 76; FS Sweeney, 'Rocks v. Islands: Natural Tensions over Artificial Features in the South China Sea' (2017) 31 *Temple International & Comparative Law Journal* 599; I Saunders, 'The South China Sea Award, Artificial Islands and Territory' (2016) 34 *Australian Year Book of International Law* 31; for historical analysis of this practice in the South China Sea, see J Zhang, F Su, and Z Ding, 'Sea Reclamation Status of Countries around the South China Sea from 1975 to 2010' (2017) 9 *Sustainability* 878.

This chapter commences with a discussion of definitions, before considering the historical legal framework and relevant state practice. Attention will then turn to the LOSC and contemporary state practice in the area, with particular reference to the South China Sea. The relationship between artificial islands, environmental impact, and land reclamation will also be considered.

II. Scope and Location of Artificial Islands

The expansive definitions of artificial islands have over time included offshore airports,[8] to anchored ships/lightships,[9] floating and sea-bed fixed sea cities and villages,[10] military installations,[11] and various types of sea-bed installations.[12] Such islands could have multiple economic and recreational purposes, including for offshore 'pirate' broadcasting.[13] A point of distinction is between building an artificial island, whatever form that may take, and land reclamation. The latter is a process extending back many centuries and can be associated with areas of coast lost to the sea, including islands, and where the coastline has been extended beyond natural limits due to port and harbour works, and associated urban expansion. Land reclamation can take place along a continental or an island coastline.[14] In 2003, for example, the International Tribunal for the Law of the Sea (ITLOS) heard in submissions that Singapore had in the previous 30 years increased its land area from 580 to 680 square kilometres (58,000 ha to 68,000 ha) as a result of land reclamation.[15] Land reclamation, which has some history as a response to rising sea levels,[16] can also be associated with the building of dykes, sea barriers and walls to halt inundation by the sea.[17] However, the latter activity is clearly designed to protect an area of land from the effects of sea-level rise, tsunami, and storm surges, rather than to extend the land frontier by way of reclamation. An artificial island

[8] N Papadakis, *The International Legal Regime of Artificial Islands* (Sijthoff 1977) 29–30.

[9] CR Symmons, *The Maritime Zones of Islands in International Law* (Martinus Nijhoff 1979) 21–22.

[10] Papadakis (n 8) 16–17; Symmons, (n 9) 28–29.

[11] Papadakis (n 8) 33–35.

[12] Symmons (n 9) 24–28.

[13] Papadakis (n 8) 35–37; which was envisaged as a way of operating effectively on the high seas beyond the reach of coastal States laws that only extended as far as territorial sea limits.

[14] See eg T Riding, 'Making Bombay Island: land reclamation and geographical conceptions of Bombay, 1661–1728' (2018) 59 *Journal of Historical Geography* 27.

[15] *Case Concerning Land Reclamation by Singapore in and around the Straits of Johor* (*Malaysia v Singapore*) (Response of Singapore) (20 September 2003) PCA Case No 2004-05, 282 [29], www.itlos.org/fileadmin/itlos/documents/cases/case_no_12/C12_Response_Singapore.pdf, discussed in T Koh and J Lin, 'The Land Reclamation Case: Thoughts and Reflections' (2006) 10 *Singapore Year Book of International Law* 1; see also with respect to land reclamation in Singapore, S Subramanian, 'How Singapore is Creating More Land for Itself', *The New York Times* (20 April 2017) www.nytimes.com/2017/04/20/magazine/how-singapore-is-creating-more-land-for-itself.html; for historical analysis of this practice in the South China Sea, see Zhang, Su, and Ding (n 7).

[16] See the discussion in chapter 10 of this volume.

[17] See eg D Byrne, 'Time on the Waterline: Coastal Reclamations and Seawalls in Sydney and Japan' (2018) 5 *Journal of Contemporary Archaeology* 53.

will always have the essential characteristic of being a feature surrounded by water, albeit one that may be connected to a mainland or another island by a bridge or tunnel.

Artificial islands are capable of being built in any maritime zone. Historically they were more likely to be built within internal waters, because of the protections offered to the islands from the sea. As technology improved and more capability was developed, it became possible to build artificial islands further offshore: first within the narrow pre-LOSC territorial sea, and then into other maritime domains. While there is a capacity to build artificial islands across any maritime space, internal waters and territorial sea are favoured locations as they offer greater access for construction and eventual utilisation, given the potential for land bridges and other transportation links.[18] An important legal issue though is that, except in the case of the high seas, an artificial island can only be built by the recognised territorial sovereign which enjoys LOSC maritime entitlements. In the high seas, all States and not only coastal States, have the legal right under LOSC Article 87 to construct artificial islands.

III. Historical Legal Framework

International courts and scholars began to consider the potential for artificial islands and associated structures in the context of territorial sea claims from the late nineteenth century onwards.[19] No detailed assessment was made of this issue until the 1930 Hague Conference for the Codification of International Law. While agreement was not reached on the issue, a view was taken in Sub-Committee II of the Special Commission (Territorial Waters) that the definition of an island did not exclude an artificial island 'provided these are true portions of territory and not merely floating works, anchored buoys, etc.'[20] In the 1950s the International Law Commission (ILC) in its work on the law of the sea directly addressed islands in draft Article 10.[21] There had been ILC discussion on certain matters associated with artificial islands,[22] but the resulting draft articles did not directly address the

[18] P Hayward and C Fleury, 'Absolute waterfrontage: Road networked artificial islands and finger island canal estates on Australia's Gold Coast' (2016) 2 *Urban Island Studies* 25.

[19] See *Fur Seals Arbitration* (*Great Britain v USA*) (15 August 1893) in JB Moore, *History and Digest of the International Arbitrations to Which the United States Has Been a Party*, vol 1 (Government Printing Office 1898) 755, 901; PC Jessup, *The Law of Territorial Waters and Maritime Jurisdiction* (GA Jennings Co 1927) 69–70.

[20] League of Nations, *Acts of the Hague Conference*, vol 3 (1930) 219; see discussion in HW Jayewardene, *The Regime of Islands in International Law* (Martinis Nijhoff 1990) 8; Johnson (n 2) 211–12.

[21] International Law Commission, 'Commentary to the articles concerning the law of the sea' in *Yearbook of the International Law Commission*, vol 2 (1956) UN Doc A/CN.4/SER.A/1956/Add.l, 265, 270, art 10, where it was observed that 'An island is understood to be any area of land …'.

[22] Jayewardene (n 20) 8; DP O'Connell, *The International Law of the Sea*, vol 1 (Clarendon Press 1982) 196.

issue. Artificial islands were alluded to in draft Article 71 concerning the exploration of the continental shelf and the associated construction and maintenance of installations. In the view of the ILC '[s]uch installations, though under the jurisdiction of the coastal State, do not possess the status of islands.'[23]

There was no precise legal regime dedicated to artificial islands arising from the First United Nations Conference on the Law of the Sea (UNCLOS I) in 1958. While direct reference was made to natural islands in the Convention on the Territorial Sea and Contiguous Zone,[24] artificial islands were not addressed. Nevertheless, clear recognition was given to the sovereignty of the coastal State over the territorial sea, which in turn conferred capacity to construct an artificial island within that area.[25] The Convention on the Continental Shelf made more express reference to the potential to construct 'installations and devices' on the continental shelf in association with exploration and exploitation of continental shelf natural resources.[26] However, it was made clear in Article 5(4) that:

> Such installations and devices, though under the jurisdiction of the coastal State, do not possess the status of islands. They have no territorial sea of their own, and their presence does not affect the delimitation of the territorial sea of the coastal State.

This variable legal status for installations and devices created several policy issues. As observed by McDougal and Burke in 1962, there remained an opportunity for coastal States to seek to utilise artificial islands as a means to extend their internal waters or the territorial sea.[27]

IV. Early State Practice

Given the lack of clarity regarding the status of artificial islands under the 1958 Geneva Conventions and the law of the sea generally in the 1960s and 1970s, it is unsurprising that some state practice developed. The first related to the development of modern technologies that permitted continental shelf resource exploitation by way of oil rigs and other facilities attached to the sea-bed. These were clear examples of the type of installations that the Convention on the Continental Shelf, Article 5 had contemplated. Second, ambiguity prevailed as to whether a naturally-formed island could also include 'man-made' structures such as lighthouses.[28] This was particularly important with respect to debates over whether a rock or a reef could become an island as a result of lighthouse works. This was reflected in state practice examples from the time. In 1971 the Minerva

[23] International Law Commission (n 21) 299, art 71(3) and accompanying commentary.
[24] Convention on the Territorial Sea and Contiguous Zone (adopted 29 April 1958, (entered into force 10 September 1964) 516 UNTS 206, art 10.
[25] ibid art 1.
[26] Convention on the Continental Shelf (adopted 29 April 1958, entered into force 10 June 1964) 499 UNTS 312, art 5(2).
[27] MS McDougal and WT Burke, *The Public Order of the Oceans* (Yale University Press 1962) 388.
[28] O'Connell (n 22) 197.

Reefs in the Pacific Ocean were the focus of attention by a non-governmental organisation that sailed to the reefs, undertook some minimal land reclamation, and proclaimed the 'Republic of Minerva'.[29] This prompted a response in 1972 from Tonga which extended to a range of activities, including the construction of two artificial islands – Teleki Tokelau and Teleki Tonga – and the publication of a territorial claim to the islands.[30] Tonga also sought to draw attention to its actions in international fora, including the Third United Nations Conference on the Law of the Sea (UNCLOS III)[31] and the South Pacific Forum.[32] Other examples of artificial island building and assertions of some form of entitlement over an 'island' relate to the actions of private citizens. These include the construction in 1968 of a platform named Insulo de la Rozoj (Rose Island) just beyond the Italian territorial sea by two Italian citizens,[33] the so-called 'Duchy of Sealand' declared in 1967 with respect to an abandoned World War II sea fort in the English Channel,[34] and attempts by US entrepreneurs to build artificial islands founded on reefs off the Florida coast during the 1960s.[35] While caution needs to be exercised in giving too much weight to the actions of private as opposed to State actors, it highlights the interest in artificial islands of whatever form and the potential legal challenges under the law of the sea and related municipal law.

V. LOSC

Given the historical legal background it is unsurprising that UNCLOS III sought to resolve a number of the core legal issues associated with artificial islands, which up to that time had been left largely unregulated. Debate at UNCLOS III over artificial islands had as a starting point the Convention on the Continental Shelf, Article 5. Deliberations commenced at the 1971 Sea-Bed Committee meetings, and extended until the final 1982 UNCLOS III sessions. Many States contributed to those debates.[36] The recognition of the exclusive economic zone (EEZ) in the LOSC, and the synergies between that regime and the continental shelf, paved the way for clarification as to the status of artificial islands and coastal State entitlements

[29] Saunders (n 7) 672.

[30] SP Menefee, 'Republics of the Reefs: Nation-Building on the Continental Shelf and in the World's Oceans' (1994) 25 *California Western International Law Journal* 81, 99–100; see also L Song, 'The Curious History of the Minerva Reefs: Tracing the Origin of Tongan and Fijian Claims Over the Minerva Reefs' (2019) 54 *The Journal of Pacific History* 417.

[31] O'Connell (n 22) 197.

[32] Saunders (n 7) 673; for more details see LA Horn, 'To Be or Not To Be: The Republic of Minerva-Nation Founding by Individuals' (1973) 12 *Columbia Journal of Transnational Law* 520.

[33] Saunders (n 7) 667–68; Menefee (n 30) 105–6.

[34] Saunders (n 7) 668–70; Menefee (n 30) 106–11; and AHE Lyon, 'The Principality of Sealand, and Its Case for Sovereign Recognition' (2015) 29 *Emory International Law Review* 637.

[35] Saunders (n 7) 670–71; Menefee (n 30) 85–95; and CW Walker, 'Jurisdictional Problems Created by Artificial Islands' (1973) 10 *San Diego Law Review* 638.

[36] These included Argentina, Belgium, Brazil, France, India, Malta, Nigeria, Peru, Uruguay, UK, USA, USSR, and States from Africa, Eastern Europe, Latin America; see SN Nandan and S Rosenne (eds), *United Nations Convention on the Law of the Sea 1982: A Commentary*, vol 2 (Martinus Nijohff

with respect to them. The principal provision is LOSC Article 60 relating to artificial islands in the EEZ, which builds upon Article 56 which makes clear the coastal State has jurisdiction with respect to 'the establishment and use of artificial islands' in the EEZ. These provisions are complemented by LOSC Article 80 which applies Article 60 *mutatis mutandis* to the continental shelf,[37] Article 87(1)(d) which extends the right to construct artificial islands to all States on the high seas,[38] and Article 246 regarding the role of artificial islands in marine scientific research within the EEZ and continental shelf.

LOSC Article 60 relevantly provides:

Article 60

Artificial islands, installations and structures in the exclusive economic zone

1. In the exclusive economic zone, the coastal State shall have the exclusive right to construct and to authorize and regulate the construction, operation and use of:
   (a) artificial islands;
   (b) installations and structures for the purposes provided for in article 56 and other economic purposes;
   (c) installations and structures which may interfere with the exercise of the rights of the coastal State in the zone.
2. The coastal State shall have exclusive jurisdiction over such artificial islands, installations and structures, including jurisdiction with regard to customs, fiscal, health, safety and immigration laws and regulations.
3. Due notice must be given of the construction of such artificial islands, installations or structures, and permanent means for giving warning of their presence must be maintained. …
4. The coastal State may, where necessary, establish reasonable safety zones around such artificial islands, installations and structures in which it may take appropriate measures to ensure the safety both of navigation and of the artificial islands, installations and structures.
5. The breadth of the safety zones shall be determined by the coastal State, taking into account applicable international standards. Such zones shall be designed to ensure that they are reasonably related to the nature and function of the artificial islands, installations or structures, and shall not exceed a distance of 500 metres around them, measured from each point of their outer edge, except as authorized by generally accepted international standards or as recommended by the competent international organization. Due notice shall be given of the extent of safety zones.
6. All ships must respect these safety zones and shall comply with generally accepted international standards regarding navigation in the vicinity of artificial islands, installations, structures and safety zones.

1993) 573–84; for additional discussion on the historical background to LOSC, art 60 see A Proelss, 'Article 60 Artificial Islands, installations and structures in the exclusive economic zone' in A Proelss (ed), *United Nations Convention on the Law of the Sea: A Commentary* (CH Beck 2017) 464, 466–69.

[37] LOSC (n 3) art 79 also addresses the interaction within the continental shelf of artificial islands and submarine cables and pipelines.

[38] This right is subject to LOSC (n 3) pt VI which reflects limitations on the capacity of any State in the high seas to construct an artificial island on the continental shelf of a coastal State that extends beyond 200nm.

7. Artificial islands, installations and structures and the safety zones around them may not be established where interference may be caused to the use of recognized sea lanes essential to international navigation.
8. Artificial islands, installations and structures do not possess the status of islands. They have no territorial sea of their own, and their presence does not affect the delimitation of the territorial sea, the exclusive economic zone or the continental shelf.

A. Analysis of LOSC Articles 60 and 80

A number of observations can be made regarding Articles 60 and 80 in their respective application to the EEZ and continental shelf. First, no definition is given as to what is an artificial island.[39] No reference is made to Article 121 and the Part VIII Regime of Islands. Nevertheless, some guidance can be taken from the Article 121(1) definition of an island being 'a naturally formed area of land, surrounded by water, which is above water at high tide.' Likewise, the Article 121(3) island/rock distinction must also be of some importance, which in the context of an artificial island would go to issues associated with size, human habitation, and economic life. The starting point in defining an artificial island is that it must possess the characteristics of an island, as distinct from Article 60 installations and structures which may be fixed to the sea-bed by way of 'legs', or floating.[40] It follows therefore than an artificial island must possess all of the characteristics of an island as understood in the LOSC, other than that it has been located or built in situ by humans.[41] Some of the questions that arise are whether the artificial island must meet a high threshold test of having all the characteristics of an Article 121(1) island with the only distinction being that it has been made artificially by way of human intervention? Would that extend to an Article 121(3) rock that through human intervention has been made into an artificial island?

Second, the right to construct the artificial island within the EEZ or continental shelf is exclusive to the coastal State, which also possesses exclusive jurisdiction over it.[42] The entitlement here rests with the coastal State which has claim to the EEZ or continental shelf. It is not an entitlement that rests generally with coastal States.

[39] For some definitions see AG Oude Elferink, 'Artificial Islands, Installations and Structures' in R Wolfrum (ed), *Max Planck Encyclopedia of Public International Law* (online edn, Oxford University Press 2013); GK Walker (ed), *Definitions for the Law of the Sea: Terms Not Defined by the 1982 Convention* (Martinus Nijhoff 2012) 104; CW Walker, 'Jurisdictional Problems Created by Artificial Islands' (1973) 10 *San Diego Law Review* 638, 638; Soons (n 2) 3.

[40] Cf *In Re Duchy of Sealand* (1989) 80 ILR 683 where reference is made to the Duchy of Sealand (Fort Roughs) – a former British anti-aircraft platform – as an island constructed by use of two concrete pillars connected to the sea-bed.

[41] See also analysis in Proelss (n 36) 470–71 which places emphasis on the feature being 'man-made'.

[42] See comment in Proelss (n 36) 469–70; the extent of the jurisdiction is further detailed in LOSC (n 3) art 208 which makes clear that the coastal State is to adopt laws and regulations with respect to protection of the marine environment in relation to any sea-bed activities associated with artificial islands.

To construct an artificial island the coastal State must therefore be the recognised coastal State with respect to that EEZ or continental shelf area.[43] Unsurprisingly the word 'exclusive' is found on multiple occasions throughout LOSC Part V dealing with the EEZ, but its use in Article 60 with respect to artificial islands is the only specific occasion it is used outside of a direct reference to the EEZ. No precise indicator is given as to how this exclusive coastal State right and jurisdiction is to be exercised. A counterpoint can be found in LOSC Article 62 where the coastal State's EEZ rights with respect to the utilization of living resources are capable of being shared with other States. Nevertheless, while the coastal State possesses these exclusive rights with respect to artificial islands, as in other aspects of the law of the sea it is within the scope of those rights to give consent or provide a licence to others to construct an artificial island.[44] The coastal State must also give notice to the other States of their construction of an artificial island.[45]

Third, an artificial island does not possess the 'status of islands', and has no territorial sea.[46] The phrase 'status of islands' is found only in LOSC Articles 60, 147 and 259. The 'status of islands' in the LOSC is broad enough to encompass all the instances where islands are referred to, especially with respect to where an island has implications for maritime rights and entitlements such as Article 7 straight baselines and Article 47 straight archipelagic baselines. That an artificial island has no territorial sea also makes clear the distinction not only from an Article 121(1) island but also from an Article 121(3) rock, where a rock does enjoy a territorial sea entitlement. Though the feature is referred to as an artificial island, it does not enjoy some of the core attributes of a juridical island. This extends not only to the law of the sea, but also to many of the general attributes of territory under international law.[47]

Fourth, the artificial island has no impact on the delimitation of the territorial sea, EEZ or continental shelf. This follows from an artificial island not having any maritime entitlements. Nor could an artificial island possessing some of the characteristics of a low-tide elevation be utilised for the purposes of measuring the breadth of the territorial sea.[48] An artificial island may be subject to a declared safety zone of a distance no greater than 500 metres. Such a coastal State safety

[43] This becomes an especially relevant factor where the legitimacy of an EEZ claim is contested, or where, if a coastal State is seeking to construct an artificial island on an area of continental shelf beyond 200 nm, that entitlement has not been subject to review by the Commission on the Limits of the Continental Shelf, and the coastal State has not proclaimed its continental shelf entitlements beyond 200 nm consistently with the Commission's recommendations as per LOSC (n 3) art 76.

[44] In this context, note LOSC (n 3) art 77(2), which provides with respect to the continental shelf that 'The rights … are exclusive in the sense that if the coastal State does not explore the continental shelf or exploit its resources, no one may undertake these activities without the express consent of the coastal State.'

[45] LOSC (n 3) art 60(3); here it is of interest that specific reference is made to the procedures associated with the abandonment or removal of installations or structures but no equivalent provisions exist with respect to artificial islands.

[46] See also comment in Proelss (n 36) 479–80.

[47] See discussion by Saunders (n 7) at 676–81 assessing the 'natural state' doctrine and its implications for how an artificial island may have some of the characteristics of a juridical island.

[48] LOSC (n 3) art 13.

zone must adhere to generally accepted international standards, and shipping is under an obligation to respect such a zone.

B. *South China Sea* Arbitration

The 2016 *South China Sea* arbitration is, to date, the leading decision of any international court or tribunal assessing the LOSC and artificial islands. The substantive background to *South China Sea* has been discussed in Chapter one, including the important aspects of the award detailing the distinction between islands and rocks. With respect to artificial islands in the South China Sea, the principal issues before the LOSC Annex VII Arbitral Tribunal were that:

- China's occupation of and construction activities on Mischief Reef were in violation of the LOSC with respect to artificial islands;
- China's occupation of and construction activities on Mischief Reef were in violation of China's duties under the LOSC to protect and preserve the marine environment; and
- China's dredging and artificial island building, and construction activities at Mischief Reef, Cuarteron Reef, Fiery Cross Reef, Gaven Reef, Johnson Reef, Hughes Reef and Subi Reef had unlawfully aggravated and extended the dispute between the Philippines and China.[49]

While the focus for the Tribunal was China's action, it was observed that other States in the South China Sea since the 1990s had undertaken a range of activities on certain features including the installation of 'buildings, wharves, helipads, and weather and communications instruments.'[50]

Mischief Reef is one of the larger reefs in the Spratly Islands group in the South China Sea. It has been described as a 'large atoll that has three natural passes (1.8m, 18m and 24m deep) into the lagoon, which has a depth of 20–27m'.[51] The status of Mischief Reef vis-à-vis China/Philippines relations[52] was highlighted by China's initial construction activities on the reef from 1995.[53] Diplomatic exchanges took place between China and the Philippines over China's ongoing activities on Mischief Reef up to the time of the 2016 arbitration award.[54] Over that 20-year period,

[49] *South China Sea* (n 6) (Final Submissions of the Philippines) 41–42 [112].

[50] ibid 388 [977].

[51] SCA Ferse, P Mumby, and S Ward, 'Assessment of the potential environmental consequences of construction activities on seven reefs in the Spratly Islands in the South China Sea, Independent Expert Report – Coral Reef Environment' (*South China Sea Annex VII Tribunal*, 26 April 2016) 19 [6] https://pcacases.com/web/sendAttach/1809.

[52] For background to the dispute over the status of the reef see D Zha and MJ Valencia, 'Mischief Reef: Geopolitics and implications' (2001) 31 *Journal of Contemporary Asia* 86; IJ Storey, 'Creeping Assertiveness: China, the Philippines and the South China Sea Dispute' (1999) 29 *Contemporary Southeast Asia* 95.

[53] *South China Sea* (n 6) 399 [996].

[54] See summary of these in ibid 399–403 [996]–[1006].

China's activities on Mischief Reef had gone through various phases with the initial focus being on installation of small structures, and intensive construction commencing in 2014. The Tribunal was presented with calculations from the Philippines indicating that China's construction work had resulted in 5,580,000 square metres of new land on the reef as at November 2015.[55] An expert report to the Arbitral Tribunal stated that approximately 48 per cent of the reef had been lost to land reclamation.[56]

As to the natural status of Mischief Reef, the Tribunal determined that it was a low-tide elevation and not a rock or an island and generated no maritime entitlements.[57] It was found to be located within the Philippines EEZ and that China had no legal basis for any entitlements to maritime zones with respect to the reef.[58] The Tribunal reaffirmed the significance of LOSC Articles 56, 60 and 80 concerning artificial islands, and observed as follows:

> These provisions speak for themselves. In combination, they endow the coastal State – which in this case is necessarily the Philippines – with exclusive decision-making and regulatory power over the construction and operation of artificial islands, and of installations and structures covered by Article 60(1), on Mischief Reef. Within its exclusive economic zone and continental shelf, only the Philippines, or another authorised State, may construct or operate such artificial islands, installations or structures.[59]

The Tribunal considered that China's activities on Mischief Reef had over time evolved from constructing installations or structures into the 'creation of an artificial island' from 'what was originally a reef platform that submerged at high tide into an island that is permanently exposed.'[60] In sum, considering the findings as to the status of Mischief Reef and the extent of China's activities, the Tribunal was of the view that China had breached LOSC Articles 60 and 80 in undertaking the construction of an artificial island without the authorisation of the Philippines.[61]

With respect to China's dredging and artificial island-building activities on Mischief Reef, Cuarteron Reef, Fiery Cross Reef, Gaven Reef, Johnson Reef, Hughes Reef and Subi Reef, the Tribunal assessed the evidence before it. The Tribunal's focus here was on the marine environmental impact of China's activities on these reefs, rather than matters associated with their status or otherwise

[55] ibid 403 [1008].
[56] Ferse, Mumby, and Ward (n 51) 30, 50.
[57] *South China Sea* (n 6) 167–68 [374], 411 [1025].
[58] ibid 411–12 [1025].
[59] ibid 414 [1035].
[60] ibid 414 [1037].
[61] ibid 415 [1043]; see also the *Dispositif*, ibid 471–77 [1203]; see also analysis in Y Tanaka, *The South China Sea Arbitration: Toward and International Legal Order in the Oceans* (Hart Publishing 2019) 147–78; JA Roach, 'Artificial islands in the South China Sea: the legal regime and implications of the Award' in S Jayakumar et al (eds), *The South China Sea Arbitration: The Legal Dimension* (Edward Elgar 2018) 206, 213–16; R Lewis, 'The Artificial Construction and Modification of Maritime Features: Piling Pelion on Ossa' (2021) 52 *Ocean Development and International Law* 239, 256–57.

as artificial islands. In this respect the expert report on China's reef construction activities observed that:

> From the area that was identified as shallow reef habitat prior to the onset of large-scale construction activity, 2% has been converted into artificial land after land reclamation was finished at Johnson Reef, 5% at Hughes and Cuarteron Reefs, 13% at Gaven Reef, 48% at Mischief Reef, and 61 and 62% at Subi and Fiery Cross Reefs, respectively.[62]

With respect to the aggravation of the dispute, the Tribunal was of the view that China's activities on Mischief Reef had 'effectively created a *fait accompli* … by constructing a large artificial island on a low-tide elevation … where only the Philippines may construct or authorise artificial islands.'[63] It was conceded by the Tribunal that Mischief Reef could not be returned to its original state due to the extent of China's construction work.[64] With respect to the other six reefs the Tribunal's focus related to the marine environment and impact arising from dredging of lagoons and damage to the reef systems. It was determined that China's construction of artificial islands on these reefs had caused irreparable harm to the coral reef habitat and had aggravated the dispute.[65]

The award provides important guidance on some core aspects of the LOSC artificial islands regime, and highlights the important environmental impact and application of LOSC Part XII environmental measures with respect to artificial islands.[66] Its significance is assessed in more detailed below.

VI. Contemporary State Practice

The most extensive contemporary state practice regarding the construction of artificial islands has occurred across the South China Sea, including in areas associated with the Paracel Islands and the Spratly Islands. That practice has, as the Tribunal in *South China Sea* acknowledged, evolved over time from a period commencing in the 1970s when a number of structures and installations were built. Those activities significantly transitioned to full-scale artificial island construction from 2010, and remain ongoing.[67] As listed in Table 2.1 (appended), as of 2021 the Asia Maritime Transparency Initiative had identified 33 maritime features in the

[62] Ferse, Mumby, and Ward (n 51) 30.
[63] *South China Sea* (n 6) 462 [1177].
[64] ibid.
[65] ibid 462–63 [1178]; Tanaka (n 61) 159–60; T Stephens, 'The Collateral Damage from China's 'Great Wall of Sand': The Environmental Dimensions of the *South China Sea Case*' (2016) 34 *Australian Year Book of International Law* 41, 48–51.
[66] LOSC (n 3) arts 208 and 214 are also applicable to artificial islands with respect to sea-bed activities. See also AW Kohl, 'China's Artificial Island Building Campaign in the South China Sea: Implications for the Reform of the United Nations Convention on the Law of the Sea' (2018) 122 *Dickinson Law Review* 917; Roach (n 61); Davenport (n 7); Saunders (n 7).
[67] For some historical background see B Dolven et al, 'Chinese Land Reclamation in the South China Sea: Implications and Policy Options' (Document No R44072, Congressional Research Service 2015).

Spratly Islands region of the South China Sea that had been subject to significant land reclamation or artificial island construction activity.[68] These islands, which included all of the seven assessed by the Arbitral Tribunal in *South China Sea*, were occupied by China, Malaysia, the Philippines, Republic of China (Taiwan), and Vietnam. In addition to being a physical presence for the various littoral States in the South China Sea, the artificial islands have airfields and associated runways, docks, small harbours, and infrastructure for personnel. All of the features have reportedly been built on a low-tide elevation such as a reef, or a rock.

Table 2.1 South China Sea features within the Spratly Islands subject to artificial island construction and/or land reclamation[69]

English Name	Occupied by	Status	Constructed and/or land reclaimed	GPS
Alison Reef	Vietnam	Low-tide elevation	No data	8° 48' 6" N, 113° 59' 18" E
Amboyna Cay	Vietnam	Rock	No data	7° 53' 30" N, 112° 55' 16" E
Ardasier Reef	Malaysia	Low-tide elevation	No data	7° 37' 3" N, 113° 56' 21" E
Barque Canada Reef	Vietnam	Rock	No data	08° 10' 30" N, 113° 18' 45" E
Collins Reef	Vietnam	Rock	No data	9° 46' 9" N, 114° 15' 23" E
Commodore Reef	Philippines	Rock	No data	08° 21' 30" N, 115° 13' 30" E
Cornwallis South Reef	Vietnam	Low-tide elevation	4.17 acres	8° 42' 44" N, 114° 11' 1" E
Cuarteron Reef	China	Rock	56 acres	8° 51' 45" N, 112° 50' 15" E
Discovery Great Reef	Vietnam	Rock	No data	10° 03' 00" N, 113° 51' 00" E
East Reef	Vietnam	Rock	No data	08° 49' 30" N, 112° 36' 00" E

(continued)

[68] The Asian Maritime Transparency Initiative (AMTI) claims as follows: 'Five claimants occupy nearly 70 disputed reefs and islets spread across the South China Sea. They have built more than 90 outposts on these contested features, many of which have seen expansion in recent years. AMTI has gathered satellite imagery of each outpost, along with other relevant information, to document their current status and any changes they have undergone in recent years': https://amti.csis.org/island-tracker/. The AMTI is an initiative of the Center for Strategic and International Studies (CSIS), Washington, DC, USA.

[69] Adopted from *South China Sea* (n 6), and Asia Maritime Transparency Initiative (n 7).

Table 2.1 ***(Continued)***

English Name	Occupied by	Status	Constructed and/or land reclaimed	GPS
Erica Reef	Malaysia	Rock	No data	8° 6' 20" N, 114° 7' 55" E
Fiery Cross Reef	China	Rock	677 acres	9° 32' 45" N, 112° 53' 15" E
Gaven Reefs	China	Rock	34 acres	10° 12' 24" N, 114° 13' 25" E
Hughes Reef	China	Low-tide elevation	19 acres	9° 54' 30" N, 114° 29' 50" E
Investigator Shoal	Malaysia	Low-tide elevation	No data	8° 7' 3" N, 114° 41' 28" E
Itu Aba Island	Republic of China	Rock	8 acres	10° 22' 35" N, 114° 21' 55" E
Johnson Reef	China	Rock	27 acres	9° 43' 1" N, 114° 16' 54" E
Ladd Reef	Vietnam	Low-tide elevation	No data	8° 39' 56" N, 111° 40' 28" E
Lansdowne Reef	Vietnam	Rock	0.24 acres	9° 46' 46" N, 114° 22' 11" E
Mariveles Reef	Malaysia	Low-tide elevation	No data	7° 58' 12" N, 113° 55' 3" E
Mischief Reef	China	Low-tide elevation	1379 acres	09° 54' 00" N, 115° 32' 00" E
Pearson Reef	Vietnam	Rock	6.03 acres	8° 57' 27" N, 113° 40' 57" E
Petley Reef	Vietnam	Rock	No data	10° 24' 38.16" N, 114° 35' 15.61" E
Sand Cay	Vietnam	Rock	9.19 acres	10° 22' 29" N, 114° 28' 48" E
Sin Cowe Island	Vietnam	Rock	26.07 acres	9° 53' 7" N, 114° 19' 47" E
South Reef	Vietnam	Rock	26.07 acres	11° 23' 15" N, 114° 17' 54" E
Southwest Cay	Vietnam	Rock	7.45 acres	11° 25' 44" N, 114° 19' 54" E
Spratly Island	Vietnam	Rock	37.19 acres	8° 38' 43" N, 111° 55' 12" E

(continued)

Table 2.1 ***(Continued)***

English Name	Occupied by	Status	Constructed and/or land reclaimed	GPS
Subi Reef	China	Low-tide elevation	976 acres	10° 55' 25" N, 114° 5' 5" E
Swallow Rock	Malaysia	Rock	No data	7° 22' 20" N, 113° 50' 43" E
Tennet Reef	Vietnam	Rock	No data	8° 51' 30" N, 114° 39' 22" E
Thitu Island	Philippines	Rock	No data	11° 3' 12" N, 114° 17' 5" E
West Reef	Vietnam	Rock	70.05 acres	8° 51' 29" N, 112° 13' 33" E

Other examples of modern artificial island-building activity can be found in the cases of Jurong Island, and Pedra Banca/Pulau Batu Puteh (Singapore),[70] Hulhamalé (Maldives),[71] the Palm Islands (United Arab Emirates (UAE)),[72] Port and Rokko Islands (Japan),[73] and the Upper Zakum Expansion Project (UAE).[74] Also under development is Forest City (Malaysia),[75] while Denmark is also developing two 'energy islands' in the North Sea.[76] These artificial islands have been

[70] Located in Singapore's territorial sea; see I Lim, 'Jurong Island' (*Singaporeinfopedia*, 1 March 2016): https://eresources.nlb.gov.sg/infopedia/articles/SIP_505_2004-12-17.html, where it is stated: 'Reclamation works for Jurong Island began in 1995 and were completed in 2009 – 20 years ahead of schedule. The reclamation amalgamated several islands comprising some 991 ha into a huge island of 3,000 ha.' In 2021 the Singapore Ministry of National Development announced that development works and land reclamation would proceed on Pedra Banca/Pulau Batu Puteh: AN Honniball, 'Singapore: Pedra Branca/Pulau Batu Puteh – Land Reclamation at Maritime Features Pending Maritime Delimitation' (2021) 6 *Asia-Pacific Journal of Ocean Law and Policy* 276.

[71] Located within the archipelagic waters of the Maldives to the south of North Male Atoll; see details at Housing Development Corporation of the Maldives, 'Hulhamalé: The City of Hope' (2016) https://hdc.com.mv/hulhumale/; and Jet Propulsion Laboratory, NASA, 'Hulhumale, Maldives' (22 January 2021) www.jpl.nasa.gov/images/hulhumale-maldives.

[72] Located within the territorial sea of the UAE, adjacent to Dubai where three Palm Islands have been constructed; see discussion in A Jalinoosi and S Moradifar, 'Analyzing the Consequences of the UAE Creating Artificial Islands in The Persian Gulf (Considering the Copenhagen School)' (2017) 1 *Journal of World Sociopolitical Studies* 281, 288.

[73] These are two artificial islands located within the Japanese internal waters of Osaka Bay for maritime port and airport infrastructure.

[74] Located within the EEZ of the UAE within the Persian Gulf, approximately 84 km north-west of Abu Dhabi and built to support the Upper Zakum Oilfield project; see A Gupta, 'Upper Zakum Offshore Oil Field Development, Abu Dhabi' (*Offshore Technology*, 5 August 2019) www.offshore-technology.com/projects/upper-zakum-offshore-uae/.

[75] Located in the Malaysian territorial sea in the Strait of Johor opposite Singapore, and comprising four man-made islands spanning 30 km^2; see details at Country Garden Pacificview, 'Forest City', www.forestcitycgpv.com/.

[76] SM Enghave, 'Energy island in the North Sea' (Danish Energy Agency) ens.dk/en/our-responsibilities/wind-power/energy-islands/energy-island-north-sea; 'Denmark to build "first energy island" in North Sea', *BBC News* (4 February 2021) www.bbc.com/news/world-europe-55931873.

constructed for a variety of purposes ranging from airports, energy generation, marine port infrastructure, and offshore oil and gas, to tourism, and urban housing. All are located in internal waters, archipelagic waters, territorial sea, or the EEZ. None raise issues with respect to the basic entitlement of the coastal State to undertake construction consistently with the LOSC. Environmental issues with respect to these artificial island-building projects are separately addressed under relevant municipal law, or where they have raised issues for neighbouring States, under international law.

VII. Artificial Islands, Rocks and Land Reclamation

While the LOSC and state practice makes clear that coastal States are entitled to construct artificial islands in their maritime domain, an issue arises as to whether a distinction exists between land reclamation and the construction of an artificial island. Land reclamation is a legitimate activity that all States are able to engage in and have done so for centuries.[77] Enhanced technological capability and responding to the impacts of climate change, including storm surges and sea-level rise, make land reclamation a realistic option for an increasing number of coastal States.[78] This raises for consideration the issue of what are the limits of land reclamation under international law and when does a legitimate act of land reclamation instead become the construction of an artificial island.[79] It also raises for consideration environmental issues associated with land reclamation and artificial island building.[80]

The LOSC alludes to land reclamation in Article 11 which provides that 'outermost permanent harbour works which form an integral part of the harbour system are regarded as part of the coast'[81] and can accordingly be utilised for determining the normal baseline where circumstances permit.[82] The seaward expansion of ports such as Rotterdam,[83] Singapore,[84] Hong Kong,[85] and Mumbai[86] illustrates

[77] For some of the literature see T Gaeth, 'Coastal Reclamation in the 21st Century' (2020) 86 *Crit* 31; D Sengupta, R Chen, and ME Meadows, 'Building beyond land: An overview of coastal land reclamation in 16 global megacities' (2018) 90 *Applied Geography* 229.

[78] See *Case Concerning Land Reclamation by Singapore in and around the Straits of Johor (Malaysia v Singapore)* (Provisional Measures) (8 October 2003) ITLOS Reports 2003, 10 (*Straits of Johor*) where neither ITLOS nor the parties contested the capacity of coastal States to engage in land reclamation.

[79] See Oude Elferink (n 39) who observed that: 'It should not be overlooked that at times it may be controversial whether a land reclamation is an artificial island or forms part of an existing coast.'

[80] SY Chee et al, 'Land reclamation and artificial islands: Walking the tightrope between development and conservation' (2017) 12 *Global Ecology and Conservation* 80.

[81] However, LOSC (n 3) art 11 also makes clear that 'Off-shore installations and artificial islands shall not be considered as permanent harbour works.'

[82] D Anderson, 'Some Aspects of the Regime of Islands in the Law of the Sea' (2017) 32 *International Journal of Marine and Coastal Law* 316, 328.

[83] Oude Elferink (n 39); see also, United States Geological Survey, 'EarthView – Expansion at the Port of Rotterdam' (22 December 2016) www.usgs.gov/news/earthview-expansion-port-rotterdam, which states 'A large infrastructure project has changed the shape of the coastline of the Netherlands while increasing the cargo capacity at Europe's largest port … the Maasvlakte 2 project, which is an expansion

state practice in this regard and the acceptance of land reclamation in customary international law for both mainland (continental) and island States.[87] Nevertheless, the Tribunal in *South China Sea* made clear that there are limits associated with land reclamation, and that one form of natural feature cannot be converted into another, when it observed that:

> Just as a low-tide elevation or area of seabed cannot be legally transformed into an island through human efforts, the Tribunal considers that a rock cannot be transformed into a fully entitled island through land reclamation. The status of a feature must be assessed on the basis of its natural condition.[88]

In addition to the South China Sea examples already noted, there are other instances of state practice where attempts have been made by States to bolster or enhance the status of certain natural features. In the case of the Arctic Ocean island of Kolbeinsey (Iceland), a helicopter landing pad was built to combat the effects of erosion and boost the island's status for the purposes of maritime boundary negotiations with Denmark.[89] Likewise, in the case of Okinotorishima (Japan) efforts have been made to halt the impact of erosion and rising sea levels by the construction of coffer dams to support the rocks,[90] which in turn has resulted in academic debate as to whether Japan's conduct amounted to constructing an artificial island or simply preserving a natural feature.[91]

Land reclamation and artificial island construction also have environmental impacts that need to be assessed against general international law and the LOSC. This was first highlighted in the 2003 *Straits of Johor* case (Malaysia/Singapore) before the International Tribunal for the Law of the Sea (ITLOS).[92] Malaysia brought

of the Port of Rotterdam. … began in 2008. About 230 million cubic meters of sand were dredged from the North Sea to create about 5,000 acres of new land.'

[84] The Tuas Next-Generation Port Phase commenced in 2019 and is the most recent phase in Singapore's land reclamation/port development infrastructure projects; see Maritime and Port Authority of Singapore, 'Development of Tuas Next-Generation Port Phase 2 begins' (4 July 2019) www.mpa.gov.sg/web/portal/home/media-centre/news-releases/detail/a2860498-ff4f-4e9c-88ac-139653ae7541.

[85] R Glaser, P Haberzettl, and RPD Walsh, 'Land reclamation in Singapore, Hong Kong and Macau' (1991) 24 *GeoJournal* 365.

[86] Seatrade Maritime News, 'Mumbai Port Trust to Build a new Container Terminal; Permission Granted by Maharashtra Coastal Zone Management' (11 May 2021) www.seatrade-maritime.com/ports-logistics/mumbai-port-build-new-container-terminal; For historical background see T Riding, '"Making Bombay Island": land reclamation and geographical conceptions of Bombay, 1661–1728' (2018) 59 *Journal of Historical Geography* 27.

[87] See also A Grydehøj, 'Island city formation and urban island studies' (2015) 47(4) *AREA* 429.

[88] *South China Sea* (n 6) 214 [508].

[89] See discussion in T Jacobsen and I Stone, 'Kolbeinsey: Iceland's Arctic island' (2006) 42 *Polar Record* 167; and BB Jia, 'A Preliminary Study of the Problem of the Isle of Kolbeinsey' (1997) 66 *Nordic Journal of International Law* 301.

[90] V Prescott and C Schofield, *The Maritime Political Boundaries of the World* (2nd edn, Martinus Nijhoff 2005) 87; AL Silverstein, 'Okinotorishima: Artificial Preservation of a Speck of Sovereignty' (1990) 16 *Brooklyn Journal of International Law* 409.

[91] See discussion in G Xue, 'How Much Can a Rock Get? – A Reflection from the Okinotorishima Rocks' (2011) 13 *China Oceans Law Review* 1; YH Song, 'Okinotorishima: A "Rock" or an "Island"? Recent Maritime Boundary Controversy between Japan and Taiwan/China' in SY Hong and JM van Dyke (eds), *Maritime Boundary Disputes, Settlement Processes, and the Law of the Sea* (Brill 2009) 145.

[92] *Straits of Johor* (n 77).

these proceedings in order to halt land reclamation works that Singapore was conducting in the Straits of Johor between the two States, concerned as to the marine environmental impact of those works and their physical location vis-à-vis Malaysia's territorial sea.[93] ITLOS accepted that land reclamation works can have marine environmental impact and issued provisional measures calling upon the parties to undertake consultations to resolve their differences.[94]

In *South China Sea* the Tribunal made extensive reference to China's land reclamation activities. This reflected the Philippines' submissions that partly focussed on China's construction of artificial islands and land reclamation with respect to the seven Spratly coral reefs. Land reclamation and construction works were considered in parallel by the Tribunal with no meaningful distinction made between the two.[95] Based on the evidence presented, both by the Philippines and from independent experts, the Tribunal gave particular attention to the environmental impact of China's land reclamation and construction works activities and LOSC Articles 192 and 194. The Tribunal found that China's conduct:

> breached its obligation under Article 192 to protect and preserve the marine environment, … conducted dredging in such a way as to pollute the marine environment with sediment in breach of Article 194(1), and … violated its duty under Article 194(5) to take measures necessary to protect and preserve rare or fragile ecosystems as well as the habitat of depleted, threatened or endangered species and other forms of marine life.[96]

Observations were also made on China's conduct with respect to land reclamation/artificial island construction and its obligations under LOSC Articles 123, 197, and 206.[97]

VIII. Conclusions

Artificial islands have since the 2000s gained additional prominence in international law and the LOSC due to a rise in state practice and the *South China Sea* arbitral award. The core fundamentals of the legal regime with respect to artificial islands are settled as a result of the advancements in the law that took place through the LOSC. A coastal State has a clear entitlement to construct artificial islands in its internal waters, archipelagic waters, and territorial sea. This is entirely consistent with the sovereignty a coastal States possesses over those waters. Likewise, the coastal State can also construct artificial islands within the EEZ and continental

[93] See also ibid (Separate Opinion of Judge Cot) 57 [2], addressing the potential impact upon navigation of Singapore's land reclamation in a strait.

[94] *Straits of Johor* (n 77) 27 [106]; where ITLOS in the *Dispositif*: 'Directs Singapore not to conduct its land reclamation in ways that might cause irreparable prejudice to the rights of Malaysia or serious harm to the marine environment, taking especially into account the reports of the group of independent experts.' See also the discussion in Koh and Lin (n 15).

[95] See eg *South China Sea* (n 7) 388 [977].

[96] ibid 394 [983].

[97] ibid 394–97 [984]–[993].

shelf, including in those areas of the continental shelf that extend beyond 200nm. Further, all States, and not just coastal States, are entitled to construct artificial islands in the high seas. While there is no evidence of state practice of such activity occurring to date, this remains a future prospect.[98]

While the LOSC makes clear that artificial islands may be constructed in multiple settings, there are significant constraints, the most important of those being, as *South China Sea* made clear, that construction can only be undertaken by the coastal State which has recognised rights over the relevant maritime zone. The Tribunal's award also suggests – though it did not have jurisdiction to determine this matter – that construction of an artificial island in breach of the entitlement of the legitimate coastal State will not confer rights upon the constructing State. In addition to the LOSC Article 60 and 80 constraints, which importantly make clear that an artificial island does not enjoy the same entitlements as a juridical island, *South China Sea* also emphasised the application of LOSC Part XII marine environmental measures. As China's conduct in the South China Sea has highlighted, construction of an artificial island can be a significant industrial activity, causing irreparable harm and damage to the associated marine environment. Such conduct will trigger for any State a number of important LOSC marine environmental obligations, and potentially distinct obligations under international environmental law.[99] These LOSC marine environmental obligations were also highlighted by ITLOS in *Straits of Johor*.

Some grey areas remain in state practice, the LOSC, and decisions of international courts and tribunals regarding land reclamation and construction of an artificial island. While both activities are subject to marine environmental protection obligations and standards, there is no clarity as to when a legitimate act of land reclamation transitions into construction of an artificial island.[100] Land reclamation traditionally occurs close to the coast within internal waters, archipelagic waters, or the territorial sea. China's conduct in *South China Sea* was determined to have been undertaken in the Philippines EEZ, which was a unique dimension of the case. However, that critical aspect was founded on the Tribunal's ruling that all of the relevant reef features were low-tide elevations and not islands or rocks subject to appropriation. Land reclamation practice in the South China Sea is therefore exceptional, and needs to be seen against the backdrop of the other territorial and maritime disputes within that region.[101]

[98] Which also raises issues with respect to the jurisdiction that can be exercised over a high seas artificial island by the constructing State, and the operation of LOSC art 60 with respect to such a feature; see RC Schmidtke, 'Artificial Islands of the Future: The Seasteading Movement and the International Legal Regimes Governing Seasteads in EEZs and on the High Seas' (2019) 21 *Asian-Pacific Law & Policy Journal* 1.

[99] See discussion in *South China Sea* (n 6) 394–95 [984]–[986] assessing the decision of the International Court of Justice in *Pulp Mills on the River Uruguay (Argentina v Uruguay)* [2010] ICJ Reps 14.

[100] The difficulty of making this distinction was acknowledged by Jessup as far back as 1927: Jessup (n 19) at 69–70.

[101] TL McDorman, 'An International Law Perspective on Insular Features (Islands) and Low-tide Elevations in the South China Sea' (2017) 32 *International Journal of Marine and Coastal Law* 298, 314.

What can also be observed as a result of *South China Sea* is that efforts to convert a natural juridical feature such as a juridical rock or a low-tide elevation into a natural juridical island will not result in a change in the feature's international law status.[102] Maintaining that distinction is especially important for the purposes of LOSC Article 121(3); otherwise a core aspect of the natural island/rock distinction will be undermined.[103] As the Annex VII Arbitral Tribunal acknowledged, a rock or a low-tide elevation can be converted into an artificial island as a result of land reclamation or construction activities. In this respect, *South China Sea* emphasised the importance of the natural state doctrine, even when the natural state of a feature may no longer exist because of damage arising from those activities. The same principle applies to the debate over the status of Okinotorishima. Critically though, an artificial island cannot gain the characteristics of a juridical island. Though its land area may be utilised for purposes equivalent to a natural island, its maritime entitlements under the LOSC will remain that of an artificial island. The endorsement in *South China Sea* of assessing features in their natural condition sets a benchmark for future courts and tribunals in considering this issue; however it remains to be seen whether it places a brake on state practice in response to a range of natural threats posed to small-island features.

[102] Tanaka (n 61) 147–48. Lewis (n 61) 243–47.
[103] Anderson (n 81) at 328 also asserts that such action could constitute an abuse of right; see LOSC (n 3) art 300.

3

Islands and Territoriality

I. Introduction

This chapter considers international law, territoriality and islands. The territorial status of islands has been significant throughout history. Islands located both close to a coast, distant from a coast, or in seas and oceans far distant from metropolitan powers have been 'discovered', claimed, and subject to dispute. Wars have been fought over islands, including in modern times. Smaller islands, including clusters of islands, have proven to be of great strategic value for certain powers. This was vividly demonstrated during World War II when in the Pacific theatre both the Americans and Japanese engaged in fierce battles to claim and reclaim small islands because of their strategic value, especially for airfields.[1] Large groups of islands, including whole archipelagos, were claimed by colonial powers, such as the Dutch in the case of the Indonesian archipelago where the Dutch East India Company (VOC) had a significant presence between the seventeenth and eighteenth centuries.[2] As European colonial powers sponsored and supported multiple different voyages of discovery throughout the world's oceans, not only were 'new' islands discovered and charted by explorers but these lands also became the subject of claim by European States. A legacy of this history of exploration followed by colonisation was various claims by European powers to islands in the Caribbean,[3] and the Atlantic, Indian, and Pacific Oceans.

Exploration and discovery of new island lands created a significant colonial legacy and was a contributing factor, amongst others, to the recognition and realisation of the rights of island peoples to self-determination post-World War II. The result was the emergence of multiple new independent States, a great many of which were island States such as those in the Pacific and the Caribbean. Some have subsequently been recognised under the LOSC as archipelagic States. The rights of peoples to self-determination had a major impact on how territoriality and islands were viewed in the latter part of the twentieth century. Prior to that time, whilst there were significant States composed solely of islands, such as Britain, Japan

[1] See GL Rottman, *World War II Pacific island guide: a geo-military study* (Greenwood Press 2001).

[2] See generally JR Bruijn, 'Between Batavia and the Cape: Shipping Patterns of the Dutch East India Company' (1980) 11 *Journal of Southeast Asian Studies* 251.

[3] See generally G Horne, *The apocalypse of settler colonialism: the roots of slavery, white supremacy, and capitalism in 17th century North America and the Caribbean* (Monthly Review Press 2017).

and New Zealand, the emergence of new island States during the United Nations (UN) era has transformed the role and significance of island States in international affairs. That these new States were required to be able to demonstrate the existence of territory over which they exercised control was a key attribute of their new statehood.[4] This meant that when these new island States emerged as fully-fledged members of the international community their territorial boundaries were settled, including land borders where they existed. In the case of Timor-Leste, this was an essential issue given the past colonial history associated with the island of Timor and the period of Indonesian occupation from 1975–1999.[5] For the most part, therefore newly independent island States that gained recognition as a result of acts of self-determination and associated processes emerged with settled borders, albeit in some instances having inherited borders that were drawn and negotiated by European powers.[6]

Territoriality with respect to islands in some instances remains unsettled, is the subject of dispute, and occasionally can become the object of armed conflict. The 1982 Falklands War between Argentina and the United Kingdom (UK) over the Falkland (Malvinas) Islands is a reminder of how significant sovereignty disputes over islands can become.[7] China's ongoing policy of seeking to reintegrate the island of Taiwan into the People's Republic of China, and the Mauritius/UK dispute over the Chagos Archipelago, are reminders of how contentious the legal and political issues associated with some islands can remain.[8]

The purpose of this chapter is to explore these issues, with a particular focus on international law as it relates to territoriality. This is a well-established body of international law which arguably has diminished in importance over time given some of the dynamics associated with decolonisation. Nevertheless, territorial disputes with respect to islands still remain. Some are being addressed through diplomatic processes and are relatively benign; others are subject to formal dispute settlement mechanisms before international courts and tribunals, while others are politically contentious and have the potential to become flashpoints subject to geopolitical circumstances. In addressing these issues, consideration will be given to international law and territoriality, and then islands and the international law of territoriality, with particular reference to the key international cases. The current law of territoriality will then be discussed, particularly as it relates to

[4] J Crawford, *The Creation of States in International Law* (2nd edn, Clarendon Press 2006) 46–52 (*Creation of States*).

[5] See A Katalin Molnar, *Timor Leste: politics, history, and culture* (Routledge 2010).

[6] In the case of Papua New Guinea, which became independent in 1975, the western border with Indonesia is a colonial era border that was determined by the Dutch (West Papua/Irian Jaya) and Germany (Papua) and Britain (New Guinea); for some background see K Nyamekye and RR Premdas, 'Papua New Guinea-Indonesian Relations over Irian Jaya' (1979) 19 *Asian Survey* 927.

[7] DG Boyce, *The Falklands War* (Palgrave Macmillan 2005); AR Coll and AC Arend (eds), *The Falklands War: lessons for strategy, diplomacy, and international law* (Allen & Unwin 1985).

[8] See discussion in TE Stolper, *China, Taiwan, and the offshore islands* (Sharpe 1985); *Legal Consequences of the Separation of the Chagos Archipelago from Mauritius in 1965* (Advisory Opinion) (25 February 2019) [2019] ICJ Reps 95 (*Chagos Advisory Opinion*).

territorial disputes concerning islands. Finally, attention will be given to a number of contemporary island territorial disputes.

II. International Law and Territoriality

The international law of territoriality is closely linked to that of statehood and international law because the possession of territory is considered to be an essential element for the recognition of a new State. As discussed in Chapter ten, it also raises important issues with respect to the potential loss of territory as a result of sea-level rise.

A. Montevideo Convention Test

The classical formulation of the criteria for statehood is found in the 1933 Montevideo Convention on the Rights and Duties of States[9] which provides as follows:

> The State as a person of international law should possess the following qualifications:
> (a) a permanent population;
> (b) a defined territory;
> (c) government; and
> (d) capacity to enter into relations with other States.

These criteria have been subject to exhaustive debate,[10] and became especially significant post-1945 during the period of decolonisation when many new States emerged into the international community as reflected in the growth in UN membership during this period.[11]

In the 1928 *Island of Palmas Case*, Arbitrator Max Huber observed that 'Territorial sovereignty … involves the exclusive right to display the activities of a State.'[12] The capacity of a governmental entity to exclusively exercise sovereign rights over territory is therefore an essential attribute. In the case of islands,

[9] Montevideo Convention on the Rights and Duties of States (adopted 26 December 1933, entered into force 26 December 1934) 165 LNTS 19, art 1.

[10] See eg J Crawford, *Brownlie's Principles of Public International Law* (Oxford University Press 2019) 118–25 (*Brownlie's Principles*); MN Shaw, *International Law* (8th edn, Cambridge University Press 2017) 157–62; TD Grant, 'Defining Statehood: The Montevideo Convention and its Discontents' (1998–1999) 37 *Columbia Journal of Transnational Law* 403; JG Starke, 'The Acquisition of Title to Territory by Newly Emerged States' (1965–1966) 41 *British Yearbook of International Law* 411.

[11] In 1945 there were a total of 51 original UN members and those numbers grew to 60 (1950), followed by decade-on-decade growth as follows 99 (1960), 127 (1970), 154 (1980), 159 (1990), 189 (2000) and 193 (2011): United Nations, 'Growth in United Nations Membership' (21 May 2021) www.un.org/en/about-us/growth-in-un-membership.

[12] *Island of Palmas Case* (*United States of America v The Netherlands*) (1928) 2 RIAA 829, 839 (*Island of Palmas*).

many of which are small in size compared to continental territories, the ability of a government to be able to exercise the attributes of sovereignty over island lands may not be as challenging as is the case with continental lands. This can be readily highlighted by considering the size of the smallest island States – Nauru (21 km^2), Tuvalu (26 km^2) – with large continental States such as Russia (17,098,242 km^2), and Canada (9,984,670 km^2).[13] A government's capacity to effectively exercise sovereignty over an island territory should, in principle be much greater than exercising similar controls over continental lands. The coastlines of islands are their natural limits, with the result that the coastline of an island State is the territorial boundary of the State. This creates a limit for an island State territory that does not exist for continental States other than those which partially front a coast.[14] A consequence of this is that island States may often possess no land boundaries because the limits of the State are solely contained within the limits of the island or islands that comprise the State. Fiji, for example, a State that comprises 332 islands, has no land boundaries. Likewise for the Philippines which is reported to have 7641 islands.[15] Australia, a State that could be classified as either a continent or an island, shares no land boundaries with other States;[16] nor do other large islands such as Greenland (Denmark). Nevertheless, islands may be the subject of territorial boundaries between different sovereigns such that the territory of the island is shared between two or more States. Modern examples arise in the case of Indonesia/Papua New Guinea (PNG), Indonesia/Timor-Leste, Ireland/UK, Dominican Republic/Haiti, and exceptionally three States in the case of the island of Borneo: Brunei/Indonesia/Malaysia.[17]

Importantly there is no limitation on the size of land that can compose the territory of a State. Accordingly, it is possible for both the Vatican and Monaco to be States at 0.4 km^2 and 1.5 km^2 respectively, as can Nauru and Tuvalu.[18] The size of the State is not critical for the purpose of international law, though there have been longstanding debates over microstates and their stability.[19] A distinct issue

[13] All figures drawn from Central Intelligence Agency (US), 'Country Comparisons – By Area' (*The World Factbook*) www.cia.gov/the-world-factbook/field/area/country-comparison/.

[14] An exception to this proposition exists with respect to Australia, a continent without any internal international boundaries, and which is sometimes referred to as both an island and a continent: E McMahon, 'Australia, the Island Continent: How Contradictory Geography Shapes the National Imaginary' (2010) 13 *Space and Culture* 178.

[15] See entries for Indonesia and the Philippines in Central Intelligence Agency (US), (*The World Factbook*) www.cia.gov/the-world-factbook/.

[16] Cf Australia's land boundaries in Antarctica where the Australian Antarctic Territory adjoins territory claimed by France, New Zealand and Norway: V Prescott and G Triggs, *International Frontiers and Boundaries* (Martinus Nijhoff 2008) 385–88.

[17] For a leading study on land boundaries, international law and territories, see Prescott and Triggs (n 16).

[18] Crawford, *Creation of States* (n 4) 47.

[19] IA Shearer, *Starke's International Law* (Butterworths 1994) 88–9; WL Harris, 'Microstates in the United Nations: A Broader Purpose' (1970) 9 *Columbia Journal of Transnational Law* 23; and TD Grant, 'Micro States' in R Wolfrum (ed), *Max Planck Encyclopedia of Public International Law* (online edn, Oxford University Press 2013) who lists the islands of Tuvalu, Nauru, Palau, Saint Kitts and Nevis, the Marshall Islands, Dominica, and Grenada as in that category. There is extensive literature

arises with respect to the loss of territory as a consequence of climate change, and this is separately considered in Chapter ten.

B. Recognition

A critical issue associated with international law and territoriality is that of recognition. This arises in two contexts. The first is associated with the recognition of a new State. While the international law test associated with statehood is found in the Montevideo Convention, unless the entity claiming to be a State is recognised by other States its capacity to operate within the international system will be compromised or non-existent. A longstanding contemporary example is Taiwan – also officially referred to as the Republic of China – which includes a main island and the adjoining Pescadores, Matsu, and Quemoy islands. The Montevideo Convention criteria are met in principle excepting the ability of the Taiwanese government to engage in international relations other than with a small number of other States. Taiwan has previously enjoyed regular diplomatic relations with a number of States, but those numbers have dwindled in the past decade.[20] This has not impaired the capacity of some States to engage in relations with Taiwan,[21] but they are not the equivalent of State-to-State diplomatic relations.[22] Other examples arise with respect to where declarations of independence have been made

on these issues; see eg J Duursma, *Fragmentation and the international relations of micro-states: self-determination and statehood* (Cambridge University Press 1996); CC Joyner and S Harden, 'Small Is Dangerous: Micro States in a Macro World' (1985) 82 *American Political Science Review* 341.

[20] As of 2021, a total of 15 States recognised Taiwan (Republic of China), see Ministry of Foreign Affairs Republic of China (Taiwan), 'Diplomatic Allies' (1 October 2021) en.mofa.gov.tw/AlliesIndex.aspx?n=1294&sms=1007; For some analysis of the state of Taiwan's diplomatic relations see TS Rich, 'Does It Matter If Taiwan Loses Formal Recognition?' (*Australian Outlook*, 9 October 2019) www.internationalaffairs.org.au/australianoutlook/does-it-matter-if-taiwan-loses-formal-recognition/.

[21] In 2021, the US Department of State website contained the following details on the status of the US-Taiwan relationship: 'The United States and Taiwan enjoy a robust unofficial relationship. The 1979 U.S.–P.R.C. Joint Communique switched diplomatic recognition from Taipei to Beijing. In the Joint Communique, the United States recognized the Government of the People's Republic of China as the sole legal government of China, acknowledging the Chinese position that there is but one China and Taiwan is part of China. The Joint Communique also stated that the people of the United States will maintain cultural, commercial, and other unofficial relations with the people of Taiwan. The American Institute in Taiwan (AIT) is responsible for implementing U.S. policy toward Taiwan': Department of State (US), 'U.S. Relations with Taiwan' (24 May 2021) www.state.gov/u-s-relations-with-taiwan/; for an analysis of the US legal position with respect to Taiwan, see L Hsieh, 'The Legal Status of Taiwan in United State Courts' (2009) 6 (2) *Taiwan International Law Quarterly* 53–84.

[22] The Australian Department of Foreign Affairs and Trade, for example, states the following with respect to relations between Australia and Taiwan: 'The terms of our Joint Communiqué dictate the fundamental basis of Australia's one China policy – the Australian Government does not recognise the ROC as a sovereign state and does not regard the authorities in Taiwan as having the status of a national government. Dealings between Australian government officials and Taiwan, therefore, take place unofficially. For example, Australia's representative office in Taiwan does not have diplomatic status nor do Taiwan's representative offices in Australia, which have the title 'Taipei Economic and Cultural Office' (TECO)': Department of Foreign Affairs and Trade (Australia), 'Australia-Taiwan relationship' (23 May 2021) www.dfat.gov.au/geo/taiwan/Pages/australia-taiwan-relationship.

by some island territories that did not receive international recognition, with the consequence that those political movements gained no international momentum or failed. Examples here include Bougainville (North Solomons) (1975),[23] East Timor (1975),[24] and West Papua (2020).[25]

The second recognition issue relates to whether the territorial claims of the island State are recognised as legitimate by others. This could arise at the point of a declaration of independence, or there may be some unresolved territorial issues associated with parts of a new or existing island State. In the case of PNG, which became independent from Australia in 1975, an issue that arose during negotiations preceding independence was the status of certain Torres Strait islands. The Torres Strait separates the northern point of Australia (Cape York) and the southern PNG coastline. Colonial maps, charts and declarations were consulted to determine which Torres Strait islands formed the northern most limits of Australia and which were to be part of the new State.[26] Once the territorial limits were resolved it became possible for Australia and PNG to negotiate Torres Strait maritime boundaries in the certain knowledge that sovereignty over islands in the strait had been settled.[27] Territorial disagreements exist between New Caledonia (France) and Vanuatu, with respect to Matthew Island and Hunter Island,[28] which can be dated to the time of Vanuatu's independence in 1980, however this does not impact upon the recognition of Vanuatu's status as a State. That an island State is engaged in a territorial dispute with a neighbour or asserts a claim over islands that is not recognised does not undermine the status of that entity as a State. This is a regular aspect of international affairs. Disputes remain over territory and there exist accepted peaceful mechanisms for the resolution of those disputes. International law accepts that the limits of a State may not be fully defined, and as such a newly emerged island State or an existing island State may possess some undefined or disputed territorial limits that are not fully recognised by the international community. As the International Court of Justice (ICJ) observed in the *North Sea Continental Shelf* cases, 'There is for instance no rule that the land frontiers of a State must be fully delimited and defined, and often in various places and for long periods they are not ….'[29]

[23] S Heathcote, 'Secession, self-determination and territorial disagreements: Sovereignty claims in the contemporary South Pacific' (2021) 34 *Leiden Journal of International Law* 653, 661.

[24] PD Elliott, 'The East Timor Dispute' (1978) 27 *International and Comparative Law Quarterly* 238.

[25] Where a provisional 'government-in-waiting' was declared in 2020: B Doherty, 'West Papua independence leaders declare "government-in-waiting"', *The Guardian* (1 December 2020) www.theguardian.com/world/2020/dec/01/west-papua-independence-leaders-declare-government-in-waiting.

[26] See SB Kaye, 'The Torres Strait Islands: Constitutional and Sovereignty Questions Post-Mabo' (1994–1995) 18 *University of Queensland Law Journal* 38.

[27] Treaty between Australia and the Independent State of Papua New Guinea concerning Sovereignty and Maritime Boundaries in the area between the two Countries, including the area known as Torres Strait, and Related Matters (Australia–Papua New Guinea) (adopted 18 December 1978, entered into force 15 February 1985) [1985] ATS 4.

[28] Heathcote (n 23) 667–64.

[29] *North Sea Continental Shelf (Federal Republic of Germany v Denmark; Federal Republic of Germany v Netherlands)* (Judgment) [1969] ICJ Rep 3, 32. This rule is as equally applicable to new States as

III. Islands and Territoriality

International affairs and modern international relations are replete with disputes over islands. These islands may be adjacent to or distant from metropolitan States, or they may be contiguous to island States. As noted above, territoriality and islands have a particular connection in some parts of the world to colonial voyages of discovery, with the result that many island territorial disputes have been between colonial powers. The analysis that follows will therefore begin with a brief review of the leading historical cases, before turning to assess some of the contemporary decisions of the ICJ and Arbitral Tribunals in this area.

A. Historical Cases, Precedents and Tests

The leading historical cases are decisions of the Permanent Court of International Justice (PCIJ), the ICJ, and arbitral tribunals during the twentieth century up to the 1950s. The chronological survey below highlights developments in the relevant international law regarding territoriality and islands.

(i) Island of Palmas Case *(1928)*

The 1928 *Island of Palmas case* (USA v Netherlands),[30] decided by Arbitrator Max Huber, remains one of the leading decisions of an international court or tribunal addressing the international law of territoriality generally, and most specifically with respect to islands. The Island of Palmas (also referred to as Miangas) is a single, isolated island located nearly equidistant from the current-day Indonesian and Philippines archipelagos in the Celebes Sea. The essence of the dispute related to the validity of any title to the island the United States (US) had acquired from Spain by way of the 1898 Treaty of Paris[31] as opposed to any title to the island possessed by the Netherlands. The principal US argument was that its title had been acquired by way of cession under the Treaty of Paris, that it had acquired all the rights of sovereignty which Spain had possessed, and the right to recognition of that claim by treaty.[32] This claim in turn was based on the US being a successor to Spain whose claim in the first instance had been based on discovery.[33] The Netherlands contended that the East India Company had acquired sovereignty

existing States; as Crawford has noted: 'Thus even a substantial boundary or territorial dispute with a new State is not enough, of itself, to bring statehood into question. The only requirement is that the State must consist of certain coherent territory effectively governed …': Crawford, *Creation of States* (n 4) 52.

[30] *Island of Palmas* (n 12).

[31] Treaty of Paris (Spain–United States) (adopted 10 December 1898, entered into force 11 April 1899) 187 CTS 100.

[32] *Island of Palmas* (n 12) 842, 846.

[33] ibid 843.

over the island as early as the seventeenth century,[34] and that sovereignty had effectively been exercised over the islands 'based on the continuous and peaceful display of State authority.'[35]

Arbitrator Huber found that the title of sovereignty claimed by the Netherlands 'acquired by continuous and peaceful display of State authority during a long period of time going probably back beyond the year 1700' was a good title and prevailed over that claimed by the US.[36] With respect to the title claimed by the US on the basis of discovery, this was characterised as an 'inchoate title, as a claim to establish sovereignty by effective occupation',[37] which had not been established on the facts. Such a title, it was observed, 'cannot prevail over a definite title founded on continuous and peaceful display of sovereignty'.[38] Importantly, given the proximity of the Philippines archipelago to the island, Arbitrator Huber also determined that title founded on contiguity, as a basis of territorial sovereignty, 'has no foundation in international law.'[39]

(ii) Clipperton Island *(1932)*

In the *Clipperton Island* case (France v Mexico),[40] the Tribunal was asked to determine sovereignty with respect to an island located in the eastern Pacific Ocean, approximately 1,120 km southwest of Mexico and reported to be six square kilometres in size.[41] The arbitrator, King Emmanuel III of Italy, found that the island had been discovered by the French in 1858 at which time a declaration of sovereignty had been made.[42] France did not undertake any subsequent significant action with respect to the island until 1897–98 at which point Mexico also indicated its interest in the island, which it asserted had been longstanding. The Tribunal considered the Mexican claim, which was itself based upon Spanish exploration and asserted title to the island. However, Spain's claim to the island was considered to be incomplete, and there was no evidence of Mexican assertions of sovereignty until 1898.[43] As a result of the status of the Mexican claim, the arbitrator was of the view that France was able to assert an alternate claim when it proclaimed sovereignty in 1858. As to France's subsequent conduct it was observed that:

> There is no reason to suppose that France has subsequently lost her right by *derelictio*, since she never had the *animus* of abandoning the island, and the fact that she has not

[34] ibid 855–56.
[35] ibid 857.
[36] ibid 869.
[37] ibid 869.
[38] ibid 869.
[39] ibid 869.
[40] *Clipperton Island (France v Mexico)* (1931) 2 RIAA 1105 (*Clipperton Island*).
[41] Central Intelligence Agency (US) 'Clipperton Island', *The World Factbook* www.cia.gov/the-world-factbook/countries/clipperton-island/.
[42] *Clipperton Island* (n 40) 391.
[43] ibid 392–93.

> exercised her authority there in a positive manner does not imply the forfeiture of an acquisition already definitively perfected.[44]

The Tribunal therefore found in favour of French sovereignty over the island,[45] and France retains its title to the uninhabited island, which it administers as a French Overseas Territory. This decision remains significant given the historical practice of some island settlements being abandoned over a period of time.

(iii) Eastern Greenland *(1933)*

In the 1933 *Legal Status of Eastern Greenland* case (Denmark v Norway)[46] the PCIJ considered the respective claims of Denmark and Norway to a part of Eastern Greenland. The case revolved around issues of continuous and effective displays of sovereignty, declarations of sovereignty, and some historical treaties with respect to an area comprising the eastern coast of Greenland.[47] The Court reviewed the history of Danish and Norwegian discovery, exploration and settlement of parts of Greenland, including the enactment of laws and decrees that sought to exercise various attributes of sovereignty during that time. While Norway was prepared to concede the existence of Danish colonies in parts of Greenland, it sought to demonstrate title to parts of Eastern Greenland that it had occupied from 1931 onwards.[48] In reliance upon the *Island of Palmas* case, Denmark sought to assert its claim on the basis of a continuous and peaceful display of State authority.[49]

The PCIJ observed that two factors were critical to being able to demonstrate a continuous display of authority: 'the intention and will to act as sovereign, and some actual exercise or display of such authority.'[50] In this respect, the Court emphasised that in instances where there were two competing claims to sovereignty the task is to determine which of the claims is stronger. In this respect, it was observed that up until 1931 there had been no claim by any State other than Denmark to sovereignty over Greenland, and that until 1921 'no Power disputed the Danish claim to sovereignty.'[51] The Court also made the following observations, which subsequently have been considered to have great significance with

[44] ibid 394.

[45] ibid 390.

[46] *Legal Status of Eastern Greenland (Denmark v Norway)* [1933] PCIJ Rep Ser A/B No 53 (*Eastern Greenland*).

[47] The status of Greenland as the world's largest island, with a landmass of 2,166,086 km^2, did not form a specific basis for the court's judgment, though it was observed that: 'It should be added that only in the last years of the XIXth century was it definitely established that Greenland is not connected by land with the other parts of the continent of America, i.e. that Greenland is an island.' ibid 26.

[48] *Eastern Greenland* (n 46) 44.

[49] ibid 45.

[50] ibid 46.

[51] ibid 46.

respect to sovereignty over polar lands,[52] and which also can equally apply to isolated islands:

> It is impossible to read the records of the decisions in cases as to territorial sovereignty without observing that in many cases the tribunal has been satisfied with very little in the way of the actual exercise of sovereign rights, provided that the other State could not make out a superior claim. This is particularly true in the case of claims to sovereignty over areas in thinly populated or unsettled countries.[53]

After a review of the relevant historical facts, the Court concluded that as at the 'critical date' of 10 July 1931, Denmark had been able to demonstrate that it possessed 'a valid title to the sovereignty over all of Greenland' and that any opposing actions taken by Norway were illegal.[54] This PCIJ decision remains of enduring significance because it is the only case involving a polar island, and for the test that was suggested for the assertion of a territorial claim over polar lands.

(iv) Minquiers and Ecrehos *(1953)*

In the 1953 *Minquiers and Ecrehos* case (France v UK),[55] the ICJ was asked to adjudge territorial sovereignty over two islands and associated rocks in the English Channel.[56] Minquiers and Ecrehos are two separate entities comprising islets and rocks between the island of Jersey (UK) and the French coast, respectively located 3.9 miles north-east of Jersey and 6.6 miles from the French coast in the case of Ecrehos, and 9.8 miles south of Jersey and 16.2 miles from the French coast in the case of Minquiers.[57] Both parties maintained they had an ancient or original title to these features dating back as far as 1066, and as such this was not a dispute over lands considered to have been *terra nullius*.[58] The Court outlined the various historical arguments made by the parties and their potential importance, but ultimately came to the view that: 'What is of decisive importance, in the opinion of the Court, is not indirect presumptions deduced from events in the Middle Ages, but the evidence which relates directly to the possession of the Ecrehos and Minquiers groups'.[59] The Court then turned to consider and assess various acts of both the UK and France in the nineteenth and twentieth centuries and sought to assess the strength of the respective claims. On the basis of the facts, the Court unanimously found it was the UK that had the stronger of the claims to the two sets of features

[52] See discussion in DR Rothwell, *The Polar Regions and the Development of International Law* (Cambridge University Press 1996) 59–60.

[53] *Eastern Greenland* (n 48) 46.

[54] ibid 64.

[55] *Minquiers and Ecrehos Case (France v United Kingdom)* (Judgment) [1953] ICJ Reps 47 (*Minquiers and Ecrehos*).

[56] The Court described the features as 'islets and rocks which are physically capable of appropriation': ibid 53.

[57] ibid 53.

[58] ibid 53.

[59] ibid 57.

and that the facts relied upon by France did not evidence sufficient intent to act as sovereign.[60] The Court made extensive reference to the historical claims and records relied upon by the parties, but gave particular prominence to more recent sovereign acts. Little reference was made to relevant decisions of international courts or tribunals.[61] While this case turned on a unique set of historical facts, it emphasises the significance of *effectivités*; discussed in more detail below.

B. Modern Cases

The foundational decisions of international courts and tribunals noted above remain important precedents. Consideration will now be given to the modern cases, principally those of the ICJ, from 1992 onwards.

(i) Land, Island and Maritime Frontier Dispute *(1992)*

In the 1992 *Land, Island and Maritime Frontier Dispute* (El Salvador v Honduras; Nicaragua intervening)[62] a Chamber of the ICJ was asked to adjudicate a number of related land and island territorial disputes, and associated maritime issues between El Salvador and Honduras in the Gulf of Fonseca. Multiple complex procedural, factual and legal issues arose in this case, including disagreement between the parties as to which of the disputed islands fell within the Court's jurisdiction. Exhaustive arguments were presented by the parties with respect to the *uti possidetis juris* principle; however, the view of the Chamber was that the material was 'too fragmented or ambiguous' for it to be able to reach a determination on those grounds.[63]

Two islands in the Gulf were the focus of the Chamber's attention. With respect to the island of El Tigre, the Chamber found that Honduras had been in effective occupation of the island since 1849 and that on the basis of subsequent historical circumstances and the espousal by Latin American States of the *uti possidetis juris* principle, Honduras was the relevant territorial sovereign.[64] With respect to the islands of Meanguera del Golfo and Meanguerita, though the islands were geographically separate, they were considered a 'singular insular entity'[65] because

[60] ibid 71; see discussion in DHN Johnson, 'The Minquiers and Ecrehos Case' (1954) 3(2) *International and Comparative Law Quarterly* 189; R St J MacDonald, 'The Minquiers and Ecrehos Case' (1952–1955) 1 *McGill Law Journal* 277.

[61] In this respect, Judge Alverez observed 'the task of the Court is to resolve international disputes by applying, not the traditional or classical international law, but that which exists at the present day and which is in conformity with the new conditions of international life, and to develop this law in a progressive spirit': *Minquiers and Ecrehos* (n 55) (Declaration of Judge Alverez) 73.

[62] *Land, Island and Maritime Frontier Dispute (El Salvador v Honduras; Nicaragua intervening)* (Judgment) [1992] ICJ Reps 351 (*Land, Island and Maritime Frontier Dispute*).

[63] ibid 563 [341]; see discussion below at section IV.E regarding the *uti possidetis juris* principle.

[64] ibid 569–70 [354]–[355].

[65] ibid 570 [365].

of the view of both parties. The Chamber, after reviewing the relevant evidence concluded that El Salvador had made a claim to the island in 1854 and subsequently remained in effective possession of the island thereafter and as such was recognised as the territorial sovereign.[66] Importantly, the Chamber was of the view that both Honduras and El Salvador had effectively succeeded to Spanish sovereignty over the respective islands.[67] While this decision did not turn on the *uti possidetis juris* principle, it highlighted its importance within Latin America and the issues that arise in applying it to island territorial disputes.

(ii) Eritrea v Yemen Arbitral Award (First Phase) *(1998)*

In the 1998 *Eritrea/Yemen Arbitral Award (First Phase)*,[68] an Arbitral Tribunal was called upon to make determinations with respect to sovereignty over several islands and some associated maritime features contested between Eritrea and Yemen in the Red Sea. The case is distinctive because of the failure of the parties to agree on the precise scope of the islands that were in dispute, so that the Tribunal was tasked with making that determination itself.[69] Considerable attention was given by the parties to making out their claims based on historic titles; however, the Tribunal was not convinced as to the merits of those arguments.[70] As a result the Tribunal turned to assess modern instances of use, possession and control of the relevant islands. The relative importance of recent acts was considered, with the Tribunal observing that: 'It is well known that the standard of the requirements of such activity may have to be modified when one is dealing, as in the present case, with difficult or inhospitable territory.'[71]

In turning to assess these issues the Tribunal observed that it was dealing in this instance with groups or subgroups of islands, some of which could be described as archipelagos, raising for consideration issues associated with the natural and physical unity of the features.[72] Applying these approaches, the Tribunal determined that the Mohabbakah islands and the Haycocks were subject to the territorial sovereignty of Eritrea, and the Zuqar–Hanish group of islands, and the Jabal al-Tayr and the Zubayr group of islands were subject to Yemeni territorial sovereignty.[73] A feature of this case was the manner in which the Tribunal was presented with significant factual evidence associated with *effectivités*. The Tribunal observed it was: 'voluminous in quantity but is sparse in useful content. This is doubtless

[66] ibid 579 [367].
[67] ibid 579 [368].
[68] *Award of the Arbitral Tribunal in the first stage of the proceedings between Eritrea and Yemen (Territorial Sovereignty and Scope of the Dispute)* (*Eritrea v Yemen*) (1998) 22 RIAA 209 (*Eritrea v Yemen*).
[69] ibid 21–25 [73]–[90].
[70] ibid 124 [447].
[71] ibid 126 [452].
[72] ibid 128–31 [460]–[466].
[73] ibid 142–3 [508] (Zuqar–Hanish Group); 126 [524] (Jabal al-Tayr and the Zubayr Group of Islands).

owing to the inhospitability of the Islands themselves and the relative meagreness of their human history.'[74]

This concluding point highlights the challenges of demonstrating *effectivités* in the case of small islands, and clusters of islands.

(iii) Qatar v Bahrain *(2001)*

In the 2001 *Maritime Delimitation and Territorial Questions between Qatar and Bahrain* case (Qatar v Bahrain),[75] the ICJ considered sovereignty over a number of land and associated island features, and the maritime boundary between Qatar and Bahrain in the Arab/Persian Gulf. The Court was asked to adjudge sovereignty with respect to the Hawar Islands, and the associated Janan Islands, which are adjacent to the main islands of Bahrain.[76] As to the Hawar Islands, the Court was of the view that a 1939 decision of Britain determining the status of the islands as resting with Bahrain was binding on the parties.[77] With respect to the Janan Islands, the Court was confronted with differing views as to the composition of this island group,[78] but elected to consider the features as a single entity. The 1939 decision by Britain was found to not deal directly with the Janan Islands, and this was confirmed by a 1947 British interpretation. Bahrain's claim to the island was not upheld and Qatar was confirmed as the territorial sovereign.[79] The case principally turned on the historical determinations made by Britain with respect to the relevant islands in the Gulf that were under consideration by the Court, which then became the basis for the respective territorial entitlements of both Bahrain and Qatar when they became independent.[80]

(iv) Pulau Ligitan and Pulau Sipadan *(2002)*

In the 2002 *Sovereignty over Pulau Ligitan and Pulau Sipadan* case (Indonesia v Malaysia)[81] the ICJ was called upon to adjudicate sovereignty over two islands in the Celebes Sea off the north-east coast of Borneo. Both islands were

[74] ibid 71 [239]; see discussion of this award in NS Marques Antunes, 'The Eritrea-Yemen Arbitration: First Stage – The Law of Title to Territory Re-Averred' (1999) 48 *International and Comparative Law Quarterly* 362; '*effectivités*' are discussed further below at section IV.A.

[75] *Maritime Delimitation and Territorial Questions between Qatar and Bahrain (Qatar v Bahrain)* (Merits) [2001] ICJ Reps 40 (*Qatar v Bahrain*).

[76] ibid 53 [35].

[77] ibid 80–82, 85 [127]–[135], [146]–[148].

[78] Bahrain sought to distinguish between two islands: Janan Island and Hadd Island: ibid 85–86 [149]–[150].

[79] ibid 90–91 [165].

[80] In the case of Bahrain – in 1971 (from the United Kingdom), in the case of Qatar – in 1971 (from the United Kingdom); for discussion of this case see KE Wiegand, 'Bahrain, Qatar, and the Hawar Islands: Resolution of a Gulf Territorial Dispute' (2012) 66 *The Middle East Journal* 78.

[81] *Sovereignty over Pulau Ligitan and Pulau Sipadan (Indonesia v Malaysia)* (Merits) [2002] ICJ Reps 625 (*Pulau Ligitan and Pulau Sipadan*).

small: Ligitan described by the Court as a very small island adjacent to a reef; Sipadan, the larger of the two, had an area of just 0.13 km^2.[82] Only Sipadan had been inhabited for the purposes of tourism since the 1980s. Both parties sought to rely upon a form of historic title as relevant successor States. For Indonesia, it was asserted that title has been attained through the Dutch and by way of colonial treaties between Britain and the Netherlands. Subsequently actions by the Dutch and Indonesia, as a successor State, had allegedly perfected title.[83] Malaysia asserted that title to the islands had originally rested with the Sultan of Sulu, and that sovereignty had been acquired by way of succession through a series of title transfers passing from Spain, to the US, Britain, and then to the new State of Malaysia.[84] Title had subsequently been confirmed by British and Malaysian *effectivités* over the islands.[85]

Upon reviewing the various bases of historical claims and titles, the Court found that none were conclusive in this instance, and in the alternative it placed emphasis upon *effectivités*. The Court reviewed the arguments of the parties and the evidence put forward in support of a claim based upon *effectivités*. Reference was made to the decision in *Eastern Greenland* on this point, and in the context of small features such as islands the Court observed that:

> In particular in the case of very small islands which are uninhabited or not permanently inhabited – like Ligitan and Sipadan, which have been of little economic importance (at least until recently) – *effectivités* will indeed generally be scarce.[86]

On a review of the evidence of Malaysian and Indonesian activities, the Court concluded that Malaysia had the stronger title based upon *effectivités*, including legislative, administrative and quasi-judicial acts over a considerable period of time. Weight was also given to the lack of protest by the Netherlands and Indonesia with respect to acts taken by Malaysia and its predecessor regarding the islands.[87] This decision also highlights the importance of *effectivités* in certain island territorial disputes, especially in the case of relatively small features that were not historically seen as strategically significant.

(v) Nicaragua v Honduras *(2007)*

In the 2007 *Territorial and Maritime Dispute between Nicaragua and Honduras in the Caribbean Sea* case (Nicaragua v Honduras)[88] the ICJ considered sovereignty

[82] ibid 634 [14].
[83] ibid 643 [32].
[84] ibid 643 [33].
[85] ibid.
[86] ibid 682 [134].
[87] ibid 685 [148]–[149]; see discussion of the case in JG Merrills, 'Sovereignty over Pulau Ligitan and Pulau Sipadan (Indonesia v Malaysia), Merits, Judgment of 17 December 2002' (2003) 52(3) *International and Comparative Law Quarterly* 797; DA Colson, 'Sovereignty over Pulau Ligitan and Pulau Sipadan (Indonesia/Malaysia)' (2003) 97 *American Journal of International Law* 398.
[88] *Territorial and Maritime Dispute between Nicaragua and Honduras in the Caribbean Sea (Nicaragua v Honduras)* (Merits) [2007] ICJ Reps 659 (*Nicaragua v Honduras*).

over certain islands and related maritime boundaries. The key islands that were the subject of dispute were Bobel Cay, Savanna Cay, Port Royal Cay and South Cay in an area of the Caribbean Sea offshore the adjacent Honduran and Nicaraguan coastlines. The Court first gave consideration to the application of *uti possidetis juris* but concluded that the principle was not conclusive in this instance.[89] It then turned to consider claims based upon *effectivités*. With respect to demonstrating sovereignty over islands, and noting with approval observations by the PCIJ in *Eastern Greenland* and the ICJ in the *Sovereignty over Pulau Ligitan and Pulau Sipadan* case, the Court observed: 'Sovereignty over minor maritime features, such as the islands in dispute between Honduras and Nicaragua, may therefore be established on the basis of a relatively modest display of State powers in terms of quality and quantity.'[90]

The Court then proceeded to consider a range of activities engaged in by the parties, including legislative and administrative control, application and enforcement of criminal and civil law, regulation of immigration, regulation of fishing, naval patrols, oil concessions, and public works.[91] On the basis of the evidence of post-colonial *effectivités*, it was concluded that Honduras had title over the four contested islands.[92] As such, *effectivités* were again a significant factor in the case of a territorial dispute over a cluster of small islands, rocks and associated maritime features.

(vi) Sovereignty over Pedra Branca/Pulau Betu Puteh, Middle Rocks and South Ledge *(2008)*

In the *Sovereignty over Pedra Branca/Pulau Betu Puteh, Middle Rocks and South Ledge* case (Malaysia v Singapore)[93] the ICJ adjudicated on a number of associated territorial and sovereignty issues with respect to islands, rocks and low-tide elevations at the eastern entrance of the Straits of Singapore. Of these various features, the island of Pedra Branca/Pulau Batu Puteh was the subject of assessment regarding territorial claims by both parties.[94] Malaysia's position was that it had a longstanding and original title over the island, while Singapore argued that in 1847 the island was *terra nullius* and as such capable of being taken possession of by the British Crown whose title was subsequently transferred to Singapore.

[89] ibid 708–11 [159]–[167].

[90] ibid 712 [174].

[91] ibid 713–22 [177]–[208].

[92] ibid 727 [227]; see assessment by CG Lathrop, 'Territorial and Maritime Dispute Between Nicaragua and Honduras in the Caribbean Sea (Nicaragua v. Honduras)' (2008) 102 *American Journal of International Law* 113.

[93] *Case Concerning Sovereignty over Pedra Branca/Pulau Betu Puteh, Middle Rocks and South Ledge (Malaysia/ Singapore)* (Merits) [2008] ICJ Reps 12 (*Pedra Branca*).

[94] Described by the Court as 'a granite island, measuring 137 m long, with an average width of 60 m and covering an area of about 8,560 sq. m at low tide': ibid 22 [16]. The two names refer to 'white rock' in Portuguese and Malay and are consistently used in tandem throughout by judgment by the ICJ: ibid.

The Court assessed various acts over different historical periods, including during colonial times and following the independence of Malaya/Malaysia (1957/1963) and Singapore (1965). Particular significance was attached to the commissioning and construction of the Horsburgh lighthouse on the island in 1850–51 and the historical events at that time when Singapore asserted that it had acquired sovereignty.[95] Though the construction and operation of the lighthouse from Singapore was important, it was not decisive. Nevertheless, it did represent a turning point in the exercise of sovereignty over the island. Considering this historical record, the Court found in favour of Singapore having sovereignty, giving weight to various acts *á titre de souverain* especially since 1953, including the investigation of marine accidents, control over visits to the island, installation of naval communication equipment, and reclamation plans.[96] In the case of Middle Rocks the ICJ considered their status separately and found sovereignty rested with Malaysia, finding that the histories of the island and the rocks were very similar until recent times, when Singapore had exercised *effectivités* over the island but not over Middle Rocks. As a result, Malaysia's ongoing claims to Middle Rocks had not been impacted by the actions of Singapore.[97] This case is distinctive because of the variety of islands, rocks and maritime features under consideration and the manner in which separate findings were made in favour of Singapore and Malaysia.

(vii) Territorial and Maritime Dispute (Nicaragua v Colombia) *(2012)*

In the 2012 *Territorial and Maritime Dispute* case (Nicaragua v Colombia)[98] the ICJ assessed sovereignty with respect to a number of islands in the Caribbean Sea, and associated maritime boundary issues. This case had a significant impact on the maritime domain in the western Caribbean because, once a determination was made as to the territorial dispute, maritime boundaries were then drawn based upon the territorial entitlements.[99]

There were a number of islands in the relevant area of the Caribbean Sea, not all of which were the subject of contested sovereignty. The Court focussed on title

[95] For background see R Haller-Trost, *Historical legal claims: a study of disputed sovereignty over Pulau Batu Puteh (Pedra Branca)* (Maritime Briefing (International Boundaries Research Unit) 1993).

[96] *Pedra Branca* (n 93) 95 [274]; for discussion see C Lathrop, 'Sovereignty over Pedra Branca/Pulau Batu Puteh, Middle Rocks and South Ledge' (2008) 102 *American Journal of International Law* 828; R Beckman, 'Case between Malaysia and Singapore concerning sovereignty over Pedra Branca/Pulau Batu Puteh, Middle Rocks and South Ledge' (2008) 14 *Asian Yearbook of International Law* 273.

[97] *Pedra Branca* (n 93) 99 [288]–[290]; where the ICJ observed at 99 [289]: 'None of the conduct reviewed in the preceding part of the Judgment which has led the Court to the conclusion that sovereignty over Pedra Branca/Pulau Batu Puteh passed to Singapore or its predecessor before 1980 has any application to the cases of Middle Rocks and South Ledge.'

[98] *Territorial and Maritime Dispute (Nicaragua v Colombia)* (Merits) [2012] ICJ Reps 624 (*Nicaragua v Colombia*).

[99] See the discussion on the maritime boundary delimitation aspect of this case in Chapter 8 of this volume.

to Albuquerque, Bajo Nuevo, East-Southeast Cays, Quitasueño, Roncador, Serrana and Serranilla, located at various distances from the Nicaraguan and Colombian coasts.[100] The Court first assessed the status of the relevant maritime features in order to determine whether they were capable of appropriation. After having completed that task, it then turned to review the respective claims of the parties. In that respect, the Court concluded that the historical records based on applicable treaties were inconclusive,[101] as were claims based on *uti possidetis juris*.[102] The Court then turned to consider the respective claims based upon *effectivités*. A critical date of 12 June 1969 was settled upon by the Court,[103] and an assessment was undertaken of relevant Colombian and Nicaraguan activities.

The Court, in assessing claims based upon *effectivités*, made particular reference to the weight that could be given to the actions undertaken by a State in their capacity as *à titre de souverain*. It was observed that these activities included, but were not limited to:

> legislative acts or acts of administrative control, acts relating to the application and enforcement of criminal or civil law, acts regulating immigration, acts regulating fishing and other economic activities, naval patrols as well as search and rescue operations.[104]

Likewise, the claims of competing States also needed to be taken into account.[105] Ultimately the Court concluded sovereignty over the islands in favour of Colombia based on a series of acts, including public administration and legislation, regulation of economic activities, public works, law enforcement, naval visits and coastal search and rescue, consular representation, alleged recognition by Nicaragua, and the position of third States.[106] This decision sees reference to both *uti possidetis juris* and *effectivités*, with ultimately the latter being much more significant in the final judgment.

IV. Current State of the Law

As the cases above have highlighted, a range of factors are taken into account to determine the best title to territory.[107] An assessment will now be undertaken as

[100] *Nicaragua v Colombia* (n 98) 640–41 [24].
[101] ibid 641 [55].
[102] ibid 651 [64]–[65].
[103] ibid 653 [71].
[104] ibid 655 [80].
[105] ibid 655 [80].
[106] ibid 656–60 [82]–[95]; for further assessment of the territorial sovereignty aspects of the case, see P Bekker, 'The World Court Awards Sovereignty Over Several Islands in the Caribbean Sea to Colombia and Fixes a Single Maritime Boundary between Colombia and Nicaragua' (15 January 2013) 17(3) *ASIL Insights*; L Palestini, 'The *Territorial and Maritime Dispute* (*Nicaragua* v. *Colombia*): On Territorial Sovereignty and the International Court of Justice's "Failure to Rule" on the Geographical Scope of the Archipelago of San Andrés' (2016) 15 *The Law and Practice of International Courts and Tribunals* 56.
[107] Crawford, *Brownlie's Principles* (n 10) 205 lists the range of competing factors a court or tribunal will have to consider.

to the current state of international law with respect to territoriality and islands, commencing with *effectivités* – increasingly the most significant legal argument for a claim to territoriality over islands – followed by a review of the additional various legal bases which can be asserted.

A. Effective Control – *Effectivités*

A consistent theme in decisions regarding territorial sovereignty for the past century has been the ability of a claimant State to assert effective control over the territory in question – increasingly referred to by the ICJ as *effectivités*.[108] The significance of the general principle has been longstanding and was stated in *Island of Palmas* as being 'the actual continuous and peaceful display of state functions is in case of dispute the sound and natural criterium of territorial sovereignty.'[109] The weight given to this approach by Arbitrator Huber reflected a view that discovery of the island had given only an inchoate title which 'must be completed within a reasonable period by the effective occupation of the region claimed to be discovered.'[110] The manner in which the general principle of effective occupation is to be applied was elaborated in *Eastern Greenland* where the PCIJ focussed upon the intention by a State to act as a sovereign, and the actual exercise and display of acts of sovereignty.[111] Writing in 2019, Crawford was of the view that '[t]his statement has not lost its force'[112] and notes how it was reinforced in *Eritrea/Yemen* by the need for 'an intentional display of power and authority over the territory, by the exercise of jurisdiction or State functions, on a continuous and peaceful basis.'[113] This reinforces the view that official acts such as the proclamation of sovereignty over an island, publication of official maps showing the island as part of the State's territory, and even the enactment of decrees, laws and regulations purporting to apply to an island, are on their own insufficient to demonstrate title unless supported by *effectivités*. A paper claim to an island without supporting physical acts is therefore insufficient.

The weight accorded to *effectivités* by the ICJ in recent decades would appear to have increased as other legal principles have diminished in significance or proven to be inconclusive. Multiple different factors have been taken into account in order to meet the required standard of *effectivités*, which in the case of the islands in question have also reflected their differing locations, accessibility, and

[108] See *Frontier Dispute (Burkina Faso v Republic of Mali)* (Merits) [1986] ICJ Reps 554 (*Burkino Faso v Mali*) 554, 586 [63] where the Court observes as follows with respect to *effectivités* as 'the conduct of the administrative authorities as proof of the effective exercise of territorial jurisdiction in the region …'.

[109] *Island of Palmas* (n 12) 840.

[110] ibid 846.

[111] *Eastern Greenland* (n 46) 46.

[112] Crawford, *Brownlie's Principles* (n 10) 10.

[113] *Eritrea v Yemen* (n 68) 268 [239].

size. Accordingly the factors considered have extended to matters such as: enactment of laws and decrees; visiting the island to undertake a range of activities, including mapping, charting and scientific exploration; settlement of the island; the building of relevant infrastructure such as lighthouses and associated maritime navigational safety aids; resource management with respect to living and non-living resources (eg, oil concessions); exercising a range of administrative controls, even if conducted remotely from a mainland or other associated larger islands; and undertaking law enforcement activities including maritime patrols relating to fishing, piracy and general maritime security. The focus has been on establishing clear and compelling evidence that a claimant has acted *á titre de souverain*.[114] In the case of islands that have been contested over a period of time, weight may be given to more recent sovereign acts,[115] subject to the relevant critical date. In *Eastern Greenland*, *Eritrea/Yemen*, and *Pulau Ligitan and Pulau Sipadan*[116] direct reference was made to the relative remoteness and inhospitability of the relevant islands, with the result that a more flexible evidential standard was applied in making out a claim based on *effectivités* compared to more temperate, accessible and populated islands.[117]

B. Historic Title

In some instances, a form of historic and original title may be the root of a modern title over islands. Such historical facts were the foundation for the claims in *Minquiers and Ecrehos*, some of which dated as far back as 1066.[118] On their own, the claims founded on historic title were not conclusive in the absence of modern evidence of the actual exercise of sovereignty, but they did provide a sound basis for the eventual claims by the UK that were upheld.[119] Claims based on forms of historic title are still advanced both with respect to territory and maritime areas and were considered in *South China Sea* (Philippines v China). Though ultimately the Annex VII Arbitral Tribunal did not possess jurisdiction to adjudicate on competing territorial claims to certain South China Sea islands, the Tribunal did

[114] *Pedra Branca* (n 93) 95 [274]; *Nicaragua v Columbia* (n 98) 655 [80]; cf the actions of private individuals not undertaken with governmental authority: see *Pulau Ligitan and Pulau Sipadan* (n 81) 683 [140].

[115] *Island of Palmas* (n 12) 857, 866–68.

[116] *Pulau Ligitan and Pulau Sipadan* (n 81) 682 [134].

[117] *Nicaragua v Honduras* (n 88) 712 [174] makes direct reference to the capacity of a claim to be made out on the basis of 'relatively modest displays of State powers in terms of quality and quantity'. In *Minquiers and Ecrehos* while the islands and associated maritime features were small, they were accessible from Jersey (UK) and the French coast; see also Crawford, *Brownlie's Principles* (n 10) 210.

[118] *Minquiers and Ecrehos* (n 55) 53, 55–6.

[119] Crawford observes that 'The concept informs the principle of "immemorial possession" and reliance on evidence of general repute or opinion as to matters of historical fact': Crawford, *Brownlie's Principles* (n 10) 209.

acknowledge the weight of the evidence presented to it which could have otherwise been relied upon to make a determination as to sovereignty over the Spratly Islands and Scarborough Shoal.[120]

C. Discovery

The principle of discovery has been the subject of much historical analysis in the cases and literature, but in no instance has it proven to be conclusive with respect to title to an island. The *Island of Palmas*, *Clipperton Island*, and *Eastern Greenland* cases considered historical evidence as to which colonial power had been the first to discover or explore the islands, and Arbitrator Huber in *Island of Palmas* considered such a root of title to be at best 'inchoate'.[121] Much more by way of the actual assertion of sovereignty was therefore required in order to solidify title to a 'discovered' island. Therefore, the act of discovery of an island, followed by an act of symbolic annexation (which may occur from afar or physically on the island), and the publication of maps showing the island as belonging to the State do not on their own provide a firm title to an island. French sovereignty over *Clipperton Island* had its basis in discovery, but was ultimately affirmed through subsequent acts actually demonstrating sovereignty over the island. This approach is also affirmed in state practice, which can be seen by the manner in which various States became the recognised territorial sovereigns of islands in the Southern Ocean and Pacific Ocean as a result of voyages of discovery by maritime explorers. In the modern era when all lands have been mapped to various degrees of specificity, an act of discovery can only have *historical* significance as the basis of title to an island. 'New' islands may emerge as a result of sea-level rise or storm surges inundating existing lands and creating new separate features, or as a result of volcanic activity. Such islands would in most instances be contiguous to existing islands or a mainland, or fall under principles of accretion.[122] In more remote areas, any 'discovery' of such a feature would most likely arise as a result of satellite imagery or other ocean monitoring systems.

[120] *In the Matter of the South China Sea Arbitration before an Arbitral Tribunal constituted under Annex VII of the 1982 United Nations Convention on the Law of the Sea (Philippines v China)* (Merits) (12 July 2016) PCA Case 2013-19, 112–113 [264]; see also comment in Crawford, *Brownlie's Principles* (n 10) 209–10.

[121] *Island of Palmas* (n 12) 846. Crawford has commented that: 'The notion of discovery only makes sense if it is placed firmly in the context of effective occupation, so the notion of inchoate title is misleading. Title exists or it does not: it is never 'inchoate', though it may be weak if it rests on slight evidence of state activity.' Crawford, *Brownlie's Principles* (n 10) 211.

[122] In 1986 the United Kingdom was prepared to recognise an island that emerged as a result of volcanic activity adjacent to the Japanese island of Iwo Jima, as Japanese territory. The following statement was made: 'We understand that the island emerged within the territorial sea of the Japanese island Iwo Jima. We take it therefore to be Japanese territory.': HL Deb 16 July 1986, vol 478, col 1005WA; see also discussion in Shaw, *International Law* (n 10) 369.

D. Contiguity

The importance of geographical unity of territory is a consideration in the principle of contiguity, whereby islands in close proximity to a mainland, or small islands that are dependencies of larger islands are considered to fall within the territorial limits of the principal or larger entity. Such an approach can also be seen in *Eastern Greenland* where Danish exploration and activity in one part of Greenland was considered sufficient to provide a sound basis of claim for the whole island.[123] This can most evidently be demonstrated with islands that are offshore or adjacent to continental States, though historical factors may be at play in some instances. The islands that make up the so-called 'Canadian Arctic Archipelago' are both geographically proximate to and in some instances at great distances from the limits of the North American continent proper. From time to time throughout the twentieth century issues were raised as to Canadian sovereignty over all of these islands, notwithstanding that they were contiguous to the Canadian mainland but over time those questions have receded.[124] Similar approaches can be seen in other geographical settings where islands that fringe a coast are in most instances part of the territory of the adjacent State. There are exceptions to this general proposition, often for historical reasons as in the case of certain Torres Strait Islands (Australia) off the PNG coast, the Channel Islands (UK) off the French coast, Greek islands adjacent to the Turkish coast, Ceuta (Spain) off the coast of Morocco, Hawar (Bahrain) off the Qatari coast, and St Martin's Island (Bangladesh) off the Myanmar coast.[125] What is unclear is how proximate the island must be to a continental or island coast for the principle to have utility. The practice of international courts and tribunals has been to consider groups of islands, clusters of islands, or larger islands and their dependencies as a single unit for the purposes of confirming title.[126] This was the approach taken in *Minquiers and Ecrehos*,[127] the *Land, Maritime and Frontier Dispute*, *Eritrea v Yemen*, *Qatar v Bahrain*, and *Nicaragua v Colombia*. In *Pedra Branca* such an approach was not taken, notwithstanding South Rocks being located only 0.6 nm to the south of the island and argument made by Singapore that the island and rocks be treated

[123] *Eastern Greenland* (n 48) 31, 62; noting that the PCIJ did observe that given the remote nature of Greenland different standards were being applied: ibid 46.

[124] DR Rothwell, 'Arctic sovereignty and its legal significance for Canada' in LC Jensen and G Hønneland (eds), *Handbook of the Politics of the Arctic* (Edward Elgar 2015) 247–61.

[125] The presence of these islands close to the coast of another State has implications for maritime boundary delimitation, discussed in more detail in Chapter 8 of this volume.

[126] *Island of Palmas* (n 12) 855 where it was observed that: 'As regards groups of islands, it is possible that a group may under certain circumstances be regarded as in law a unit, and that the fate of the principal part may involve the rest.'

[127] While separate considerations were made of Minquiers, and Ecrehos, their associated dependent islets and rocks were considered together with the main islands; the ICJ made numerous references to the 'islets and rocks of the Minquiers and Ecrehos groups': as reflected in Article 1 of the Special Agreement conferring jurisdiction on the Court: *Minquiers and Ecrehos* (n 55) 52.

as a group.[128] The ICJ accepted it was possible to distinguish between Pedra Branca and Middle Rocks because of the different positions taken by the parties, especially Singapore and its exercise of *effectivités* over Pedra Branca but not the rocks.[129]

E. *Uti Possidetis*

The *uti possidetis* principle is one that seeks to retain previous administrative and other associated boundaries from the colonial era, with the result that newly independent States acquire those boundaries. As observed by the ICJ in 1986:

> The essence of the principle lies in its primary aim of securing respect for the territorial boundaries at the moment when independence is achieved. Such territorial boundaries might be no more than delimitations between different administrative divisions or colonies all subject to the same sovereign.[130]

The principle has been particularly asserted in Latin America and Africa in reliance upon Spanish colonial boundaries.[131] The effect of *uti possidetis* is to seek to ensure certainty and stability in international boundaries, which was of particular significance during the decolonisation era. Island States that emerged during this period rarely sought to rely upon the principle, partly because their territorial limits had been determined by former colonial powers and they rarely shared land boundaries with neighbouring States. If new island States did share land boundaries, they were often not contested at independence because they were well settled. The application of the *uti possidetis* principle has therefore most commonly been applied to islands in the context of territorial disputes between continental States where disagreements have arisen over certain islands, often very small and often significant in the context of maritime boundary delimitation. Consideration by the ICJ of claims based on *uti possidetis* in the *Land, Island and Maritime Frontier Dispute*,[132] *Nicaragua v Honduras*, and the *Territorial and Maritime Dispute (Nicaragua v Colombia)* resulted in none of the island claims being upheld in reliance on the principle.

[128] *Pedra Branca* (n 93) 22 [18], 97 [280]–[282].

[129] ibid 99 [288]–[290].

[130] *Burkino Faso v Mali* (n 108) 566 [23]; see also *Land, Island and Maritime Frontier Dispute* (n 62) 388.

[131] See discussion in the context of Africa in MN Shaw, *Title to Territory in Africa: International Legal Issues* (Oxford University Press 1985); and generally SR Ratner, 'Drawing a Better Line: *Uti Possidetis* and the Borders of New States' (1996) 90 *American Journal of International Law* 590.

[132] Cf *Land, Island and Maritime Frontier Dispute* (n 62) 569 [355] where the Chamber observed: 'Given the firm and consistent attachment of the States of Central America to the principle of the *uti possidetis juris*, the Chamber considers also that these events support the conclusion that that contemporary assumption implied also belief that Honduras was entitled to the island of El Tigre by succession from Spain; or, at least, that such succession by Honduras was not contradicted by any known Spanish colonial title in favour of one of the other two States of the Gulf.'

F. Annexation

Islands have also been the subject of annexation where an existing State has asserted a claim over land that was previously controlled by another sovereign.[133] Annexation of territory in these circumstances is often associated with the unilateral use of force and a violation of Article 2(4) of the UN Charter. Such an act would more than likely be condemned by the UN Security Council.[134] As such, the acquisition of title to an island in these circumstances would not be consistent with international law and not be recognised as such.[135] The 1982 seizure of the Falkland Islands by Argentina is illustrative of this proposition as at the time the UK was the recognised sovereign over the islands, albeit that claim was contested by Argentina.[136] In 1975 Indonesia sought to occupy East Timor which it eventually annexed. Portugal, the previous colonial power in East Timor, had gradually begun to withdraw from the administration of that territory between 1974 and 1975. In the absence of Portugal as the relevant territorial sovereign, Indonesia sought to militarily intervene and take control of East Timor and it became an Indonesian province in 1976.[137] Indonesia's sovereignty over East Timor was recognised by some States, including by Australia which concluded a maritime boundary agreement with Indonesia in 1989 in the area between East Timor and Australia.[138] Following a 1999 UN facilitated plebiscite, a process was set in place which resulted in independence in 2002 of the new State of Timor Leste.

G. Cession

Cession involves the peaceful transfer of territory from one State to another. For the transfer to successfully occur, the transferring State must have a good title to the territory under international law. The acceptance of the transfer of title to territory would normally be effected by way of a treaty or other

[133] An example is the annexation by Iraq of Kuwait, including Kuwaiti islands in the Red Sea, in 1990; see C Greenwood, 'Iraq's Invasion of Kuwait: Some Legal Issues' (1991) 47 *The World Today* 39; for background on the border issues see J Horner, 'The Iraq-Kuwait Border dispute' (1992) 7 *Journal of Borderlands Studies* 1.

[134] See UNSC Res 662 (9 August 1990) UN Doc S/RES/662 following the annexation by Iraq of Kuwait.

[135] Crawford, *Creation of States* (n 4) 131–33; also noting the non-recognition of the Turkish Republic of Northern Cyprus as within this category.

[136] See discussion in DW Greig, 'Sovereignty and the Falkland Islands Crisis' (1983) 8 *Australian Year Book of International Law* 20.

[137] See JS Hoadley, 'Indonesia's Annexation of East Timor: Political, Administrative, and Developmental Initiatives' (1977) *Southeast Asian Affairs* 133; M Leifer, 'Indonesia and the Incorporation of East Timor' (1976) 32 *The World Today* 347.

[138] See Treaty between Australia and the Republic of Indonesia on the Zone of Cooperation in an Area between the Indonesian Province of East Timor and Northern Australia (Australia-Indonesia) (adopted 11 December 1989, entered into force 9 February 1991) [1991] ATS 9.

equivalent international instrument.[139] Historically an act of cession may have occurred within the framework of a peace treaty following a war;[140] however, there are instances where, due to a lack of precision in such treaties, there has been uncertainty as to which islands and island groups within poorly defined geographic areas have been the subject of such a transfer. This was one of the contentious issues that arose in *Island of Palmas*, namely whether the 1898 Treaty of Paris clearly included Palmas. Likewise, under the 1951 San Francisco Peace Treaty[141] a number of issues have arisen as to the islands that actually fall within the remit of the treaty and where sovereignty rested.[142] The cession of island territories under these circumstances, especially post World War II, must also be questioned as to their legitimacy given the element of victor's justice that arises at the end of a war. One common form of cession of island territories has been between colonial powers, between colonial powers and their dominions, or colonial powers and successor and/or newly independent States. Examples include the 1890 cession by Great Britain to Germany of the Heligoland islands off the northwest coast of Germany,[143] the Spanish cession of the Philippines to the US (1898) as discussed in *Island of Palmas*, cession by Denmark of the Caribbean islands of St John, St Thomas and St Croix to the US (1916),[144] cession by the Netherlands to Indonesia of West Irian (1962),[145] cession by India to Sri Lanka of Katchatheevu (1974),[146] and cession of Ashmore and Cartier Islands (1933), Heard and McDonald Islands (1947), Cocos (Keeling) Islands (1955), and Christmas Island (1958) from the UK to Australia.[147] Transfer of territory by cession frequently occurred in the past, and today would be exceptional. Nevertheless, in 2016 Egypt reached agreement with Saudi Arabia to cede the Tiran and Sanafir islands in the Red Sea, thereby resolving longstanding tensions over the status of those islands.[148]

[139] Crawford, *Brownlie's Principles* (n 10) 215 where the weight to be accorded to treaties concluded between indigenous people and the State is qualified; a point reinforced in the *Island of Palmas* where it is observed that 'In substance, it is not an agreement between equals': *Island of Palmas* (n 12) 858.

[140] Shaw, *International Law* (n 10) 369.

[141] Treaty of Peace with Japan (adopted 8 September 1951, entered into force 28 April 1952) 136 UNTS 45.

[142] See eg S Lee, 'The 1951 San Francisco Peace Treaty with Japan and the Territorial Disputes in East Asia' (2002) 11 *Pacific Rim Law and Policy Journal* 63.

[143] C Hattenhauer, 'Heligoland' in R Wolfrum (ed), *Max Planck Encyclopedia of International Law* (online edn, Oxford University Press 2013).

[144] Convention between the United States and Denmark (United States–Denmark) (adopted 4 August 1916, entered into force 17 January 1917) 7 USTIA 56.

[145] Agreement (with Annex) concerning West New Guinea (West Irian) (Indonesia–Netherlands) (adopted 15 August 1962, entered into force 21 September 1962) 437 UNTS 273.

[146] J Stephen and A Menon, 'Fluid territories: Rethinking state territorialisation in Palk Bay, South Asia' (2016) 70 *Norsk Geografisk Tidsskrift – Norwegian Journal of Geography* 263, 269.

[147] For a discussion of the cession of islands from Britain to Australia see H Burmester, 'Island Outposts of Australia' in WSG Bateman and MW Ward (eds), *Australia's Offshore Maritime Interests* (Centre for Maritime Studies 1985) 54; AC Castles, 'International Law and Australia's Overseas Territories' in DP O'Connell (ed), *International Law in Australia* (Law Book Co 1966) 292.

[148] See discussion in Global Security, 'Tiran and Sanafir Islands' (7 March 2018) www.globalsecurity.org/military/world/war/tiran.htm; and KA Kebaish, 'Tiran and Sanafir: A Historical and Constitutional Argument Opposing the Territorial Cession of the Tiran and Sanafir Islands to Saudi Arabia' (2019) 97 *Texas Law Review* 835.

H. Role of Intertemporal Law

A recurring theme in many island territorial disputes with respect to islands which have been the subject of claims that extend back in time, such as *Minquiers and Ecrehos* where claims dated back to the eleventh century, is whether title established under the law at one time remains valid in the modern era when the law may have been modified. The general position adopted under the intertemporal law rule, is that title to territory that was made out to be sufficient under existing law at the time a claim was made should continue to be respected. However, the difficulty with this rule is that modern international law may not give as much weight to certain principles that previously were considered significant or even decisive. An example of such a principle that historically was prominent in island territorial disputes is discovery. Arbitrator Huber considered this in *Island of Palmas* as follows:

> As regards the question which of different legal systems prevailing at successive periods is to be applied in a particular case (the so-called intertemporal law), a distinction must be made between the creation of rights and the existence of rights. The same principle which subjects the act creative of a right to the law in force at the time the right arises, demands that the existence of the right, in other words its continued manifestation, shall follow the conditions required by the evolution of the law.[149]

The role of intertemporal law is therefore that whilst the law at the time a claim was made out will be respected and upheld as much as possible, a flexible approach will be taken so as to account for subsequent developments in both the law and the practice of the relevant States.[150]

I. Critical Date

A feature of many territorial disputes is the determination by a court or tribunal of a 'critical date' up to which the various acts of the claimants can be legitimately considered as relevant in the determination of a territorial claim.[151] Events occurring after that date will therefore, normally not be considered to be significant. The critical date may relate to an official act (proclamation of title, enactment of a law, conclusion of a treaty) or a turning point in the events associated with a dispute over territory between the parties.[152] There is no precise legal rule that is applied to determine the critical date and it will very much depend on the facts, though occasionally the parties to a dispute may agree upon such a date. In *Eastern Greenland*, the PCIJ took the critical date as 10 July 1931 because that was the date

[149] *Island of Palmas* (n 12) 845.
[150] Crawford, *Brownlie's Principles* (n 10) 206–7; Shaw, *International Law* (n 10) 377–78.
[151] Cf the critical date at which a dispute between the parties is said to have crystallised; see discussion in *Pedra Branca* (n 93) 28 [33], [35], 70 [179].
[152] Shaw, *International Law* (n 10) 378.

when Norway first sought to assert its title. The Court then sought to determine the strength of the Danish title to Eastern Greenland up to and as at that date.[153]

J. Boundary Treaties and Awards

Previous colonial boundary treaties, or boundary treaties between the States contesting an island territory will be taken into account. The caveat is that the treaties must be sufficiently precise to enable a clear determination as to who the territorial sovereign is of a particular island. Historical boundary treaties often lack that precision and as a result are often not decisive. Similarly, any awards, determinations, or rulings by any authoritative body may be of assistance, subject again to their level of precision with respect to the particular island features.[154] In *Qatar v Bahrain* the ICJ was of the view that a 1939 administrative report of a 'British Political Agent', subsequently endorsed by the British government and communicated to the relevant interested parties, was a sound basis for determining the status of certain islands as resting with Bahrain.[155] This suggests that detailed administrative reports and inquiries, even those conducted solely by government officials, may be determinative if relied upon by the parties.

K. Historical Consolidation

In light of the previous analysis of *effectivités*, some consideration can be given to whether there is any weight in a doctrine of historical consolidation as it may apply to islands. Certainly international courts and tribunals have occasionally sought to apply such an approach as a means of affirming a view they have formed as to who is the legitimate territorial sovereign.[156] This is particularly relevant in the context of the attitude taken by other States, and was a factor in the *Territorial and Maritime Dispute (Nicaragua v Colombia)* case.[157] Crawford cautions, however, that 'consolidation does not exist as a concept independent of the established rules …'.[158]

L. Subsequent Conduct

A number of additional factors may be taken into account that reflect upon distinctive aspects of a particular case. The doctrine of prescription places weight upon

[153] *Eastern Greenland* (n 48) 45; see also *Nicaragua v Colombia* (n 98) 653 [71].

[154] See the discussion of the significance of the 1900 Loubet Award in *Nicaragua v Colombia* (n 98) 657–58 [86], [88].

[155] *Qatar v Bahrain* (n 75) 80–82, 85 [127]–[135], [146]–[148].

[156] *Eritrea v Yemen* (n 68) 244 [126].

[157] *Nicaragua v Colombia* (n 98) 659–60 [91]–[95].

[158] Crawford, *Brownlie's Principles* (n 10) 223.

the subsequent conduct of a party in acquiring title to territory that may be dubious, unlawful, or where the circumstances relating to acquisition cannot be clearly demonstrated.[159] There are clear parallels with the principles associated with *effectivités*; however, Shearer's view is that title acquired by prescription 'is the result of the peaceable exercise of de facto sovereignty for a very long period over territory subject to the sovereignty of another, and this may be as the consequence of the immemorial exercise of such sovereignty'.[160] This suggests that one sovereign had not completed the process of perfecting title to an island, and another sovereign asserted a de facto competing claim.[161] In the alternative, it raises the prospect of whether an abandonment of territory has taken place,[162] resulting in the island being *terra nullius*.[163] Abandonment would mean that the former presumptive sovereign has relinquished their claim. While such a finding would be exceptional in the twenty-first century, it is clear that the arbitrator in *Clipperton Island* gave some consideration to whether this was exactly what France had done as a result of its failure to exercise *effectivités*.[164] Nevertheless, in an era of climate change where islands are being impacted by sea-level rise, it cannot be ruled out that certain islands may become uninhabitable and effectively abandoned by a State whilst being retained as part of the territory of that State. Certain subsequent types of conduct by the States competing for recognition of title over an island may also be influential, including acts equating to recognition of the title of the other State.[165] In *Pulau Ligitan and Pulau Sipadan* weight was given to acquiescence by the Netherlands and Indonesia in the face of Malaysia undertaking various sovereign acts with respect to the islands.[166] While estoppel may also be relevant, effectively barring the capacity of a competing State to make a claim over territory as a result of its previous actions, the threshold for a State being estopped is high.[167]

M. Distinctive Territorial Features

Finally, islands raise some distinctive territorial issues that are not always present in continental territorial disputes. This was famously highlighted in *Eastern Greenland* by the reference to 'thinly populated or unsettled countries', effectively

[159] Shaw, *International Law* (n 10) 374.
[160] Shearer (n 19) 153; see also Shaw, *International Law* (n 10) 375.
[161] There is no conclusive position on the status of prescription by the ICJ or amongst scholars; see Shearer (n 19) 154; J Wouters and S Verhoeven, 'Prescription' in R Wolfrum (ed), *Max Planck Encyclopedia of International Law* (online edn, Oxford University Press 2008).
[162] Shaw, *International Law* (n 10) 375.
[163] Crawford, *Brownlie's Principles* (n 10) 217.
[164] *Clipperton Island* (n 40) 394.
[165] See generally *Nicaragua v Colombia* (n 98) 655–60 [82]–[95].
[166] *Pulau Ligitan and Pulau Sipadan* (n 81) 685 [148]–[149].
[167] *Chagos Marine Protected Area Arbitration (Mauritius v United Kingdom)* (Award) (18 March 2015) PCA Case No 011-03, 174 [438]; see also Shaw, *International Law* (n 10) 384–85.

acknowledging that a lower standard would be applied in such instances compared to more temperate lands.[168] This is especially significant if another State cannot make out a 'superior claim.'[169] An additional, unique factor, in *Eastern Greenland*, was the size of the territory involved, where the PCIJ suggested that a different standard would be applied given the challenges in exercising sovereignty over such a vast territory.[170] The inhospitability of certain islands and their history of scarce human occupation,[171] and the limited historical economic importance of certain small islands[172] have also been taken into account where the facts allowed.

V. Contemporary Island Territorial Disputes

Brief consideration will now be given to contemporary island territorial disputes. This review is not intended to be comprehensive of all island territorial disputes but rather is designed to provide an overview of some of the most prominent disputes and also reflect a variety of the issues that arise across disputes in various parts of the world.[173] The analysis seeks to provide some of the background and history to the disputes and an outline of the relevant legal issues.

A. Aegean Sea/Mediterranean Sea (Greece v Turkey)

There are a number of territorial disputes between Greece and Turkey with respect to islands and rocks in the Aegean Sea which have had particular implications for the finalisation of maritime boundaries. One dispute relates to the islets of Gavdos and Gavdopula which are to the south of Crete in the Mediterranean Sea. Greece rests its claim on the bases of contiguity to Crete, Turkey's acquiescence, and a culmination of *effectivités* in recent decades. Turkey claims the islands were formerly part of the Ottoman Empire, are not referenced in any subsequent treaties dealing with territory in the region, and it relies on its status as a successor State.[174] Tensions have previously flared over the status of the islands during NATO

[168] *Eastern Greenland* (n 48) 46.
[169] ibid; this view still holds weight see *Nicaragua v Colombia* (n 98) 655 [80]–[81].
[170] *Eastern Greenland* (n 48) 45.
[171] *Eritrea v Yemen* (n 68) 71 [239]; *Nicaragua v Honduras* (n 88) 712 [174].
[172] *Pulau Ligitan and Pulau Sipadan* (n 81) 682 [134].
[173] Other island disputes are those between Iran and UAE over Greater Tunb, Lesser Tunb, and Abu Musa: see M Eslami and S Sotoudehfar, 'Iran–UAE Relations and Disputes Over the Sovereignty of Abu Musa and Tunbs,' in FJBS Leandro, C Branco, and F Caba-Maria (eds), *The Geopolitics of Iran* (Palgrave Macmillan 2021) 343; Marshall Islands and US over Wake Island (Enen-Kio): see Heathcote (n 23) 674.
[174] JM Van Dyke, 'An Analysis of the Aegean Disputes under International Law' (2005) 36 *Ocean Development and International Law* 63, 70; JM Van Dyke, 'Aegean Sea' in R Wolfrum (ed), *Max Planck Encyclopedia of International Law* (online edn, Oxford University Press 2010) [8]; see also E Anyanova, 'Delimitation of the Aegean Sea' (2013) 3 *International Journal of Public Law and Policy* 210.

exercises in the region.[175] Another dispute exists with respect to the Kardak/Imia Rocks located in the Aegean Sea off the coast of Turkey and claimed by Greece. The status of these islets and rocks was highlighted in 1995 when a Turkish bulk carrier *Figen Akat* grounded on the rocks. Greece claims they are dependent islands of Kalimnos (Greece), which is 5.5 nm distant, and therefore relies upon principles of contiguity and *effectivités*. Turkey asserts that the treaties relied upon confirming sovereignty over these and other islands in the Aegean Sea are unclear, and has also countered with its own claim based on contiguity given the islands are only 3.8 nm from the Turkish coast.[176] There are no indications of diplomatic attempts to settle this dispute.[177]

B. Chagos Archipelago (Mauritius v United Kingdom)

The Chagos Archipelago is located in the Indian Ocean and consists of a number of islands and atolls, the largest of which is Diego Garcia.[178] Until 1965, the Chagos Archipelago was part of the islands historically comprising Mauritius. From that date, the Chagos Archipelago became part of the island groups that compose the British Indian Ocean Territory (BIOT).[179] Mauritius was occupied by the Dutch (1638–1710) and the French (1715–1810), and following the 1814 Treaty of Paris, French interests were ceded to Britain.[180] The islands of the Chagos Archipelago were administered as part of Mauritius from 1814–1965, until such time as the BIOT was formed in 1965. Mauritius gained independence from the UK in 1968, but the Chagos Archipelago remained islands of the BIOT. The UK position is that it acquired the 58 islands of the Chagos Archipelago through a legitimate act of cession from France, and has since continued to act as sovereign by way of *effectivités*. Mauritius asserts that the 1965 detachment of the Chagos Archipelago was contrary to international law, and that as the successor to the UK's claims over all of the islands that were previously part of Mauritius it is the legitimate sovereign of them. It points to numerous resolutions by the UN and its associated bodies, and other international organisations such as the Organisation of African Unity calling for the return of the islands to Mauritius. In 2019 the ICJ in the *Legal Consequences of the Separation of the Chagos Archipelago from Mauritius in 1965* Advisory Opinion concluded the islands were unlawfully detached from

[175] Van Dyke, 'An Analysis of the Aegean Disputes' (n 174) 70.
[176] ibid 69.
[177] See the position of Turkey at Ministry of Foreign Affairs (Turkey), 'The Kardak Dispute', www.mfa.gov.tr/the-kardak-dispute.en.mfa; for some recent analysis of these disputes and related issues see G Dalay, 'Turkey, Europe, and the Eastern Mediterranean: Charting a Way Out of the Current Deadlock' (*Policy Briefing* (Brookings Doha Center), January 2021) www.brookings.edu/wp-content/uploads/2021/01/Turkey-Europe-and-the-Eastern-Mediterranean.pdf.
[178] *Chagos Advisory Opinion* (n 8).
[179] ibid 108 [33].
[180] ibid 107 [27].

Mauritius, and that the UK was under an obligation to bring to an end its administration of the archipelago.[181] In 2021 a Special Chamber of the International Tribunal of the Law of the Sea was called upon to consider aspects of this dispute in *Dispute Concerning Delimitation of the Maritime Boundary between Mauritius and Maldives in the Indian Ocean.*[182] The Special Chamber reviewed the history of the matter and the ICJ's Advisory Opinion and reaffirmed the view that there exists a sovereignty dispute over the islands.[183] The dispute remains under active review in UN fora.

C. Cyprus

The Mediterranean island of Cyprus is divided between the dominant Greek Cypriot government that controls much of the island, and the 'Turkish Republic of Northern Cyprus' (TRNC) established in 1983 and only recognised by Turkey.[184] The existence of the TRNC has not impacted upon the status of Cyprus as an independent island State and reinforces the position that a recognised State in international law may not control all its territory and may have disputed borders. There have been ongoing efforts to reach a political settlement with respect to the situation on Cyprus, including the potential for a 'two-state solution',[185] which would result in a formal territorial division of the island and recognition of the respective territorial claims and entitlements of two entities.[186]

D. Dokdo/Takeshima (Japan v Republic of Korea)

The Dokdo islands are located in the East Sea (Sea of Japan) between the Republic of Korea (ROK) and Japan. The islands comprise two co-located rocky outcrops and 32 smaller features. The islands are located 87.4 km from the island of Ulleungo (ROK) and 157 km from the Oki Islands (Japan).[187] The islands are currently

[181] ibid 138–39 [177], 140 [183].

[182] *Dispute Concerning Delimitation of the Maritime Boundary between Mauritius and Maldives in the Indian Ocean (Mauritius v The Maldives)* (Preliminary Objections Judgment) (28 January 2021) ITLOS Reports 2020–21, to be published (*Mauritius and Maldives*).

[183] ibid 71 [242]; see also discussion in Chapter 9, section IV.A of this volume.

[184] The declaration was declared 'legally invalid' by UNSC Res 541 (8 November 1983) UN Doc S/RES/541.

[185] T Gumrukcu, 'North Cyprus leader backs two-state proposal for U.N. talks', *Reuters* (26 April 2021) www.reuters.com/world/middle-east/north-cyprus-leader-backs-two-state-proposal-un-talks-2021-04-26/; for more detailed background see C Rumpf, 'Comments on the Legal Status of Cyprus: Issues of Conflict and their Causes' in T Giegerich (ed), *The EU Accession of Cyprus-Key to the Political and Legal Solution of an 'Insoluble' Ethnic Conflict?* (Nomos 2005) 37.

[186] For earlier consideration of recognition of the TRNC see S Palmer, 'The Turkish Republic of Northern Cyprus: Should the United States Recognize it as an Independent State' (1986) 4 *Boston University International Law Journal* 423.

[187] S Lee and HE Lee (eds), *Dokdo: Historical Appraisal and International Justice* (Martinus Nijhoff 2011) ix.

occupied by the ROK where a lighthouse is maintained, patrols of surrounding waters are undertaken, and a small number of civilians are located.[188] The Japanese claim to the islands is based on annexation in 1905 on the grounds they were *terra nullius*, at a time when Japan was engaged in establishing a protectorate over parts of the Korean Peninsula. That claim was maintained in various forms until the end of World War II after which Japan's control of the islands diminished as a result of the 1951 San Fransisco Peace Treaty.[189] The ROK's claim is based on various levels of historical control over a number of centuries, Japanese recognition of that claim during the nineteenth century, and strong assertion of a claim following independence in 1952, which has since been continued.[190] The ROK claim has in recent decades increasingly been based upon *effectivités*.[191] The status of the islands continues as a diplomatic issue between Japan and the ROK and impacts the bilateral relationship.[192] Japan has suggested that the matter be submitted to the ICJ for resolution, but the ROK has not agreed.[193]

E. Falkland (Malvinas) Islands (Argentina v United Kingdom)[194]

The Falkland Islands comprise two main islands and approximately 200 adjacent smaller islands located in the South Atlantic approximately 500 km from the coast of Argentina. The islands have a population of just over 3,000 persons and their current status is that of a self-governing Overseas Territory of the UK.[195] The islands were first discovered in the late sixteenth century, with East Falkland colonised by France in 1764 and West Falkland by Britain in 1766. These two settlements

[188] S Lee, 'Dok Do/Takeshima Islands from a Korean Perspective' in R Wolfrum (ed), *Max Planck Encyclopedia of Public International Law* (online edn, Oxford University Press 2014) [18].

[189] JM Van Dyke, 'Addressing and Resolving the Dokdo Matter' in S Lee and HE Lee (eds), *Dokdo: Historical Appraisal and International Justice* (Martinus Nijhoff 2011) 29, 29–30; for more detail on this issue also see JM Van Dyke, 'Legal Issues Related to Sovereignty over Dokdo and Its Maritime Boundary' (2007) 38 *Ocean Development and International Law* 157.

[190] Van Dyke, Addressing and Resolving the Dokdo Matter' (n 189) 29–30.

[191] Which has been the subject of analysis by legal commentators, see eg NJ Schrijver and V Prislan, 'Cases Concerning Sovereignty over Islands before the International Court of Justice and the Dokdo/Takeshima Issue' (2015) 46 *Ocean Development and International Law* 281.

[192] KE Wiegand, 'The South Korean–Japanese security relationship and the Dokdo/Takeshima islets dispute' (2015) 28 *The Pacific Review* 347.

[193] Van Dyke, Addressing and Resolving the Dokdo Matter' (n 174) 30; see also M Selden, 'Japanese territorial disputes with Korea and China: Small islets, enduring conflicts' in J Kingston (ed), *Critical Issues in Contemporary Japan* (2nd edn, Routledge 2019) 145, 145–8.

[194] This analysis does not include the Falkland Island Dependencies which encompass islands to the south of the Falkland Islands (South Georgia, South Shetland Islands, South Orkney Islands, South Sandwich Islands) and parts of the Antarctic continent; see discussion in CHM Waldock, 'Disputed Sovereignty in the Falkland Islands Dependencies' (1948) 25 *British Year Book of International Law* 311.

[195] Central Intelligence Agency (US), 'Falkland Islands' (*The World Factbook*) www.cia.gov/the-world-factbook/countries/falkland-islands-islas-malvinas/.

failed or were withdrawn, and succeeded by Spain, which controlled both islands from around 1770 onwards.[196] Spain also withdrew from the islands around 1811 and there followed a period where control was indeterminate, with Argentina also seeking to assert its interests in the early nineteenth century. Britain took control of both islands in 1833 and a governor was installed a year later. Argentina at various times subsequently contested British sovereignty over the islands, and was successful in drawing attention to the status of the islands in the UN General Assembly.[197] In April 1982 Argentine military forces occupied and took control of the islands. A British expeditionary force sailed from the UK and an armed conflict resulted until Argentine forces surrendered in June 1982.[198] The islands have remained under British control since that time. The Argentine claim over the islands is based upon discovery by Spain, English and French recognition of Spanish sovereignty, occupation by Spain from 1774 until Argentine independence in 1816, succession of States, recognition of Argentine independence by Britain in 1825, and a period of occupation and administration by Argentina.[199] The position of the UK at the time of the 1982 conflict was that its sovereignty over the islands was based upon discovery, settlement, Spain's withdrawal from West Falkland in 1811, diplomatic protests to various Argentine acts in the early nineteenth century, British repossession of the islands in 1832–33, and subsequent continuous effective and peaceful occupation amounting to *effectivités*.[200] Some diplomatic exchanges continue between Argentina and the UK over the status of the Falkland Islands. In a March 2013 referendum over 99 per cent of those Falkland Islanders who voted indicated a desire that the Islands remain an Overseas Territory of the UK.[201]

F. Hans Island (Tartupaluk) (Canada v Denmark)

Hans Island is a small island of no more than 1.25 km^2 located in the Kennedy Channel portion of Nares Strait between Ellesmere Island (Canada) and Greenland.[202] The dispute over the island only arose in 1973 during negotiations

[196] J Goebel, *The Struggle for the Falkland Islands* (Yale University Press 1982) xiii.

[197] UNGA Res 2065 (4 January 1966) UN Doc A/RES/2065; UNGA Res 3160 (29 January 1974) UN Doc A/RES/3160.

[198] For discussion of the Falklands War see DG Boyce, *The Falklands War* (Palgrave Macmillan 2005); M Parsons, *The Falklands War* (Sutton 2000).

[199] R Perl, *The Falkland Islands Dispute in International Law and Politics: A Documentary Sourcebook* (Oceana 1983) 23.

[200] ibid 28.

[201] R Edwards, 'Statement (Falkland Islands (Malvinas))', (Caribbean regional seminar on the implementation of the Third International Decade for the Eradication of Colonialism: accelerating decolonization through renewed commitment and pragmatic measures, Saint George's, Grenada, 2–4 May 2019) www.un.org/dppa/decolonization/sites/www.un.org.dppa.decolonization/files/2019_2_falkland_islands_malvinas_crs_2019_crp.8.pdf.

[202] PR Dawes and T Tukiainen, 'Hans Ø, celebrated island of Nares Strait between Greenland and Canada: from dog-sledge to satellite mapping' (2008) 15 *Geological Survey of Denmark and Greenland Bulletin* 77, 77.

over the Nares Strait maritime boundary when negotiators became aware of differing views as to the island's status.[203] Because the island was uninhabited and its capacity to generate any significant maritime entitlements was compromised because of the adjacent lands on either side of the strait, little serious attention had been given to clarifying whether the island was Canadian or Danish. Hans Island was not directly referred to by the PCIJ in *Eastern Greenland*; however, Denmark has referenced the reliance placed by the Court upon a 1920 note from Britain acting on behalf of Canada recognising Danish sovereignty over Greenland.[204] Canada's claim is based on the transfer to it of certain Arctic islands, other than Greenland, from Britain in 1880 and subsequent occasional use and occupation for scientific research.[205] There has been no strong diplomatic momentum to resolve the status of the island given its remote location, that it is uninhabited, and that it is only occasionally visited by scientists. This may change if Greenland seeks to become independent from Denmark, but for the time being the dispute appears to be one that is diplomatically being managed by Canada and Denmark without resort to formal mechanisms.[206]

G. Kuril Islands (Japan v Russian Federation)

The Kuril Islands are located to the north of the Japanese main island of Hokkaido and straddle the North Pacific Ocean and the Sea of Okhotsk; they are the subject of dispute between Japan and the Russian Federation. There are four islands and their associated rocks and features in dispute: Kunashiri, Etorofu, Shikotan, and Habomais. They are the southern-most islands in the Kuril Island chain, and are sometimes referred to as the 'Southern Kurils' or 'Lesser Kuril' chain.[207] Japan refers to the islands as the 'Northern Territories'.[208] The islands range in size from 102 km^2 to 3139 km^2, and the Habomais group are as close as 5 km from the northern tip of Hokkaido.[209] Japan's claim to the islands is based upon discovery and upon historical nineteenth-century treaties with Russia that determined the

[203] M Byers, *International Law and the Arctic* (Cambridge University Press 2013) 11.

[204] *Eastern Greenland* (n 46) 59; discussed by Byers (n 203) 11.

[205] Byers (n 203) 12.

[206] In 2018 Canada and Denmark convened a joint task force to progress discussions over Hans Island: S Frizzell, 'Truce? Canada, Greenland, Denmark inch closer to settling decades-old spat over Hans Island', *CBC News* (28 May 2018) www.cbc.ca/news/canada/north/canada-denmark-battle-ownership-hans-island-1.4679142; see analysis by Byers (n 203) 10-16; C Stevenson, 'Hans Off: The Struggle for Hans Island and the Potential Ramifications for International Border Dispute Resolution' (2007) 30 *Boston College International and Comparative Law Review* 263.

[207] Y Zinberg, 'Kuril Islands' in R Wolfrum (ed), *Max Planck Encyclopedia of International Law* (online edn, Oxford University Press 2011) [1]–[3].

[208] T Burrett, 'Great expectations: Domestic Politics and the Russo–Japanese Northern Territories Dispute' in J Kingston (ed), *Critical Issues in Contemporary Japan* (2nd edn, Routledge 2019) 158, 158.

[209] AB Quillen, 'The "Kuril Islands" or the "Northern Territories": Who Owns Them? – Island Territorial Dispute Continues to Hinder Relations between Russia and Japan' (1993) 18 *North Carolina Journal of International Law and Commercial Regulation* 633, 635.

status of the Kuril Island chain and placed the four most southern islands under Japanese control. Japan subsequently occupied and administered the islands until they were seized by the then USSR in 1945.[210] Russia's claim, as a successor State to the USSR, is based upon its occupation of the islands since 1945, the 1951 San Francisco Peace Treaty in which Japan renounced its rights to the Kuril Islands, and consequent *effectivités*.[211] Japan contests the Russian interpretation of the 1951 Peace Treaty, which has been the subject of ongoing negotiations in recent decades, though little substantive progress has been made.[212]

H. Matthew (Umaenupne) and Hunter (Leka) Islands (France v Vanuatu)

Matthew and Hunter Islands are two uninhabited South Pacific Islands that are situated to the east of New Caledonia in the Southwest Pacific. Their principal significance is the maritime claims they generate consistent with the LOSC.[213] The islands had been considered to be a part of the French Overseas Territory of New Caledonia from 1853 when France annexed the numerous islands composing that expansive territory.[214] Since its independence in 1980, Vanuatu has asserted its entitlement to the islands.[215] The background to the dispute rests with joint British and French control of the South Pacific islands making up the New Hebrides, which was formalised under a 1914 Anglo-French Condominium in which Matthew and Hunter Islands were not named. In 1929, France annexed the islands for New Caledonia and since has undertaken varying levels of administration. Britain occupied the islands in 1965, and Vanuatu succeeded to that entitlement upon its independence.[216] The French claim would appear to be based upon annexation and *effectivités*, while that of Vanuatu is based upon competing *effectivités* by Britain and Vanuatu as the successor State. There is also a suggestion that the indigenous peoples of Vanuatu have over time visited the islands for cultural purposes.[217] There have been ongoing minor incidents since 1980. Attempts at negotiations over the status of the islands occurred in 2018, which will

[210] ibid 639–42.

[211] Zinberg (n 207) [6]–[8]; see also Quillen (n 209) 642–45.

[212] See discussion in EV Neverova, 'The Southern Kuril Deadlock: effectiveness v. protest' (2019) 3 *Moscow Journal of International Law* 47; Burrett (n 208) 168–69 discussing recent developments.

[213] Prescott and Triggs (n 16) 103 who estimated the maritime entitlements of the islands as 59,400 nm^2.

[214] Heathcote (n 23) 667; ibid 103.

[215] M Mosses, 'Revisiting the Matthew and Hunter Islands Dispute in Light of the Recent Chagos Advisory Opinion and Some Other Relevant Cases: An Evaluation of Vanuatu's Claims relating to the Right to Self-Determination, Territorial Integrity, Unlawful Occupation and State Responsibility Under International Law' (2019) 66 *Netherlands International Law Review* 475.

[216] ibid 477.

[217] ibid 478.

take on additional urgency if New Caledonia moves towards independence from France.[218]

I. Senkaku/Diaoyu Islands (China v Japan)

The Senkaku Islands are located in the East China Sea and are composed of a main island – Uotsurijima – and seven other associated smaller features. The closest land – the Yaeyama Islands (Japan) – is 150 km distant.[219] The islands are presently under Japanese control and are uninhabited, though they have been the subject of some small-scale economic activity and occasional visitation. China's claim to the islands is based on a form of historic title acquired over many centuries, and asserts that Japan's nineteenth-century acquisition of the islands was by way of an unequal treaty. Both China and the Republic of China (Taiwan) asserted a formal claim over the islands in 1971.[220] Japan's claim is based upon a view the islands were effectively *terra nullius* prior to Japanese incorporation in 1895,[221] that the islands were not included in any renunciation of territorial claims under the 1951 San Francisco Peace Treaty, and were returned to Japan following the end of American post-World War II occupation. Diplomatic exchanges have taken place between China and Japan over the islands' status, but no resolution has been reached. In the past decade, China has become more assertive with respect to its claim to the islands.[222]

J. South China Sea Islands (China, Malaysia, Philippines, Vietnam)

There are numerous disputes between littoral States in the South China Sea over islands, rocks, reefs, and shoals.[223] The principal areas of dispute relate to the Paracel Islands, to the east of Vietnam and south of Hainan Island (China), and the Spratly Islands which are in a central area of the South China Sea approximately

[218] A Dayant, 'Not one, but two new points of tension for France in the Pacific' (*The Interpreter* (Lowy Institute), 19 March 2019) www.lowyinstitute.org/the-interpreter/not-one-two-new-points-tension-france-pacific; ibid 478.

[219] M Asada, 'Senkaku/Diaoyu Islands' in R Wolfrum (ed), *Max Planck Encyclopedia of International Law* (online edn, Oxford University Press 2007) [1].

[220] Selden (n 193) 151.

[221] ibid.

[222] See also analysis in G McCormack, 'Much Ado over Small Islands: The Sino-Japan confrontation over Senkaku/Diaoyu' in TF Liao, K Hara, and K Wiegand (eds), *The China-Japan Border Dispute: Islands of Contention in Multidisciplinary Perspective* (Ashgate 2015) 15; Y Matsui, 'International Law of Territorial Acquisition and the Dispute over the Senkaku (Diaoyu) Islands' (1997) 40 *Japanese Annual of International Law* 3.

[223] Only those claims relating to islands and rocks are considered; for claims to lesser maritime features see LG Cordner, 'The Spratly Islands Dispute and the Law of the Sea' (1994) 25 *Ocean Development and International Law* 61, 68 (Brunei).

mid-way between the Vietnamese coast and the Philippines archipelago. The largest claimant is China which occupies several of the larger features and in the past decade has built artificial islands in the area.[224] The Chinese claim is framed around longstanding historic rights and interests throughout the whole South China Sea, which include both the islands and other maritime features and waters adjacent to and between those waters. The claim is principally reflected in the so-called 'Nine-Dash Line', which increasingly has been understood as a claim to both the land within the confines of the Line and to all of the maritime areas.[225] The maritime element of that claim was not upheld by an Annex VII Arbitral Tribunal in the 2016 *South China Sea Arbitration*;[226] however, as the Tribunal lacked jurisdiction to assess land claims China's island territorial claims were not considered. The Republic of China (Taiwan) also asserts claims in the region, and occupies one of the larger features – Itu Abu. These claims are closely aligned with those of China.[227] Malaysia's claims to islands and rocks in the southern part of the Spratly Islands are based principally on notions associated with its continental shelf entitlements – by which it asserts claims to land features located within its continental shelf – and on control based on *effectivités*.[228] The Philippines claim relates to the Kalayaan Island Group,[229] which encompasses 53 islands in the West Philippine Sea.[230] The basis of this claim appears to be discovery of *terra nullius* lands, the limits established under the 1951 San Francisco Peace Treaty, and a form of *effectivités*.[231] Vietnam claims sovereignty over all the Paracel and Spratly Islands based on historical evidence, claims made by France, its status as a successor State, and a form of *effectivités*.[232] Some attempts have been made to settle these claims through the Association of Southeast Asian Nations (ASEAN), which in 2002 reached agreement with China on a Declaration on the Conduct of Parties in the South China Sea.[233] Negotiations have since stalled.

[224] See the discussion in Chapter two of this volume.

[225] See generally F Dupuy and P-M Dupuy, 'A Legal Analysis of China's Historic Rights Claim in the South China Sea' (2013) 107 *American Journal of International Law* 124.

[226] *In the Matter of the South China Sea Arbitration before an Arbitral Tribunal constituted under Annex VII of the 1982 United Nations Convention on the Law of the Sea (Philippines v China)* (Merits) (12 July 2016) PCA Case 2013-19, [5]; see also *In the Matter of the Arbitration before an Arbitral Tribunal constituted under Annex VII of the 1982 United Nations Convention on the Law of the Sea (Philippines v China)* (Award on Jurisdiction and Admissibility) (29 October 2015) PCA Case 2013-19, [8].

[227] Cordner (n 223) 62–5.

[228] ibid 67.

[229] Permanent Mission of the Republic of the Philippines to the United Nations, 'Note Verbale No. 11-00494' (5 April 2011) www.un.org/depts/los/clcs_new/submissions_files/vnm37_09/phl_re_chn_2011.pdf.

[230] See Presidential Decree No. 1596 (11 June 1978) (Philippines); and discussion in JR Coquia, 'Maritime Boundary Problems in the South China Sea' (1990) 24 *University of British Columbia Law Review* 117, 119.

[231] Cordner (n 223) 66.

[232] Permanent Mission of the Socialist Republic of Viet Nam to the United Nations, 'Note Verbale No. 77/HC-2011' (3 May 2011) www.un.org/Depts/los/clcs_new/submissions_files/mysvnm33_09/vnm_2011_re_phlchn.pdf; Coquia (n 230) 119; Cordner (n 223) 65–66.

[233] ASEAN, 'Declaration on the Conduct of the Parties in the South China Sea (4 November 2002)' https://asean.org/declaration-on-the-conduct-of-parties-in-the-south-china-sea-2/.

VI. Conclusions

International law, islands and territoriality has evolved over the past century. Many of the earlier disputes were between colonial powers contesting claims in parts of the world significantly distant from the metropolitan State. Particular emphasis was given to acts of discovery, formal proclamations of title, and publication of maps.[234] Few of those disputes gave any prominence to the potential maritime entitlements of the islands, reflective of the state of the law of the sea at the time. Towards the end of the twentieth, and certainly in the twenty-first century, much greater weight in island disputes has been given to their potential maritime entitlements. This has been reflected by the manner in which States with competing island claims have especially used diplomatic exchanges with the UN to stall Article 76 LOSC claims before the Commission on the Limits of the Continental Shelf. The emergence of mixed land and maritime disputes before international courts and tribunals also highlights how islands, territoriality and law of the sea have increasingly become intertwined. A review of the relevant international decisions and the current state of the law demonstrates how there has been an increasing shift towards *effectivités* as being one of the most significant factors a court or tribunal will consider when making determinations as to islands and territoriality. The *Island of Palmas* award highlighted the need for effective occupation. Arbitrator Huber was careful to not give decisive weight to discovery and found that it resulted in only an inchoate title. It is perhaps inevitable that, as States have acquired greater capacity to exercise effective control and sovereignty over islands, the threshold for demonstrating *effectivités* has risen. Whether such a high standard will be expected of even the most remote islands far distant from any significant populations remains to be seen. In that respect, some caution needs to be exercised in placing too much reliance upon the observations in *Eastern Greenland* in the modern digital and satellite era. A review of the ongoing island territorial disputes also suggests that States are giving increasing weight to demonstrating *effectivités*. Certainly in the most contentious and high-profile island disputes, States which are in occupation are engaging in multiple activities to demonstrate that title to the island has been perfected by the actual exercise of sovereignty. In parts of the South China Sea this has extended to the building of significant infrastructure, such as airstrips, harbour facilities, and forms of land reclamation which can also be characterised as artificial island building.

The international law in this area must always be seen against the backdrop of the general international law with respect to territoriality. In that regard international courts and tribunals make very little distinction between continental and island lands, and the claims of continental and island States. Nevertheless, there are some very distinctive legal and geopolitical issues. In the case of East Asian

[234] On maps, see generally *Island of Palmas* (n 12) 852 (esp).

island disputes there remains the historical legacy of twentieth-century conflict: issues arising as to which islands were removed from Japanese control under the 1951 San Francisco Peace Treaty, and resulting ongoing tensions between Japan and its neighbours over these islands. The geographical unity of islands, especially small co-located clusters of islands, is another distinctive aspect of how the law has evolved in this area. States engaged in island territorial disputes need to closely observe the general international law with respect to territoriality; however, as this chapter has demonstrated, there is now a considerable body of international law in this area which reflects upon the particular circumstances of islands.

4

Islands, Status and Statehood

I. Introduction

Islands raise some distinctive issues with respect to statehood and their status within political units. With the emergence of the League of Nations and then the United Nations (UN), paralleled by the growth of international human rights law, these issues became more relevant during the twentieth century. While many of the general legal principles relating to matters such as islands and statehood, including the status of archipelagic States, have been settled, these principles remain significant in the twenty-first century. They raise issues with respect to the historic legal status of islands, their current status as States or other forms of legal or political entities under international law, and the implications of that status for the ongoing standing of the islands and their peoples.

For the purposes of this discussion three categories of islands, including parts of islands, can be identified. The first is those islands that remain under colonial domination and the rights of island peoples to self-determination. Contemporary examples include the Falkland Islands (UK), Guam (US), New Caledonia (France), and Tokelau (New Zealand). The UN Special Committee on Decolonization has also been monitoring the situation in Puerto Rico,[1] which is currently an 'unincorporated, organized territory' of the United States. If some of these island communities eventually emerge via self-determination processes to seek independence, then questions will arise as to whether they should be recognised as States for the purposes of international law. In the case of small islands with small populations this will particularly raise issues regarding statehood and their viability. This category of islands falls within the oversight of the UN under Chapter XI of the UN Charter.[2]

The second category comprises islands, and groups of islands, that do not aspire to statehood, and have a form of legal and political association with a continental State. This raises issues with respect to the status of these islands within the larger State. Islands that fall into this category include Aruba (Netherlands), the Cook

[1] Special Committee on Decolonization (United Nations), 'Special Committee on Decolonization Approves Text Calling upon United States to Promote Puerto Rico's Self-Determination, Eventual Independence' (18 June 2021), Press Release GA/COL/3346.

[2] Charter of the United Nations (adopted 26 June 1945, entered into force 24 October 1945) 1 UNTS XV (UN Charter).

Islands (New Zealand), Isle of Man (Mann) (United Kingdom (UK)), Hawaii (US), Norfolk Island (Australia), and Reunion Island (France). The constitutional status of these island territories under national laws is unique. As discussed in Chapter nine, some also have a distinct status under international law either because of an act of self-determination or because their island territories are the home to peoples as recognised in international law.

There is a third category of islands which form part of a continental or island State which have been integrated into the metropolitan State and constitutionally are treated no differently from other parts of that State. There are numerous islands that fall into this latter category, many of which are very small and uninhabited; however, there are also much larger islands with significant populations. Examples here include the Andaman and Nicobar Islands (India),[3] Crete (Greece), Hainan Island (China), Jeju (Republic of Korea), Okinawa (Japan), Prince Edward Island (Canada),[4] Sicily (Italy), Tasmania (Australia),[5] Vancouver Island[6] (Canada), and the Isle of Wight (UK).[7]

This chapter is principally concerned with those islands that fall into the first and second categories and proceeds by considering issues associated with islands and the international system, before progressing to assess the status of islands within the UN system with particular reference to UN Charter Chapter XI Non-Self-Governing Territories and Chapter XII Trust Territories. With that background an assessment will then be undertaken of the current status of islands as independent States, constituent units of a State, islands in free association or that have been integrated, UN listed 'non self-governing' territories, the ocean territories of France, the UK and US, and some sui generis categories.

II. Islands and the International System

The status of island territories increasingly came under the international spotlight throughout the twentieth century. This arose due to parallel processes: through the League of Nations followed by the UN, and with the rise of international human rights law and its recognition of the rights of peoples to self-determination.[8] This focus was not upon already existing island States such as Great Britain or Japan, but rather island territories that were part of colonies or had some form of associated status with major powers. Many of these islands were located across parts of the Pacific, or clustered in distinct geographic regions such as the Caribbean.

[3] A Union Territory of India.
[4] Prince Edward Island is one of the 10 Canadian provinces.
[5] Tasmania is one of the six Australian states.
[6] Vancouver Island is part of the Canadian province of British Colombia.
[7] The Isle of Wight is an island county in the southern UK.
[8] UN Charter (n 2) arts 1(2), 55.

The international concern over these territories was first reflected in the system of League of Nations Mandates (League Mandates) that were provided for under Article 22 of the Covenant of the League of Nations.[9] Three types of 'Mandates' were envisaged, of which the so-called 'C' Mandates included all of the territories that were detached from Germany following the Treaty of Versailles.[10] These territories, composed principally of islands, were described as ones that:

> owing to the sparseness of their population, or their small size, or their remoteness from the centres of civilisation, or their geographical contiguity to the territory of the Mandatory, and other circumstances, can be best administered under the laws of the Mandatory as integral portions of its territory, subject to the safeguards above mentioned in the interests of the indigenous population.[11]

The islands and associated territories that fell within the 'C' Mandate (and their Administering State) were New Guinea (Australia), Nauru (British Empire: Australia, New Zealand, UK), Western Samoa (New Zealand), and Pacific Islands (Japan/US).[12]

However, while the status of these distinctive island territories was the focus of the League Mandates, there were other island territories that came within the purview of the international system during the period of the League of Nations. Some of these islands were the subject of territorial disputes,[13] and issues of territoriality were considered by the Permanent Court of International Justice as occurred with the *Legal Status of Eastern Greenland*,[14] or in international arbitrations such as *Clipperton Island*,[15] or the *Island of Palmas*.[16] A unique special regime was also created in the case of the Spitsbergen/Svalbard archipelago.[17]

With respect to the right of island peoples to self-determination,[18] while the concept was to a degree embedded in the League Mandates system, its legal status was ambiguous. Nevertheless, the question of self-determination was raised in the case of the Aaland Islands in a matter brought before the League of Nations and referred to the International Committee of Jurists. The Aaland Islands are located in

[9] The Treaty of Peace Between the Allied and Associated Powers and Germany (adopted 28 June 1919, entered into force 10 January 1920) 225 CTS 188 (Covenant of the League of Nations) pt 1.

[10] The Treaty of Peace Between the Allied and Associated Powers and Germany (adopted 28 June 1919, entered into force 10 January 1920) 225 CTS 188 (Treaty of Versailles) arts 118–199.

[11] Covenant of the League of Nations (n 9) art 22.

[12] The Japanese Mandate was from 1920 to 1944, and from 1947 the Mandate rested with the US. The islands were occupied and used as a military base first by Japan and then the US during World War II. The only other 'C' Mandate territory was South West Africa (South Africa).

[13] See discussion of these issues and cases in Chapter 3 of this volume.

[14] *Legal Status of Eastern Greenland (Denmark v Norway)* (1933) PCIJ Ser A/B No 53.

[15] *Clipperton Island (France v Mexico)* (1931) 2 RIAA 1105.

[16] *Island of Palmas (Netherlands v United States of America)* (1928) 2 RIAA 829.

[17] See the discussion in section V of this chapter.

[18] Described by Crawford as 'perhaps the most controversial and contested of the many controversial and contested terms in the vocabulary of international law': J Crawford, 'The Right of Self-Determination in International Law: Its Development and Future' in P Alston (ed), *People's Rights* (Oxford University Press 2001) 7, 7 ('The Right of Self-Determination').

the Gulf of Bothia and at the conclusion of World War I were the subject of a dispute between Finland and Sweden, partly provoked by the Swedish-speaking population not wishing to remain under Finnish control. The residents of the islands claimed a right of self-determination and desire to be reunified with Sweden. However the International Committee of Jurists, while conceding that 'the principle of self-determination of peoples plays an important part in modern political thought', noted that it was not mentioned in the Covenant of the League of Nations and concluded that '[t]he recognition of this principle in a certain number of international treaties cannot be considered as sufficient to put it upon the same footing as a positive rule of the Law of Nations.'[19] While the International Committee of Jurists were unable to find in favour of a claim by the islanders to be associated with Sweden by way of their entitlement to self-determination, the special status of the Aaland Islands was upheld in other respects, including that they remain demilitarised.[20]

At the time of the formation of the UN, only six founding members were islands or comprised groups of islands: Cuba, Dominican Republic, Haiti, New Zealand, Philippines, and the UK. By 1950 they had been joined by Iceland and Indonesia. Other founding UN members contained islands or island groups as parts of their territories such as Australia, Canada, China, Denmark, France, Netherlands, Portugal, USSR and the US; however these were all continental States.

III. Chapter XI Non-Self-Governing Territories and Chapter XII Trust Territories

The UN Charter ushered in a new era with respect to the previous League Mandate territories, and colonial territories that either pre-dated World War II or had come under colonial occupation as a result of expansionist activities prior to and during the War. These territories were broadly classified into two groups: those that fell under a newly devised trusteeship system, and those that were non-self-governing. Both groups contained significant island territories.

A. International Trusteeship System

Chapters XII and XIII of the UN Charter dealt with the new UN 'International Trusteeship System' and was designed to be the successor to the League Mandates.[21]

[19] 'Report of the International Committee of Jurists entrusted by the Council of the League of Nations with the task of giving an advisory opinion upon the legal aspects of the Aaland Islands question' [October 1920] *League of Nations Official Journal* 3, 5 (Report of the International Committee of Jurists); for Crawford's view on this matter and the status of self-determination at the time see Crawford, 'The Right of Self-Determination' (n 18) 11–15.

[20] Report of the International Committee of Jurists (n 19) 19; and see the discussion below that elaborates this point.

[21] UN Charter (n 2) art 77(1).

The objectives of the trusteeship system, consistent with the purposes of the UN, included:

- Furthering international peace and security;
- Promoting the political, economic, social and educational advancement of the inhabitants of trust territories;
- Promoting the progressive development towards self-government or independence for the peoples of those territories;
- Respect for human rights and equal treatment in social, economic and commercial matters.[22]

A Trusteeship Council, established under Chapter XIII, exercised general oversight of these arrangements, with distinctive roles also anticipated for the General Assembly (UNGA) and the Security Council (UNSC).[23] Article 77 of the Charter envisaged three types of territories being placed under trusteeship arrangements: territories currently held under mandate, territories detached from an enemy State as a result of World War II, and territories voluntarily placed under the system by the States responsible for their administration.[24] A total of 11 trust territories resulted from these processes, of which the island territories and their administering States were Western Samoa (New Zealand), New Guinea and Nauru (Australia),[25] and the Pacific Islands (US).[26]

All of these trusteeship arrangements have been terminated during the UN era, and in the case of the relevant islands independence was achieved by Nauru (1968), Papua New Guinea (PNG) (1975),[27] and Samoa (1962).[28] The Trust Territory of the Pacific Islands proved to be more problematic partly due to its status as a 'strategic area'.[29] Notwithstanding an expectation that the territory would eventually emerge as a single independent State, eventually three independent States and an associated State were formed:

- Federated States of Micronesia (1986);
- Palau (1994);[30]

[22] ibid art 76a–d.
[23] See eg ibid arts 83, 84.
[24] ibid art 77(1).
[25] The formal administering States of New Guinea and Nauru were Australia, New Zealand and the UK, but in practice it was administered by Australia alone. For an assessment of Australia's international legal obligations with respect to New Guinea and Nauru see AC Castles, 'International Law and Australia's Overseas Territories' in DP O'Connell (ed), *International Law in Australia* (Law Book 1965) 292, 304–7.
[26] UNSC Resolution 21 (1947) UN Doc S/RES/21; see also MN Shaw, *International Law* (8th edn, Cambridge University Press 2017) 176; R Jennings and A Watts (eds), *Oppenheim's International Law: Volume 1 Peace* (9th edn, Longman 1992) 311–12.
[27] New Guinea was joined with the non-self-governing territory of Papua to create the new State of PNG.
[28] Upon independence known as 'Western Samoa', reverted to 'Samoa' in 1997.
[29] UN Charter (n 2) art 82; see discussion in Jennings and Watts (n 26) 313.
[30] UNSC Resolution 956 (1994) UN Doc S/RES/956.

- Republic of the Marshall Islands (1986); and
- Commonwealth of the Northern Mariana Islands in association with the US (1975).[31]

Appendix 1 to this volume provides details on the current status of former UN Charter Chapter XII island Trust Territories.

B. Non-Self-Governing Territories

The second group referred to above were Chapter XI 'non-self-governing' territories (NSGT). These were those 'whose peoples have not yet attained a full measure of self-government' and over which UN members 'which have or assume responsibilities for the administration of territories' thus acquired responsibilities towards the peoples of those territories. This was described in Article 73 as a 'sacred trust' to promote to 'the utmost' the 'well-being of the inhabitants of these territories'. The relevant responsibilities of the metropolitan State towards a NSGT included:

- Respect for the culture of the peoples and their political, economic, social and educational advancement;
- To develop self-government and take account of their political aspirations;
- To promote international peace and security; and
- To promote constructive measures of development.[32]

UN member States had obligations under Article 73e to transmit information to the UN Secretary-General regarding the 'economic, social and educational conditions in the territories' for which they were responsible, other than those which fell within the ambit of Chapters XII and XIII.[33]

A critical issue for Chapter XI was the distinction between 'territories' and 'metropolitan areas', as only territories fell within the ambit of being NSGTs,[34] and given the lack of definition in the terms and the potential for geographical ambiguity, there was considerable scope for debate. In that regard Crawford observed, with specific reference to islands:

> The term 'metropolitan' is presumably a reference to the history of the area concerned as part of a State and to its geographical contiguity with the rest of the State. But while

[31] See UNSC Resolution 683 (1990) UN Doc S/RES/683; United Nations Trusteeship Council Resolution 2183 (LIII) (28 May 1986) UN Doc T/RES/2183(LIII); and the discussion in Shaw (n 26) 176.

[32] UN Charter (n 2) art 73a, b, c, d; cf similarities in the language of the text of art 76 outlining the objectives of the International Trusteeship System.

[33] ibid art 73e.

[34] ibid art 74, provides: 'Members of the United Nations also agree that their policy in respect of the territories to which this Chapter applies, no less than in respect of their metropolitan areas, must be based on the general principle of good neighbourliness, due account being taken of the interests and well-being of the rest of the world, in social, economic and commercial matters.'

> a separate area of land such as an island might be considered 'metropolitan' because it had been part of a State for as long as the State had existed, 'territory' as such can neither be 'self-governing' or 'non-self-governing': only people or groups can govern and be governed.[35]

It was therefore important to identify the existence of people on a territory for the Chapter XI criteria to be met, because as Crawford has also observed: 'Uninhabited islands, even if acquired by traditional colonial powers on the other side of the world, have never been treated as Chapter XI territories in their own right.'[36] Article 73e NSGTs were first recognised in 1946 in UNGA Resolution 66 (I) where a total of 72 territories under eight different administering States were listed.[37] The number of territories on the list continued to rise in subsequent years either as a result of Article 73e reporting or via decisions of the UNGA.[38]

Closely linked to the capacity of NSGTs to evolve as self-governing was the principle of self-determination. The importance of the right of peoples to self-determination was regularly reinforced by the UN, including by UNGA Resolution 1514 (VX) Declaration on the Granting of Independence to Colonial Countries and Peoples which reaffirmed that: 'All peoples have the right to self-determination; by virtue of that right they freely determine their political status and freely pursue their economic, social and cultural development.'[39] The UNGA in 1961 subsequently established a Special Committee for the implementation of UNGA Resolution 1514 (VX), initially with 17 members and then 24.[40] The 'Special Committee on Decolonization' or C-24[41] annually reviewed the list of territories to which UNGA Resolution 1514 (VX) applied and the status of NSGTs. That work remains ongoing.[42]

[35] J Crawford, *The Creation of States in International Law* (2nd edn, Clarendon Press 2006) 606 (*Creation of States*).

[36] ibid 606; this is particularly applicable in the case of uninhabited islands in the Arctic Ocean, Southern Ocean and parts of the Pacific Ocean; however, the fact that a group of islands that form a distinct entity include one or more uninhabited islands does not disqualify them from being a Chapter XI NSGT, as is the case with some of the smaller islands that comprise the Falkland/Malvinas Islands.

[37] ibid 608; and generally MM Mbengue, 'Non-Self-Governing Territories' in R Wolfrum (ed), *Max Planck Encyclopedia of Public International Law* (online edn, Oxford University Press 2013).

[38] See generally Crawford, *Creation of States* (n 35) 608–10.

[39] UNGA Resolution 1514 (VX) (14 December 1960) UN Doc A/RES/1514(XV), in which the Resolution's Preamble recited: 'Considering the important role of the United Nations in assisting the movement for independence in Trust and Non-Self-Governing Territories.'

[40] UNGA Resolution 1654 (XVI) (27 November 1961) UN Doc A/RES/1654(XVI).

[41] Formally known as the 'Special Committee on the Situation with regard to the Implementation of Declaration on the Granting of Independence to Colonial Countries and Peoples' (or C-24).

[42] See UN, 'The United Nations and Decolonization: Special Committee on Decolonization' www.un.org/dppa/decolonization/en/c24/about, where the current work of the Committee is described as 'The C-24 annually reviews the list of Non-Self-Governing Territories to which the Declaration is applicable. It also hears statements from representatives of the Non-Self-Governing Territories at its annual sessions, dispatches visiting missions to Non-Self-Governing Territories and annually organizes regional seminars.'

The importance of the linkage between colonial territories and the right of peoples to self-determination was justified by Crawford as follows:

> It was thus, for purely historical reasons, that the category of colonial territories fell into two groups. The first group included those territories which had been mandates and which (if they had not achieved independence) were brought under the trusteeship system. The remaining colonial territories were covered by Chapter XI. All these territories were seen as falling in some sense under the rubric of self-determination.[43]

In 1995 the status of the peoples of East Timor and their rights of self-determination were considered by the International Court of Justice (ICJ).[44] While the *East Timor* case did not turn on that question, the Court was unambiguous as to its views regarding the status of self-determination when it observed:

> Portugal's assertion that the right of peoples to self-determination, as it evolved from the Charter and from UN practice, has an *erga omnes* character, is irreproachable. The principle of self-determination of peoples has been recognized by the United Nations Charter and in the jurisprudence of the Court; it is one of the essential principles of contemporary international law.[45]

The Court expressly made a connection between East Timor's status for the parties as a NSGT and its people having a right to self-determination,[46] which became an important element in the eventual transition of East Timor from its 1995 status as a province of Indonesia to independence in 2002.

In addition to the entitlement of peoples to the right of self-determination, the other critical element to the interpretation of Article 73 has been UNGA Resolution 1541 (XV), the annex to which outlined 12 Principles to guide UN members as to whether there existed an obligation to provide information on a NSGT. The Principles recognised that Chapter XI of the UN Charter embodied territories that were in 'a dynamic state of evolution and progress towards a "full measure of self-government"',[47] which importantly was recognised as being achieved by one of three measures:

- Emergence as a sovereign independent State;
- Free association with an independent State;
- Integration with an independent State.[48]

[43] Crawford, 'The Right of Self-Determination' (n 19) 15–16.

[44] *Case Concerning East Timor (Portugal v Australia)* (Judgment) [1995] ICJ Reps 90; see also *Legal Consequences for States of the Continued Presence of South Africa in Namibia* (Advisory Opinion) [1971] ICJ Reps 16; *Western Sahara* (Advisory Opinion) [1975] ICJ Reps 12, especially 31–33 [54]–[59] with respect to self-determination and a non-self-governing territory; *Legal Consequences of the Construction of a Wall in the Occupied Palestinian Territory* (Advisory Opinion) [2004] ICJ Reps 136, 171–72; *Kosovo* (Advisory Opinion) [2010] ICJ Reps 403, 436.

[45] *Case Concerning East Timor (Portugal v Australia)* (n 44) 102 [29].

[46] ibid 103 [31].

[47] UNGA Resolution 1541 (XV) (15 December 1960) UN Doc A/RES/1541(XV) Annex, Principle II.

[48] ibid Annex, Principle VI.

The processes associated with the recognition of territories in free association and integration with an independent State are outlined in more detail in Principles VII, VIII and IX. They are as follows:

Principle VII

(a) Free association should be the result of a free and voluntary choice by the peoples of the territory concerned expressed through informed and democratic processes. It should be one which respects the individuality and the cultural characteristics of the territory and its peoples, and retains for the peoples of the territory which is associated with an independent State the freedom to modify the status of that territory through the expression of their will by democratic means and through constitutional processes.

(b) The associated territory should have the right to determine its internal constitution without outside interference, in accordance with due constitutional processes and the freely expressed wishes of the people. This does not preclude consultations as appropriate or necessary under the terms of the free association agreed upon.

Principle VIII

Integration with an independent State should be on the basis of complete equality between the peoples of the erstwhile Non-Self-Governing Territory and those of the independent country with which it is integrated. The peoples of both territories should have equal status and rights of citizenship and equal guarantees of fundamental rights and freedoms without any distinction or discrimination; both should have equal rights and opportunities for representation and effective participation at all levels in the executive, legislative and judicial organs of government.

Principle IX

Integration should have come about in the following circumstances:

(a) The integrating territory should have attained an advanced stage of self-government with free political institutions, so that its peoples would have the capacity to make a responsible choice through informed and democratic processes;

(b) The integration should be the result of the freely expressed wishes of the territory's peoples acting with full knowledge of the change in their status, their wishes having been expressed through informed and democratic processes, impartially conducted and based on universal adult suffrage. The United Nations could, when it deems it necessary, supervise these processes.

The significance of Principles VII, VIII and IX is that they make clear that the transitioning of a NSGT to independence is not the only status envisaged under the processes contemplated by Article 73 and given effect to in both the practice of States and the UN. It also reflects that self-determination can take many forms. As Jennings and Watts observed:

[W]hile the terms of Chapter XI rest on the concept of self-government, the spirit in which that Chapter has in practice been applied has drawn its inspiration from the

> wider principle of self-determination, to the development of which that practice has in turn greatly contributed.[49]

UN practice, especially the role of the C-24, has therefore been critical over the decades as island NSGTs have transitioned either to a state of independence, free association, or integration with a metropolitan State. Likewise, the continuing exercise of UNGA 'procedural discretion' by way of its oversight of the remaining NSGTs has been important.[50] The UN list includes 17 territories,[51] of which 15 are island territories. Appendix 1 provides details on the status of former and current NSGTs.

IV. Current Status of Islands

Following on from the above analysis it is now possible to categorise islands under current international law through seven categories.

A. Independent States

The most significant category is that of independent island States. Of the six founding island State members of the UN, that number has now grown to a total of 42. This includes recognised archipelagic States under Part IV of the 1982 United Nations Convention on the Law of the Sea (LOSC)[52] such as Mauritius and PNG, and also States that comprise parts of islands shared with others such as Ireland (with the UK) and Timor Leste (with Indonesia). Some islands are shared between multiple States as in the case of Borneo which comprises Brunei, five Indonesian provinces (North Kalimantan, East Kalimantan, South Kalimantan, West Kalimantan, and Central Kalimantan), and two Malaysian states (Sabah and Sarawak). As a result of the process of decolonisation and through acts of self-determination, contemporary island States have attained statehood through a variety of processes. While these political and legal processes may now be seen purely in historical terms, they serve to highlight some of the legal and political foundations for modern

[49] Jennings and Watts (n 26) 285; see also Crawford, 'The Right to Self-Determination' (n 18) 15–37; UN Economic and Social Council Official Records, 'The Principle of Self-Determination in Relation to Chapters XI, XIII and XIII of the Charter of the United Nations' (16 April 1952) 8th session UN Doc E/CN.4/662, agenda items 3 and 4; E Rodríguez-Santiago, 'The Evolution of Self-Determination of Peoples in International Law' in FR Tesón (ed), *The Theory of Self-Determination* (Cambridge University Press 2016) 201–40.

[50] Crawford, *Creation of States* (n 35) 605.

[51] See UN, 'The United Nations and Decolonization: Non-Self-Governing Territories' www.un.org/dppa/decolonization/en/nsgt.

[52] United Nations Convention on the Law of the Sea (adopted 10 December 1982, entered into force 16 November 1994) 1833 UNTS 397 (LOSC).

island States which in some instances have created important legacies. Vanuatu for example, which attained independence in 1980, had been subject to British and French settlement in the nineteenth century and in 1906 became an Anglo-French Condominium over what was then known as the 'New Hebrides'. However, the territory was not a British colony, and following World War II the administrative arrangements evolved under NSGT status with the UK acting as administering power to allow for more substantive engagement from the local peoples until independence.[53] In the case of Timor Leste, a former Portuguese colony recognised as a NSGT, following Portugal's withdrawal in 1974–75 an attempt was made to declare independence as 'East Timor'. However East Timor was never recognised as an independent State prior to Indonesian military occupation on 27 December 1975 and the declaration of the territory as a province of Indonesia.[54] A plebiscite conducted under UN auspices held on 30 August 1999 voted in favour of greater autonomy, after which Indonesia withdrew and the territory fell under the oversight of the United Nations Transitional Administration in East Timor (UNTAET)[55] until independence on 20 May 2002.[56]

A major threshold issue for the emergence of any new State, whether it be island or continental, is whether it will gain recognition as a State. As a result the Montevideo Convention criteria of a State possessing a permanent population, a defined territory, government, and capacity to enter into relations with other States are important thresholds.[57] The Montevideo criterion of a permanent population raises two particular issues for islands. The first relates to whether a minimum number of persons is required to constitute a permanent population. Here the status of the Vatican, albeit an exceptional case, highlights that even an entity with a population on average of no more than 1000 persons is considered by some States to meet the statehood criterion.[58] Island States with very small populations such as Nauru (9,770)[59] and Tuvalu (11,448)[60] also meet the relevant criteria.[61] Ultimately it would appear that the size of the population is not determinative, but rather the stability of the population and its capacity to form a coherent social group and political community.

[53] Shaw (n 25) 179–80; see also DP O'Connell, 'The Condominium of the New Hebrides' (1968–1969) 43 *British Yearbook of International Law* 71.

[54] The western part of the island of Timor had been, and remains a part of Indonesia, and is referred to as 'West Timor'.

[55] UNSC Res 1272 (1999) UN DOC S/RES/1272.

[56] See discussion in Shaw (n 26) 183; and generally I Martin, *Self-Determination in East Timor: The United Nations, the Ballot, and International Intervention* (Lynne Rienner 2001).

[57] Montevideo Convention on the Rights and Duties of State (adopted 26 December 1933, entered into force 26 December 1934) 165 LNTS 19, art 1.

[58] Crawford, *Creation of States* (n 35) 222–23.

[59] Central Intelligence Agency (US) 'Nauru' (*The World Factbook*) www.cia.gov/the-world-factbook/countries/nauru/.

[60] Central Intelligence Agency (US) 'Tuvalu' (*The World Factbook*) www.cia.gov/the-world-factbook/countries/tuvalu/.

[61] Shaw (n 26) 158.

In the case of some islands, while territory is often simply defined by the geographic limits of the island, the capacity of the recognised sovereign State to exercise control over all of that territory may be compromised. Cyprus illustrates this proposition where, as a result of Turkish military intervention in 1974, circumstances were created for the establishment of the 'Turkish Republic of Northern Cyprus' (TRNC) in 1983.[62] However, the TRNC is only recognised by Turkey and, as noted by Shaw, 'it cannot be regarded as a sovereign state, but remains a de facto administered entity within the confines of the Republic of Cyprus and dependent upon Turkish assistance.'[63] The TRNC has not impacted upon the status of Cyprus as an independent island State, though it has impacted upon the political stability of the island, a UN peacekeeping mission having been present on Cyprus since 1964, with its mission expanded in 1974 in respect to the Turkey's military intervention and the establishment of the TRNC.[64]

B. Constituent Units of a State

An island may also be a constituent unit within a continental State, in which the island territory exercises a significant degree of autonomy within a constitutional compact. Prominent examples include Tasmania, which was a founding state of Australia in 1901, and Prince Edward Island, a founding province of Canada in 1867. The US state of Hawaii has a different history in this regard, as it was a recognised NSGT before becoming a state in 1959. While technically, this is an example of integration of a NSGT within a State, consistent with Principles VIII and IX of UNGA Resolution 1541 (XV), Hawaii's entitlements under the US constitution giving it constitutional equivalency to the original 13 founding US states place it in a category distinct from that of integration into a metropolitan State.

Constituent units of a federation or confederation are characterised by being part of a legal and political system governed by a constitution, and which themselves have their own constitutions, laws and courts systems.[65] However, islands may also be a constituent part of a State, including federations, without possessing any distinctive legal or political status other than for the purposes of municipal or local government. Prominent examples here include Vancouver Island (part of the Canadian province of British Colombia), the Florida Keys (islands that form part of the US state of Florida), the multiple islands of the Norwegian skjærgaard along its west coast, and Greek and Turkish islands in the Aegean Sea. There are also examples of islands that fall between these different categories, principally as they transition to a higher level of self-government. Tokelau, a self-administering

[62] The declaration was declared 'legally invalid' by UNSC Resolution 541 (1983) UN Doc S/RES/541.
[63] Shaw (n 26) 185.
[64] For background on the 'United Nations Peacekeeping Force in Cyprus' (UNFICYP) see unficyp.unmissions.org/about.
[65] See Constitution Act 1934 (Tasmania) (Australia); Constitution of the State of Hawaii 1959 (US).

Pacific island territory of New Zealand with a population of 1,500 persons, falls into this category.[66] A 2007 UN-sponsored referendum that would have seen Tokelau transition to free association with New Zealand did not succeed and it remains an Article 73 NSGT.[67]

C. Free Association

'Free Association' exists where an island territory exercises a high degree of autonomy under its own laws and constitution, and the associated State having responsibility for defence and foreign affairs of the island territory. Crawford has identified the following characteristics of Free Association:

1. The association is freely accepted by the inhabitants of the territory;
2. The terms of the association are set down in a form binding on the parties;
3. The associated territory has substantial powers of internal self-government;
4. The reserved powers of the 'metropolitan' State do not include substantial discretions to intervene in the reserved or internal affairs of the associated territory;
5. There is a procedure for the termination of the association.[68]

There are currently five island territories that clearly enjoy free association: Cook Islands and Niue (with New Zealand), and the Federated States of Micronesia, Republic of the Marshall Islands and Palau (with the US). While the Northern Mariana Islands and Puerto Rico, both of which enjoy commonwealth status in the US, have some of the characteristics of free association, neither territory is independent or asserts a high degree of autonomy over its affairs.[69]

The Cook Islands' status as a self-governing State in free association with New Zealand was achieved in 1965.[70] Under the terms of the Cook Islands Constitution Act 1964 (NZ), the status of the Cook Islands as self-governing is made clear;[71] however, foreign affairs and defence responsibilities rest with New Zealand following consultations between the two countries.[72] While the Cook

[66] See UN, 'The United Nations and Decolonization: Non-Self-Governing Territories – Tokelau' www.un.org/dppa/decolonization/en/nsgt/tokelau.

[67] A Townend, 'Tokelau's 2006 Referendum on Self-Government' (2007) 5 *New Zealand Journal of Public and International Law* 12; UN Mission to Tokelau, 'Report of the United Nations Mission to observe the October 2007 referendum on self-determination of Tokelau' (3 December 2007) UN Doc A/AC.109/2007/19.

[68] Crawford, *Creation of States* (n 35) 632–33.

[69] See the discussion in M Igarashi, *Associated Statehood in International Law* (Kluwer Law International 2002) 44–62, 212–15.

[70] See generally Isaacus and the Editorial Committee, 'The Cook Islands' in MA Ntumy (ed), *South Pacific Islands Legal Systems* (University of Hawaii Press 1993) 3–25.

[71] Cook Islands Constitution Act 1964 (NZ) s 3.

[72] ibid s 5.

Islands has evolved since independence and possesses full executive powers, significant links are retained with New Zealand, including citizenship.[73]

Niue's self-governing State in free association status with New Zealand was attained in 1974,[74] under the Niue Constitution Act 1974 (NZ).[75] New Zealand remains responsible for defence and foreign affairs, though only exercised at the request of the Government of Niue.[76] Again, similarly to the case of the Cook Islands, significant links are retained between Niue and New Zealand including citizenship.[77] It is estimated that 24,000 Niueans live in New Zealand, compared to 1,700 living in Niue.[78]

The Federated States of Micronesia (FSM), Republic of the Marshall Islands (RMI), and Palau all achieved associated status with the US following the dissolution of the Trust Territory of the Pacific Islands. In the case of FSM, a 'Compact of Free Association' was entered into with the US in 1986 upon independence and renewed in 2004. Micronesians enjoy the right to migrate to and settle in the US. Defence responsibilities rest with the US. RMI has a similar history to FSM, with independence and a 'Compact of Free Association' entered into in 1986. Likewise, defence responsibilities rest with the US. Palau is a Presidential Republic also in free association with the US, with that status commencing in 1994. Defence remains the responsibility of the US with the US military having access to the islands.

As a general observation, the international legal personality of 'Free Association' territories is ambiguous.[79] For example, in 1993 it was observed that the 'status of the Cook Islands as an independent State capable of entering into international relations is controversial.'[80] However, this situation is fluid and capable of change. In 2020 the New Zealand Ministry of Foreign Affairs and Trade observed: 'While not fully independent, the Cook Islands and Niue are recognised as "states" at international law. Since the mid-1980s they have generally conducted their own treaty making'.[81] Both the Cook Islands and Niue continue to mature in their international relations through engagement in a range of international fora, and the

[73] Ministry of Foreign Affairs and Trade (New Zealand), 'Cook Islands: Constitutional Status and International Personality' (May 2005) cookislandslawsociety.com/solicitors.html; Cook Islanders do not have additional Cook Island citizenship.

[74] See generally AH Angelo, 'Niue' in Ntumy (n 70) 158–79.

[75] Niue Constitution Act 1974 (NZ) s 3.

[76] ibid s 6; Central Intelligence Agency (US) 'Niue' (*The World Factbook*) www.cia.gov/the-world-factbook/countries/niue/.

[77] Niue Constitution Act 1974 (NZ) s 5.

[78] Foreign Affairs and Trade (New Zealand), 'Niue' www.mfat.govt.nz/en/countries-and-regions/australia-and-pacific/niue/; Central Intelligence Agency (US), 'Niue' (n 76).

[79] See the views of Crawford, *Creation of States* (n 35) 633.

[80] Isaacus and the Editorial Committee (n 70) 12.

[81] Ministry of Foreign Affairs and Trade (New Zealand), 'International Treaty Making: Guidance for government agencies on practice and procedures for concluding international treaties and arrangements' (September 2020) 41, www.mfat.govt.nz/assets/About-us-Corporate/Treaties-Model-instruments/International-Treaty-Making-Guide-2020.pdf.

establishment of diplomatic relations.[82] In this respect, States in free association will over time evolve as their institutions develop and capacities expand so that they exercise all of the attributes of a State, albeit still contracting out certain activities such as defence.[83]

D. Integration

Integration was envisaged as one way in which NSGTs would realise self-determination consistent with the aims of Article 73 of the UN Charter and UNGA Resolution 1541 (XV). Consistent with those processes, integration should only arise in cases where the integrating territory has attained an 'advanced stage of self-government' and is the result of the 'freely expressed wishes' of the territory's peoples.[84] The Faroe Islands and Greenland are both examples of integration and have become part of the 'Danish Realm'[85] under 'Home Rule'. In the case of the Faroe Islands, Home Rule from Denmark was established in 1948 as 'an autonomous nation within the Danish Kingdom'[86] with its own democratically elected legislative assembly, the Løgting. Under these arrangements the Faroe Islands have assumed responsibilities with respect to matters such as conservation and management of marine resources, protection of the environment, trade relations and financial policy, taxation and customs, social security, and education.[87] These powers were further extended by the Takeover Act of the Faroe Islands (2005)[88] which gave to the Faroe Islands the capacity to unilaterally exercise certain legislative and administrative powers not already within the ambit of its powers, excepting the constitution, citizenship, Supreme Court, and foreign, security, and defence policy.[89] The Foreign Policy Act 2005[90] further extends the competence of the Faroe Islands. Matters relating to defence or security, or which generally relate

[82] Eg both are members of the Pacific Islands Forum, and the Pacific Agreement on Closer Economic Relations Plus (PACER Plus) (adopted 14 June 2017, entered into force 13 December 2020) [2020] ATS 12; and the South Pacific Nuclear Free Zone Treaty (adopted 6 August 1985, entered into force 11 December 1986) [1986] ATS 32.

[83] The Marshall Islands, notwithstanding its status as an Associated State in a Compact of Free Association with the US, commenced ICJ proceedings: *Obligations concerning Negotiations relating to Cessation of the Nuclear Arms Race and to Nuclear Disarmament (Marshall Islands v UK)* (Preliminary Objections Judgment) [2016] ICJ Reps 833.

[84] UNGA Resolution 1541 (XV) (15 December 1960) UN Doc A/RES/1541(XV) Principle IX.

[85] The 'Danish Realm' consists of Denmark, Greenland and the Faroe Islands; see JA Jensen, 'The Position of Greenland and the Faroe Islands Within the Danish Realm' (2003) 9 *European Public Law* 170.

[86] See Faroes Home Rule Act (1948) (Act No 137) (Denmark); a general overview of these developments concerning the Faroe Islands can be found in S Dosenrode, 'Spill-back: The Faroe Islands' Zigzag towards Independence' in S Dosenrode (ed), *Limits to Regional Integration* (Routledge 2015) 197–214.

[87] Faroe Islands, 'The constitutional status of the Faroe Islands' (14 May 2018) www.faroeislands.fo/government-politics/constitutional-status/.

[88] Takeover Act of the Faroe Islands 2005 (Act No 578) (Denmark).

[89] Faroe Islands, 'The constitutional status' (n 87).

[90] Faroe Islands Act 2005 (Act No 80) (Denmark).

to the international relations of Denmark, are excluded from the competence of the Faroe Islands in this respect.[91]

Greenland, a NSGT, became part of the Danish Realm in 1953 which resulted in its removal from the NSGT list in 1954.[92] Home Rule status was attained in 1978 under the Greenland Home Rule Act.[93] Under that arrangement Greenland was recognised as a 'distinct community within the Kingdom of Denmark'.[94] While the Greenland assembly had extensive capacities similar to those of the Faroe Islands, matters within the 'foreign relations of the Realm' rested with the Danish government.[95] An exception was made for treaties that particularly affected 'Greenland interests' which are referred to Home Rule authorities for comments.[96] The subsequent Act on Greenland Self-Government (2009) extended Greenland's Home Rule status. In international affairs the government of Greenland, known as the Naalakkersuisut, may negotiate and conclude agreements under international law with other States and international organisations which 'exclusively concern Greenland'.[97] This entitlement can be extended in the case of matters that exclusively concern Greenland and the Faroe Islands, which both governments can jointly negotiate on behalf of the Danish Realm.[98] In matters where Denmark retains responsibility, the Naalakkersuisut is to be consulted before negotiations are initiated regarding agreements under international law.[99]

E. UN Listed NSGTs

Consistent with the processes noted above under Article 73 of the UN Charter, and the practice of the C-24, 15 island territories remain on the current UN list of 17 NSGTs.[100] Those islands and their administering power are:

- Anguilla, Bermuda, British Virgin Islands, Cayman Islands, Falkland Islands (Malvinas), Montserrat, Pitcairn, Saint Helena, and Turks and Caicos Islands (UK);
- American Samoa, Guam, and United States Virgin Islands (US);

[91] Faroe Islands, 'The constitutional status' (n 87); see also Faroe Islands, 'The Faroe Islands in the International Community' available at www.faroeislands.fo/government-politics/foreign-relations/.

[92] UNGA Resolution 849 (IX) (22 November 1954) UN Doc A/RES/849(IX).

[93] Greenland Home Rule Act 1978 (Act No 577) (Denmark); see generally I Foighel, 'Home Rule in Greenland' (1979) 48 *Nordisk Tidsskrift for International Ret* 4–9.

[94] Greenland Home Rule Act (n 93) s 1.

[95] ibid s 11.

[96] ibid s 13.

[97] Act on Greenland Self-Government 2009 (Act No 473) (Denmark) s 12(1).

[98] ibid s 12(2).

[99] ibid s 13(1).

[100] The other two NSGTs on the list are Gibraltar and Western Sahara.

- French Polynesia, and New Caledonia (France); and
- Tokelau (New Zealand).[101]

All of the islands are located in the Atlantic/Caribbean region, and the Pacific Ocean. All have populations of less than 100,000 excepting French Polynesia (271,800), Guam (159,358), New Caledonia (268,767) and the United States Virgin Islands (103,700). The size of the islands is also small, with all less than 1000 km^2 other than the Falkland Islands, French Polynesia and New Caledonia. Consistent with the ongoing mandate of the C-24, its work remains ongoing and the status of the various NSGT islands remains under review. In addition to island territories being removed from the list, there remains the potential that new islands may be added. In 2016 Norfolk Island (Australia) petitioned the C-24 for its inclusion on the NSGT list and that request remains under review.[102]

F. French, UK and US Ocean Territories[103]

As noted above, France, the UK and US retain responsibility for 14 of the remaining 15 island NSGTs and have additional island ocean territories over which they enjoy territorial entitlements. The very distinctive constitutional, legal and political arrangements in place for those islands justify separate analysis.

(i) French Categories

France has three categories under its municipal law and constitution that relate to overseas island territories:

- DROM – *départments et régions d'outre-mer*;
- COM – *collectivités d'outre-mer*; and
- POM – *pays d'outre-mer au sein de la République*.[104]

[101] For reference to the status of New Zealand treaties with respect to Tokelau, see Ministry of Foreign Affairs and Trade (New Zealand), 'International Treaty Making: Guidance for government agencies on practice and procedures for concluding international treaties and arrangements' (September 2020) 7, 25, 40–41, www.mfat.govt.nz/assets/About-us-Corporate/Treaties-Model-instruments/International-Treaty-Making-Guide-2020.pdf; for a discussion of Tokelau and territorial disputes see S Heathcote, 'Secession, self-determination and territorial disagreements: Sovereignty claims in the contemporary South Pacific' (2021) 34 *Leiden Journal of International Law* 653, 679–80.

[102] Heathcote (n 101) 665, 680.

[103] For an assessment of the Pacific island territories in particular, see ibid 665–67, 674–80.

[104] For a discussion of these categories see N Mrgudovic, 'The French Overseas Territories in transition' in P Clegg and D Killingray (eds), *The non-independent territories of the Caribbean and the Pacific: continuity and change* (University of London, Institute of Commonwealth Studies 2012) 85–103; and G Novak, 'Overseas Territories, Australia, France, Netherlands, New Zealand, United Kingdom, United States of America' in R Wolfrum (ed), *Max Planck Encyclopedia of Public International Law* (online edn, Oxford University Press 2017).

The two Article 73 NSGTs for which France is the administering power, French Polynesia and New Caledonia, fall into these categories; however, each has a distinct status. Since 1988 New Caledonia has been considered a 'sui generis' collectivity of France. It has a unicameral territorial congress with a head of government and cabinet. New Caledonia also has representation in both the French Senate and National Assembly, and has acquired significant autonomy in a range of matters other than policing, monetary policy, tertiary education, immigration, defence and foreign affairs. French Polynesia has a similar status, with a head of government supported by a cabinet and a unicameral assembly. It has acquired autonomy in the same areas as New Caledonia and also has the same exceptions. Whereas New Caledonia is considered a POM because of its higher level of autonomy, French Polynesia is more of a hybrid COM/POM. The legal status of other French island territories is as follows: Guadeloupe, Martinique, French Guiana, Réunion Island, Mayotte (DROM), Saint-Martin, Saint-Barthélemy, Saint Pierre and Miquelon, and Wallis and Futuna (COM).

There is a further category into which certain French island territories in the Southern Ocean and adjacent waters fall, the Territory of the French Southern and Antarctic Lands (TAAF[105]). Overseas territories since 1955, none of the TAAF islands have indigenous peoples or permanent populations and they are only visited by French military and government civilians. The islands that make up these territories include: Ile Amsterdam, Ile Saint Paul, Iles Crozet, Iles Kerguelen, Bassas da India,[106] Europa Island, Glorioso Island, Juan de Nova Island, and Tromelin Island.[107] The major distinction regarding the governance of the TAAF islands and the DROM islands is that the latter have a permanent population and a local economy.

(ii) UK Categories

The UK classifies all of its overseas territories that are not a part of Great Britain and Northern Ireland as 'Overseas Territories' which also includes the NSGTs for which the UK is responsible. Excepting Gibraltar, all of these territories are islands. Accordingly it is possible to divide the UK island 'Overseas Territories' into two categories: Article 73 NSGTs and those that are not. The territories are as follows: Anguilla, Bermuda, British Virgin Islands, Cayman Islands, Falkland Islands, Montserrat, Pitcairn Islands, Saint Helena, and Turks and Caicos Islands (NSGT); and British Indian Ocean Territory, and South Georgia and the South Sandwich

[105] *Terres australes et antarctiques françaises* (TAAF).

[106] There is a question as to whether this feature is a LOSC (n 52) art 121 juridical island or a juridical rock; Central Intelligence Agency (US), 'French Southern and Antarctic Lands' (*The World Factbook*) www.cia.gov/the-world-factbook/countries/french-southern-and-antarctic-lands/ describes the feature as 'a volcanic rock surrounded by reefs and is awash at high tide.'

[107] Central Intelligence Agency (US), 'French Southern and Antarctic Lands' ibid; the TAAF also include the French claimed portion of the Antarctic continent, Adelie Land.

Islands. For completeness, it should also be noted that the UK military bases of Cyprus, which comprise the 'Sovereign Base Area of Akrotiri and Dhekelia', are a separate and distinct form of UK overseas island territory. A common feature of all UK Overseas Territories is that the Queen is the Head of State, represented at the local level by a Governor. All of the listed Article 73 UK NSGTs have a unicameral house of assembly or equivalent, with a Premier or equivalent as head of government. The two Overseas Territories that are not on the NSGT list are uninhabited other than by military or government civilians, and are administered remotely. The British Indian Ocean Territory (BIOT) comprises 58 islands scattered throughout the central Indian Ocean,[108] of which the largest of the islands and archipelagos, Diego Garcia, is the home to a significant joint UK/US military base. The British Antarctic Territory (BAT) principally encompasses the UK claim to continental Antarctica but also includes offshore islands such as the South Shetland Islands and South Orkney Islands. The adjacent islands of South Georgia and the South Sandwich Islands, all of which are beyond the territorial reach of the 1959 Antarctic Treaty, are governed under separate administrative arrangements as an Overseas Territory.

(iii) US Categories

The US has up to six different categories under its municipal law describing the legal and constitutional status of an 'insular area'; that is, an area that is neither a part of a US state or Federal district.[109] These categories include Commonwealth status, incorporated territory, unincorporated territory, organized territory, and unorganized territory.[110] A separate category extends to islands in a Compact of Free Association.

The US has three Article 73 NSGTs: American Samoa, Guam, and United States Virgin Islands. Each island is an unincorporated territory of the US,[111] with a Governor, Lieutenant Governor and a legislature. The US Secretary of the Interior has jurisdiction over the islands, which are managed by the Office of Insular Affairs. Separate from these three NSGTs, the US also has responsibilities for the Federated States of Micronesia, Republic of the Marshall Islands, and

[108] This includes the Chagos Archipelago, which was the subject of an ICJ Advisory Opinion in *Legal Consequences of the Separation of the Chagos Archipelago from Mauritius in 1965* (Advisory Opinion) [2019] ICJ Reps 95; this issue is discussed in more detail in Chapters 3 and 9 of this volume.

[109] As a result, islands that are offshore of a US state and included within the limits of the state are excluded; ie, Santa Catalina Island (California), Long Island (New York), Martha's Vineyard (Massachussetts), Florida Keys (Florida).

[110] Office of Insular Affairs, Department of the Interior (US), 'Definitions of Insular Area Political Organizations' www.doi.gov/oia/islands/politicatypes.

[111] An 'unincorporated territory' is 'A United States insular area in which the United States Congress has determined that only selected parts of the United State Constitution apply': Office of Insular Affairs (n 110); of these territories Guam and the United States Virgin Islands are 'organized, unincorporated territories' and American Samoa is an 'unorganized, unincorporated territory.'

Palau, all of which emerged from the former Pacific Trust Territories and are in a Compact of Free Association relationship with the US.

Two US island territories have 'Commonwealth' status: the Commonwealth of the Northern Mariana Islands, and the Commonwealth of Puerto Rico.[112] The Commonwealth of the Northern Mariana Islands emerged from the former Trust Territory of the Pacific Islands, with US federal law making the islands a US territory in 1976.[113] A constitution was adopted in 1977, with the first government taking office in 1978.[114] The relationship of NMI with the US is described as being a 'commonwealth in political union with the US',[115] in which the US holds all responsibility for foreign affairs and defence. With the attainment of the objectives of the Trusteeship Agreement as it applied to the islands, the UN Security Council terminated those arrangements for the islands in 1990.[116]

The Commonwealth of Puerto Rico is considered to be an 'unincorporated, organized territory of the US with commonwealth status.'[117] This status was initially recognised in the Puerto Rican Federal Relations Act 1950 (US), after which the Commonwealth Constitution was adopted on 6 February 1952, and entered into force on 25 July 1952. Those events were recognised by the UNGA as acts of self-determination resulting in the people of Puerto Rico having been 'invested with attributes of political sovereignty which clearly identify the status of self-government attained by the Puerto Rican people as that of an autonomous political entity.'[118] The US has responsibility for defence and foreign affairs, and Puerto Ricans enjoy US citizenship. In 2021 the US Congress had before it for debate the Puerto Rico Self-Determination Act,[119] and the proposed law remains under review. Notwithstanding these events, the C-24 continues to review the status of Puerto Rico.[120]

[112] The US Department of the Interior defines a 'commonwealth' as: 'An organized United States insular area, which has established with the Federal Government, a more highly developed relationship, usually embodied in a written mutual agreement': Office of Insular Affairs (n 110).

[113] Covenant to Establish a Commonwealth of the Northern Mariana Islands in Political Union with the United States of America 1976 (48 USC § 1801) (US). The Covenant was approved by the US through a joint resolution adopted by the House of Representatives on July 21, 1975, and the Senate on February 24, 1976. It was signed by President Ford on March 24, 1976.

[114] See details at Office of Insular Affairs, Department of the Interior (US), 'Commonwealth of the Northern Mariana Islands' www.doi.gov/oia/islands/cnmi.

[115] Central Intelligence Agency (US) 'Northern Mariana Islands' (*The World Factbook*) www.cia.gov/the-world-factbook/countries/northern-mariana-islands/.

[116] UNSC Resolution 683 (1990) UN Doc S/RES/683.

[117] Central Intelligence Agency (US) 'Puerto Rico' (*The World Factbook*) www.cia.gov/the-world-factbook/countries/puerto-rico/; the US Department of the Interior defines an 'unincorporated territory' as: 'A United States insular area in which the United States Congress has determined that only selected parts of the United States Constitution apply': Office of Insular Affairs, Department of the Interior (US), 'Definitions of Insular Area Political Organizations' www.doi.gov/oia/islands/politicatypes.

[118] UNGA Resolution 748 (VIII) (27 November 1953) UN Doc S/RES/748 (VIII).

[119] Puerto Rico Self-Determination Act 2021 (US), H.R. 2070, 117th Congress (2021–2022) www.congress.gov/bill/117th-congress/house-bill/2070/text.

[120] See Special Committee on Decolonization (UN) (n 1); Crawford, *Creation of States* (n 35) 610.

The US also has a distinct status for a number of small reefs, islands and atolls scattered throughout the Pacific which fall within the 'United States Pacific Island Wildlife Refuge'. These islands include Baker Island, Howland Island, Jarvis Island, Johnston Atoll, Kingman Reef, and Midway Islands. All are unincorporated territories of the US and administered by the US Department of the Interior as part of the National Wildlife Refuge System. Wake Island in the Pacific Ocean, and Navassa Island in the Caribbean are also unorganized, unincorporated territories of the US, with the latter island also a part of the Caribbean Islands National Wildlife Refuge. Palmyra Atoll is an exception as it has the status of an incorporated territory, arising from its previous connection with Hawaii. When Hawaii was admitted as a US state, Palmyra Atoll remained an incorporated territory.[121] There are no indigenous inhabitants on these Pacific or Caribbean islands, though in some of the islands US military personnel and government officials have been located there from time to time.[122]

G. Sui Generis Categories

There remain other distinctive categories of islands that are sui generis, either because of their historical connection with a continental State or the unique legal and political association they enjoy with a State or a monarch. The status of these islands has changed over time, especially given developments under the UN Charter and the general international movement towards decolonisation and self-determination that characterised post-World War II international affairs. As a result, these categories are often a result of historical legacies or unique legal and political circumstances.

The Crown Dependencies of the Bailiwick of Jersey, the Bailiwick of Guernsey, and the Isle of Man are within this category. Each of these Crown Dependencies, which are geographically proximate to Great Britain, is a self-governing dependency of the Crown. This means that they are not a part of the UK. They each have their own elected legislature, legal, and administrative system. They have never been colonies of the UK and have no representation in the UK Parliament. The status of these dependencies is one that is 'maintained through the Crown and is not enshrined in a formal constitutional document'.[123] The historical backgrounds to these Crown Dependencies and the laws and administration of the islands have been inherited from the Middle Ages, and can be adjusted only under very

[121] See Office of Insular Affairs, Department of the Interior (US), 'Palmyra Atoll' www.doi.gov/oia/islands/palmyraatoll; Central Intelligence Agency (US), 'United States Pacific Wildlife Refuges' (*The World Factbook*) www.cia.gov/the-world-factbook/countries/united-states-pacific-island-wildlife-refuges/.

[122] For detailed information on these islands see Central Intelligence Agency (US) (n 121).

[123] Ministry of Justice (UK), 'Fact sheet on the UK's relationship with the Crown Dependencies' assets.publishing.service.gov.uk/government/uploads/system/uploads/attachment_data/file/863381/crown-dependencies-factsheet-february-2020.pdf.

limited circumstances by the UK Parliament.[124] Each has separate constitutional arrangements, which in the case of Guernsey extends to the three smaller adjacent islands of Alderney, Sark and Herm.[125] As the British sovereign is the Head of State for each of the dependencies, the sovereign's 'heirs and successors' automatically accede to that position,[126] consistent with the islands being 'Crown Dependencies' and not UK dependencies. The independence of the islands from the UK has from time to time been highlighted as a result of the UK's engagement with the European Community/Union and in matters associated with taxation. In 1971 for example, Guernsey petitioned the Queen:

> That if Your Majesty's Government legislates for the Bailiwick of Guernsey in any taxation matter or in any other matter which has long been accepted as the responsibility and concern of the Insular Authorities such legislation will be an infringement of the UN General Assembly Resolution 1514 (XV) of 14th December, 1960.[127]

The UK has raised international law issues regarding these islands before international courts, as was highlighted in the *Minquiers and Ecrehos* case before the ICJ.

The Republic of China (ROC) encompasses the island of Taiwan and adjacent islands and is another sui generis category. The ROC exists as a result of the historical circumstances that prevailed in China immediately following the end of World War II when, following a civil war, the then Nationalist government retreated from mainland China and established itself in Taiwan. As a result China had two governments: the ROC in Taiwan, and the People's Republic of China (PRC) led by the Chinese Communist Party on the mainland. The ROC held the 'China seat' at the UN until 1971 when the PRC and the Beijing government were acknowledged. The ROC has continued to exist on Taiwan, and while China views it as a breakaway province and seeks reunification with the mainland, the nationalist government continues to survive, albeit at times only with the support of powerful allies such as the US. Based on the Montevideo criteria, the ROC meets many of the requirements of a State for the purposes of international law, but the reality is that its status as a State is not widely recognised which compromises its ability to enter into international relations. Taiwan therefore exists in something of a twilight zone as a non-State which has many of the characteristics of a State,[128] including as a member of fishing conventions where is it known as the 'Fishing Entity of Taiwan'.[129]

[124] R Aldrich and J Connell, *The Last Colonies* (Cambridge University Press 1998) 31–32.

[125] ibid 32, fn 19; aspects of the constitutional arrangements and history of these islands, especially Jersey, were considered by the ICJ in *Minquiers and Ecrehos* case *(France v United Kingdom)* (Judgment) [1953] ICJ Reps 47, 53, 55–58.

[126] Aldrich and Connell (n 124) 32.

[127] Order in Council in the Royal Court of the Island of Guernsey (23 November 1971) www.guernseylegalresources.gg.

[128] See the discussion in Chapter 3, section II.B of this volume.

[129] See Commission for the Conservation of Southern Bluefin Tuna, at www.ccsbt.org/en/content/home; and A Serdy, 'Bringing Taiwan into the International Fisheries Fold: The Legal Personality of a Fishing Entity' (2005) 75 *British Yearbook of International Law* 183.

V. Special Regimes

One of the most distinctive special regimes developed for islands in international law is that with respect to Svalbard (Spitsbergen).[130] Svalbard is an archipelago comprising two large islands and a number of outer islands situated about 400 miles to the north of Norway in the Arctic Ocean.[131] The islands were originally uninhabited and discovered by the Dutch in 1596, with sovereignty subsequently claimed by the Danish-Norwegian and English Kings. The Netherlands, France and Spain asserted a right to hunt on the islands, and during the nineteenth century it was claimed the islands were *terra nullius* and not subject to any State's sovereignty.[132] Efforts to resolve the status of the islands failed prior to World War I, after which diplomatic efforts were resumed, resulting in the conclusion in Paris in 1920 of the Treaty Concerning the Archipelago of Spitsbergen.[133] The treaty recognised the 'full and absolute sovereignty of Norway over the Archipelago'[134] subject to the provisions of the treaty. Norway's qualified sovereignty over the islands is reflected in a series of rights and entitlements enjoyed by other State parties including:

- Fishing and hunting in the islands and the 'territorial waters';[135]
- Access and entry for 'any reason or object whatever' to the waters, fjords, and ports of the islands;[136] and
- Continued recognition of certain rights previously acquired by foreign nationals, including mining rights.[137]

Norway also agreed not to establish a naval base on the islands, or construct any fortifications.[138]

As Churchill and Ulfstein have observed: 'What is unique about the Svalbard Treaty is that while Norway enjoys "full and absolute sovereignty," all states of the world may become parties to the Treaty and thereby enjoy certain non-discriminatory rights.'[139] This has been reflected by recent interest in Svalbard where the Treaty has attracted

[130] 'Svalbard' is the modern Norwegian name for the islands, whereas 'Spitsbergen' or 'Spitzbergen' was the older English or Dutch name; see R Churchill and G Ulfstein, 'The Disputed Maritime Zones around Svalbard' in M Nordquist, JN Moore and TH Heidar (eds), *Changes in the Arctic Environment and the Law of the Sea* (Martinus Nijhoff 2010) 551, 552.

[131] A good description of the islands and its features can be found in a handbook prepared by the Foreign Office (Great Britain), *Spitsbergen* (HM Stationery Office 1920).

[132] Churchill and Ulfstein (n 130) 551, 552; drawing upon the more expansive analysis found in G Ulfstein, *The Svalbard Treaty: From Terra Nullius to Norwegian Sovereignty* (Scandinavian University Press 1995) 34–38.

[133] Treaty Concerning the Archipelago of Spitsbergen (adopted 9 February 1920, entered into force 14 August 1925) 2 LNTS 7.

[134] ibid art 1, which precisely identified the islands that composed the archipelago.

[135] ibid art 2.

[136] ibid art 3.

[137] ibid arts 6, 7, 8.

[138] ibid, art 9.

[139] Churchill and Ulfstein (n 130) 551, 555.

new parties including most recently China, Republic of Korea, and the Democratic People's Republic of Korea.[140] Nevertheless, issues have arisen regarding the status of the maritime zones around the archipelago given the expansion in maritime entitlements since the 1920s under the modern law of the sea and the LOSC.[141] The islands are currently administered as a territory of Norway through a resident Governor.

The Aaland Islands in Finland also have a distinctive status. The 1920 Report of the International Committee of Jurists considered whether the Aaland Islanders enjoyed a right to self-determination, as it was then understood in international law, and then assessed the status of an 1856 Convention on the Aaland Islands that provided for demilitarisation.[142] It was concluded that the Convention remained in force and that the demilitarisation 'provisions were laid down in European interests. They constituted a special international status relating to military considerations for the Aaland Islands.'[143] The demilitarisation of the islands had not been respected during World War I,[144] and following the Committee's 1920 Report a more contemporary treaty was agreed upon for ongoing demilitarisation of the islands, the 1921 Convention Respecting the Non-Fortification and Neutralisation of the Aaland Islands.[145] The Convention defined the islands included within its scope,[146] and included an obligation on the part of Finland not to fortify the islands,[147] including limitations on the building of military or naval establishments[148] and – subject to the exception of the right of innocent passage – the exclusion of all foreign military, naval or air forces.[149] The demilitarised status of the islands was subsequently reinforced by a 1940 Agreement between Finland and the USSR,[150] and the 1947 Paris Peace Treaty.[151] The Aaland Islands have continued to enjoy this distinctive demilitarised status into the twenty-first century, albeit as a self-governing province of Finland where the official language is Swedish.[152] The region consists of more than 6,700 islands.

[140] There are currently 46 parties to the Treaty.

[141] Churchill and Ulfstein (n 130) 551; T Pedersen, 'The Svalbard Continental Shelf Controversy: Legal Disputes and Political Rivalries' (2006) 37 *Ocean Development and International Law* 339; CR Rossi, 'A Unique International Problem: The Svalbard Treaty, Equal Enjoyment, and Terra Nullius: Lessons of Territorial Temptation from History' (2015) 15 *Washington University Global Studies Law Review* 93.

[142] Paris Convention between France and Great Britain and Russia respecting the Aaland Islands (adopted 30 March 1856, entered into force 27 April 1856) 114 CTS 405.

[143] Report of the International Committee of Jurists (n 19) 19 (Conclusions).

[144] L Hannikainen, 'The Continued Validity of the Demilitarised and Neutralised Status of the Åland Islands' (1994) 54 *Zeitschrift für ausländisches öffentliches Recht und Völkerrecht* 614.

[145] Convention Respecting the Non-Fortification and Neutralisation of the Aaland Islands (adopted 20 October 1921, entered into force 6 April 1922) 9 LNTS 213.

[146] ibid art 2.

[147] ibid art 1.

[148] ibid art 3.

[149] ibid art 4.

[150] Agreement Between Finland and the Soviet Union Concerning the Aaland Islands (adopted 11 October 1940, entered into force 13 March 1948) 67 UNTS 139.

[151] Treaty of Peace with Finland (adopted 10 February 1947, entered into force 15 September 1947) 48 UNTS 203.

[152] Ministry of Foreign Affairs of Finland, 'The special status of the Åland Islands', um.fi/the-special-status-of-the-aland-islands.

VI. Conclusions

The UN era has been characterised by decolonisation and the emergence of many independent States, including island States of which some also fall within the special category of LOSC archipelagic States.[153] However, there remain many island territories with widely varying constitutional, legal and political status under both international law and municipal law. This chapter has highlighted the spectrum of overseas territories that arise from the distinctive legal and constitutional arrangements that are in place under national laws in States such as Denmark, France, and the US, to UN NSGT. In some instances, island territories may still be engaged in a process of moving towards self-determination (Greenland, New Caledonia), while in other instances there is no incentive to disturb the status quo (Pitcairn, Saint Pierre and Miquelon). The spectrum not only permits multiple models, but also variations within those models. Formal characterisation of an island under constitutional or municipal law arrangements may not reflect the reality of the political practice. Greenland's 'Home Rule' arrangements are not dissimilar to the Cook Islands and its Free Association with New Zealand. An important distinction, however, is that the Cook Islands enjoys diplomatic relations with over 50 States.

At the UN, the legal and political status of islands remains dominated by processes associated with NSGTs and the work of the C-24. Whether many of the remaining 15 island NSGTs transition off the UN list in the near future may be problematic for a variety of reasons, including their size, population, economic, political and social issues. To that end, while self-determination was a right and legitimate aspiration for some island territories over recent decades, there still exist constraints for some islands undertaking that step. As an alternative, Free Association or Associated State status has proven to be an effective hybrid model in which a high degree of self-government can be exercised under the defence and foreign affairs umbrella of a larger State. Independence is not viable for all island territories, but along the spectrum there remain multiple models that have proven successful and are capable of being developed within national legal frameworks so as to recognise the legitimate aspirations of island communities and peoples to their political independence.

[153] Discussed in more detail in Chapter 5 of this volume.

5

Archipelagic States*

I. Archipelagos and International Law

The law of the sea developed around the rights and interests first of maritime States which were interested in ensuring the freedom of the seas so as guarantee rights of navigation to support their trading ambitions, and then certain coastal States which began to press claims for the recognition of maritime zones such as the territorial sea. In nearly all instances, the States that promoted these claims and sought to advance the development of state practice, which eventually became customary international law, were continental or mainland States in Europe or the Americas. Britain was an exception. While it was an island State and this influenced certain aspects of practice, it was also a major maritime power that strongly advocated for the freedom of navigation. Island States that may have been considered archipelagos, such as Japan, were not thought of as such in juridical terms. Rather, as international law and the law of the sea developed, these States were considered to be coastal States with all of the entitlements that flowed from that. Exceptions to this such as Spitsbergen (Norway), were dealt with by way of separate legal regimes which did not specially address any distinctive law of the sea entitlements.[1]

In the period immediately following the end of World War II the status of island States began to take on greater significance, as a result of decolonisation and the rapid emergence of new States, especially in Southeast Asia, the Pacific, and the Caribbean. Indonesia and the Philippines were prominent States in these processes. Gradually emerging from independence achieved from the Netherlands in 1945, Indonesia was a mid-ocean archipelago[2] comprising 13,466 islands, of which only 922 were inhabited, and with a total coastline of 54,716 km.[3] Some of the larger islands were at that time also shared with neighbouring countries, including Portugal

* This chapter is drawn from DR Rothwell and T Stephens, *The International Law of the Sea* (2nd edn, Bloomsbury 2016) ch 8.

[1] See Treaty Concerning the Archipelago of Spitsbergen (adopted 9 February 1920, entered into force 14 August 1925) [1925] ATS 10, art 2 which refers to the territorial waters of the archipelago.

[2] The term 'mid-ocean archipelago' is a geographic descriptor indicating an archipelago distant from a continental mainland, in contrast to a coastal archipelago comprising islands close to a mainland coast; while the term has no contemporary legal significance it has been used in previous legal discourse, eg. DP O'Connell, 'Mid-Ocean Archipelagos in International Law' (1971) 45 *British Yearbook of International Law* 1.

[3] Central Intelligence Agency (US), 'Indonesia' (*The World Factbook*) www.cia.gov/the-world-factbook/countries/indonesia/.

(East Timor), Australia (Papua-New Guinea), and Great Britain (North Borneo). Notwithstanding some of these boundaries with other States, Indonesia was principally a State composed of an archipelago. The geographical and political situation of the Philippines was even clearer. Emerging from World War II as an independent State in 1946, the Philippines archipelago comprised 7,641 islands spread throughout the South China Sea, Philippine Sea, Sulu Sea and Celebes Sea, giving the new country a total coastline of 36,289 km.[4] The claims of these two countries to recognition as archipelagic States had a profound influence on the development of the law of sea in the latter part of the twentieth century, fundamentally changing the way in which international law recognised mid-ocean archipelagos.

Archipelagos take varying forms. There are coastal archipelagos which are composed of multiple islands which effectively form an outer edge of the coastline, such as the Norwegian *skjaergaard*. In other cases, a coastal archipelago may result in the effective extension of the coastline via a series of islands, cays and reefs, of which the Florida Keys are an example. More common is where a cluster of islands of varying sizes and shapes fringe a coastline.[5] The Recherche Archipelago off the south coast of Western Australia (Australia) is an example. In some instances, such as the islands which make up the Canadian Arctic Archipelago, the landmass of these islands may be extensive and clearly represent an extension of adjacent continents. In other cases, the islands are much smaller and may be simply remnants of coastal headlands. Mid-ocean archipelagos are distinctive in that they are separated from continental landmasses by a significant body of water such as a sea or ocean. Most of the islands within the Caribbean Sea, while proximate to the American continent, would fall into this category. Many comprise large islands with scattered outlying islands, of which Cuba is a prominent example. Japan is also an archipelago, with one of its distinctive features being the size of the four main islands. The Pacific Ocean also features many archipelagos. The Hawaiian Islands are a classic example of a tightly clustered group of related islands, while in other instances islands may be more scattered as is the case with Vanuatu, French Polynesia, the Marshall Islands and the Federated States of Micronesia.[6] These latter examples highlight some of the issues associated with States that are composed of individual islands and groups of islands, and the political dimension associated with how the peoples that inhabit those islands may constitute a State for the purposes of international law.

[4] Central Intelligence Agency (US), 'Philippines' (*The World Factbook*) www.cia.gov/the-world-factbook/countries/philippines/.

[5] *Maritime Delimitation and Territorial Questions between Qatar and Bahrain (Qatar v Bahrain)* (Merits) [2001] ICJ Reps 40 [214] (*Qatar v Bahrain*) where the ICJ refers to a 'cluster of islands' or an 'island system' in the context of offshore fringing islands.

[6] M Munavvar, *Ocean States: Archipelagic Regimes in the Law of the Sea* (Martinus Nijhoff 1995) 14–23; HP Rajan, 'The Legal Regime of Archipelagos' (1986) 29 *German Yearbook of International Law* 137, 139.

This chapter commences with an historical review of the law of the sea and archipelagos, including consideration of debates prior to and at the First United Nations Conference on the Law of the Sea (UNCLOS I), and the Third United Nations Conference on the Law of the Sea (UNCLOS III) leading to adoption of the 1982 United Nations Convention on the Law of the Sea (LOSC).[7] Attention will then turn to the interpretation and application of LOSC Part IV and archipelagic States, and relevant state practice.

II. Early Legal Developments

While the status of the territorial sea attracted the attention of the major international law bodies in the late nineteenth century, little consideration was given to the issue of either coastal or mid-ocean archipelagos. This was despite the fact that by this time law officers in both Great Britain and the United States had considered the status of offshore fringing islands in the context of maritime claims.[8] The first serious review of the issue by the community of international legal experts took place in the 1920s, when the Institut de Droit International, International Law Association, and the American Institute of International Law all separately considered the impact of islands upon territorial sea claims.[9] The American Institute suggested that in the case of an archipelago, the islands 'shall be considered as forming a unit', with the territorial sea measured from the 'islands farthest from the center of the archipelago'.[10] At the 1930 Hague Codification Conference there was support amongst the experts for the American Institute of International Law's views that archipelagos could be considered as a single unit, but this was met with a mixed response from certain governments and no concluded position was reached on this question.[11]

When the International Law Commission (ILC) considered this issue the first report of the Special Rapporteur, Professor François, proposed that in the case of 'a group of islands (archipelago) and islands situated along the coast' straight baselines no longer than 10 miles could be adopted to connect those islands, with the effect that the 'waters included within the group shall constitute inland waters'.[12]

[7] United Nations Convention on the Law of the Sea (adopted 10 December 1982, entered into force 16 November 1994) 1833 UNTS 397 (LOSC).

[8] O'Connell (n 2) 2–3.

[9] J Evensen, 'Certain Legal Aspects Concerning the Delimitation of Territorial Waters of Archipelagos' in *United Nations Conference on the Law of the Sea: Official Records*, vol 1 (United Nations 1958) 289, 290–91.

[10] American Institute of International Law, 'Text of Projects' (1926) 20 *American Journal of International Law Special Supplement* 318, 319; being art 7 of a set of draft articles on the 'National Domain'; a similar view was promoted by Jessup: PC Jessup, *The Law of Territorial Waters and Maritime Jurisdiction* (GA Jennings 1927) 457.

[11] CF Amerasinghe, 'The Problem of Archipelagoes in the International Law of the Sea' (1974) 23 *International and Comparative Law Quarterly* 539, 541; Evensen (n 9) 292.

[12] International Law Commission, 'Regime of the Territorial Sea' reprinted in *Yearbook of the International Law Commission*, vol 2 (1952) UN Doc A/CN.4/53, 31; see also Evensen (n 9) 292.

By his third report, François had adopted a less ambitious, but nonetheless still novel approach towards islands making up an archipelago. He proposed that:

> The term 'groups of islands', in the juridical sense shall be determined to mean three or more islands enclosing a portion of the sea when joined by straight lines not exceeding five miles in length, except that one such line may extend to a maximum of ten miles.[13]

Ultimately the ILC as a whole did not endorse these proposals and its 1956 *Articles concerning the Law of the Sea with commentaries*[14] made no direct reference to archipelagos. All that remained of some elements of the François drafts was reference in Article 10 to islands having their own territorial sea and an acknowledgment in the accompanying commentary of the difficulties associated with reaching agreement on the issues raised by archipelagos.[15] The only draft article which had significance for the future recognition of archipelagic claims was Article 5 dealing with 'Straight Baselines' which the ILC's commentary acknowledged could be relied upon to draw baselines to 'islands situated in the immediate vicinity of the coast'.[16]

III. UNCLOS I

Despite the ILC's ultimate position with respect to archipelagos, it seemed inevitable that UNCLOS I would need to give some consideration to the issues arising in both the case of coastal and mid-ocean archipelagos. The 1951 *Fisheries Case*[17] between the UK and Norway had certainly set an important precedent in the case of coastal archipelagos, while the initial archipelagic claims by Indonesia and the Philippines clearly indicated to the major maritime powers that the status of archipelagos in international law was a rapidly emerging issue. Expectations as to the intentions of UNCLOS I with respect to archipelagos were further raised by the preparation of a paper in 1957 by the Norwegian lawyer, Jens Evensen, on 'Certain legal aspects concerning the delimitation of the Territorial Waters of Archipelagos' which was included in the Preparatory Documents for the conference.[18] Evensen's paper reviewed relevant state practice with respect to coastal archipelagos[19] and mid-ocean archipelagos,[20] and assessed the significance of the *Fisheries Case*.

[13] International Law Commission, 'Regime of the Territorial Sea' reprinted in *Yearbook of the International Law Commission*, vol 2 (1954) UN Doc A/CN.4/77, 1; and see Evensen (n 9) 293.

[14] International Law Commission, *Yearbook of the International Law Commission*, vol 2 (1956) UN Doc A/CN.4/SER.A/1956/Add.l, 265.

[15] ibid 270.

[16] ibid 268; though in the case of Article 10 'Bays' the Commentary observed at 270 that 'article 5 may be applicable to groups of islands lying off the coast'.

[17] *Fisheries Case (United Kingdom v Norway)* (Judgment) [1951] ICJ Reps 116 (*Fisheries Case*).

[18] Evensen (n 9) 289.

[19] Referring to the practices adopted with respect to 'Norway, Iceland, Denmark, Sweden, Finland, Yogoslavia [sic], Saudi Arabia, Egypt, Cuba, the United Kingdom, Australia, and USA': ibid 295–97.

[20] Referring to the practices adopted with respect to 'the Faeroes, Svalbard, Iceland, Bermudas, Galapagos, Philippines, Fiji, Cook Island and the Hawaiian Islands': ibid 297–99.

Summing up this review of state practice and the developments in the law, Evensen asserted that 'no hard and fast rules exist as to the delimitation of the territorial waters of archipelagos',[21] but he nonetheless made recommendations for future consideration at the Conference.[22]

Notwithstanding Evensen's paper and what may have appeared to be an impetus for UNCLOS I to deal with archipelagos, the Conference avoided any sustained discussion of the issue. Ultimately, the 1958 Convention on the Territorial Sea and Contiguous Zone[23] contained no provisions of particular application to archipelagos, other than generic articles dealing with straight baselines,[24] and Article 10 which sought to define an island and confirm the method for determining its territorial sea. The Philippines did make a bold proposal to confirm the status of archipelagos, including that the waters on the landward side of baselines would be considered internal waters,[25] however the US firmly indicated its opposition, noting that the consequence of this proposal being accepted would be that 'areas of the high seas formerly used by ships of all countries would be unilaterally claimed as territorial waters or possibly even internal waters'.[26] Attempts were made to revive the debate within the First Committee, with Denmark and Iceland urging further consideration of the issue in the context of Article 10 of the Convention; however, Sir Gerald Fitzmaurice (UK) put forward the view that given the complexity of the issues, especially with respect to 'oceanic archipelagos' it was preferable to have the matter deferred for further study. This ultimately was the position adopted at the Conference.[27] Notwithstanding that in 1960 the Second United Nations Conference on the Law of the Sea (UNCLOS II) followed soon after UNCLOS I, and that there was a further attempt by the Philippines to introduce substantive debate on the question of archipelagos, no detailed consideration was given to the matter at that conference.[28]

IV. The Indonesian and Philippines Claims

As the two leading advocates for international legal recognition of the special status of archipelagic States, it is instructive to review the legislative history of the archipelagic claims asserted by Indonesia and the Philippines. Both had considerable

[21] ibid 301.

[22] ibid 302.

[23] Convention on the Territorial Sea and Contiguous Zone (adopted 29 April 1958, entered into force 10 September 1964) 516 UNTS 206.

[24] ibid art 4.

[25] 'Philippines: Proposal (article 5)', reprinted in *United Nations Conference on the Law of the Sea: Official Records*, vol 3 (United Nations 1958) UN Doc A/CONF/13/C.1/L.98, 239; see also the 'Yugoslavia: Proposal (article 5)' UN Doc A/CONF/13/C.1/L.58, 227.

[26] ibid UN Doc A/CONF.13/C.1/SR.6–10 'Summary Records of the 6th to 10th Meetings of the First Committee', 25.

[27] ibid 162–63.

[28] O'Connell (n 2) 21–22.

influence not only in the development of state practice, but also in how the law was eventually shaped through the negotiations of UNCLOS III and in the final outcomes of Part IV of the LOSC.

A. Indonesia

Indonesia has long advocated that its status as an archipelago should be given international recognition in the law of the sea. In support of this claim Indonesian governments have consistently argued, both domestically and internationally since Indonesia gained independence in 1945, that the Indonesian islands and waters between them constituted a single, unified nation.[29] This was reflected in the concept of *wawasan nusantara* which aims for the unification of the land, waters and the people of Indonesia.[30] This concept encapsulates the attitude adopted by Indonesians towards their country, one in which they regard:

> all of their islands, and the waters around them and interconnecting those islands as one entity. The term fatherland in Indonesian is *tanah air* which means 'land and water'. The nationhood of Indonesia is built on the concept of unity between the Indonesian islands and the inter-connecting waters. Those seas are regarded as a unifying, not a separating, element.[31]

Wawasan nusantara was first officially expressed by Indonesia in the 1957 Djuanda Declaration which affirmed the concept of the Indonesian archipelago as an entity, encompassing the islands and waters.[32] It stated that:

> all waters around, between and connecting, the islands or parts of islands belonging to the Indonesian archipelago irrespective of their width or dimension are natural appurtenances of its land territory and therefore an integral part of the inland or national waters subject to the absolute sovereignty of Indonesia. The peaceful passage of foreign vessels through these waters is guaranteed as long and insofar as it is not contrary to the sovereignty of the Indonesian state or harmful to her security.
>
> The delimitation of the territorial sea, with a width of 12 nautical miles, shall be measured from straight base lines connecting the outermost points of the islands of the Republic of Indonesia.[33]

[29] These assertions became more developed in the light of the ICJ decision in *Fisheries Case* (n 17); JG Butcher, 'Becoming an Archipelagic State: The Juanda Declaration of 1957 and the "Struggle" to gain International Recognition of the Archipelagic Principle' in R Cribb and M Ford (eds), *Indonesia beyond the Water's Edge* (Institute of Southeast Asian Studies 2009) 28, 34–35.

[30] *Wawasan* means outlook; *nusantara* refers to people.

[31] N Wisnomoerti, 'Indonesia and the Law of the Sea' in C-H Park and JK Park (eds), *The Law of the Sea: Problems from the East Asian Perspective* (Law of the Sea Institute 1987) 392.

[32] Butcher (n 29) 38–40.

[33] MM Whiteman, *Digest of International Law*, vol 4 (United States Department of State 1965) 284; cf alternative translations of the Indonesian text: JJG Syatauw, *Some Newly Established Asian States and the Development of International Law* (Martinus Nijhoff 1961) 173–74.

Despite diplomatic protests from Australia, France, Japan, the Netherlands, New Zealand, the UK and the US,[34] the Declaration was implemented internally in 1960. Act No 4 of 18 February 1960 indicated that 'Indonesian waters consist of the territorial sea and the internal waters of Indonesia'[35] and that Indonesian internal waters were those lying within the baselines. The baselines were to be 'straight lines connecting the outermost points of the low-water mark of the outermost islands or part of such islands comprising Indonesian territory'.[36] Whilst this claim had little basis in the then law of the sea following UNCLOS I, Article 1(3) of the accompanying Government Regulation No 4 did permit innocent passage by foreign vessels through these 'internal' waters, suggesting that Indonesia was seeking to develop a form of internal waters/territorial sea hybrid within its archipelago. However, in a clarification of the regulations also issued at the same time, Indonesia sought to distinguish innocent passage through the territorial sea and innocent passage within 'interior waters' which noted that this latter form of innocent passage 'constitutes a certain facility granted intentionally by Indonesia, while innocent passage in territorial waters constitutes a right of the foreign ships which is recognized by international law'.[37] Indonesia's position with respect to internal waters encompassing those waters on the landward side of the baselines drawn around the edge of the Indonesian archipelago was further reinforced by a Reservation which accompanied its ratification of the 1958 Convention on the High Seas,[38] which restated the Indonesian concept of internal waters.[39]

As O'Connell observed, Indonesia's indication that innocent passage was 'a "facility" rather than a right had an ominous implication, and seemed to indicate that Indonesia would resist passage through the enclosed seas when it was deemed necessary for national security to do so'.[40] Nevertheless, innocent passage was subsequently regulated by government ordinance in 1962 with the enactment of a Government Regulation concerning 'Innocent Passage by Foreign Water Vehicles within Indonesian Waters'. Article 1 of that regulation affirmed that innocent passage of foreign vessels was guaranteed within Indonesian waters, while the remainder of the regulation substantially implemented the innocent passage

[34] Whiteman (n 33) 284–85; DP O'Connell, *The International Law of the Sea*, vol 1 (Clarendon Press 1982) 249.

[35] Act Concerning Indonesian Waters (Act No 4 of 1960) (Indonesia) art 1(1), reprinted in Syatauw (n 33) 176.

[36] ibid art 1(2). Indonesia has conceded that the Declaration was 'prepared in some haste' in order to achieve recognition of archipelagic waters prior to UNCLOS II: *Sovereignty over Pulau Ligitan and Pulau Sipadan (Indonesia v Malaysia)* (Merits) [2002] ICJ Reps 625 [130] (*Pulau Ligitan and Pulau Sipadan*).

[37] Article-by-Article Clarification, annexed to Government Regulation No 4, 1960, in lieu of an Act concerning Indonesian Waters; O'Connell, 'Mid-Ocean Archipelagos' (n 2) 40; Syatauw (n 33) 180–82 uses the terms 'inland', 'interior' and 'national' waters interchangeably with 'internal waters'.

[38] Convention on the High Seas (adopted 29 April 1958, entered into force 30 September 1962) 450 UNTS 11.

[39] O'Connell, 'Mid-Ocean Archipelagos' (n 2) 40.

[40] ibid 41.

regime of the Convention on the Territorial Sea and Contiguous Zone.[41] A significant point of distinction from the innocent passage regime of the Convention was that in Article 4(1) of the 1962 Regulation Indonesia sought to retain a right to 'place a temporary ban in innocent passage on certain parts of Indonesia's waters'. However, it appears that Indonesia never sought at that time to rely upon this provision to actually close its waters to innocent passage.[42]

The Djuanda Declaration marked a historic step in Indonesia's national development and was pivotal in laying the foundation for its claim to be recognised as an archipelagic State. Legally it set an important precedent, and although the major maritime powers clearly indicated their objections between 1957 and 1962, there was a gradual acceptance of the Indonesian claim, even extending to informal notification of the passage of warships through Indonesian waters.[43] The Indonesian claim also needed to be seen in the context of Indonesian national politics at the time, when concerns over internal security were especially sensitive and when the West also had its own concerns over whether Indonesia would fall to the communists.[44] The West had an incentive to see the development of a strong Indonesia, robust enough to resist communism. This was reflected in the recognition of not only Indonesian territorial claims but also maritime claims to the waters within the archipelago.

B. The Philippines

The position of the Philippines with respect to its recognition as an archipelagic State differs from Indonesia in two major respects. The first is geographic in that the Philippines is a more compact group of islands than Indonesia, and accordingly is often referred to as an 'island studded sea' rather than a group of interconnected islands.[45] The second is historic, and is based on a series of treaties and related instruments drawn up by colonial powers in the late nineteenth and early twentieth centuries which, the Philippines asserts, make clear that recognition was granted to rights over the waters that connect the islands of the archipelago. These claims commence with the 1898 Treaty of Paris,[46] where Article III provided that 'Spain cedes to the United States the archipelago known as the Philippines Islands' and the islands which fall within certain coordinates. The subsequent 1900 Treaty between

[41] DR Rothwell, 'The Indonesian Straits Incident: Transit or Archipelagic Sea Lanes Passage?' (1990) 14 *Marine Policy* 491, 496–97.

[42] M Kusumaatmadja, 'The Concept of the Indonesian Archipelago' (1982) 10 *Indonesian Quarterly* 12, 15.

[43] Butcher (n 29) 43.

[44] ATH Tan, *Security Perspectives of the Malay Archipelago* (Edward Elgar 2004) 201–3.

[45] Munavvar (n 6) 21.

[46] Treaty of Peace between Spain and the United States (Treaty of Paris) (adopted 10 December 1898, entered into force 11 April 1899) 187 CTS 100.

Spain and the US for the Cession of Outlying Islands of the Philippines sought to clarify which islands were ceded by Spain to the US; however, no direct reference is made to the waters that lay between the islands as also having been transferred. A later 1930 colonial treaty between the UK and the US is also relied upon by the Philippines to support its claims to the waters within defined coordinates.[47] However, the treaty clarified the southern extent of the Philippines and the northern extent of the British Malay territory of Borneo and it is doubtful whether there was an intention thereby to confer sovereignty over the waters.[48]

The first international indication of the extent of the Philippines' claim to the waters between the islands of the archipelago came in 1955 and this was reinforced in 1956 during communications with the United Nations (UN) in response to the ILC's draft articles on the law of the sea.[49] In commenting on the definition of the high seas, a *note verbale* lodged by the Philippines stated that:

> All waters around, between and connecting different islands belonging to the Philippine Archipelago, irrespective of their width or dimension, are necessary appurtenances of its land territory, forming an integral part of the national or inland waters, subject to the exclusive sovereignty of the Philippines.[50]

The *note verbale* further provided that all of the 'natural deposits or occurrences of petroleum or natural gas in public and/or private lands' within the archipelago and 'seaward from the shores of the Philippines which are not within the territories of other countries' belong to the Philippines 'subject to the right of innocent passage of ships of friendly foreign States over those waters'.[51]

While the Philippines made these assertions in the 1950s, it did not at that time enact laws seeking to give effect to such a claim. This did not occur until 1961, with the adoption of the Republic Act No 3046.[52] In seeking to define for the first time the baselines that composed the outer limits of the Philippines' claim, Republic Act No 3046 reaffirmed aspects of the 1955 and 1956 *notes verbales*, including the historical basis for the claim, and asserted that:

> Whereas, all the waters within the limits set forth in the above-mentioned treaties have always been regarded as part of the territory of the Philippine Islands;
>
> Whereas, all the waters around, between and connecting the various islands of the Philippine archipelago, irrespective of their width or dimension, have always been

[47] Convention regarding the Boundary between the Philippine Archipelago and the State of North Borneo (adopted 2 January 1930, entered into force 13 December 1932) 137 LNTS 297.

[48] O'Connell, 'Mid-Ocean Archipelagos' (n 2) 26–27; Munavvar (n 6) 62–63. These treaties and agreements are also reviewed by the ICJ in *Pulau Ligitan and Pulau Sipadan* (n 36).

[49] 'Note Verbale Dated 20 January 1956 from the Permanent Mission of the Philippines to the United Nations' in *Yearbook of the International Law Commission*, vol 2 (1956) 69–70.

[50] ibid.

[51] ibid.

[52] 'An Act to Define the Baselines of the Territorial Sea of the Philippines', reprinted in SH Lay, R Churchill and M Nordquist (eds), *New Directions in the Law of the Sea*, vol 1 (Oceana Publications 1973) 27.

> considered as necessary appurtenances of the land territory, forming part of the inland or internal waters of the Philippines.[53]

Whilst the Republic Act No 3046 proceeded to identify the baselines from which the Philippines' claim was being asserted, of particular concern to maritime powers was the failure to state unambiguously the position regarding innocent passage through these waters. The Philippines denied recognition of a customary international law right of innocent passage by warships, and this became a particularly sensitive issue. Australia, the UK and the US all raised their concerns over the new Philippines law; however, the US was on firmer ground in insisting on the navigational rights of its warships due to pre-existing bilateral arrangements.[54] Uncertainty remained over this issue for much of the 1960s and a number of minor incidents occurred involving British and Australian naval vessels.[55] Further reinforcement of the Philippines' position regarding its claim over the waters within the archipelago was made in the 1973 Philippines Constitution, in which Article 1 asserted that 'The waters around, between and connecting the islands of the archipelago, irrespective of their breadth and dimensions, form part of the internal waters of the Philippines.'[56]

The Philippines took a more robust position than did Indonesia during the UNCLOS I and UNCLOS II negotiations on the issue of archipelagos and the need for recognition in the law of the sea of archipelagic baselines. Whilst these proposals failed to win support at the time, the Philippines did not retreat from continuing to assert some form of archipelagic status.[57]

V. UNCLOS III

By the time UNCLOS III commenced in 1973, it had been nearly 15 years since both Indonesia and the Philippines had first asserted a form of archipelagic claim. Though the broad extent of the claims had not been widely recognised,[58] they had provoked debate amongst the international community and interest from other States which believed they could make similar claims. Prior to the commencement of UNCLOS III, Fiji and Mauritius joined Indonesia and the Philippines to form a small bloc of States supporting wider recognition of the interests of States comprising mid-ocean archipelagos. Within the Group of 77, these views

[53] ibid.
[54] JA Roach and RW Smith, *Excessive Maritime Claims* (3rd edn, Martinus Nijhoff 2012) 211–13.
[55] O'Connell, 'Mid-Ocean Archipelagos' (n 2) 33–36.
[56] Munavvar (n 6) 64.
[57] See comment by O'Connell, 'Mid-Ocean Archipelagos' (n 2) 37.
[58] ED Brown, 'Maritime Zones: A Survey of Claims' in R Churchill, KR Simmonds and J Welch (eds), *New Directions in the Law of the Sea*, vol 3 (British Institute of International and Comparative Law 1973) 157, 160 observing 'There is increasing evidence of sympathy for the arguments skilfully deployed by Indonesian and Philippino spokesmen.'

generated considerable additional support, and accordingly there was a great deal of momentum behind UNCLOS III addressing the issue of archipelagos by the time the Conference convened.[59]

Given that there had been so little progress on issues associated with archipelagos at either UNCLOS I or II, much remained to be accomplished if new provisions were to be agreed upon at UNCLOS III. Nevertheless, there existed some key foundations upon which a new legal framework could be based, including the legacy of the *Fisheries Case* with respect to straight baselines, the work of the ILC and other expert groups considering the status of archipelagos, and Indonesian and Filipino state practice. Two of the principal issues were whether any distinctive status should be accorded to States comprising one or more archipelagos, and navigational rights through any waters that may become enclosed through the drawing of baselines connecting up the islands of the archipelago. However, these issues could not be seen in isolation and were closely connected to other pivotal issues requiring resolution during UNCLOS III, including the breadth of the territorial sea and the navigational regime through international straits.

Once a decision was made to include the topic of 'Archipelagos' on the UNCLOS III agenda, Fiji, Indonesia, Mauritius and the Philippines sought to advance debate by introducing proposals which outlined the principles for an archipelagic regime which included a limited right of innocent passage through sea lanes within an archipelago.[60] These formed the basis for formal proposals eventually put before the conference in 1974.[61] An initial threshold issue which arose related to the eligibility of a State to make certain claims. This was highlighted not only because of the great geographical variety among States made up of archipelagos, but also because of concerns that the definition could be expanded to cover a multitude of cases. The fact that the Bahamas, PNG and Tonga also expressed their interest in having their claims recognised, and that the Bahamas put forward separate proposals for the recognition of its particular status as an archipelago, fuelled fears that the debate regarding archipelagos could become unwieldy and divisive. Nevertheless, the major maritime powers were prepared to recognise these archipelagic claims, in return for unimpeded navigational rights, and accordingly much of the debate at UNCLOS III was focussed on seeking to accommodate these positions.[62]

[59] RP Anand, *Origin and Development of the Law of the Sea* (Martinus Nijhoff 1983) 202–3. The 'Group of 77', or G-77, was a negotiating bloc originally composed of 77 less-developed or developing UN member States who sought to use their numbers to advance international negotiations to their advantage.

[60] ibid 203.

[61] 'Fiji, Indonesia, Mauritius, and Philippines: Draft Articles relating to Archipelagic States', in *Third United Nations Conference on the Law of the Sea, Official Records*, vol 3 (United Nations 1975) UN Doc A/CONF.62/C.2/L.49, 226.

[62] Described as 'The Archipelago Package': C Ku, 'The Archipelagic States Concept and Regional Stability in Southeast Asia' (1991) 23 *Case Western Reserve Journal of International Law* 463, 471–74.

The pivotal UNCLOS III definitional issue was whether the new Convention should only apply to mid-ocean archipelagos, or continental archipelagos, or both. Whilst the debate and development of state practice had predominantly been driven by the interests of mid-ocean archipelagos such as Indonesia and the Philippines, a group of States with continental archipelagos put forward proposals for draft articles in which they sought the extension of some of the principles under consideration to groups of outer-lying islands offshore continental land masses.[63] An important breakthrough in the negotiations occurred in 1975 when the Bahamas introduced a document titled '18 Principles for Inclusion in Archipelagic Articles',[64] which had the effect of crystallising the debate with respect to those States possibly entitled to archipelagic status, and sought to give clarity to the issues associated with the drawing of baselines. By 1976, it was clear that agreement had been reached within UNCLOS III that the archipelagic regime would focus on mid-ocean archipelagos, and not those archipelagos associated with a continental State. By the time of the final 1982 UNCLOS III session, a number of States during concluding debates sought to declare their status as archipelagic States, including the Bahamas, Cape Verde, Fiji, Indonesia, Netherlands Antilles, PNG, the Philippines and the Solomon Islands.[65]

VI. The LOSC and Archipelagic States

Reflective of the eventual significance that came to be associated with the question of archipelagos during UNCLOS III, the LOSC devotes Part IV to archipelagic States. Part IV contains key definitional provisions concerning the characterisation and identification of archipelagic States, the drawing of archipelagic baselines, the rights and entitlements of archipelagic States, and navigation and overflight within archipelagos. The discussion which follows immediately below focuses on the characterisation and identification of archipelagic States.

A. Status of Archipelagic States

The fact that Part IV of the LOSC is headed 'Archipelagic States' is both symbolic and of great significance for the law of the sea and international law generally. Throughout contemporary international law the international system has

[63] This group included States such as Canada, Chile, Iceland, India, Mexico, New Zealand and Norway: SN Nandan and S Rosenne (eds), *United Nations Convention on the Law of the Sea 1982: A Commentary*, vol 2 (Martinus Nijhoff 1993) 402.

[64] ibid 405.

[65] Office for Ocean Affairs and the Law of the Sea (UN), *The Law of the Sea: Archipelagic States* (United Nations 1990) 108–13.

increasingly accorded to States ever greater privileges and entitlements, and during the UN era this has been heightened by the 'State-centric' system which has been perpetuated under the UN Charter. The criteria for statehood by island States, including archipelagic States, were considered in Chapter four and the discussion that follows is framed upon the entitlements of recognised States under international law. Nevertheless, as with all States, there is the potential that parts of the territory of the State, including islands, may be the subject of competing claims or that the entitlements of a particular State may not be recognised.[66]

Article 46 of the LOSC defines both an 'archipelagic State' and 'archipelago'. The two definitions are linked and to understand the former it is first important to comprehend the juridical definition accorded to the term archipelago.[67] This definition, while focussing on the geographic features of an island group, also incorporates additional dimensions. Article 46(b) provides that an archipelago:

> means a group of islands, including parts of islands, interconnecting waters and other natural features which are so closely interrelated that such islands, waters and other natural features form an intrinsic geographical, economic and political entity, or which have historically been regarded as such.

This definition clearly reflects some of the essential elements that emerged in the campaign during the 1950s and 1960s for recognition of archipelagic status, with its focus not only upon the land but also the waters of the archipelago, and the notion that the two are 'closely interrelated'. A number of the elements require further elaboration.

The first is that an archipelago includes a 'group of islands'. No threshold is set for this criterion and accordingly an archipelago could comprise only two islands, though this would be exceptional. The second is that the definition encompasses 'parts of islands' and as such includes islands that have two or more sovereign states. Examples include Borneo (Brunei/Malaysia/Indonesia), Hispaniola (Dominican Republic/Haiti), New Guinea (Indonesia/PNG), and Timor (Indonesia/Timor-Leste). The third component to note is the inclusion of 'interconnecting waters and other natural features' within the archipelago. Given the maritime focus, this includes all waters that are between the islands, irrespective of the designation they may have previously had under international law, and other features including atolls, cays, reefs, rocks, shoals and low-tide elevations. Artificial islands are not included. The fourth component is that these features – land in the form of islands, smaller associated maritime features, and the waters between them – must be so

[66] In *Pulau Ligitan and Pulau Sipadan* (n 36) the ICJ was asked to determine sovereignty over the islands of Ligitan and Sipadan in the Celebes Sea off the north-east coast of Borneo.

[67] LL Herman, 'The Modern Concept of the Off-Lying Archipelago in International Law' (1985) 23 *Canadian Yearbook of International Law* 172, 179–85.

'closely inter-related' that together they 'form an intrinsic geographical, economic and political entity, or which have historically been regarded as such.' The connection between the islands composing the archipelago can therefore be on multiple levels. The inclusion of economic and political factors is significant and emphasises that geography is not the sole determining factor in identifying the existence of an archipelago, and that islands which either historically have been an intrinsic entity, or which as a result of economic or political factors have become such an entity, may be recognised as an archipelago. Peoples from different groups of islands may therefore come together to create a juridical archipelago, which subject to other factors may be recognised as an archipelagic State.

Article 46(a) defines an 'archipelagic State' as a State 'constituted wholly by one or more archipelagos and may include other islands'. There are important geographical limitations associated with this definition. The first, self-evidently, is that the State must consist of at least one archipelago. The definition is also wide enough to encompass a State comprising more than one archipelago. The second is that the State can only be composed of islands, and as such no part of the archipelagic State can include parts of a continental landmass. Islands located offshore a continent are, however, acceptable providing those islands are part of a distinct political entity. The Hawaiian islands that make up the state of Hawaii (US) are an example of an archipelago that meets the Article 46 definition in all respects other than the fact that the US as the relevant metropolitan State is a continental State. The result is that the Hawaiian archipelago cannot be a part of an archipelagic State as currently constituted.[68] The LOSC does not define a continental or mainland State and accordingly an issue that may arise is the distinction between an island and a continent for the purposes of Article 46.[69] The third element is that the archipelago is composed of islands as defined by law. To that end the Article 121 definition of an island, including that it is naturally formed, is important.[70]

Article 46 excludes continental States that have offshore archipelagos adjacent to their coast, such as Canada with its northern islands in the Arctic,[71] and the Norwegian *skjærgaard* along its west coast.[72] Likewise, France is unable

[68] N Barron, 'Archipelagos and Archipelagic States under UNCLOS III: No Special Treatment for Hawaii' (1981) 4 *Hastings International and Comparative Law Review* 509.

[69] Greenland, for example is considered an island, while Australia is considered a continent; see Central Intelligence Agency (US), 'Australia' (*The World Factbook*) www.cia.gov/the-world-factbook/countries/australia/; 'Greenland' (*The World Factbook*) www.cia.gov/the-world-factbook/countries/greenland/.

[70] This raises issues as to whether it is possible for an archipelagic State to build artificial islands within archipelagic baselines; see discussion in Chapter 10, section V with respect to the Maldives and building the artificial island of Hulhumalé.

[71] Though Canada has sought to proclaim straight baselines around these islands: JB McKinnon, 'Arctic Baselines: *A Litore Usque ad Litus*' (1987) 66 *Canadian Bar Review* 790.

[72] Considered by the ICJ in *Fisheries Case* (n 17), where the Court upheld the validity of the Norwegian straight baseline system that had been employed to connect up the islands, which ultimately has become reflected in LOSC (n 7) art 7.

to claim archipelagic status notwithstanding that several of its overseas territories would be considered to be archipelagos.[73] Importantly, an archipelagic State may comprise one or more archipelagos, and States may still be able to claim archipelagic status based on several archipelagos, or a central archipelago and a number of distant outlying islands.[74] As the situation of Indonesia and PNG highlights, it is also possible for two archipelagic States to share a common island, which is the case with New Guinea, and rely upon that part of the island over which they exercise sovereignty for the purpose of drawing LOSC archipelagic baselines. To that end, it is clear that the LOSC definition seeks to provide flexibility as to the groups of island States that may be entitled to claim archipelagic State status.

In addition to Indonesia and the Philippines, by 1982 a number of additional States had taken steps towards achieving archipelagic status, either by way of enacting new laws providing a framework for archipelagic claims including the recognition of archipelagic waters, or by actually having declared baselines and proclaimed archipelagic waters.[75] These States included Cape Verde,[76] Fiji,[77] PNG,[78] Sao Tome and Principe,[79] and Vanuatu.[80] Soon after the conclusion of the LOSC, Prescott observed that '[t]he requirement for the islands and the waters to be closely interrelated is a matter for subjective judgement and there are 35 archipelagic States which could be considered to meet the definition of Article 46', of which only 17 had the capacity to proclaim legitimate archipelagic baselines.[81]

[73] For example, French Polynesia and New Caledonia.

[74] Office for Ocean Affairs and the Law of the Sea (UN), *The Law of the Sea: Baselines* (United Nations 1989) 37 (*Baselines*).

[75] For a review of that practice see B Kwiatkowska, 'The Archipelagic Regime in Practice – Making or Breaking International Law?' (1991) 6 *International Journal of Estuarine and Coastal Law* 1.

[76] Decree-Law No 126/77 delimiting the territorial sea of the Republic of Cape Verde 1977 (Cape Verde), reprinted in M Nordquist, SH Lay and KR Simmonds (eds), *New Directions in the Law of the Sea*, vol 7 (Oceana Publications 1980) 363 declaring 'straight baselines' (art 2) and archipelagic waters (art 3).

[77] Marine Spaces Act 1977 (Fiji), reprinted in Nordquist, Lay and Simmonds (n 76) 391, declaring archipelagic waters to be subsequently proclaimed by further declaration of baselines (s 4).

[78] National Seas Act 1977 (PNG), reprinted in Nordquist, Lay and Simmonds (n 76) 485, describing archipelagic waters (s 7), and an 'Interim Delimitation of Archipelagic Waters' (s 9).

[79] Decree-Law No 148/82 amending art 2 of Decree-Law No 14/78 (Sao Tome and Principe), reprinted in Nordquist, Lay and Simmonds (n 76) 5 declaring 'straight lines' (art 2) and archipelagic waters (art 3).

[80] Maritime Zones Act 1982 (Act No 23 of 1981) (Vanuatu), reprinted in *The Law of the Sea: Current Developments and State Practice* (United Nations 1987) 124 declaring archipelagic waters (s 4) and archipelagic baselines (sch).

[81] JRV Prescott, 'Straight and Archipelagic Baselines' in G Blake (ed), *Maritime Boundaries and Ocean Resources* (Croom Helm 1987) 38, 46–47; cf Kwiatkowska (n 75) 3 referring to the potential claim of 24 archipelagic States.

Table 5.1 Archipelagic States

No	State	Legislation/Proclamation	Date	No	Ratio	% ABL >100nm	ABL <125nm	Art 47 C
1	Antigua and Barbuda	Maritime Areas Act 1982 (Act No 18)	01/09/1982	1	7.91:1	0/22: 0%	Yes	Yes
2	The Bahamas	The Archipelagic Waters and Maritime Jurisdiction 1993; modified by The Archipelagic Waters and Maritime Jurisdiction (Archipelagic Baselines) Order 2008	04/01/1996; 08/12/2008	1	6.86:1	2/95: 2.11%	Yes	Yes
3	Cape Verde	Decree Law No. 60/IV 92	21/12/1982	1	8.92:1	0/25: 0%	Yes	Yes
4	Comoros	Law No 82-005 (1982); Presidential Decree No 10-092 (2010)	06/05/1982; 13/08/2010	1	5.99:1	0/13: 0%	Yes	Yes
5	Dominican Republic	Act 66-07 (2007)	22/05/2007	1	1.03:1 (cf UK, US)	0/20: 0%	Yes	Yes (cf UK, US)
6	Fiji	Marine Spaces Act 1978; Marine Spaces (Archipelagic Baselines and Exclusive Economic Zone) Order, Legal Notice No 117 of 1981	01/12/1981	1	2.98:1	1/33: 3.03%	Yes	Yes
7	Grenada	Territorial Sea and Maritime Boundaries Act 1989; Statutory Rules and Orders No 31 of 1992	25/04/1989; 16/12/1992	1	1.61:1	0/23: 0%	Yes	Yes
8	Indonesia	List of geographical coordinates of points of archipelagic baselines, Government Regulation No 38 of 2002 (as amended by Government Regulation No 37 of 2008)	19/05/2008	1	1.61:1	5/197: 2.53%	Yes	Yes

9	Jamaica	The Maritime Areas Act, 1996; Exclusive Economic Zone (Baselines) Regulation (1992)	12/10/1982	1	2.00:1	0/28: 0%	Yes	Yes
10	Kiribati	Maritime Zones (Declaration) Act 2011; Baselines around the Archipelagos of Kiribati Regulations 2014	01/07/2011; 04/11/2014	2	8.72:1 8.47:1	0/10 0/4	Yes	Yes
11	Maldives	Maritime Zones Act No 6/96	27/06/1996	1	2.63: 1	3/37: 8.1%	Yes	No
12	Marshall Islands	Republic of the Marshall Islands Maritime Zones Declaration Act 2016; Baselines and Maritime Zones Outer Limits Declaration 2016	18/03/2016; 18/04/2016	2	8.54:1 9.56:1	1/53: 1.88% 0/33: 0%	Yes	No
13	Mauritius	Maritime Zones Act 2005; Maritime Zones (Baselines and Delineating Lines) Regulations 2005	05/08/2005	2	2.84:1 7.5:1	0/3: 0% 0/32: 0%	Yes	Yes
14	Papua New Guinea	National Sea Act 1977; Offshore Seas Proclamation 1978; Declaration of the baselines by method of coordinates of base points for purposes of the location of archipelagic baselines 2002	25/07/2002	1	1.22:1	1/74: 1.35%	No: 1 x 174.78 nm	No
15	Philippines	Republic Act No 3046 (1961); Republic Act No 9522 (2009)	10/03/2009	1	1.98:1	3/101: 2.97%	Yes	Yes
16	Saint Vincent and the Grenadines	Archipelagic Closing Lines and Baselines of Saint Vincent and the Grenadines (Notice No 60/2014)	01/04/2014	1	3.81:1	0/33: 0%	Yes	Yes
17	São Tomé and Principe	Law No 1/98	31/03/1998	1	4.03:1	0/14: 0%	Yes	Yes

(continued)

Table 5.1 (Continued)

No	State	Legislation/Proclamation	Date	No	Ratio	% ABL >100nm	ABL <125nm	Art 47 C
18	Seychelles	Maritime Zones Act 1999; Maritime Zones (Baselines) Order, 2008 (as amended)	06/11/2008	4	10.5:1 239:1 44.5:1 5.15:1	0/45: 0% 0/48: 0% 0/29: 0% 0/35: 0%	Yes	No
19	Solomon Islands	The Delimitation of Marine Waters Act (No 32 of 1978); Declaration of Archipelagos of Solomon Islands, 1979	31/08/1979	5	4.06:1 4.44:1 29.9:1 7.03:1 3.57:1	1/37: 2.7% 0/10: 0% 0/13: 0% 0/15: 0% 0/8: 0%	Yes	No
20	Trinidad and Tobago	Archipelagic Waters and Exclusive Economic Zone Act (No 24 of 1986)	11/11/1986	1	1.39:1	0/11: 0%	Yes	Yes
21	Tuvalu	Tuvalu Maritime Areas Act 2012; Declaration of Archipelagic Baselines 2012	04/05/2012; 22/11/2012	1	7.58:1	0/30: 0%	Yes	Yes
22	Vanuatu	Maritime Zones Act (No 6 of 2010); Amendments of the Schedule of the Maritime Act (29 July 20090	18/06/2009	1	5.83: 1	0/59: 0%	Yes	Yes

Key:
Art 47 C – LOSC Art 47 compliance.
No – number of archipelagic straight baseline systems used to enclose islands and parts of islands of the archipelagic State.
Ratio – whether the straight baseline systems are consistent with the area of water to land ratio of 9:1 to 1:1 in LOSC Art 47(1).
SBL <125nm – whether all of the archipelagic baselines are less than the maximum length of 125 nm as per LOSC Art 47(2).

Source: Data from DR Rothwell and T Stephens, *The International Law of the Sea* (2nd edn, Hart Publishing 2016) 198–99 based on analysis in JA Roach and RW Smith, *Excessive Maritime Claims* (3rd edn, Martinus Nijhoff 2012) 206–8 as updated by Department of State (US), *Limits in the Sea* Nos. 98, 101, 125, 126, 128, 129, 130, 131, 132, 133, 134, 135, 136, 137, 138, 139, 140, 141, 142, 144, 145, 146; United Nations, *Law of the Sea Bulletin* No 86, 87, 91.

B. Recognition of Archipelagic States

A total of 22 States have sought to proclaim themselves as archipelagic States (see Table 5.1), and legal issues have been raised with respect to proclaimed archipelagic baselines which are considered further below. It can be observed, however, that five States have declared more than one set of archipelagic baseline systems: Kiribati, Marshall Islands, Mauritius, Seychelles, and Solomon Islands. This state practice emphasises that an archipelagic State may consist of more than one archipelago. Consistently with Article 46, there are also examples of States that comprise both archipelagos and separate islands, as in the case of Mauritius. The principal island is Mauritius, where the capital, Port Louis, is located. In addition there are three smaller islands (Rodrigues Island, Agalega Island, Tromelin Island), and two claimed archipelagos which have been enclosed by archipelagic baselines: the Chagos Archipelago, and the Chargados Carajos Shoals (Saint Brandon).[82] However, sovereignty over the Chagos Archipelago is contested between Mauritius and the UK.[83] As a result not all elements of the Mauritius archipelagic State claim are recognised.[84] The Dominican Republic, Indonesia, and Papua New Guinea claims also include parts of islands over which sovereignty is shared with neighbouring States; uniquely in the case of Indonesia and PNG, the two *archipelagic* States share sovereignty over New Guinea.

Declarations of archipelagic State status have not directly been considered by international courts or tribunals. However, in 2001 the International Court of Justice (ICJ) in *Qatar v Bahrain* considered Bahrain's contention that it was a 'multi-island' State characterised by a cluster of islands off the coast of its main islands and that as such it was a de facto archipelagic State.[85] The issue arose in the context of Bahrain's drawing of straight baselines around certain islands. Bahrain is composed of 33 islands in the Gulf of Bahrain and is an archipelago consistent with Article 46(b) of the LOSC.[86] When the Court considered Bahrain's claim that it was a 'multi-island State', a term that is not found in the LOSC or in common usage in international law, the Court observed that such an assertion does not allow the State 'to deviate from the normal rules for the determination of baselines unless the relevant conditions are met.'[87] Bahrain's claim was equated with one of being a de facto archipelagic State; however, the Court observed that only

[82] Department of State (US), *Mauritius: Archipelagic and Other Maritime Claims and Boundaries (Limits in the Sea No 140)* (Department of State 2014) 4, 11.

[83] *Dispute Concerning Delimitation of the Maritime Boundary between Mauritius and Maldives in the Indian Ocean (Mauritius v The Maldives)* (Preliminary Objections Judgment) (28 January 2021) ITLOS Reports 2020–21, to be published [116]–[246] at www.itlos.org/fileadmin/itlos/documents/cases/28/preliminary_objections/C28_Judgment_prelimobj_28.01.2021_orig.pdf (*Mauritius and Maldives*).

[84] This is the position taken by the US: Department of State (US), *Mauritius: Archipelagic and Other Maritime Claims and Boundaries* (n 82) 5.

[85] *Qatar v Bahrain* (n 5) [181].

[86] Central Intelligence Agency (US), 'Bahrain' (*The World Factbook*) www.cia.gov/the-world-factbook/countries/bahrain/ refers to Bahrain as 'an archipelago in the Persian Gulf'.

[87] *Qatar v Bahrain* (n 5) [213].

those States which had declared themselves to be archipelagic States were entitled to draw archipelagic baselines.[88] Notwithstanding that neither Article 46 nor LOSC Part IV make reference to a State declaring itself to be an archipelagic State, the Court placed emphasis upon such a declaration if a State sought to rely upon LOSC Article 47 to draw archipelagic baselines. More recently in the 2016 *South China Sea* arbitration before a LOSC Annex VII Tribunal,[89] a question arose as to whether China was an archipelagic State. The context was again an issue related to the drawing of baselines that could have been assimilated with Article 47 archipelagic baselines. The Tribunal observed that the use of archipelagic baselines is 'strictly controlled by the Convention' and that their use is limited to archipelagic States,[90] and that as China was principally a mainland Asian State it did not meet the definition of an archipelagic State. Such an approach is consistent with the interpretation of Article 46(a).

VII. Archipelagic State Entitlements

An archipelagic State enjoys certain entitlements under the LOSC, the most significant of which is the ability to draw straight archipelagic baselines so as to effectively enclose the islands of the archipelago, and the ability to exercise sovereignty over the waters of the archipelago: known as 'archipelagic waters'. These aspects of archipelagic State entitlements are discussed below.

A. Archipelagic Baselines

Article 46 provides the basis for recognition as an archipelagic State; however, the capacity to enjoy all of the rights and privileges of an archipelagic State ultimately rests with the ability of the State to proclaim archipelagic baselines consistent with the provisions of Article 47.[91] The ICJ in *Qatar v Bahrain* made it clear that Part IV archipelagic straight baselines can only be relied upon by a declared archipelagic State.[92] In response to Bahrain's assertion that it was a de facto archipelagic State, Judge ad hoc Torres Bernárdez observed that there is 'no such thing in

[88] ibid.

[89] *In the Matter of the South China Sea Arbitration before an Arbitral Tribunal constituted under Annex VII of the 1982 United Nations Convention on the Law of the Sea (Philippines v China)* (Merits) (12 July 2016) PCA Case 2013-19 (*South China Sea*).

[90] ibid 236 [573].

[91] This is reflected in the wording of LOSC (n 7) art 47(1) which notes that the 'archipelagic State may draw straight archipelagic baselines'.

[92] *Qatar v Bahrain* (n 5) 103 [214]; suggesting at [213] strict application of the baseline criteria; in this instance Bahrain had not declared itself an archipelagic State and was therefore unable to avail itself of the provisions of Part IV.

conventional or general international law as a "secret archipelagic State" appearing in or disappearing from general international judicial proceedings or international relations in general.'[93] Therefore, even if a State meets all the generic criteria of Article 46, if the State is unable to comply with the specific requirements of the archipelagic baseline regime, its ability to proclaim itself as an archipelagic State will be compromised. This would not, however, impact upon the ability of that State to draw straight baselines consistent with Article 7.[94]

The Article 47 archipelagic baselines provisions are founded upon the general LOSC straight baselines provisions that have developed over time in the law of the sea, including state practice following the *Fisheries Case* and the 1958 Convention on the Territorial Sea and Contiguous Zone. They also reflect some of the specific state practice found in the Indonesian and Philippines baseline claims. While there is no direct link between Articles 7 and 47, certain common principles apply with respect to the drawing of straight and archipelagic baselines.

The core elements of the archipelagic baseline provisions in Article 47 specify five criteria.[95] The baselines must:

1. connect the outermost points of the outermost islands and drying reefs of the archipelago[96] and include the main islands;[97]
2. result in a ratio of the area of water to land of between 1 to 1 and 9 to 1;[98]
3. with the exception mentioned below, be no longer than 100 nm in length;[99]
4. be no longer than 125 nm in length, with only three per cent of the total number of baselines to be within a range of 101 to 125 nm in length;[100] and
5. not depart to any appreciable extent from the general configuration of the archipelago.[101]

A number of observations can be made regarding these criteria. First, they make clear that the archipelagic baselines are to enclose the main islands and extend to the outermost points of the archipelago, thereby thwarting any attempts to enclose

[93] ibid (Dissenting Opinion of Judge ad hoc Torres Bernárdez) 280 [56].
[94] See comment in *South China Sea* (n 89) 237 [575]–[576].
[95] Prescott (n 81) 46 observed that: 'Three of the five tests are incapable of consistent objective interpretation.'
[96] Cf LOSC (n 7) art 6 where the term 'fringing reefs' is used; Nandan and Rosenne (n 63) 430.
[97] Office for Ocean Affairs and the Law of the Sea (UN), *Baselines* (n 74) 35 [82] comments: 'The expression "main islands" could be interpreted in a variety of ways. For different countries the main islands might mean the largest islands, the most populous islands, the most economically productive islands, or the islands which are pre-eminent in an historical or cultural sense.'
[98] LOSC (n 7) art 47(7) clarifies what 'land' can be included for the purpose of computing the water to land ratio, and is drawn from the '18 Principles for Inclusion in Archipelagic Waters' paper introduced by the Bahamas during UNCLOS III; Nandan and Rosenne (n 63) 405, 432.
[99] LOSC (n 7) art 47(2).
[100] ibid art 47(2).
[101] ibid art 47(3).

small separate clusters of islands that may be distant from a larger island or groups of large islands.[102] Islands that form part of the archipelagic State but which are not part of an archipelago are not capable of being enclosed within straight archipelagic baselines, though it may be possible to draw Article 7 straight baselines around such islands. The requirement that the baselines include the 'main islands' raises issues of interpretation as to whether this criterion is adjudged on the basis of size, population, economic or political significance. Mauritius is an interesting example in this regard as the island of Mauritius is subject to Article 7 straight baselines notwithstanding that Mauritius is the predominant island in the State including where the capital, Port Louis, is located. Mauritius then draws straight archipelagic baselines around two separate archipelagos that are at some distance from the main island.[103] There may also be a need to make adjustments to archipelagic baselines as a result of a change in the recognised sovereign over certain islands. Indonesia was faced with the need to adjust its archipelagic baselines following the 2002 independence of East Timor/Timor-Leste, and the 2002 ICJ decision in the *Sovereignty over Pulau Ligitan and Pulau Sipadan* case between Indonesia and Malaysia, which clarified sovereignty over certain disputed islands.[104]

Second, the minimum water-to-land ratio requirement of 1 to 1 ensures that the archipelagic State is not dominated by very large islands with minimal ocean space between them. The effect of this provision is to exclude states such as Japan, New Zealand, and the UK which despite being States composed of islands, would not meet the minimum 1 to 1 area of water to area of land ratio given the size of the landmass compared to waters that may be enclosed within legitimate baselines. Likewise, island States which comprise one large island such as Cuba, Iceland, Ireland and Madagascar are generally excluded,[105] even though there may exist some small coastal islands and islets. An exception is Jamaica, which comprises one main island and a collection of smaller rocks, islets, and cays which nevertheless have been enclosed within Article 47 straight archipelagic baselines.[106] A concession is made in Article 47(7) for how the water-to-land ratio is to be

[102] Kiribati expressed its concern about this provision in its LOSC Declaration where it stated: 'Part IV calculations for archipelagic waters do not allow a baseline to be drawn around all the islands of each of the three Groups of islands that make up the Republic of Kiribati. These Group of islands are spread over an expanse of over three million square kilometres of ocean, and the existing formula … will divide Kiribati's three island groups into three distinct exclusive zone waters and international waters': 'Declarations and Statements' at www.un.org/Depts/los/convention_agreements/convention_declarations.htm.

[103] See analysis in Department of State (US), *Mauritius: Archipelagic and Other Maritime Claims and Boundaries* (n 82).

[104] *Pulau Ligitan and Pulau Sipadan* (n 36).

[105] Prescott (n 81) 47, listed 15 States prevented from drawing archipelagic baselines because they could not enclose an area of water equal to the area of land: Australia, Cuba, Haiti, Iceland, Ireland, Japan, Madagascar, Malta, New Zealand, Singapore, Sri Lanka, Taiwan, Trinidad and Tobago, and the UK and Western Samoa; though this does not bar those States from drawing straight baselines consistent with LOSC (n 7) art 7.

[106] Department of State (US), *Bahamas: Archipelagic and Other Maritime Claims and Boundaries (Limits in the Sea No 125)* (Department of State 2014) 3–4.

computed in special cases such that land areas may include waters lying within fringing reefs of islands and atolls, including certain waters of limestone island chains and associated drying reefs. The Bahamas has relied upon this provision in determining its water-to-land ratio.[107]

Third, in recognition of the size of some archipelagos and the distance that may exist between some of the islands, Article 47(2) provides that archipelagic baselines shall not exceed 100 nm,[108] except that up to three per cent of the total number of baselines which enclose the archipelago may extend up to a maximum length of 125 nm. This provision is both technical and strict; however, there is nothing to prevent the drawing of multiple straight archipelagic baselines to and from appropriate basepoints to ensure the number of baselines measuring between 101 and 125 nm are less than three per cent of the total.[109] In that regard, Article 47(4) makes clear that baselines are not to be drawn to and from low-tide elevations unless lighthouses or similar installations permanently above sea level have been built there, or that the feature is within the breadth of the territorial sea of the nearest island.

Fourth, the baselines are also not to depart to 'any appreciable extent' from the general configuration of the archipelago.[110] However, this provision is capable of flexible interpretation due to the potential for there to be more than one set of straight archipelagic baseline systems which allow for more than one archipelago within the archipelagic State.[111] The general configuration of the archipelago may also be subject to the limitations set down within Article 47 for the drawing of straight archipelagic baselines such that distant islands, beyond 125 nm, may not be encompassed within the baselines.

Other notable elements within Article 47 include that straight archipelagic baselines are not to cut off high seas or EEZ access from the territorial sea of another State.[112] This applies in the case of Indonesia where some of the main Indonesian islands share land boundaries with Brunei, Malaysia, PNG, and Timor-Leste. Archipelagic baselines are to be shown on charts, and due publicity is to be given to them including the deposit of charts and relevant geographic coordinates with the UN.[113] A number of the States that assert archipelagic status and which

[107] See analysis in Department of State (USA), *Jamaica's Maritime Claims and Boundaries (Limits in the Sea No 128)* (Department of State 2014) 2–3.

[108] There does not appear to have been any firm grounding in prior state practice for the identification of 100 nm as the length of archipelagic baselines: Munavvar (n 6) 131–32.

[109] Office for Ocean Affairs and the Law of the Sea (UN), *Baselines* (n 74) 35, noting that: 'Since there is no restriction on the number of segments a country can draw, and since the more segments used the closer the system is likely to be to the general configuration of the archipelago, it will usually be possible to adjust the number of segments to secure the necessary number of very long baselines.'

[110] LOSC (n 7) art 47(3).

[111] The Solomon Islands has established archipelagic baselines around five separate groups of islands: Department of State (US), *Solomon Islands: Archipelagic and other Maritime Claims and Boundaries (Limits in the Sea No 136)* (Department of State 2014) 2.

[112] ibid art 47(5).

[113] ibid arts 47(8), (9).

have proclaimed straight archipelagic baselines have lodged details of those claims with the Division of Ocean Affairs and the Law of the Sea (DOALOS) and that data is available on the UN website.[114] Baselines once declared are not fixed and may be subject to subsequent adjustment.[115]

B. Archipelagic Waters and Maritime Zones

Once archipelagic baselines have been drawn, an archipelagic State enjoys two distinctive rights. The first, consistent with its ongoing status as a coastal State – albeit one which is recognised as an archipelagic State for the purposes of the LOSC – is the entitlement in Article 48 to determine the breadth of its maritime zones from its straight archipelagic baselines. While in principle this right is no greater an entitlement than that enjoyed generally by other coastal States, its significance rests with the manner in which straight archipelagic baselines have been drawn, giving the State an ability to assert claims to a territorial sea, contiguous zone, EEZ and continental shelf over areas of the ocean that previously would have been considered high seas.[116] In this respect those archipelagic States that comprise many distant islands, such as Tuvalu and Vanuatu, connected by long, straight archipelagic baselines are particular beneficiaries of this entitlement, compared to more compact archipelagic States such as Grenada and Indonesia.

The second distinctive right, which is sui generis to the LOSC, is that waters that fall within archipelagic baselines are considered to be 'archipelagic waters' over which the archipelagic State is able to exercise its sovereignty, extending not only to the waters but also to the air space above and the seabed below.[117] This sovereignty is exercised irrespective of the depth of the waters or their distance from the coast, making it clear that the juridical status of archipelagic waters differs from the other LOSC maritime spaces. Archipelagic waters are therefore waters over which the archipelagic State exercises sovereignty in nearly the same manner that a coastal State exercises sovereignty over waters on the landward side of the baselines such as rivers, lakes, and internal waters. Importantly for the archipelagic State, this includes sovereignty over the living and non-living resources found within those waters and the seabed and subsoil, the regulation and control of marine scientific research, and the ability to exercise security controls within those waters. The exercise of this sovereignty is not, however, absolute and is subject to LOSC Part IV. This includes making allowance for foreign ships not

[114] See DOALOS, Office of Legal Affairs, United Nations Secretariat at www.un.org/Depts/los/LEGISLATIONANDTREATIES/depositpublicity.htm.

[115] This is raising issues for sea-level rise as discussed in Chapter 10, section V of this volume.

[116] As discussed in Chapter 7, a juridical island generates all of the maritime claims that a continental landmass does; nevertheless, as an archipelagic State can draw archipelagic baselines of up to 125 nm between certain islands, the maritime claims generated from those baselines encompass larger areas of ocean space than if baselines of such length were not capable of being drawn.

[117] LOSC (n 7) art 49(1), (2).

only to exercise a right of innocent passage generally within those waters, but also to exercise a right of archipelagic sea lanes passage (ASLP) within archipelagic sea lanes designated by the State or routes normally used for international navigation where no sea lanes have been designated. This right, however, is not one that in other respects affects the status of archipelagic waters.[118] However, the capacity of the archipelagic State to enforce its laws and regulations against vessels engaged in those different navigational rights, and the related prescriptive and enforcement jurisdiction of the archipelagic State, do raise some issues with respect to the adoption of jurisdictional regimes designed to apply within the territorial sea.[119] Consistent with its sovereignty over the air space, the archipelagic State also exercises complete sovereignty with respect to overflight of both the archipelagic landmass and archipelagic waters. Archipelagic sea lanes passage, however, does permit a right of overflight along sea lanes by aircraft.[120]

An archipelagic State may also draw closing lines for the purpose of delimiting internal waters within archipelagic waters,[121] and this may be considered desirable especially for the purposes of regulating access to and from port and harbour facilities that exist within the archipelago.[122] That internal waters may exist within archipelagic waters raises for direct consideration the distinction that exists between these bodies of water. It is clear from the early Indonesian and Philippine claims that the waters within baselines were equated by both States with their internal waters, even though rights of innocent passage were recognised. When it came to the negotiation of the LOSC, and the recognition in Part IV of 'archipelagic waters', it was therefore important to make clear the extent of not only archipelagic State sovereignty and jurisdiction over archipelagic waters, but to also distinguish the new regime from previous practice.

Therefore, whilst the sovereignty of a State over internal waters and archipelagic waters is closely aligned, there are some important distinctions. The most significant is the prima facie right of navigation that exists through archipelagic waters, extending to innocent passage and ASLP. There is no equivalent right of navigation

[118] ibid art 49(4), 52; see discussion which follows below.

[119] EJ Molenaar, *Coastal State Jurisdiction over Vessel-Source Pollution* (Kluwer Law International 1998) 342–45; a clear example would be differential interests in the case of vessels carrying hazardous cargoes principally because of the much longer period of time that it could be anticipated such vessels would be within archipelagic waters, compared to vessels within the territorial sea, either for the purposes of a port visit or whilst undertaking some form of transit through the archipelago.

[120] LOSC (n 7) art 53.

[121] ibid art 50, which makes clear that the baselines may be drawn in accordance with LOSC, arts 9–11, thereby excluding LOSC, art 7 straight baselines; cf LOSC (n 7) art 8(1), which makes clear that the general provisions regarding internal waters being on the landward side of the baseline do not apply in the context of Part IV.

[122] Given the size and scale of the Indonesian and Philippine archipelagic claims, and some of the industrial and other port developments that are taking place within their archipelagic waters, this provision has particular application. Indonesian law makes allowance for the drawing of such closing lines: Act No 6 of 8 August 1996 regarding Indonesian Waters, art 7; see analysis in Department of State (US), *Indonesia: Archipelagic and Other Maritime Claims and Boundaries (Limits in the Sea No 141)* (Department of State 2014) annex 3.

through internal waters. Not only does the recognition of these navigational rights permit the passage of foreign vessels through archipelagic waters, it also places certain limitations on the laws and regulations which can be applied to foreign ships within archipelagic waters. This is to be contrasted with the plenary powers that a coastal State has over its internal waters. The other distinction between the two regimes is that the archipelagic State is also bound to recognise 'existing rights and all other legitimate interests' which immediately adjacent neighbouring States may have 'traditionally exercised' in what are now archipelagic waters,[123] including pre-existing fishing agreements and 'traditional fishing rights',[124] and previously laid submarine cables which pass through what have become archipelagic waters.[125] These provisions collectively seek to address issues that arise when archipelagic waters of one State are located between two parts of a neighbouring country, which occurs in the case of Indonesian archipelagic waters located between East and West Malaysia.[126]

C. Archipelagic State Practice

Table 5.1 summarises key elements of the archipelagic State claims of 22 States. Given the significance associated with their claims, and the size of their archipelagos, the state practice of Indonesia and the Philippines is closely observed. In 2009 Indonesia deposited with the UN a revised set of geographical coordinates of points consistent with LOSC Article 47(9). These coordinates are based on Government Regulation No 38 (2002) as amended by Government Regulation No 27 (2008).[127] A total of 192 baselines are identified in the Indonesian coordinates, which include a mix of normal and archipelagic baselines. The baselines range in length from as little as 0.51 nm to 122.75 nm with a total length of 6,920 nm, enclosing an area of 4,986,325 km^2 of which the water area is 3,081,756 km^2 making for a water-to-land ratio of 1.61 to 1.[128] In 2009 the Philippines also deposited with the UN a set of geographical coordinates of points, which for the first

[123] LOSC (n 7) art 47(6). This provision sought to reflect concerns Malaysia had raised over Indonesia's archipelagic claim: Nandan and Rosenne (n 63) 431.

[124] LOSC (n 7) art 51(1); this latter term is not defined: Rajan, 'The Legal Regime of Archipelagos' (n 6) 149–50.

[125] LOSC (n 7) art 51(2) extends the rights with respect to submarine cables to their maintenance and replacement, subject to notification.

[126] Office for Ocean Affairs and the Law of the Sea (UN), *Baselines* (n 74) 36; addressed by the Treaty between Malaysia and the Republic of Indonesia relating to the Legal Regime of Archipelagic State and the Rights of Malaysia in the Territorial Sea and Archipelagic Waters as well as in the Airspace above the Territorial Sea, Archipelagic Waters and the Territory of the Republic of Indonesia lying between East and West Malaysia (Jakarta Treaty) (adopted 25 February 1982, entered into force 25 May 1984).

[127] United Nations, 'Deposit by the Republic of Indonesia of a list of geographical coordinates of points, pursuant to article 47, paragraph 9, of the Convention' (25 March 2009) UN Doc MZN67.2009.

[128] See the analysis in Department of State (US), *Indonesia: Archipelagic and Other Maritime Claims and Boundaries* (n 122) 2–3.

time proclaimed archipelagic baselines consistent with the LOSC.[129] These baselines were based upon Republic Act No 9522 which had in turn amended earlier Philippine legislation.[130] The Philippines identified a total of 101 basepoints and baselines which range in length from 0.08 nm to 122.83 nm with a total length of 2,808 nm, enclosing 887,909 km^2 of which the water area is 589,739 km^2 making for a water-to-land ratio of 1.98 to 1.[131] Republic Act No 9522 also reaffirms in section 3 that the Philippines 'has dominion, sovereignty and jurisdiction over all portions of the national territory as defined in the Constitution'. A separate declaration is also made in Republic Act No 9522 with respect to the islands that form the Kalayaan Island Group and Scarborough Shoal, which are determined as a 'Regime of Islands' for the purposes of Article 121 of the LOSC.[132] China has protested the Philippines' baselines and provisions of Republic Act No 9522 in the context of their contested sovereignty over Huangyan Island, and the islands and reefs of the Nansha Islands (which the Philippines refer to as the Kalayaan Island Group).[133]

Unsurprisingly, given there are 22 declared archipelagic States whose geographic and maritime circumstances vary considerably, different approaches have been taken in applying and interpreting Part IV. Consistently with Article 50, Antigua and Barbuda, Fiji, Grenada, Mauritius, Saint Vincent and the Grenadines, and Tuvalu have sought to delimit internal waters within their archipelagic waters.[134] Tuvalu has also sought to mix its use of archipelagic baselines in the case of some atolls that are located within the archipelago, with Article 6 in the case of isolated atolls.[135] Papua New Guinea's declared archipelagic baselines do not connect with New Guinea, but rather commence at a point approximately 40 nm off the northern coast in the Bismark Sea and terminate on Suau Island in the Coral Sea off the southern New Guinea coast.[136] Whilst these baselines effectively enclose New Guinea they do not connect with the New Guinea coast at either

[129] MA Palma, 'The Philippines as an Archipelagic and Maritime Nation: Interests, Challenges and Perspectives' (2009) *RSIS Working Paper* No 182, 4–5. Under the previous baselines, for example, a baseline across Moro Gulf was 140.05 nm in length.

[130] United Nations, 'Deposit by the Republic of the Philippines of a list of geographical coordinates of points, pursuant to article 47, paragraph 9, of the Convention' (21 April 2009) UN Doc MZN 69.2009.

[131] Department of State (US), *Philippines: Archipelagic and Other Maritime Claims and Boundaries (Limits in the Sea No 142)* (Department of State 2014) 3.

[132] Republic Act No 9522 of 2009 (Philippines) s 3.

[133] Communication from the Government of China received by the Secretary-General of the United Nations, CML/12/2009 (13 April 2009); which in turn promoted a response from Vietnam with respect to China's assertions of sovereignty: Communication from the Government of Vietnam received by the Secretary-General of the United Nations, No 86/HC-2009 (8 May 2009); at www.un.org/Depts/los/LEGISLATIONANDTREATIES/STATEFILES/PHL.htm.

[134] K Baumert and B Melchior, 'The Practice of Archipelagic States: A Study of Studies' (2015) 46 *Ocean Development and International Law* 60, 71.

[135] Department of State (US), *Limits in the Seas: No 139 Tuvalu's Maritime Claims and Boundaries* (Department of State 2014) 3, 7, 18.

[136] Baumert and Melchior (n 134) 63–64.

their commencement or terminus points. In the case of the lengths of archipelagic straight baselines, Table 5.1 generally highlights a high degree of compliance with the exception of:

- PNG having a straight archipelagic baseline of 174.78 nm, in excess of the 125 nm limit;
- Kiribati having a water-to-land ratio of 9.31 to 1 in one of its proclaimed straight archipelagic baseline systems;
- Seychelles having three of its four proclaimed archipelagic straight baselines systems in excess of the required water-to-land ratio;
- Solomon Islands having one of its proclaimed straight archipelagic baselines systems at a water-to-land ratio of 29.9 to 1;
- Maldives having more than 3 per cent of its straight archipelagic baselines in excess of 100 nm; and,
- Marshall Islands straight archipelagic baselines enclosing an area greater than the 9 to 1 ratio permissible under Article 47(1).

Some maritime States have been sensitive to the manner in which certain archipelagic baselines have been proclaimed and have challenged their consistency with the LOSC. The US has been particularly vigilant in monitoring claims by archipelagic States,[137] including instances where continental States which do not meet the Article 46 definition of an archipelagic State have sought to enclose clusters of offshore islands in a manner similar to an archipelagic claim.[138] In 1980, the US protested Cape Verde's claim to be an archipelagic State on the basis that the water-to-land ratio arising from that State's archipelagic baselines was 12.54 to 1, with the result that the baselines were modified to conform with the LOSC.[139] In 2007 following the declaration by the Dominican Republic that it was an archipelagic State,[140] the UK and the US issued a joint *demarche* indicating they did not accept the Dominican Republic's claim and challenging the reliance by the Dominican Republic upon certain low-tide elevations as basepoints for archipelagic baselines. The UK and US asserted that these features were not above water at high tide and did not meet the particular requirements of Article 47.[141] In 2012, Timor-Leste

[137] See generally Baumert and Melchior (n 134) assessing recent US studies of archipelagic state practice.

[138] Roach and Smith (n 54) 208, referring to US protests following claims by Canada, Denmark, Ecuador, Portugal, Spain, and the UK.

[139] ibid 209.

[140] Law No 66–07 2007 (Dominican Republic); see S Kopela, '2007 Archipelagic Legislation of the Dominican Republic: An Assessment' (2009) 24 *International Journal of Marine and Coastal Law* 501.

[141] 'Text of a Joint Demarche Undertaken by the United Kingdom of Great Britain and Northern Ireland and the United States of America in relation to the Law of the Dominican Republic Number 66-07 of 22 May 2007, Done on 18 October 2007' (2008) 66 *Law of the Sea Bulletin* 98–99, which also asserts that as the turning points relied upon 'do not qualify as turning points under article 47, paragraph 1, of the Convention, and that the Dominican Republic does not meet the other requirements of article 47 to be an archipelagic State'.

sought to raise its concerns with respect to aspects of Indonesia's archipelagic straight baseline system as they directly impacted upon its interests as a neighbouring State, particularly highlighting that Indonesia had not taken into account the provisions of Article 47(5) with respect to the Timor-Leste enclave of Oecussi and its access to the EEZ and high seas.[142]

There has also been some tension over the manner in which archipelagic States have sought to interpret their rights with respect to archipelagic waters. A Philippines declaration upon LOSC signature, and confirmed on ratification, regarding its interpretation of archipelagic status in a manner consistent with the Philippines Constitution and previous treaties ceding sovereign rights over the islands that compose the Philippines, has been particularly contentious.[143] The Philippines' Declaration provided:

> 7. The concept of archipelagic waters is similar to the concept of internal waters under the Constitution of the Philippines and removes straits connecting these waters with the economic zone or the high seas from the rights of foreign vessels to transit passage for international navigation.

A number of States responded to aspects of the Philippines' Declaration, including Australia, Bulgaria, the Ukraine and the Soviet Union. The US protested the Declaration in January 1986 as follows:

> The Government of the United States wishes to observe that, as generally understood in international law, including that reflected in the 1982 Law of the Sea Convention, the concept of internal waters differs significantly from the concept of archipelagic waters. Archipelagic waters are only those enclosed by properly drawn archipelagic baselines and are subject to the regimes of innocent passage and archipelagic sea lanes passage.[144]

In the *South China Sea* arbitration the Annex VII Tribunal considered the utilisation of straight archipelagic baselines by a State that had not proclaimed itself to be an archipelagic State for the purposes of Part IV. The issue was considered because of Chinese statements which could have been interpreted to suggest that the Spratly Islands in the South China Sea could be enclosed by a system of straight archipelagic baselines. The Tribunal observed that the use of straight archipelagic baselines is 'strictly controlled by the Convention' and that their use is limited to archipelagic States,[145] and that as China was principally a mainland Asian State it did not meet the definition of an archipelagic State. Notwithstanding that the Philippines is an archipelagic State, the Tribunal was also of the view that the

[142] Timor-Leste, Diplomatic Note NV/MIS/85/2012 (6 February 2012) www.un.org/Depts/los/LEGISLATIONANDTREATIES/PDFFILES/DEPOSIT/communicationsredeposit/mzn67_2009_tls.pdf.

[143] 'Declarations and Statements' at: www.un.org/Depts/los/convention_agreements/convention_declarations.htm.

[144] Roach and Smith (n 54) 214; see also the Australian protest of 3 August 1988 reproduced in (1992) 12 *Australian Year Book of International Law* 383.

[145] *South China Sea* (n 89) 236 [573].

Philippines could not declare archipelagic baselines around the Spratly Islands, as the ratio of water to land would 'greatly exceed 9:1 under any conceivable system of baselines.'[146] These comments are significant as they suggest that international courts and tribunals will take a strict approach towards the interpretation of LOSC Article 47. The Tribunal's position on this has been subsequently endorsed by a number of States in separate diplomatic notes to the UN Secretary-General with respect to submissions to the Commission on the Limits of the Continental Shelf regarding the South China Sea.[147]

D. Regulation of Navigation and Overflight

One of the principal goals of UNCLOS III, once agreement was reached on the definition of an archipelago, was to determine the regulation of navigation and overflight within archipelagic waters. As an archipelagic State was entitled to the same maritime zones beyond the territorial sea baselines as any other coastal State, navigation and overflight within the territorial sea and adjacent maritime zones were the same as for all States. As the LOSC provided that archipelagic States were able to claim sovereignty over the waters within the limits of their archipelagic baselines, which also extended to the air space,[148] the sovereignty of the archipelagic State was to be exercised in conformity with Part IV of the Convention, which made express allowance for a range of navigational and overflight regimes within archipelagic waters. In sum those regimes are:

- Innocent passage for the ships of all States within archipelagic waters; and
- ASLP for foreign ships and aircraft through designated sea lanes and air routes within archipelagic waters.

The various aspects of these regimes for navigation and overflight will now be considered.

(i) Innocent Passage within Archipelagic Waters

Innocent passage within archipelagic waters is the default navigation regime for those ships not otherwise undertaking ASLP. Article 53 makes clear that subject to certain exceptions, within archipelagic waters the ships of all States enjoy the

[146] ibid 237 [574].
[147] See Commission on the Limits of the Continental Shelf (CLCS), 'Outer limits of the continental shelf beyond 200 nautical miles from the baselines: Submissions to the Commission: Partial Submission by Malaysia in the South China Sea – diplomatic notes by US' (1 June 2020), Australia (23 July 2020), UK, France and Germany (16 September 2020), Japan (19 January 2021) and New Zealand (3 August 2021), at www.un.org/Depts/los/clcs_new/submissions_files/submission_mys_12_12_2019.html.
[148] LOSC (n 7) art 49.

right of innocent passage and that this right is to be applied in accordance with the relevant LOSC articles found in Part II dealing with innocent passage.[149] Therefore, for the purposes of navigation within archipelagic waters, the innocent passage regime effectively applies in the same way as it does within the territorial sea. Hence ships of all States have the right of passage through archipelagic waters irrespective of whether they are calling at a local port, or simply passing through from an entry to an exit point, provided that the passage is innocent and not prejudicial to the peace, good order and security of the archipelagic State and in conformity with any relevant laws and regulations the archipelagic State may have adopted. In this respect all of the relevant aspects of the innocent passage regime that generally apply within the territorial sea of a coastal State also apply within archipelagic waters.[150]

Innocent passage within archipelagic waters is therefore essentially identical to that enjoyed within the territorial sea, subject to two qualifications that are distinctive to an archipelagic State.[151] First, like the innocent passage regime within the territorial sea, the archipelagic State may temporarily suspend innocent passage within specified areas of its archipelagic waters 'if such suspension is essential for the protection of its security'.[152] There is a minor variation in the wording between Article 52(2) and the equivalent Part II provision for coastal States in Article 25(3) that adds the words 'including weapons exercises'; however, this omission is more than likely a drafting oversight and unlikely to place any particular limitations on the archipelagic State in this regard. Such suspension is to only take effect after having been duly published. Accordingly, an archipelagic State may from time to time, and with appropriate notice, completely close areas of its archipelagic waters to international shipping. The LOSC places few limitations on this right other than it be non-discriminatory, and a temporal and notification requirement. This provides the archipelagic State with considerable latitude in how it interprets this provision,[153] including its capacity to suspend navigation in waters which are at

[149] LOSC (n 7) arts 17–32.

[150] See the detailed discussion in DR Rothwell and T Stephens, *The International Law of the Sea* (2nd edn, Hart Publishing 2016) 229–39; JE Noyes, 'The Territorial Sea and Contiguous Zone' in DR Rothwell, AG Oude Elferink, KN Scott and T Stephens (eds), *The Oxford Handbook of the Law of the Sea* (Oxford University Press 2015) 91, 98–102.

[151] This is made clear by LOSC (n 7) art 52(1) which states that the right of innocent passage is '[s]ubject to article 53 [right of archipelagic sea lanes passage] and without prejudice to article 50 [delimitation of internal waters]'. In the case of Indonesia, 'Government Regulation No 37 on the Rights and Obligations of Foreign Ships and Aircraft Exercising the Right of Archipelagic Sea Lanes Passage through Designated Sea Lanes (28 June 2002)' (2003) 52 *Law of the Sea Bulletin* 20, art 13 contemplates the exercise of the right of innocent passage within an archipelagic sea lane.

[152] LOSC (n 7) art 52(2).

[153] The equivalent provision in LOSC (n 7) art 25(3) provides that the coastal state may temporarily suspend innocent passage 'if such suspension is essential for the protection of its security, including weapons exercises'. The omission of a reference to weapons exercises in art 52(2) does not appear significant; for examples of relevant state practice see UN Division of Ocean Affairs and Law of the Sea 'Suspension of innocent passage', at: https://www.un.org/Depts/los/convention_agreements/innocent_passages_suspension.htm.

a considerable distance from any of the islands that fall within archipelagic baselines. Given the history of internal security issues in Indonesia, the Philippines, and the Solomon Islands,[154] and the particular dynamic of varying security challenges arising within and amongst the multiple islands and their populations that make up an archipelago, the capacity of an archipelagic State to suspend innocent passage on security grounds is an important entitlement. Secondly, the innocent passage regime is without prejudice to the ability of the archipelagic State to draw closing lines for the delimitation of internal waters within the archipelago.[155] Nevertheless, innocent passage may still be enjoyed between archipelagic waters and the internal waters of the archipelago where a ship is proceeding to or from those internal waters, such as in the case of a port facility.[156]

In addition to the right of innocent passage within archipelagic waters, innocent passage also applies within the territorial sea of an archipelagic State, which lies on the seaward side of the normal baselines and archipelagic baselines. Therefore, foreign ships which enter into the territorial sea of an archipelagic State would enjoy an ongoing right of innocent passage as they passed from the territorial sea into archipelagic waters and then passed through the archipelago back out into the territorial sea as part of a continuous journey.

Some archipelagic States have sought to legislate so as to recognise the right of innocent passage within archipelagic waters, including Antigua and Barbuda,[157] Bahamas,[158] Cape Verde,[159] Comoros,[160] the Dominican Republic,[161] Grenada,[162] Indonesia,[163] Kiribati,[164] Mauritius,[165] the Solomon Islands,[166] the Seychelles,[167] Trinidad and Tobago,[168] Tuvalu,[169] and Vanuatu.[170] In some instances these States have indicated that prior permission or notification is required for the passage

[154] For example, internal security within the Solomon Islands became so fragile that between 2003 and 2017 a 'Regional Assistance Mission to the Solomon Islands' (RAMSI) was deployed to assist the Solomon Islands to restore internal stability and security.

[155] LOSC (n 7) arts 50, 52(1).

[156] Using the language and the provisions found in LOSC (n 7) art 18(1)(b).

[157] Maritime Areas Act 1982 (Act No 18) (Antigua and Barbuda).

[158] An Act respecting the territorial sea, archipelagic waters, internal waters and the exclusive economic zone 1993 (Act No 37) Bahamas).

[159] Law No 60/IV/92 of 21 December 1992 (Cape Verde).

[160] Law No 82-005 relating to the delimitation of the maritime zones of the Islamic Federal Republic of the Comoros of 6 May 1982 (Comoros).

[161] Law No 66-07 of 22 May 2007 (Dominican Republic).

[162] Chapter 318 Territorial Sea and Maritime Boundaries Act 1989 (Act No 25) (Grenada).

[163] Act of the Republic Regarding Indonesian Waters (Act No 6 of 1996) (Indonesia).

[164] Marine Zones (Declaration) Act 2011 (Kiribati).

[165] Maritime Zones Act 2005 (Mauritius).

[166] Delimitation of Marine Waters Act 1978 (Act No 32) (Solomon Islands).

[167] Maritime Zones Act 1999 (Act No 2) (Seychelles).

[168] Archipelagic Waters and Exclusive Economic Zone Act (Act No 24) (Trinidad and Tobago).

[169] Maritime Zones Act 2012 (Tuvalu).

[170] Maritime Zones Act 2010 (Act No 6) (Vanuatu).

of *warships* through archipelagic waters,[171] which has provoked protests from the US.[172]

(ii) Archipelagic Sea Lanes Passage

The most significant distinctive navigational regime that applies within archipelagic waters is ASLP, which is outlined in Article 53 but which borrows heavily from the LOSC Part III transit passage regime, even to the extent of applying some of the provisions of the transit passage regime *mutatis mutandis*.[173] Within archipelagic sea lanes all ships and aircraft enjoy a right of ASLP.[174] The right is one that can be exercised for the purpose of 'continuous, expeditious and unobstructed transit' between one part of the high seas or an EEZ and another part of the high seas or an EEZ,[175] and extends from a territorial sea entry point, through archipelagic waters, to a territorial sea exit point.[176] ASLP duplicates key aspects of the transit passage regime within international straits in that it is designed to facilitate the passage of both ships and aircraft through and over the waters of the archipelagic State so that they can freely move through the archipelago as they continue their journey. In this respect, emphasis is given to the regime being one which promotes continuous and expeditious transit. Vessels that interrupt their navigation to call at a port within archipelagic waters therefore do not exercise ASLP, but rather revert to the innocent passage regime noted above.[177]

(a) Navigation and Overflight in the 'Normal Mode'

Ships and aircraft are to exercise ASLP in the 'normal mode' with Article 39 from the transit passage regime applied *mutatis mutandis* (by virtue of Article 54). This can raise significant issues, especially in the case of foreign warships,[178] where an

[171] See s 14(2), Maritime Areas Act 1982 (Act No 18) (Antigua and Barbuda); s 16(2) Maritime Zones Act 1999 (Act No 2) (Seychelles); s 5 Maritime Zones Act No 6 of 2010 (Vanuatu).

[172] Department of State (US), *Antigua and Barbuda: Archipelagic and Other Maritime Claims and Boundaries (Limits in the Sea No 133)* (Department of State 2014) 3–4; Department of State (US), *Seychelles: Archipelagic and Other Maritime Claims and Boundaries (Limits in the Sea No 132)* (Department of State 2014) 6.

[173] ibid art 54.

[174] LOSC (n 7) art 53(2). Writing in 1991, B Kwiatkowska and ER Agoes, *Archipelagic Waters Regime in the Light of the 1982 United Nations Law of the Sea Convention and State Practice* (ICLOS, UNPAD 1991) 43 asserted that the right of 'non-suspendable archipelagic sea lanes passage of all ships and aircraft, … is alongside with the innocent passage of warships the most controversial element of [sic] archipelagic state regime'.

[175] LOSC (n 7) art 53(3).

[176] ibid art 53(4).

[177] ibid art 38(2), which anticipates a vessel or aircraft in transit passage entering, leaving or returning from a State which borders a strait, does not have an equivalent provision in the ASLP regime. This is understandable given that within archipelagic waters there exists a mixed regime of innocent passage for some ships and ASLP for other ships.

[178] Kwiatkowska and Agoes (n 174) 44, 54; Munavvar (n 6) 168. Upon its signature of the LOSC in 1983, Sao Tome and Principe lodged a LOSC (n 7) art 310 declaration which in part provided: 'The

archipelagic State may have a legitimate sensitivity to the presence of such ships within its archipelagic waters. Likewise, it is arguable that because ASLP along an archipelagic sea lane may be a lengthy voyage that could take many hours and even days, 'normal modes' of operation for warships should be allowed a more flexible interpretation, especially in the case of submarines and aircraft carriers.[179] In any event, normal modes of operation for warships and many foreign military aircraft would permit the gathering of data and other intelligence while passage was taking place.

(b) Navigation and Overflight within Archipelagic Sea Lanes

Unlike the transit passage regime, where the coastal State has little capacity to influence where ships and aircraft exercise the right of transit other than in designated sea lanes, the right of ASLP is one by which the LOSC conferred significant capacity upon the archipelagic State so as to designate sea lanes within which ASLP can be exercised. However, it is important to note that an archipelagic State 'may designate sea lanes and air routes thereabove'[180] and as such there is no *requirement* to do so. There is also a linkage between sea lanes and air routes, with the latter located above the sea lanes. Designated sea lanes and air routes must include 'all normal passage routes used as routes for international navigation and overflight' and in the case of ships 'all normal navigational channels'.[181] Recognising that the waters within many archipelagic States would previously have been either high seas, or straits within which a right of international navigation prevailed, the clear intent of the LOSC is to preserve these previously existing navigation routes, and this is emphasised by the repeated use of the word 'normal' in the context of the passage routes and channels. This key provision as to where ASLP may be enjoyed sought to retain the status quo with respect to navigation routes that existed through some of the major archipelagos prior to the conclusion of the LOSC. Accordingly, for principal Indonesian straits such as Sunda and Lombok, the entry into force of ASLP provisions did not have a major impact upon traditional navigation routes. Nevertheless, irregularly used routes such as those which may be selected by foreign yachts undertaking a pleasure cruise through an archipelago would not fall into the category of a 'normal' route. The inclusion in archipelagic sea lanes of 'all

Government of the Democratic Republic of Sao Tome and Principe reserves the right to adopt laws and regulations relating to the innocent passage of warships through its territorial sea or its archipelagic waters and to take any other measures aimed at safeguarding its security': United Nations Division for Ocean Affairs and the Law of the Sea, 'Declarations and Statements' www.un.org/Depts/los/convention_agreements/convention_declarations.htm.

[179] BH Oxman, 'Transit of Straits and Archipelagic Waters by Military Aircraft' (2000) 4 *Singapore Journal of International and Comparative Law* 377, 393 observed that 'certain maritime powers, such as the United States regarded the inclusion … of the clause "in the normal mode" … as an important reminder regarding the operation of naval task forces employing defensive screens, evasive tactics, air cover and submerged submarines through the vast areas involved.'

[180] LOSC (n 7) art 53(1).

[181] ibid art 53(4).

normal navigational channels' is subject to an exception arising in the case where there may have previously existed a number of duplicate routes of similar convenience. The effect here is that only one sea lane is required for designation within any one particular body of water. In addition, the designation of particular sea lanes may also need to take into account interactions between foreign ships undertaking ASLP, and local commercial navigation moving within the archipelago.[182]

(c) Designation of Archipelagic Sea Lanes

Article 53 of the LOSC envisages that the archipelagic State will designate sea lanes consistent with the procedures provided for in the Convention. However, in recognition that sea lanes may not have been designated, there is a default provision that ASLP 'may be exercised through the routes normally used for international navigation'.[183] Not only could this be relied upon in instances where an archipelagic State delays its designation of sea lanes or air routes after becoming bound by the LOSC, but it also applies where an archipelagic State either refuses to designate sea lanes or is content to accept the default position imposed by the LOSC. Whilst these provisions guarantee an ongoing right of ASLP through an archipelago even in the absence of sea lanes designation, there is the potential for varying interpretations as to what are the routes which have been 'normally used for international navigation' through an archipelago. At the major entry and exit points into the archipelago, which in most instances would be straits, it will be possible to rely upon previous state practice. However, in the case of some declared and recognised archipelagic States, there may be little clear state practice as to which navigation routes have previously been utilised, due to the fact that these waters would formerly have been high seas and there would have been minimal obligations upon international shipping to use any particular route.[184]

It is therefore clearly beneficial for an archipelagic State to designate sea lanes and air routes, which are to be identified by a series of continuous axis lines from entry to exit points throughout the archipelago, and are to be clearly indicated on charts to which due publicity shall have been given.[185] Both ships and aircraft are required not to deviate more than 25 nm either side of the axis lines, with the effect that a sea lane may be up to 50 nm in width, subject to constraints which may be imposed by islands or navigational hazards.[186] However, archipelagic waters

[182] JL Batongbacal, 'Barely Skimming the Surface: Archipelagic Sea Lanes Navigation and the IMO' in AG Oude Elferink and DR Rothwell (eds), *Oceans Management in the 21st Century: Institutional Frameworks and Responses* (Martinus Nijhoff 2004) 49, 65.

[183] LOSC (n 7) art 53(12). In contrast to LOSC, art 53(4) the words 'or overflight' are not included in LOSC, art 53(12), leading to some ambiguity, however as the paragraph also refers to the failure of the archipelagic State to 'designate … air routes' the necessary implication is that the provision also extends to air routes used for overflight as well as sea lanes.

[184] Munavvar (n 6) 168.

[185] LOSC (n 7) art 53(10).

[186] ibid art 53(5).

may contain islands of varying size and in some instances these inner islands may impinge upon the corridor within which ASLP can be exercised. In recognition of the sovereign interests of the archipelagic State, LOSC Article 53(5) provides that ships and aircraft are to not navigate closer to the coasts than 10 per cent of the distance between the nearest points of the islands bordering the sea lane. Accordingly, if adjacent islands are 10 nm distant from each other and a sea lane passes between them, then shipping may navigate no closer to the islands than 1 nm, which in turn narrows the breadth of the sea lane to only 8 nm. In addition to the designation of archipelagic sea lanes, the archipelagic State may also designate traffic separation schemes for the safe passage of ships through 'narrow channels' in the sea lanes.[187] This has particular relevance in the case where a sea lane has been considerably narrowed as a result of islands within the archipelago and application of the 10 per cent rule.

(d) Obligations while Undertaking Archipelagic Sea Lanes Passage

Whilst LOSC Part IV outlines in some detail the ASLP regime, many of the rights, duties and obligations of both the user State and archipelagic State are left silent. The exception is Article 54, which makes clear that the provisions of Articles 39, 40, 42 and 44 apply *mutatis mutandis* to ASLP, which is a further reinforcement of the linkage between the transit passage and ASLP regimes. Accordingly, both ships and aircraft engaged in ASLP are required to proceed without delay and to refrain from any threat or use of force against the sovereignty or territorial integrity of the archipelagic State.[188] Article 39(1)(c) reinforces that passage is to be undertaken in the normal mode. Ships and aircraft also have obligations to comply with appropriate safety at sea and marine environmental provisions, while civil aircraft must comply with International Civil Aviation Organization (ICAO) Rules of the Air and state aircraft must have due regard to the safety of navigation, whilst also monitoring designated air traffic control authorities. Foreign ships engaged in ASLP are also not to undertake marine scientific research, including any survey activities, without prior authorisation.[189] There is likewise an obligation upon foreign ships and aircraft to comply with the relevant laws and regulations of the archipelagic State. In the case of ships these may deal with safety of navigation, pollution control, stowage of fishing gear, and activities contrary to customs, fiscal, immigration or sanitary laws and regulations.[190] That the same category of laws and regulations which apply to ships in transit passage also apply in ASLP

[187] ibid art 53(6).

[188] ibid art 39(1)(a)(b). This is reflected also in Indonesian law: Indonesian Government Regulation No 37 on the Rights and Obligations of Foreign Ships and Aircraft Exercising the Right of Archipelagic Sea Lanes Passage through Designated Sea Lanes, arts 4, 6.

[189] LOSC (n 7) art 40.

[190] LOSC (n 7) art 42(1). The safety of navigation and regulation of maritime traffic provisions cross-refer back to Article 41, which would also apply in the case of ASLP, which makes allowance for the possible designation of a traffic separation scheme within an archipelagic sea lane.

is a significant concession to international maritime traffic, given the comparative length of time ships may spend within archipelagic waters as opposed to the territorial sea whilst in transit passage. Of some note here is that no express provisions are included to deal with the case of warships, and like the Part III provisions dealing with transit passage, the ASLP provisions remain silent on whether any distinction can be made between warships and other ships exercising ASLP.[191]

(e) Obligations of the Archipelagic State

The obligations of the archipelagic State with respect to ASLP are likewise transposed from Article 44 within Part III and as such they are to not hamper transit passage, to give appropriate publicity to any danger of which they have knowledge, and not to suspend ASLP. These obligations upon the archipelagic State are further reinforced by the Article 53 reference to ASLP being 'unobstructed'. Accordingly, other than for permissible laws and regulations which the archipelagic State may enact consistent with the LOSC, an archipelagic State must permit ASLP to be enjoyed by all vessels and aircraft other than those not acting in conformity with their Article 39 obligations. In the latter case, such vessels or aircraft are not legitimately undertaking ASLP and could have their continued right of navigation or overflight revoked by intervention from the archipelagic State. The obligation to give publicity to any dangers to navigation and overflight is potentially significant, given the size of some archipelagic States, and is only qualified to the extent that it applies only to those dangers of which 'they have knowledge'. Both Indonesia and the Philippines have faced internal disruption as a result of the actions of insurgent groups and these have had the potential to pose dangers to navigation and overflight.[192] Since the 1990s there have also been pirate attacks within the waters of both archipelagos.[193] Not only do these events trigger obligations to warn, but may also result in the need to adjust sea lanes in order to ensure safe passage. Bearing in mind that ASLP cannot be suspended altogether, in the case of significant ongoing threats especially to ships, there may be a need to substitute designated sea lanes with other sea lanes on a temporary basis.[194]

[191] Under Indonesian Government Regulation No 37 on the Rights and Obligations of Foreign Ships and Aircraft Exercising the Right of Archipelagic Sea Lanes Passage through Designated Sea Lanes, art 4(4) purports to restrict the right of warships and aircraft engaged in ASLP from conducting war exercises. A further distinction exists with respect to submarine navigation, which whilst undertaking *innocent passage* is to navigate on the surface (LOSC, art 20), yet whilst engaged in *ASLP* can do so in 'normal mode'; see comment by Batongbacal, 'Barely Skimming the Surface' (n 182) 62.

[192] In the case of the Philippines these incidents have included the 2000 bombing of the inter-island ferry *MV Our Lady of Mediatrix*, and bombing of the *MV SuperFerry 14* in Manila Bay in 2004: MA Palma (n 129) 21.

[193] RA Witular, 'Java Sea, Lombok Strait Becoming More Dangerous, Government Says', *The Jakarta Post* (3 August 2005) 13; 'Pirates in South-East Asia: Malacca buccaneers', *The Economist* (June 27, 2015) 24.

[194] Some allowance is made for the need to substitute sea lanes in LOSC (n 7) art 53(7).

One of the clearest obligations which archipelagic States have with respect to ASLP is not to suspend passage and this duplicates a similar obligation of strait States with respect to transit passage within international straits. The obligation is significant. It means that at all times the waters within the archipelago will be subject to navigation and overflight through the sea lanes such that there may always be a foreign presence within the waters of the archipelagic State, especially if the archipelago sits in the midst of major shipping lanes. This dual nature of the non-suspendable ASLP regime and the suspendable innocent passage regime within archipelagic waters may result in confusion as to which regime applies in essentially the same body of water. This would especially be the case as ships engaging in innocent passage may legitimately have the need to enter and exit archipelagic waters via an archipelagic sea lane, or to intersect a sea lane whilst moving from one part of the archipelago to the other. In 1988 Indonesia temporarily closed the Sunda and Lombok Straits to navigation in order to conduct weapons exercises. This action brought about diplomatic protests from several countries, including Australia, West Germany and the US.[195] Whilst at the time Indonesia had ratified the LOSC, the Convention had yet to enter into force, creating challenges in assessing the content of Indonesia's obligations under both treaty law and customary international law to give effect to the ASLP regime. Whilst Indonesia has not attempted to close passage through these or other straits in recent years, this incident did highlight the sensitivity associated with how the LOSC sought to balance the interests of maritime States wanting to maintain the freedom of navigation in the Convention with the rights and interests of archipelagic States.[196]

(f) State Practice Designating Archipelagic Sea Lanes

An important aspect of the operationalisation of the ASLP regime in Part IV is the designation of archipelagic sea lanes. No archipelagic State had designated sea lanes at the time of the Convention's 1994 entry into force, with the effect that the default provisions applied and ASLP was recognised through routes within those archipelagic States that were 'normally used for international navigation'.[197] Although in effect this resulted in ongoing application of the status quo within the major navigation routes through archipelagos, it did create the potential for disputes to arise between user States and archipelagic States as to what those routes actually were.

Soon after the entry into force of the LOSC, Indonesia began a process to designate archipelagic sea lanes. This created an immediate challenge, as Article 53 makes clear that there is no unilateral right of sea lanes designation and that the

[195] N Chanda and N Holloway, 'Troubled Waters: Indonesia's Neighbours Consider Responses to Closure of Straits', *Far Eastern Economic Review* (10 November 1988) 18.

[196] Rothwell, 'The Indonesian Straits Incident' (n 41) 491–506.

[197] LOSC (n 7) art 53(12).

archipelagic State is to 'refer proposals to the competent international organization with a view to their adoption'.[198] However, as archipelagic sea lanes were a creature of the LOSC there was no previous experience for any international organisation in the designation of such sea lanes, and the Convention did not create any new organisation to fulfil that task. In 1996 Indonesia proposed to the International Maritime Organization (IMO) the adoption of archipelagic sea lanes, and as this referral was not met with objection by other LOSC parties, it was clear that a consensus view had developed that the IMO was the most appropriate international organisation to fulfil this role.[199] At the IMO the Indonesian proposals were considered by the Maritime Safety Committee, and the Safety of Navigation Sub-Committee. Indonesia also held a series of bilateral meetings with key user States including Australia and the US.

With no previous experience in considering the LOSC archipelagic sea lanes provisions, the IMO determined the need for internal procedures to be devised for the designation process. This resulted in the 1998 adoption of the General Provisions on the Adoption, Designation and Substitution of Archipelagic Sea Lanes (GPASL). The GPASL not only sought to reflect the IMO experience in considering the Indonesian proposals, but were also designed to guide future deliberations under the Article 53 process.[200] The Philippines, however, made clear during the IMO deliberations that it did not consider the GPASL to represent a precedent for future archipelagic sea lane designations.[201] Some of the main issues which arose with the Indonesian proposal were concerns expressed by major maritime States as to the direction of the sea lanes, and whether there were adequate North South and East-West sea lanes under consideration. In addition, there were issues as to the interpretation of the 10 per cent rule, the role of the ICAO with respect to overflight of the sea lanes, and whether the designated sea lanes could be subject to subsequent variation or modification. Following eventual IMO endorsement in 1998, Indonesia proclaimed archipelagic sea lanes. However, an understanding was reached with major user States such as Australia and the US that ASLP could continue to be exercised throughout routes normally used for international navigation.[202] Indonesia therefore completed a partial archipelagic sea lanes designation and there remain other 'routes normally used for international navigation' within Indonesian waters in which ASLP rights apply. Accordingly, user States are able to rely upon an interpretation of Article 53(12) to support their ongoing use of routes through the Indonesian archipelago which they previously used for

[198] LOSC (n 7) art 53(9).

[199] R Balkin, 'The Role of the International Maritime Organization in the Settlement of International Disputes' in DR Rothwell and S Bateman (eds), *Navigational Rights and Freedoms and the New Law of the Sea* (Martinus Nijhoff 2000) 293, 310–13.

[200] R Warner, 'Implementing the Archipelagic Regime in the International Maritime Organization' in Rothwell and Bateman (n 199) 170, 174.

[201] Batongbacal, 'Barely Skimming the Surface' (n 182) 58.

[202] Warner (n 200) 176–84.

international navigation. As the first archipelagic State to designate archipelagic sea lanes consistent with the processes outlined in LOSC Article 53, Indonesia adopted in 2002 Government Regulation No 37 dealing with the rights and obligations of foreign ships and aircraft in passage.[203] The Indonesian Regulation directly refers to ASLP by foreign ships and aircraft as a right recognised under Indonesian law by Act No 6 regarding Indonesian Waters.[204]

In the Philippines, the House of Representatives and Senate have debated versions of a 'Philippines Archipelagic Sea Lanes Act' since 2015. Passage of this law would permit the declaration of archipelagic sea lanes. As of 2021, no Philippines archipelagic sea lanes had been declared consistent with the Article 53 and IMO procedures noted above.[205] Matters to be considered by the Philippines as a part of the process of declaring archipelagic sea lanes include assessing the already existing routes which are currently being used for international navigation, the existing multiple internal routes used for domestic trade and transport, and maritime safety and security.[206] A number of other archipelagic States have enacted laws and regulations that allow for the designation of archipelagic sea lanes and related air routes but none have formally been designated by way of the IMO GPASL process.[207]

VIII. Conclusions

The archipelagic State regime was one of the most significant achievements of UNCLOS III. It gave legal recognition to the political, economic and social entitlements of peoples of archipelagic nations, many of which only emerged as independent States following 1945. Nevertheless, the LOSC Part IV definition of an archipelagic State has been described by Crawford as 'arbitrary' and 'amounts to discrimination and is a deviation from formal equality under international law'.[208]

[203] Indonesian Government Regulation No 37 on the Rights and Obligations of Foreign Ships and Aircraft Exercising the Right of Archipelagic Sea Lanes Passage through Designated Sea Lanes (28 June 2002) (2003) 52 *Law of the Sea Bulletin* 20.

[204] Act No 6 of 8 August 1996 regarding Indonesian Waters (Indonesia); see also ibid art 2.

[205] F Principe Gamboa and J Teodoro, 'The role of archipelagic sea lanes in the Philippines' national security' (*Philippine Strategic Forum*, 30 November 2020) www.stratforumph.com/post/the-role-of-archipelagic-sea-lanes-in-the-philippines-national-security.

[206] Palma, 'The Philippines as an Archipelagic and Maritime Nation' (n 129) 7–9.

[207] See eg Maritime Areas Act 1982 (Act No 18) (Antigua and Barbuda) s 20C; An Act respecting the territorial sea, archipelagic waters, internal waters and the exclusive economic zone 1993 (Act No 37) (Bahamas) s 11; Chapter 318 Territorial Sea and Maritime Boundaries Act 1989 (Act No 25) (Grenada) s 20; Marine Zones (Declaration) Act 2011 (Kiribati) s 12; Maritime Zones Act 2005 (Mauritius) s 10; Delimitation of Marine Waters Act 1978 (Act No 32) (Solomon Islands) s 10; Maritime Zones Act 1999 (Act No 2) (Seychelles) s 19; Archipelagic Waters and Exclusive Economic Zone Act 1986 (Act No 24) (Trinidad and Tobago) s 32; Maritime Zones Act 2012 (Tuvalu) s 16(1)(a).

[208] J Crawford, *Chance, Order, Change: The Course of International Law* (Brill 2014) 326 [421]; see also O'Connell (n 34) 256.

Aspects of this critique are highlighted in the case of dependent archipelagos which are considered in the following chapter.

While there is an inevitable and appropriate focus on the largest archipelagic States such as Indonesia and the Philippines, it also needs to be recognised that smaller States such as the Marshall Islands and Tuvalu have also benefitted from recognition as an archipelagic State. There are only 22 generally recognised archipelagic States meaning that there is limited state practice with respect to the interpretation of LOSC Part IV. The ICJ in *Qatar v Bahrain*, and the *South China Sea* arbitration highlighted legal and political sensitivities associated with the declaration of de facto archipelagic State status or Article 47 archipelagic baselines. Generally, the declared archipelagic States have adhered to the constraints of Article 47 in their drawing of straight archipelagic baselines. In some instances declarations of archipelagic State status have been contested due to the manner in which Article 47 baselines have been drawn, as in the case of the Dominican Republic. There have also been related issues with respect to competing territorial claims to islands that compose an archipelago, as in the case of Mauritius and its claim to the Chagos Archipelago. The highly sensitive issue of navigational rights and freedoms and the mixed LOSC innocent passage/ASLP regime within archipelagic waters has also not proven to be particularly contentious. In this regard, the exercise of navigational rights and freedoms through archipelagos that straddle major shipping routes has been the focal point of attention for the major maritime nations and there have been no significant issues for international navigation through the Philippines or Indonesian archipelagic waters.

While there have only been limited opportunities for international courts and tribunals to assess aspects of the LOSC Part IV regime, when they have done so a strict approach has been adopted. This suggests that international courts and tribunals are concerned to limit archipelagic State status and entitlements to only those States which meet the geographic, maritime, and political criteria laid down in Articles 46 and 47. The stated criteria for a juridical archipelago on the basis of state practice and that of international courts and tribunals have generally been interpreted within the spirit of the LOSC and the intentions of its negotiators. However, it needs to be kept in mind that the capacity of island nations to claim entitlements as an archipelagic State under LOSC Part IV may attract new archipelagic claimants in the future and, as such, archipelagic State practice will potentially evolve with the emergence of new States.

6

Dependent Archipelagos

I. Introduction

Archipelagos have a special status in international law and the law of the sea because of the regime created for archipelagic States in the LOSC.[1] As outlined in Chapter five, this creates a unique set of international law rules applicable to archipelagic States that encompasses not only their status under the law of the sea but also gives them a distinctive standing under international law. An archipelagic State comprises archipelagos and encompasses islands and parts of islands,[2] but not all archipelagos will be part of an archipelagic State. There are numerous illustrations of such island groups that do not form an archipelagic State, including the Aaland Islands (Finland), the Bijagos Archipelago (Guinea-Bissau), the Dahlak Archipelago (Eritrea), the Hawaiian islands (US), the Ryukyu islands (Japan), and Svalbard (Norway). All of these features, irrespective of how they are named, are unquestionably archipelagos, but they do not have any distinctive legal status as archipelagos in international law as they do not constitute an archipelagic State. Rather, as they are associated with mainland and island States, they simply possess the status of islands under international law and the LOSC without having the entitlement of a juridical archipelago. While the LOSC Part VIII regime of islands is of importance for the status of these features, that regime predominantly relates to the maritime entitlements of the islands as individual islands rather than island groups.

This raises for consideration the status of features that are archipelagos – but not LOSC Article 46 juridical archipelagos – and what distinctive international law issues may arise with respect to these features, especially under the law of the sea. These islands have increasingly become referred to as dependent archipelagos. The issues arising with respect to dependent archipelagos are amply illustrated by how LOSC Article 7 refers to a fringe of islands with respect to the potential drawing of straight baselines. Clearly, there is the potential that a fringe of islands adjacent to a coast may be an archipelago and as such have implications for how a coastal State may be able to draw straight baselines. There are also

[1] United Nations Convention on the Law of the Sea (adopted 10 December 1982, entered into force 16 November 1994) 1833 UNTS 397 (LOSC) pt IV.

[2] ibid art 46.

examples from state practice, where some coastal States seek to draw straight baselines around archipelagos, that reflect a hybrid approach blending aspects of LOSC Article 7 and Article 47 straight baselines. These approaches have been the subject of comment by international courts and tribunals.[3] The purpose of this chapter is to assess these issues by focussing first on the relevant maritime geography, law and political status of dependent archipelagos. Detailed consideration will then be given to baselines, before an assessment of maritime entitlements. Illustrative examples of relevant state practice will also be assessed before drawing conclusions.

II. Characterisation

A. Geography

An archipelago may be defined as a: 'Group of islands; a sea containing many scattered small islands.'[4] This suggests three important dimensions. The first is that there must be more than one island. To constitute an archipelago three or more islands would appear to be a minimum requirement, although a group of two islands together with associated rocks and reefs may be named an archipelago, in which case much would depend on the number of such associated maritime features. The second dimension is that the islands are located in the sea, beyond internal waters which could include waters immediately adjacent to the coast, the territorial sea and other coastal State maritime zones. Island groups that have historically been located within internal waters pre-dating the LOSC,[5] or located within a delta system,[6] are therefore excluded. The third requirement is that there is some level of proximity between the islands so they are in some manner interconnected. How closely clustered the islands of an archipelago may be will depend upon multiple variables, including whether the islands are close to a mainland or whether they are mid-ocean islands. Care needs to be exercised, however, in placing too much emphasis upon particular names that have been given to groups of islands referred to as an 'Archipelago'. A great range of titles have been given to groups of islands with no uniformity in how the descriptive noun has been used.[7] Likewise, as was also observed in the preparatory

[3] See eg *In the Matter of the South China Sea Arbitration before an Arbitral Tribunal constituted under Annex VII of the 1982 United Nations Convention on the Law of the Sea (Philippines v China)* (Merits) (12 July 2016) PCA Case 2013-19, 237 [575] (*South China Sea*).

[4] M Allaby, *A Dictionary of Geology and Earth Sciences* (5th edn, Oxford University Press 2020).

[5] The Gulf Islands, British Colombia (Canada) and the San Juan Islands, Washington (US) located within the Strait of Georgia fall into this category.

[6] The islands forming the Mouths of the Ganges (Bangladesh/India) fall into this category.

[7] This is illustrated by how the Admiralty Islands (Papua New Guinea) sit within the Bismarck Archipelago (Papua New Guinea).

documents for the 1958 First United Nations Conference on the Law of the Sea: 'One glance at the map is sufficient to show that the geographical characteristics of archipelagos vary widely.'[8]

B. Law

The legal definition of a *dependent* archipelago encompasses two dimensions. The first is the status of the islands and whether they are recognised in law as an archipelago. While guidance can clearly be taken from LOSC Article 46, it needs to be recalled that the definition sets a high threshold for the purposes of determining the existence of an archipelagic State.[9] Nevertheless, the distinction provided for between Article 46(a) – which focusses on the existence of the 'State' – and Article 46(b) which emphasises geographic characteristics is helpful. Article 46(b) states that 'an archipelago' means:

> a group of islands, including parts of islands, interconnecting waters and other natural features which are so closely inter-related that such islands, waters and other natural features form an intrinsic geographical, economic and political entity, or which have historically been regarded as such.

This definition gives emphasis to the territorial dimension of the islands including connected natural features, the waters between them, and associated economic, historical, and political features. In that regard, the fact that a group of islands has historically been regarded as an archipelago and has been referred to as such is important. Here a distinction in law can be made between a LOSC Article 46 archipelago and a LOSC Article 7 fringe of islands. Adjacency is also a critical factor. Hodgson and Alexander have observed that '[i]f the islands, islets, or rocks are located a considerable distance from each other, then the inter-island waters are hardly "adjacent" to the land.'[10] For the purposes of this analysis, it is important to distinguish between some of the historical legal studies conducted on so-called 'mid-ocean archipelagos' and those under consideration here.[11] Mid-ocean archipelagos were studied because of their potential to have a distinctive legal regime, and they have been duly recognised as such under LOSC Part IV.[12]

[8] United Nations Conference on the Law of the Sea, 'Certain Legal Aspects Concerning the Delimitation of the Territorial Waters of Archipelagos' vol 1 (Preparatory Document No 15, 27 November 1957) UN Doc. A/CONF.13/18, 290.

[9] See the discussion in Chapter 5, section VI of this volume.

[10] RD Hodgson and LM Alexander, *Towards an Objective Analysis of Special Circumstances: Bays, Rivers, Coastal and Oceanic Archipelagos and Atolls* (Occasional Paper No 13, Law of the Sea Institute, University of Rhode Island 1972) 45.

[11] See discussion in DP O'Connell, 'Mid-Ocean Archipelagos in International Law' (1971) 45 *British Yearbook of International Law* 1; see also DP O'Connell, *The International Law of the Sea*, vol I (Clarendon Press 1982) 236–58.

[12] For the use of the term in the context of an archipelagic State see P Tangsubkul and DJ Dzurek, 'The Emerging Concept of Midocean Archipelagos' (1982) 3 *Ocean Yearbook* 386; and generally B Hart Dubner, *The Law of Territorial Waters of Mid-Ocean Archipelagos and Archipelagic States* (Martinus Nijhoff 1976).

However, as noted in Chapter five there are only 22 recognised archipelagic States, with the result that there remain many archipelagos that do not enjoy that status for some of the reasons noted above.[13] It therefore seems appropriate to retain the use of the geographic descriptor of a 'dependent mid-ocean archipelago' in distinction to a juridical Part IV archipelago.

C. Political Status

The political status of the islands and their connection with a State are critical for the purposes of determining the existence of a dependent archipelago. Setting aside archipelagos that make up a LOSC Article 46 archipelagic State, a dependent archipelago may include:

- An archipelago that is close to the mainland of its coastal State (Aaland Islands, Finland);
- An archipelago that is distant from the mainland of its coastal State (Faroe Islands, Denmark);
- An archipelago that is close to the main island/islands of an island State (Bay of Islands, New Zealand); and,
- An archipelago that is distant from the main islands/island of an island State (New Hebrides, UK)

These archipelagos may in turn have their own distinctive status as sub-units in the relevant political system of the State, as in the case of the Falkland/Malvinas Islands (UK/Argentina), Hawaii (US), and New Caledonia (France). The political status of the islands is equally as important as their characterisation as archipelagos, as this will impact upon the manner in which the State views the islands and any particular economic and political status they are granted.

D. Multiple Forms of Dependent Archipelagos

A dependent archipelago may take a number of forms. The island group may be close to a mainland coast, distant from a mainland coast, or may itself be associated with an island State. The size, population, economic importance, and social and political history of the islands will all be factors as to how the State views the significance of the islands. However, what is clear is that the development of the law of the sea and the recognition that islands can generate significant maritime entitlements has increased their legal and political importance.[14]

[13] Examples include the Åland Islands (Finland), Andaman and Nicobar Islands (India), and Falkland/Malvinas Islands (UK/Argentina).

[14] V Prescott and C Schofield, *The Maritime Political Boundaries of the World* (2nd edn, Martinus Nijhoff 2005) 57.

The name given to the islands will not be decisive, as there are many examples of island groups that meet the geographic criteria of an archipelago but do not bear that name. Nevertheless, some historic association between the islands that constitute the archipelago and the peoples of the islands may be a factor in how they are viewed.

For the purposes of the analysis that follows it seems appropriate to characterise the features under consideration as:

- Dependent coastal archipelagos – an archipelago that is close to the mainland of its coastal State, eg Dampier Archipelago, Australia; or
- Dependent mid-ocean archipelagos – an archipelago that is distant from the mainland of its coastal State, eg Arquipélago dos Açores (Azores) Portugal.

III. Baselines

The principal issue that arises with respect to baselines is the potential for a State to draw straight baselines around a dependent archipelago. The LOSC recognises the capacity of a coastal State to utilise three types of baselines:

1. Normal baseline (low-water mark): Article 5
2. Straight baseline: Article 7
3. Archipelagic baseline: Article 47

Additional factors that can be taken into account include baselines with respect to reefs (Article 6), bays (Article 10), and low-tide elevations (Article 13).[15] For the purposes of this analysis, attention will be given to straight baselines and archipelagic baselines.

A. Straight Baselines

A key issue with respect to dependent archipelagos is how LOSC Article 7 straight baselines may be drawn from the coast to the islands. The key points when considering the Article 7 rule in this context are that:

- There is a fringe of islands along the coast (Article 7(1));
- The straight baselines must not depart to any appreciable extent from the general direction of the coastline (Article 7(3));

[15] For an assessment by the International Law Association of the legal issues with these baselines, see CG Lathrop, JA Roach, and DR Rothwell (eds), *Baselines under the International Law of the Sea: Reports of the International Law Association Committee on Baselines under the International Law of the Sea* (Brill 2018) 2.1–2 The Law of the Sea 1 (*ILA Report*).

- The waters lying within the baselines must be sufficiently linked to the land domain so as to be subject to the regime of internal waters (Article 7(3)); and
- The drawing of straight baselines may take into account the economic circumstances peculiar to the region (Article 7(5).

The application of this rule with respect to dependent archipelagos raises issues with respect to three distinct geographic issues: a fringe of islands, a coastal archipelago, and a mid-ocean archipelago.[16]

(i) Fringe of Islands

The International Court of Justice (ICJ) in the *Fisheries Case*[17] considered and upheld a system used by Norway of drawing straight baselines along the islands of the Norwegian *skjærgaard*[18] that form a barrier between the mainland and Atlantic Ocean.[19] This decision in turn had an impact upon the work of the International Law Commission on the law of the sea, and was reflected in the 1958 Convention on the Territorial Sea and Contiguous Zone.[20] That background formed the basis for LOSC Article 7 with respect to both deeply indented coastlines and fringing islands.

That LOSC Article 7(1) contemplates the drawing of straight baselines where there is a fringe of islands has raised a number of issues. The first is characterisation. In 1989 the United Nations Office for Ocean Affairs and the Law of the Sea published a study on baselines (1989 UN Study) that explains several terms in Article 7.[21] As to the characterisation of a fringe of islands, the 1989 UN Study

[16] See also the classification employed in M Munavvar, *Ocean States: Archipelagic Regimes in the Law of the Sea* (Martinus Nijhoff 1995) 14–45; HW Jayewardene, *The Regime of Islands in International Law* (Martinus Nijhoff 1990) 63–78.

[17] *Fisheries Case (United Kingdom v Norway)* (Judgment) [1951] ICJ Reps 116 (*Fisheries Case*).

[18] Which the Court also referred to as a 'rock rampart': ibid 127. For O'Connell's assessment of the significance of this aspect of the decision for islands and archipelagos see O'Connell, 'Mid-Ocean Archipelagos' (n 11) 14–16.

[19] The ICJ observed with respect to the *skjærgaard* that: 'The number of insular formations, large and small, which make up the "skjærgaard", is estimated by the Norwegian Govenment to be one hundred and twenty thousand. … Within the "skjærgaard", almost every island has its large and its small bays; countless arms of the sea, straits, channels and mere waterways serve as a means of communication for the local population which inhabits the islands as it does the mainland. The coast of the mainland does not constitute, as it does in practically all other countries, a clear dividing line between land and sea. What matters, what really constitutes the Norwegian coast line, is the outer line of the "skjærgaard"': *Fisheries Case* (n 17) 127.

[20] Convention on the Territorial Sea and Contiguous Zone (adopted 29 April 1958, entered into force 10 September 1964) 516 UNTS 206 art 4.

[21] United Nations Office for Ocean Affairs and the Law of the Sea, *Baselines: An Examination of the Relevant Provisions of the United Nations Convention on the Law of the Sea* (UN 1989) (*1989 UN Study*); the UN study was subject to review by a Group of Technical Experts on Baselines who commented on a preliminary draft of the publication as prepared by the United Nations Office for Ocean Affairs and the Law of the Sea.

observes that '[t]here is no uniformly identifiable objective test which will identify for everyone islands which constitute a fringe in the immediate vicinity of the coast. States should, however, be guided by the general spirit of article 7.'[22] Two examples were given to illustrate where a fringe of islands is likely to exist. The first is one which relates to the circumstances of the *Fisheries Case* and where the islands appear to 'form a unity with the mainland'.[23] The other is where the islands may be some distance from the coast and 'form a screen which masks a large proportion of the coast from the sea.'[24] As to the distance of the islands from the coast and being within the 'immediate vicinity', the view was that location within a distance of 24 miles would be satisfactory.[25] It was also observed that the concept applies to the inner edge of the islands because the fringe may be of considerable width.[26]

Since the 1989 UN Study, the ICJ has had occasion to consider certain aspects of Article 7 in *Qatar v Bahrain*.[27] Bahrain contended that it was a multiple-island State characterised by a cluster of islands off the coast of its main islands and that as such it was a de facto archipelagic State.[28] Bahrain applied the method of straight baselines, maintaining that the external fringe should serve as the baseline for the territorial sea.[29] However, the ICJ observed that:

> the method of straight baselines, which is an exception to the normal rules for the determination of baselines, may only be applied if a number of conditions are met. This method must be applied restrictively. Such conditions are primarily that either the coastline is deeply indented and cut into, or that there is a fringe of islands along the coast in the immediate vicinity.[30]

Directly referring to Bahrain's claim that it was a 'multiple-island State', the Court went on to observe that such an assertion does not allow the State 'to deviate from the normal rules for the determination of baselines unless the relevant conditions are met.'[31] The Court rejected Bahrain's contention that the maritime features off the coast of its main islands could be assimilated to a fringe of islands, noting that the islands were relatively small and that they would only be a part of a 'cluster of islands' or 'island system' if Bahrain's main islands were included.[32] This reinforces the ICJ's conservative position on LOSC Article 7(1) straight baselines.

[22] ibid 20 [42].
[23] ibid 20 [44].
[24] ibid 20 [45]; where the Recherche Archipelago (Australia) was cited as an example.
[25] ibid 21 [46].
[26] ibid.
[27] *Maritime Delimitation and Territorial Questions between Qatar and Bahrain (Qatar v Bahrain)* (Merits) [2001] ICJ Rep 40 *(Qatar v Bahrain)*.
[28] ibid 96 [181].
[29] ibid 103 [210]–[211].
[30] ibid 103 [212].
[31] ibid 103 [213].
[32] ibid 103 [213]–[214]; here the Court was referring to the Hawar islands/Hawar archipelago, located 10 nm to the south east of the principal islands of Bahrain, just off the coast of Qatar: ibid, 52–54 [35]; see also discussion in P Mojtahed-Zadeh and B Zarei, 'Maritime Boundary Delimitations in the Persian Gulf' (2017) 14(2) *International Studies Journal* 49, 61.

In the view of the US, providing the islands in question meet the criteria under Article 121(1), then three further criteria must be met for Article 7(1) to apply:

1. The most landward point of each island lies no more than 24 nm from the mainland coastline;
2. Each island to which a straight baseline is drawn is not more than 24 nm apart from the island from which the straight baseline is drawn; and
3. The islands, as a whole, mask at least 50 per cent of the mainland coastline in any given locality.[33]

Relying upon the above criteria, the US has protested the straight baseline claims of China, Cuba, Djibouti, Ecuador, Honduras, Italy, Japan, Mexico, Oman, Portugal, South Korea and Thailand.[34] The US is distinctive in having a precise and public position on these issues.

Prescott and Schofield have commented that:

> While the intent of the phrase ['immediate vicinity'] is clear enough, Article 7 fails to deliver a clear-cut, objective test by which to judge whether certain islands are close enough to a mainland in order to be considered in its immediate vicinity.[35]

Reisman and Westerman are of the view that LOSC Article 7(1) introduces three cumulative tests. The first is a quantitative and spatially distributional test in that there must be a number of islands that are spatially related to each other so as to create a 'fringe'. The second is a spatial test with regard to the relation of the islands and coast in that they must be distributed 'along' the coast. The third is a relational element as between the islands and coast in terms of their proximity.[36]

(ii) Coastal Archipelago

A coastal archipelago can also equate to a fringe of islands, and the ICJ in the *Fisheries Case* used the terms archipelago and *skjærgaard* interchangeably.[37] The fringe of islands criterion suggests very close proximity between the islands and the outer limits of the coast proper. This was emphasised in the *Fisheries Case*, though again care needs to be taken given the distinctive configuration of the Norwegian *skjærgaard*.[38] A point of distinction relates to the distance of the

[33] JA Roach and RW Smith, *Excessive Maritime Claims* (3rd edn, Martinus Nijhoff 2012) 62–63.
[34] ibid 98–107.
[35] Prescott and Schofield (n 14) 147; see also Y Tanaka, *The International Law of the Sea* (3rd edn, Cambridge University Press 2019) 60.
[36] WM Reisman and GS Westerman, *Straight Baselines in International Maritime Boundary Delimitation* (MacMillan 1992) 82–90.
[37] *Fisheries Case* (n 17) 129; see also *1989 UN Study* (n 21) 21 [41] where it is suggested that text of LOSC art 7(1) regarding a fringe of islands in the immediate vicinity 'appears to be a widening of the phrase used in the Judgment'.
[38] *Fisheries Case* (n 17) 127.

islands from the coast.[39] In the *Fisheries Case* this matter was not given much consideration due to the obvious physical proximity of those islands; however, this does become a relevant factor if a coastal archipelago requires the drawing of straight baselines that may be considered to exceed an acceptable length. In this respect, LOSC Article 7 is silent as to the permissible length of straight baselines and this is a matter of contention in the literature and state practice.

Prescott and Schofield noted the longest straight baseline endorsed by the ICJ in the *Fisheries Case* was 43.6 nm and suggest that the maximum acceptable limit would not be less than this.[40] Trümpler supports a straight baseline limit of between 24 and 48 nm.[41] The 1989 UN Study also observed that the literature, as a general rule, has proposed a maximum baseline length of 48 nm.[42] Length of the baseline is on its own not the only relevant criterion to be taken into account, and the other qualifying factors outlined in LOSC Article 7 need to be considered.[43] In its 2018 study on this topic, the International Law Association declined to specify a limit to the length of straight baselines, but did note that the ICJ in *Qatar v Bahrain* had promoted a restrictive approach to straight baselines and that LOSC Part IV archipelagic straight baselines were constrained to 100 nm with a length of 125 nm only permitted in very limited instances.[44]

A coastal archipelago that is located at some distance from the coast can be the subject of straight baselines drawn to and from the adjacent mainland coast. Proximity to the mainland will be pivotal in determining the legitimacy of the straight baselines, especially with respect to how long those baselines are. Excessive straight baseline length would be impermissible and inevitably be subject to protest from other coastal States. Likewise States protesting such baselines would continue to exercise the right of innocent passage within waters that the coastal State may now consider to be internal waters.

There are two additional factors that need to be accounted for. The first is that the baselines drawn from the coast to the archipelago are not to depart from the general direction of the coastline. Accordingly, the general location of the archipelago in this instance will be a critical consideration. If the archipelago is generally proximate to the contours of the coastline such that it is either enveloped within the sweep of the coastline or the location of the islands is such that they situate within the coastline's general direction, this criterion will be met.[45] Issues arise with the application of this criterion in seeking to determine the general direction

[39] On this point of distinction between a fringe of islands and a coastal archipelago, see D Pharand, *Canada's Arctic Waters in International Law* (Cambridge University Press 1988) 133–34.

[40] Prescott and Schofield (n 14) 146.

[41] K Trümpler, 'Article 7 Straight Baselines' in A Proelss (ed), *United Nations Convention on the Law of the Sea: A Commentary* (CH Beck 2017) 65, 75.

[42] *1989 UN Study* (n 21) 21 [46].

[43] RR Churchill and AV Lowe, *The Law of the Sea* (3rd edn, Manchester University Press 1999) 37.

[44] *ILA Report* (n 15) 119–20 [109].

[45] This reinforces the reference in article 7(1) to a 'fringe of islands' or what is also often referred to as a 'shield of islands'.

of the coast, or attempting to apply a precise mathematical formula.[46] An archipelago located directly off the coast, requiring the drawing of straight baselines to and from the islands that may be in the range of 40–50 nm in length, would raise objections as to whether the resulting baseline system does in fact follow the coast's general direction or whether it represents a significant deviation.[47] The second factor is that the waters that fall within the straight baselines must be 'sufficiently closely linked to the land domain' to be part of the regime of internal waters.[48] Straight baselines drawn directly off the coastline so as to encompass a coastal archipelago would not immediately fulfil this requirement.[49] This is where additional factors such as size of the population on the coastal archipelago, economic activity between the archipelago and the mainland, and the existence of vessel traffic may become relevant.

(iii) Mid-Ocean Archipelago

In the case of a mid-ocean archipelago the starting point with the application of the LOSC Article 7 straight baseline rule is to consider from which coastlines straight baselines can be drawn. In this respect Article 7 refers to islands being within the vicinity of a 'coastline' and a 'coast'. There is no reference to a mainland,[50] and as such it is entirely possible that straight baselines could be drawn from one island to another. Likewise there is no reference to a 'main island' within an offshore fringe of islands, or within an archipelago. Demonstrating the existence of a main island in a mid-ocean archipelago with its own fringe of islands may in some instances be problematic.[51] Rather, the threshold requirement is the existence of a coastline.

An island coastline may have a fringe of islands in the same way as a continental coastline.[52] This interpretation of Article 7 makes appropriate allowances for island States and the drawing of baselines to their adjoining islands in instances when that State does not meet the LOSC Article 46 archipelagic State criteria. Distinguishing between continental States and island States with respect to

[46] *1989 UN Study* (n 21) 24 [54]–[55].

[47] While the ICJ did not directly comment on this in *Qatar v Bahrain*, this would have been the result if straight baselines had been drawn from the main islands of Bahrain to the Hawar archipelago; see also *1989 UN Study* (n 21) 20 [43] which observes that the 'along the coast' requirement would not apply in the case of 'islands arranged like stepping-stones perpendicular to the coast'.

[48] LOSC (n 1) art 7(3).

[49] This is alluded to by the ICJ in *Qatar v Bahrain* (n 27) 110 [223] with respect to the Hawar Islands (Bahrain) and the right of innocent passage being enjoyed in the territorial sea between the islands and the main islands of Bahrain; see also *1989 UN Study* (n 21) 25 [57].

[50] Cf LOSC (n 1) art 13 which makes a distinction between a mainland and an island in the context of a low-tide elevation.

[51] In the case of the Hawaiian islands (US), the largest island – Hawaii – is at the south eastern edge while the capital, Honolulu, is located on the more central island of Oahu.

[52] SD Murphy, *International Law Relating to Islands* (Brill/Nijhoff 2017) 133.

the application of Article 7 is therefore not appropriate, and both large (Japan, New Zealand) and small (Cuba,[53] Palau) mid-ocean archipelagos are able to utilise the Article 7 straight baseline rule. However, the application of the Article 7 straight baseline rule remains subject to all of the constraints and limitations that have been noted above, including the ICJ's observations in *Qatar v Bahrain*.

B. Archipelagic Baselines

The rule and principles for the drawing of archipelagic baselines were assessed in Chapter five. Critically, only an archipelagic State may draw LOSC Article 47 archipelagic baselines. A coastal State that is not a recognised archipelagic State or which does not meet the LOSC Article 46 criteria of an archipelagic State, is unable to draw archipelagic baselines. This applies just as much to a continental State as it does to an island State, and the ICJ made clear in *Qatar v Bahrain* that it would not give weight to claims of de facto archipelagic State status.[54] In *South China Sea* discussion arose regarding whether it would be permissible for China to enclose the Spratly Islands by a system of straight or archipelagic baselines 'surrounding the high-tide features of the group, and accorded an entitlement to maritime zones as a single unit'.[55] China had not formally drawn a system of archipelagic baselines, nor had it made a claim that it was an archipelagic State. Nevertheless, the Tribunal observed:

> The use of archipelagic baselines (a baseline surrounding an archipelago as a whole) is strictly controlled by the Convention, where Article 47(1) limits their use to 'archipelagic states'. Archipelagic States are defined in Article 46 as States 'constituted wholly by one or more archipelagos and may include other islands.' The Philippines is an archipelagic State (being constituted wholly by an archipelago), is entitled to employ archipelagic baselines, and does so in promulgating the baselines for its territorial sea.[56]

The Tribunal then considered the application of Article 7 straight baselines, and observed that 'the Tribunal is aware of the practice of some States in employing straight baselines with respect to offshore archipelagos to approximate the effect of archipelagic baselines.'[57] Two views were expressed on this matter: one technical and the other relating to the overall application of the LOSC. The Tribunal made clear that Article 7 straight baselines could not be drawn in the case of an offshore

[53] For an assessment see Department of State (USA), *Straight Baselines: Cuba (Limits in the Seas No. 76)* (Department of State 1977).

[54] *Qatar v Bahrain* (n 27) at 96 [180].

[55] *South China Sea* (n 3) 236 [573]; this question was discussed in the context of statements made by China indicating that it claimed a territorial sea, EEZ and continental shelf 'based on the Nansha Islands as a whole.' ibid, 235–36 [571].

[56] ibid.

[57] ibid 237 [575].

archipelago where the relevant conditions did not exist. In this regard the Tribunal noted:

> Although the Convention does not expressly preclude the use of straight baselines in other circumstances, the Tribunal considers that the grant of permission in Article 7 concerning straight baselines generally, together with the conditional permission in Articles 46 and 47 for certain States to draw archipelagic baselines, excludes the possibility of employing straight baselines in other circumstances, in particular with respect to offshore archipelagos not meeting the criteria for archipelagic baselines. Any other interpretation would effectively render the conditions in Articles 7 and 47 meaningless.[58]

Through this assessment and review of the specific and general provisions of the LOSC with respect to the drawing of straight and archipelagic baselines the Tribunal made clear that a restrictive approach should be taken towards the drawing of such baselines in the case of mid-ocean dependent archipelagos.

C. Flexible Straight Baseline Rules

The straight baseline rules set down in Article 7 provide a degree of flexibility for coastal States in drawing baselines in the case of a fringe of islands, an offshore archipelago, and a mid-ocean archipelago. There is no precise mathematical formula applied for the drawing of straight baselines, though there are a number of disqualifying criteria. The existence of islands does not allow for a liberal interpretation of the LOSC straight baseline provisions by a coastal State. This conservative position is also reflected with respect to archipelagic baselines, which are reserved for archipelagic States. On the basis of what is admittedly limited jurisprudence, courts and tribunals have also indicated that they do not support some form of hybrid approach that blends elements of Articles 7 and 47.

IV. Maritime Entitlements[59]

The maritime entitlements of dependent archipelagos are determined consistently with the LOSC and the customary international law of the sea. Assuming the legitimacy of Article 7 straight baselines that have been drawn and that they are not the subject of protest, there are two principal scenarios. The first is where a dependent coastal archipelago has been enclosed with straight baselines drawn from the mainland. In that situation all of the maritime entitlements will be the same as those of the mainland and the delineation of maritime claims

[58] ibid.
[59] See the more detailed discussion in Chapter 7 of this volume.

will proceed consistently with the LOSC. This was precisely the outcome that arose in the *Fisheries Case*, albeit under the then customary international law of the sea pre-dating the 1958 Geneva Conventions. The second is the case of a dependent mid-ocean archipelago which has also been subject to straight baselines. Maritime entitlements would be determined from the baselines. In both instances, consistently with LOSC Article 14, combinations of Article 5 normal baselines and Article 7 straight baselines could be relied upon. In the case of either a dependent coastal archipelago or a dependent mid-ocean archipelago not capable of being subject to the LOSC Article 7 straight baseline regime, then those islands will retain their entitlement to generate maritime clams consistently with the LOSC Article 121 regime of islands. An exception to both scenarios arises if the archipelago comprises juridical islands and juridical rocks, in which case the rocks will only generate a 12 nm territorial sea. If this were to occur in the case of a *coastal* archipelago the combination of the various maritime zones generated from the mainland and the juridical islands of the coastal archipelago would more than likely compensate for the reduced entitlement of the juridical rocks due to the proximity of the maritime features and their enveloping claims. With respect to a *mid-ocean* archipelago, this will very much depend on its configuration but there is certainly potential that rocks located within such an archipelago would only enjoy a territorial sea while being located within an exclusive economic zone (EEZ) or continental shelf generated from the islands within the group.

V. State Practice

Following the above assessment of the relevant LOSC provisions, more detailed assessment can now be given to state practice. A total of nine prominent dependent archipelagos have been selected for analysis.[60]

A. Canada (Arctic)

The Canadian Arctic Archipelago is a dependent coastal archipelago comprising 73 major islands and 18,114 smaller Canadian islands adjacent to the northern

[60] See also analysis in S Kopela, *Dependent Archipelagos in the Law of the Sea* (Martinus Nijhoff 2013); and related discussion of examples of state practice in JA Roach, 'Offshore Archipelagos Enclosed by Straight Baselines: an Excessive Claim?' (2018) 49 *Ocean Development and International Law* 176; Chinese Society of International Law, 'The South China Sea Arbitration Awards: A Critical Study' (2018) 17 *Chinese Journal of International Law* 207, 492; E Franckx and M Benatar, 'Straight baselines around insular formations not constituting an archipelagic state' in CJ Jenner and TT Thuy (eds), *The South China Sea: A Crucible of Regional Cooperation or Conflict-making Sovereignty Claims?* (Cambridge University Press 2016) 186; and United Nations Conference on the Law of the Sea, 'Certain Legal Aspects' (n 8) at 295–99 for relevant state practice up to 1957.

tip of the North American continent.[61] Whether the archipelago is an Article 7 fringe of islands or a coastal archipelago has been the subject of some debate.[62] Canada's longstanding position with respect to the waters between the continental mainland and the islands is that they are historic waters.[63] In addition, Canada also sought to bolster its claim in 1985 by proclaiming straight baselines around the archipelago as part of a series of measures to respond to increasing US interest in navigation through the Northwest Passage.[64] Canada's straight baselines around the Canadian Arctic Archipelago have been justified on the basis of either an historic waters claim, or LOSC Article 7 straight baselines.[65] Scholarly assessment of the Canadian claim supports the legitimacy of the baselines as founded on an interpretation of LOSC Article 7.[66] The United States continues to reject the Canadian position, principally it would seem, because of the implications it has for navigational rights within the Northwest Passage.[67]

B. Chile (Pacific Coast)

Chile has a long coastal front to the Pacific Ocean where the continental coastline is shielded by islands that form a dependent coastal archipelago. By a 1977 decree Chile established a straight baseline system of 75 points along its Pacific coast,[68] where the baseline lengths range from 1 nm to 65 nm.[69] In a 1978 analysis of the straight baseline system the US Department of State observed that the southern Chilean coastline 'is deeply indented with fjord-like embayments, and the mainland is virtually masked in its entirety by thousands of major and minor islands and rocks'.[70] There are significant similarities between the Chilean Pacific coast and the Norwegian Atlantic mainland coast with respect to the relationship between fringing islands – including areas properly described as archipelagos – and the coastline.

[61] D Pharand, *Canada's Arctic Waters* (n 39) 160.
[62] ibid 160–61.
[63] TL McDorman, *Salt Water Neighbors: International Ocean Law Relations between the United States and Canada* (Oxford University Press 2009) 233–34.
[64] House of Commons Debates (Canada) 10 September 1985, vol V, 6,463; see analysis in JB McKinnon, 'Arctic Baselines: *A Litore Usque Ad Litus*' (1987) 66 *Canadian Bar Review* 790.
[65] See the exhaustive assessment of both claims in D Pharand, 'The Arctic Waters and the Northwest Passage: A Final Revisit' (2007) 38 *Ocean Development and International Law* 3.
[66] Kopela (n 60) 79–81; Pharand, 'The Arctic Waters and the Northwest Passage' (n 65) 28.
[67] McDorman (n 63) 240; Roach and Smith (n 33) 111–12, 318–28.
[68] Decree No 416 1977 (Chile).
[69] Department of State (US), *Straight Baselines: Chile (Limits in the Seas No 80)* (Department of State 1978) 4–5.
[70] ibid 5; see also discussion in T Scovazzi, 'Bays and Deeply Indented Coastlines: The Practice of South American States' (1995) 26 *Ocean Development and International Law* 161, 167.

C. China (South China Sea)

The status of China's claimed islands in the South China Sea and the capacity of China to draw baselines around those islands was, as noted above, the subject of discussion in *South China Sea*. That analysis has attracted widespread commentary both in support of and in disagreement with the Tribunal's award.[71] China has indicated its intention to eventually draw baselines around its claimed islands in the South China Sea, including Dongsha Qundao (Pratas), Xisha Qundao (Paracels), Zhongsha Qundao (Scarborough Shoal and Macclesfield Bank), Nansha Qundao (Spratlys) and all the other islands it claims.[72] These features would be characterised as dependent mid-ocean archipelagos. In response to China's position the US via a 2016 Diplomatic Note to China observed that:

> Consistent with international law as reflected in the Law of the Sea Convention, including Articles 5, 7, 46, and 47, China cannot claim straight or archipelagic baselines in the Paracel Islands, Pratas Island, Macclesfield Bank, Scarborough Reef, or the Spratly Islands.[73]

A detailed 2018 study by the Chinese Society of International Law has argued that there is sufficient state practice to support China's claim to draw straight baselines around these islands on the basis of customary international law.[74] There have since been further diplomatic exchanges on this issue via the Commission on the Limits of the Continental Shelf (CLCS) over 2019–21. In response to a 2019 Malaysian submission to the CLCS regarding an area of continental shelf beyond 200 nm in the South China Sea,[75] China restated its position regarding the drawing of baselines around its South China Sea claimed islands.[76] China's statement

[71] See eg Roach (n 60); C Whomersley, 'Offshore Archipelagos Enclosed By Straight Baselines: A Reply to J. Ashley Roach' (2018) 49 *Ocean Development and International Law* 203; MH Loja, 'The Spratly Islands as a Single Unit Under International Law: A Commentary on the Final Award in Philippines/China Arbitration' (2016) 47 *Ocean Development and International Law* 309.

[72] The State Council (PRC), 'China Adheres to the Position of Settling Through Negotiation the Relevant Disputes Between China and the Philippines in the South China Sea' (13 July 2016), english.www.gov.cn/state_council/ministries/2016/07/13/content_281475392503075.htm, [34].

[73] CLD Guymon (ed), *Digest of United States Practice in International Law* (Department of State 2017) https://2017-2021.state.gov/wp-content/uploads/2019/05/2016-Digest-United-States.pdf, 522.

[74] Chinese Society of International Law (n 60) 479–510; for an assessment of some of relevant analysis on these points see Roach (n 60) 183–87.

[75] Commission on the Limits of the Continental Shelf (CLCS), 'Outer limits of the Continental Shelf beyond 200 nautical miles from the baselines: Submissions to the Commission: Partial Submission by Malaysia in the South China Sea' (United Nations Division for Ocean Affairs and the Law of the Sea, 12 December 2019), www.un.org/depts/los/clcs_new/submissions_files/submission_mys_12_12_2019.html.

[76] 'China – Communication received with respect to the submission of Malaysia, Commission on the Limits of Continental Shelf, CML/14/2019' (United Nations Division for Ocean Affairs and the Law of the Sea, 12 December 2019), www.un.org/depts/los/clcs_new/submissions_files/mys85_2019/CML_14_2019_E.pdf.

was subsequently rejected in further diplomatic exchanges from the US, Australia, France, Germany and the UK, Japan, and New Zealand.[77]

D. Denmark (Faroe Islands)

Denmark has established a straight baseline system around the 18 islands that make up the Faroe Islands,[78] a dependent mid-ocean archipelago in the North Atlantic. In 1991 the US lodged a diplomatic note with Denmark over these baselines on the basis that they constituted straight baselines connecting the outer islands of the archipelago, and that Denmark was not an archipelagic State.[79] The US did concede that some of the Faroe Islands that were fringed with islands could be the subject of straight baselines consistently with international law.[80] Denmark responded to the US note by observing that the straight baseline system was consistent with international law due to the 'compact nature of the group of islands involved' and due to the particular economic circumstances of the islands.[81]

E. Ecuador (Galapagos Islands)

Ecuador has proclaimed a series of straight baselines around the Galapagos Islands in the Pacific Ocean, a dependent mid-ocean archipelago.[82] There are a total of eight baseline segments, 552 nm in length, ranging from 32 to 126 nm which connect up eight islands and enclose others.[83] The islands do not possess any deep indentations, so a principal issue is their proximity and whether they can be considered a fringe in relation to each other, particularly with respect to their location vis-à-vis the largest of the islands – Isla Isabela. A 2020 US Department of State analysis rejects the legitimacy of the baselines set against the criterion of

[77] See Commission on the Limits of the Continental Shelf (CLCS), 'Outer limits of the continental shelf beyond 200 nautical miles from the baselines: Submissions to the Commission: Partial Submission by Malaysia in the South China Sea – diplomatic notes by US' (1 June 2020), Australia (23 July 2020), UK, France and Germany (16 September 2020), Japan (19 January 2021) and New Zealand (3 August 2021), www.un.org/Depts/los/clcs_new/submissions_files/submission_mys_12_12_2019.html.

[78] Ordinances Nos 598 and 599 (Denmark); the status of the Faroe Islands is discussed in more detail in Chapter 9 section IV.D of this volume.

[79] Roach and Smith (n 33) 108–9.

[80] ibid 108.

[81] ibid 109; see also analysis in AG Oude Elferink, 'Maritime Delimitation between the United Kingdom and Denmark/Faroe Islands' (1999) 14(4) *International Journal of Marine and Coastal Law* 541, 548–49; Kopela (n 60) 126.

[82] Supreme Decree No 959-A Prescribing Straight Baselines for the Measurement of the Territorial Sea 1971 (Ecuador).

[83] Department of State (US), *Ecuador Maritime Claims and Boundaries (Limits in the Seas No 147)* (Department of State 2020) 10.

LOSC Articles 7 and 47.[84] Ecuador is not an archipelagic State and has a significant Latin American continental coastline. On becoming a LOSC party in 2012, Ecuador lodged an Article 310 declaration which sought to justify the baselines position it had taken with respect to the Galapagos Islands.[85] Ecuador's declaration was the subject of diplomatic objection and protest from other LOSC parties including Belgium, the European Union, Ireland, Germany, Greece, Latvia, Netherlands, Spain, Sweden, and the UK.[86]

F. Myanmar (Myeik Kyunzu)

Myanmar in 1977 proclaimed a series of straight baselines along its western coast fronting the Andaman Sea.[87] The baselines connect up 11 islands and rocks at the far western edge of Myeik Kyunzu (Mergui Archipelago) – a dependent coastal archipelago – along the Tenasserim coast.[88] The US in 1982 protested the Myanmar claim and placed particular emphasis on how the baselines departed from the general direction of the coastline.[89] A characteristic of the archipelago is a cluster of larger islands within a distance of approximately 20 nm from the coast, and an outer ring of much smaller islands. It is the latter islands that were selected for the basepoints of the straight baselines, which measure up to 80 nm. There are differing views in the academic literature as to the validity of these baselines, especially as to whether they follow the general direction of the coast.[90]

G. Norway (Svalbard)

As discussed above, Norway is a prominent coastal State with respect to the drawing of straight baselines and its practice in the field has historic legacies.[91] Norway in 2001 proclaimed a new series of straight baselines with respect to the Svalbard dependent mid-ocean archipelago which consisted of 196 points connected

[84] ibid 10; see also analysis in VE Arellano Rodriguez, 'The Legal Status of Mid-Ocean Archipelagos of Mainland States under International Law: The Case of the Galapagos' (2017) 6(2) *UCL Journal of Law and Jurisprudence* 71; Roach (n 60) 197–98; Scovazzi (n 70) 166–67; Reisman and Westerman (n 36) 154, 156.

[85] Ecuador, 'Declarations and Reservations' (*United Nations Convention on the Law of the Sea*) www.un.org/depts/los/convention_agreements/convention_declarations.htm.

[86] Division for Ocean Affairs and the Law of the Sea, Office of Legal Affairs (UN) (2014) 83 *Law of the Sea Bulletin* 14–19.

[87] Territorial Sea and Maritime Zones Law 1977 (Myanmar).

[88] Roach and Smith (n 33) 116–17; Kopela (n 60) 268 (Figure 6).

[89] Roach and Smith (n 33) at 117; see also analysis in M Aung Myoe, 'Myanmar's maritime challenges and priorities' in J Ho and S Bateman (ed), *Maritime Challenges and Priorities in Asia* (Routledge 2012) 83, 92–94.

[90] See Kopela (n 60) 82; cf Reisman and Westerman (n 36) 168, 172.

[91] For a contemporary assessment of Norway's Article 7 straight baselines drawn around its continental coast, Svalbard, and Jan Mayen, see Department of State (US), *Norway Maritime Claims and Boundaries (Limits in the Seas No 148)* (Department of State 2020).

by geodetic lines around five separate islands or island groups: (1) Hopen, (2) Bjørnøya, (3) Kong Karls Land, (4) Kvitøya, and (5) the main Svalbard islands, including Spitsbergen.[92] The baselines connecting Spitsbergen and the associated islands of Nordaustlandet, Edgeøya, and Barentsøya are the most extensive, with 101 points, and extend in total for 888 nm. Characterising the island coastlines is challenging as they are all deeply indented, have many fjords, and face other islands in the archipelago. The islands in this system are no more than 5 nm apart.[93] The Kong Karls Land 116 nm straight baseline system connects three principal islands separated by between 7–12 nm with 29 points and segments.[94] Norway does not connect these two baseline systems, notwithstanding the relative geographic proximity of the Svalbard islands, 35 nm to 50 nm, to Kong Karls Land.[95] A 2020 US Department of State analysis generally endorsed the baseline system adopted for the main Svalbard islands, but disputed the legitimacy of that employed in the case of Kong Karls Land.[96]

H. Spain (Canary Islands)

Spain has a longstanding series of baselines for the Canary Islands,[97] a dependent mid-ocean archipelago in the Atlantic Ocean off the coast of Africa. The Canary Islands consist of eight main islands and some smaller offshore islands with an east-west extent of approximately 270 nm and north-south of approximately 100 nm.[98] Five of the main islands are the subject of straight baselines, with only one set of islands – Isla Graciosa, Lanzarote, and Fuerteventura – joined by connecting baselines between 9.4 and 27.3 nm in length.[99] A 2020 US Department of State analysis of the Canary Island baseline system with respect to Isla Graciosa, Lanzarote, and Fuerteventura is of the view that the baselines are not consistent with LOSC Article 7 because of the linear location of the islands, that they are not fringing each other, and do not meet the other relevant criteria.[100] In 2010, Law 44/2010 proclaimed a 'perimeter' around the Canary

[92] Norway, 'Regulations relating to the limits of the Norwegian territorial sea around Svalbard' (Royal Decree of 1 June 2001), at 'Deposit of the list of geographical coordinates of points for drawing the baselines for measuring the width of the territorial sea around Svalbard, as contained in: Regulations of 1 June 2001 relating to the limit of the Norwegian territorial sea around Svalbard' (*UN Convention on the Law of the Seas*) www.un.org/Depts/los/LEGISLATIONANDTREATIES/PDFFILES/mzn_s/mzn38.pdf; Department of State (US), *Norway Maritime Claims* (n 91) 13; for a previous assessment see Department of State (US), *Straight Baselines: Svalbard (Limits in the Seas No 39)* (Department of State 1972).

[93] Department of State (US), *Norway Maritime Claims* (n 91) 19.

[94] ibid 16.

[95] ibid 19.

[96] ibid 16–20, 31.

[97] Royal Decree No 2510/1977 (Spain).

[98] Department of State (US), *Spain Maritime Claims and Boundaries (Limits in the Seas No 149)* (Department of State 2020) 12.

[99] ibid 15–16.

[100] ibid 16; see also Reisman and Westerman (n 36) 156, 158.

Islands; however, this does not appear to have been an attempt to create the equivalent of archipelagic status for the islands but rather is purely for Spanish municipal law purposes.[101]

I. Vietnam (Tho Chu Archipelago)

Vietnam in 1982 declared a series of straight baselines around its coast, starting in the Gulf of Tonkin through to the Gulf of Thailand.[102] The baselines are principally based on offshore islands and features, including the Thu Chu Archipelago, Con Dao group of islands, and the Phu Quy group (Catwick Islands), which are dependent coastal archipelagos.[103] A 1983 US Department of State analysis observed that the island basepoints averaged 39.4 nm from the nearest mainland points, are a maximum of 80.7 nm, and that the Tho Chu Archipelago, the Con Dao group, and the Phu Quy group are all at least 50 nm from the mainland and adjacent island groups.[104] Academic analysis has also queried the legitimacy of this straight baseline system as it relates to Vietnam's offshore archipelagos.[105]

VI. Conclusions

International law with respect to baselines is longstanding and has a firm basis in the law of the sea. The ICJ set an important precedent in the *Fisheries Case* with respect to coastal archipelagos and straight baselines. That was a catalyst for key rules with respect to straight baselines adopted in both the Convention on the Territorial Sea and the LOSC, and which paved the way for state practice to develop with respect to archipelagos and eventual adoption of the Part IV Archipelagic State regime. These law of the sea developments each had implications for dependent archipelagos. In the case of a fringe of islands properly characterised as a dependent coastal archipelago, LOSC Article 7 directly addressed their existence. Mid-ocean dependent archipelagos were seen by some States and publicists as having been ignored by the LOSC.[106] Yet, it is clear that even the US accepts that

[101] ibid 16-18; see also discussion in Kopela (n 60) 247–52.

[102] Vietnam, 'Statement on the Territorial Sea, the Contiguous Zone, the Exclusive Economic Zone, and the Continental Shelf of Vietnam' (12 May 1977) which indicates that the baselines are ones which link 'the furthest seaward points of the coast and the outermost points of Vietnamese offshore islands, and which is the low-water line along the coast', and Vietnam, 'Declaration on Baseline of Territorial Waters' (12 November 1982).

[103] Department of State (US), *Straight Baselines: Vietnam (Limits in the Seas No 99)* (Department of State 1983) 12.

[104] ibid 8, 12.

[105] MJ Valencia and JM Van Dyke, 'Vietnam's National Interests and the Law of the Sea' (1994) 25 *Ocean Development and International Law* 217, 221–22; Roach and Smith (n 33) 99–100; Reisman and Westerman (n 36) 133, 136; JH Nossum, 'What Vietnam could gain from redrawing its baselines' (Winter 2001–2002) *IBRU Boundary and Security Bulletin* 97.

[106] J Crawford, *Chance, Order, Change: The Course of International Law* (Brill 2014) 326 [421].

straight baselines can be drawn around these islands subject to relevant Article 7 criteria being met. Other criteria may be relevant in assessing the legitimacy of straight baselines drawn around dependent coastal and mid-ocean archipelagos, including the existence of historic waters and LOSC Article 7(5) economic interests.

State practice associated with dependent archipelagos and the application of Article 7 and de facto application of Article 47 have proven contentious.[107] An increasing number of States have publicly protested excessive claims.[108] Some States may raise their concerns bilaterally without putting their objections into the public domain. There may be multiple reasons why straight baselines associated with dependent archipelagos are proving contentious.[109] The decisions of international courts and tribunals assessing the LOSC provisions, albeit few in number, have taken a conservative view, especially with respect to the interpretation of the Part IV archipelagic State regime. Both the ICJ and a LOSC Annex VII Arbitral Tribunal have indicated they are not prepared to support de facto archipelagic States drawing the equivalent of archipelagic baselines around their dependent archipelagos. Nevertheless, this does not stop state practice evolving in the area. The diplomatic exchanges occurring over certain South China Sea islands highlight that some States may be seeking to advance the law of the sea though an evolution of customary international law.[110] Others are resisting this change. This may partly be a consequence of an ambiguity in the law of the sea with respect to certain dependent archipelagos. In that respect, the evolution of the law of the sea through both state practice within the LOSC framework and separately through customary international law cannot be ignored.

[107] See also the analysis with respect to straight baselines declared/proposed by India (Andaman and Nicobar Islands) in JM Smith, 'UNCLOS: China, India, and the United States Navigate an Unsettled Regime' (30 April 2021) 3608 *Asian Studies Center Backgrounder* 13, 13–14; the UK (Falkland Islands) in Scovazzi (n 70) 169; and Djibouti (Seba Islands), Portugal (Azores), UK (Turks and Caicos Islands) in Roach and Smith (n 33) 104–15.

[108] In addition to those noted above, see also Roach (n 60) 180–81 listing protests from Bangladesh, Belgium, Germany, Philippines, Senegal, Spain, Sweden, UK, US, Vietnam and the EC.

[109] See C Schofield, 'Departures from the Coast: Trends in the Application of Territorial Sea Baselines under the Law of the Sea Convention' (2012) 27 *International Journal of Marine and Coastal Law* 723.

[110] A number of scholars have accepted the potential for customary international law to continue to play a role in this area of the law of the sea notwithstanding the finalisation of the LOSC; see Kopela (n 60) 259–60; Pharand, *Canada's Arctic Waters* (n 39) 133–34.

7

Islands and Maritime Entitlements

I. Introduction

One of the essential characteristics of the law of the sea as it has developed over the centuries has been the recognition of the rights of coastal States to various forms of maritime entitlements. Initially these entitlements began in the nineteenth century with the territorial sea over which coastal States exercised sovereignty in much the same way as that over the land excepting the right of foreign ships to exercise innocent passage. By the 1950s, following developments in customary international law, those entitlements were extended to the continental shelf, which following the adoption of the 1958 Geneva Conventions were given a firm basis in treaty law. A contiguous zone adjacent to the territorial sea was also recognised. The negotiations that resulted in the 1982 United Nations Convention on the Law of the Sea (LOSC)[1] quickly ushered in an era when those maritime entitlements were joined by the endorsement and recognition accorded to the exclusive economic zone (EEZ). By the time of the entry into force of the LOSC in 1994, if not beforehand,[2] these core maritime zones which make up the suite of entitlements of coastal States under the law of the sea were well understood in modern international law. They were also accompanied by the distinctive entitlements the LOSC gave to islands by way of the Part VIII Regime of Islands, and the even more expansive entitlements of the Part IV provisions for archipelagic States. The effect of these developments in the law of the sea and the LOSC was that, with the exception of Article 121(3) juridical rocks, all juridical islands enjoyed the same maritime entitlements as a mainland.

The enhanced LOSC maritime entitlements of islands resulted in maritime areas previously considered high seas becoming subject to a variety of maritime claims. While this phenomenon parallels that of mainland States which had sought to assert new maritime claims consistent with developments in the law of the sea between the 1960s and 1980s, the entitlements and maritime claims of archipelagic and island States were particularly pronounced because of their

[1] United Nations Convention on the Law of the Sea (adopted 10 December 1982, entered into force 16 November 1994) 1833 UNTS 397 (LOSC).

[2] See *Continental Shelf (Libyan Arab Jamahiriya v Malta)* (Judgment) [1985] ICJ Reps 13, 33 [34] acknowledging the status of the EEZ as reflective of customary international law only three years after the conclusion of the LOSC.

impact upon large portions of high seas areas of the ocean. As Prescott and Schofield have observed:

> if no maritime neighbours were within 400 nm of the feature, an island has the potential to generate 125,664 nm^2 (431,014 km^2) of territorial sea, EEZ and continental shelf rights, making the potential value of disputed islands difficult to underestimate.[3]

This phenomenon is highlighted in the Pacific Ocean – which has many small island States and newly recognised archipelagic States – and to a lesser extent in the Caribbean Sea. Artificial islands, on the other hand, enjoy no maritime entitlements as per LOSC Article 60.[4]

While juridical islands have the same maritime entitlements as a mainland both the LOSC and state practice highlight the distinctive impact of islands upon maritime entitlements. This can be seen by the impact islands have historically had upon the drawing of straight baselines and also the manner in which islands have been central to historic waters and historic title claims. Contemporary state practice and debate in this area is highlighted in the Northwest Passage (Canada),[5] and South China Sea (China).[6] Islands have also had an impact on maritime entitlements in the case of both the continental shelf and EEZ: first, because coastal States have been able to make submissions to the Commission on the Limits of the Continental Shelf (CLCS) based upon oceanic islands distant from the metropolitan State, which can generate LOSC Article 76 entitlements beyond 200 nm; and second, because of the distinctive environmental and fisheries management issues raised by EEZ claims from islands.

The chapter will assess these issues by considering distinctive island issues that arise with respect to baselines, and then move on to an assessment of matters related to historic waters, bays, and internal waters. Each coastal State maritime zone will then be assessed, commencing with the territorial sea and contiguous zone, the continental shelf, and the EEZ. Distinctive issues associated with the maritime entitlements of archipelagic States are addressed in Chapter five above. The focus is on Article 121(1) juridical islands, but where relevant the status of Article 121(3) juridical rocks will be noted.

II. Baselines

A first critical issue for determining maritime entitlements is ascertaining from where maritime claims are asserted. The baselines from which the territorial sea and all subsequent maritime claims are measured can be either the low-water

[3] V Prescott and C Schofield, *The Maritime Political Boundaries of the World* (2nd edn, Martinus Nijhoff, 2005) 249.

[4] See discussion in Chapter 2 of this volume.

[5] D Pharand, *Canada's Arctic Waters in International Law* (Cambridge University Press 1988).

[6] See generally Y Tanaka, *The South China Sea Arbitration: Toward an International Legal Order in the Oceans* (Hart Publishing 2019) ch 3.

mark, as provided for under LOSC Article 5 or, subject to special circumstances being met, straight baselines drawn along the coast consistent with LOSC Article 7. The application of the low-water line normal baseline rules around islands presents no more distinctive issues than those that arise for other lands. The only exception arises in the case where islands are situated on atolls or have fringing reefs as per Article 6, in which case the baseline is the seaward low-water line of the reef. This may raise issues in circumstances where a reef has been damaged as a result of storm surges or where the low-water line around the reef has contracted as a result of sea-level rise. A question arises as to whether Article 6 permits all islands, irrespective of size, that have fringing reefs to take advantage of this rule. Would, for example, larger islands such as Cyprus and Madagascar be entitled to include reefs in their baseline system? Trümpler has argued against such an interpretation, observing that such an approach would 'contradict the history and purpose of Art. 6. Both indicate a limitation to islands where the need for special protection and the interdependence of atoll/lagoon/reef are inherent in the insular formation.'[7] This would appear the better view.

A. *Fisheries Case*

LOSC Article 7 raises some distinctive issues associated with islands. The provision originated from the 1951 *Fisheries Case*,[8] where the International Court of Justice (ICJ) assessed Norway's straight baseline system connecting islands of the *skjærgaard* along the Norwegian west coast. The *Fisheries Case* was relied upon by the International Law Commission (ILC) in proposing the Draft Articles on the Law of the Sea, which then became the basis for deliberations at the First United Nations Conference on the Law of the Sea (UNCLOS I) resulting in adoption of the 1958 Convention on the Territorial Sea and the Contiguous Zone.[9]

The *Fisheries Case* arose out a claim by the United Kingdom (UK) that the Norwegian straight baseline system was not supportable under international law. Norway's straight baseline system connected the islands of the *skjærgaard* along the west coast including both large and small islands and in some instances reefs, rocks and islets only above water at low tide.[10] The UK argued that Norway was unable to draw baselines other than from the low-water mark on

[7] K Trümpler, 'Article 6 Reefs' in A Proelss (ed), *United Nations Convention on the Law of the Sea: A Commentary* (CH Beck/Hart/Nomos 2017) 60, 63.

[8] *Fisheries Case (United Kingdom v Norway)* (Judgment) [1951] ICJ Reps 116 (*Fisheries Case*).

[9] Convention on the Territorial Sea and the Contiguous Zone (adopted 29 April 1958, entered into force 10 September 1964) 516 UNTS 206.

[10] *Fisheries Case* (n 8) 127 where the Court observed: 'Within the "skjærgaard", almost every island has its large and its small bays; countless arms of the sea, straits, channels and mere waterways serve as a means of communication for the local population which inhabits the islands as it does the mainland. The coast of the mainland does not constitute, as it does in practically all other countries, a clear dividing line between land and sea. What matters, what really constitutes the Norwegian coastline, is the outer line of the "skjærgaard".'

permanently dry land, and contested Norway's definition of a bay and historic waters. The Court upheld the international law legitimacy of Norway's method for the delimitation of its fisheries zone, and its reliance upon the straight baselines drawn around the *skjærgaard*.[11] The Court noted the distinctive nature of the Norwegian coastline as being one in which the 'coast of the mainland does not constitute, as it does in practically all other countries, a clear dividing line between land and sea',[12] and in recognition of the particular geographic nature of the Norwegian coastline, endorsed the use of straight baselines which could 'within reasonable limits' depart from the 'physical line of the coast'.[13] The Court agreed that a straight baseline could also be drawn between islands, islets and rocks that make up the *skjærgaard* even if those waters do not fall within the conception of a bay.[14] Nevertheless, the ICJ was not prepared to concede that the delimitation of these areas of the sea was merely a unilateral act of the coastal State which could be undertaken without any reference to international law, and certain basic considerations were identified which courts could apply in assessing the legitimacy of straight baselines. These included: the close dependence of the territorial sea upon the land domain; that the baselines must not depart to any appreciable extent from the general direction of the coast; the close relationship between certain sea areas and the adjoining land formations; and the economic interests peculiar to the region which may be evidenced by long usage.[15] The Court concluded that the acceptability of the method of straight baselines used by Norway was the result of the particular geography of the coastline, and that Norway's approach had been historically consolidated through long practice which had not been contested by other States as being contrary to international law.[16]

Following the *Fisheries Case* the ILC considered the question of baselines during its analysis of the law of the sea between 1949 and 1956, which eventually resulted in four draft articles found within the ILC *Articles concerning the Law of the Sea with commentaries* (ILC Draft).[17] The 1958 First United Nations Conference on the Law of the Sea (UNCLOS I) drew upon the work of the ILC in codifying the law with respect to straight baselines, as reflected in the 1958

[11] ibid 143 by respective majorities of ten votes to two, and eight votes to four; Judges McNair and Read wrote dissenting opinions.

[12] ibid 127.

[13] ibid 129.

[14] ibid 130.

[15] ibid 133; on this last point Norway was able to point to various Royal decrees and other orders dating back to 1812 which reflected the use of a baseline system for some of the waters within the *skjærgaard*.

[16] ibid 139; for detailed assessment see H Lauterpacht, *The Development of International Law by the International Court* (Stevens 1958) 45, 190–99; DP O'Connell, *The International Law of the Sea*, vol 1 (Clarendon 1982) 199–206; WM Reisman and GS Westerman, *Straight Baselines in International Maritime Boundary Delimitation* (Macmillan 1992) 19–37.

[17] International Law Commission, 'Articles concerning the Law of the Sea with commentaries' in *Yearbook of the International Law Commission*, vol 2 (1956) 265, 266–71.

Convention on the Territorial Sea and the Contiguous Zone, where Article 4 addressed straight baselines.

B. LOSC Article 7 Straight Baselines

During UNCLOS III negotiations on the question of straight baselines, emphasis was given to seeking to repeat the essential elements of Article 4 of the Convention on the Territorial Sea and the Contiguous Zone, albeit with appropriate modifications to reflect changes in the structure of the draft Convention negotiating text. LOSC Article 7 retains many of the core elements found in Article 4. Coastal States can rely upon the method of straight baselines in three instances:

1. Where a coastline is deeply indented and cut into;[18]
2. When there is a fringe of islands along the coast in its immediate vicinity;[19] or
3. Where because of the presence of a delta or other natural conditions the coastline is highly unstable.[20]

These criteria are not cumulative and any one of these three geographic circumstances will be sufficient for the coastal State to become entitled to use the straight baseline method. However, a coastal State does not have a unilateral right to draw straight baselines, which remain subject to several Article 7 controlling factors.[21]

Article 7 therefore establishes the current legal rules with respect to the drawing of straight baselines, and has been subject to assessment by various bodies, courts, and publicists and has also been impacted by state practice. In 1989 the United Nations Office for Ocean Affairs and the Law of the Sea published a study on baselines which gave an explanation for several of the relevant terms found within Article 7.[22] That study provided as follows:

> 'Straight baselines' are a system of straight lines joining specified or discrete points on the low-water line, usually known as straight baseline tuning points. A 'straight line' is mathematically the line of shortest distance between two points.

As to the characterisation of a fringe of islands, the UN study observes that '[t]here is no uniformly identifiable objective test which will identify for everyone islands which constitute a fringe in the immediate vicinity. States should, however, be guided by the general spirit of article 7.'[23] Two examples were given to illustrate

[18] LOSC (n 1) art 7(1).

[19] ibid.

[20] ibid art 7(2).

[21] These include that the baseline is not to depart to an appreciable extent from the general direction of the coast, ibid art 7(3); and limitations on the drawing of a baseline to and from low-tide elevations, ibid art 7(4).

[22] United Nations Office for Ocean Affairs and the Law of the Sea, *Baselines: An Examination of the Relevant Provisions of the United Nations Convention on the Law of the Sea* (United Nations 1989).

[23] ibid 20 [42].

this proposition where a fringe of islands is likely to exist. The first relates to the circumstances of the *Fisheries Case* and where the islands appear to form a unity with the mainland. The other is where the islands may be a distance from the coast and 'form a screen which masks a large proportion of the coast from the sea.'[24] As to the distance of the islands from the coast and being within the 'immediate vicinity', the view of the UN study was that a maximum distance of 24 miles would be satisfactory.[25] It was also observed that the concept applies to the inner edge of the islands because the fringe may be of considerable width.[26]

States have taken different views as to what constitutes a fringe of islands for the purposes of Article 7(1). The US position is that providing the islands in question meet the criteria under Article 121(1), then three further conditions must be met:

1. The most landward point of each island lies no more than 24 miles from the mainland coastline;
2. Each island to which a straight baseline is drawn is not more than 24 miles apart from the island from which the straight baseline is drawn; and
3. The islands, as a whole, mask at least 50 per cent of the mainland coastline in any given locality.[27]

The US is distinctive in having a precise positon on this issue, which has resulted in US diplomatic protests regarding the straight baseline claims of China, Cuba, Djibouti, Ecuador, Honduras, Italy, Japan, Mexico, Oman, Portugal, South Korea and Thailand.[28] The US is also of the view that the straight baselines drawn by Mauritius to and from islands and rocks off its mainland are not consistent with Article 7.[29]

An issue closely related to the interpretation of Article 7 and the drawing of straight baselines to and from islands is the length of the baselines. However, Article 7 is silent as to the length of straight baselines and there is considerable variance in state practice.[30] Whether or not a fringe of islands exists – allowing Article 7 straight baselines to be drawn to and from those islands – may become contentious during the delimitation of maritime boundaries. The status of three

[24] ibid 20 [45]; an example of such islands is given as the Recherche Archipelago off the coast of Western Australia, Australia.

[25] ibid 21 [46]; cf *Maritime Delimitation in the Black Sea (Romania v Ukraine)* (Judgment) [2009] ICJ Reps 61 [149] where the ICJ considered that Serpents' Island, at a distance of 20 nautical miles from the Ukrainian coast, could not be considered to be a part of the Ukraine's coastal configuration.

[26] ibid 21 [46].

[27] JA Roach and RW Smith, *Excessive Maritime Claims* (3rd edn, Martinus Nijhoff 2012) 62–63.

[28] ibid 98–107.

[29] Department of State (US), *Mauritius: Archipelagic and Other Maritime Claims and Boundaries (Limits in the Sea No 140)* (Department of State 2014) 5; see also discussion in Chapter 5 section III.A.(i) of this volume.

[30] See the discussion in International Law Association (ILA), *Committee on Baselines under the International Law of the Sea: Final Report* (Sydney 2018); and for an assessment of US state practice see Roach and Smith (n 27) 63–67.

islands in the Gulf of Riga was an aspect of the maritime delimitation between Estonia and Latvia. Estonia had in place a system of straight baselines drawn between three islands, one of which was located 37 nm from the coastline and which were at their closest 24.4 nm apart. This system of straight baselines to and from these islands was not relied upon for the purposes of a 1996 maritime boundary concluded between the two States.[31]

C. Straight Baselines and Courts and Tribunals

Since adoption and eventual entry into force of the LOSC, courts and tribunals have had a number of occasions to review Article 7 straight baselines and in doing so have considered issues associated with islands. In the *Eritrea/Yemen Arbitration*,[32] the status of the Dahlaks, a 'tightly knit group of islands and islets', and the capacity of the islands making up that group to be subject to straight baselines consistent with Article 7 were considered.[33] While the Tribunal and both of the parties agreed that the Dahlaks were an appropriate island group for the establishment of a straight baseline system, ultimately the validity of the actual baselines proposed by the parties was not a matter the Tribunal was called upon to decide.[34] In *Qatar v Bahrain*,[35] Qatar instituted proceedings against Bahrain in respect of disputes between the two States relating to sovereignty over certain islands and shoals, and the delimitation of the maritime areas between the two States. As to the method of determining straight baselines, Bahrain contended that it was a multi-island State characterised by a cluster of islands off the coast of its main islands and that as such it was a de facto archipelagic State.[36] Bahrain applied the method of straight baselines, maintaining that the external fringe should serve as the baseline for the territorial sea.[37] However, the ICJ observed that:

> the method of straight baselines, which is an exception to the normal rules for the determination of baselines, may only be applied if a number of conditions are met. This method must be applied restrictively. Such conditions are primarily that either the coastline is deeply indented and cut into, or that there is a fringe of islands along the coast in the immediate vicinity.[38]

[31] JI Charney and RW Smith, *International Maritime Boundaries*, vol 4 (Martinus Nijhoff, 2002) 3007.

[32] *Second stage of the proceedings between Eritrea and Yemen (Maritime Delimitation)* (Arbitral Award) (1999) 22 RIAA 335 (*Eritrea v Yemen*).

[33] ibid 367 [139].

[34] ibid 367 [140]–[142].

[35] *Maritime Delimitation and Territorial Questions between Qatar and Bahrain (Qatar v Bahrain)* (Judgment) [2001] ICJ Reps 40 (*Qatar v Bahrain*).

[36] ibid 96 [181].

[37] ibid 103 [210]–[211].

[38] ibid 103 [212].

Directly referring to Bahrain's claim that it was a 'multi-island State', the ICJ went on to observe that such an assertion does not allow the State 'to deviate from the normal rules for the determination of baselines unless the relevant conditions are met.'[39] The Court rejected Bahrain's contention that the maritime features off the coast of its main islands could be assimilated to a fringe of islands, noting that the islands were relatively small and that they would only be a part of a 'cluster of islands' or 'island system' if Bahrain's main islands were included.[40]

In *South China Sea* discussion arose regarding whether it would be permissible for China to enclose the Spratly Islands by a system of straight or archipelagic baselines 'surrounding the high-tide features of the group, and accorded an entitlement to maritime zones as a single unit'.[41] The Tribunal indicated that it did not agree with such a claim.[42] The Tribunal then turned to consider the application of Article 7 straight baselines, and observed that 'the Tribunal is aware of the practice of some States in employing straight baselines with respect to offshore archipelagos to approximate the effect of archipelagic baselines.'[43] Two views were expressed on this matter: one technical and the other relating to the overall application of the LOSC. The Tribunal made clear that Article 7 straight baselines could not be drawn in the case of an offshore archipelago as the relevant conditions of deeply indented or 'cut into' coastlines, or where there is a fringe of islands, do not exist.[44] The Tribunal then went on to observe:

> Although the Convention does not expressly preclude the use of straight baselines in other circumstances, the Tribunal considers that the grant of permission in Article 7 concerning straight baselines generally, together with the conditional permission in Articles 46 and 47 for certain States to draw archipelagic baselines, excludes the possibility of employing straight baselines in other circumstances, in particular with respect to offshore archipelagos not meeting the criteria for archipelagic baselines. Any other interpretation would effectively render the conditions in Articles 7 and 47 meaningless.[45]

While acknowledging the existence of contrary state practice, the Tribunal was firmly of the view that there was no evidence that any deviations had amounted to the formation of a new rule of customary international law justifying 'a departure from the express provisions of the Convention.'[46]

[39] ibid 103 [213].
[40] ibid 103 [213]–[214].
[41] *In the Matter of the South China Sea Arbitration before an Arbitral Tribunal constituted under Annex VII of the 1982 United Nations Convention on the Law of the Sea (Philippines v China)* (Merits) (12 July 2016) PCA Case No 2013-19, 236 [573] (*South China Sea*); this question was discussed in the context of statements made by China indicating that it claimed a territorial sea, EEZ and continental shelf 'based on the Nansha Islands as a whole.': ibid 235 [571].
[42] ibid 236 [573]; discussed in more detail in Chapter 5, section VII.C of this volume.
[43] ibid 237 [575].
[43] ibid.
[44] ibid.
[45] ibid.
[46] Ibid.

This review of the relevant cases highlights that international courts and tribunals have adopted a conservative position in their interpretation of Article 7 and its application in the case of islands, and a similar approach has been taken by some of the leading publicists in the field. For example, Prescott and Schofield have observed that:

> The reference to the fringe of islands being in the immediate vicinity of the coast must be construed to mean the landward edge of the fringe … While the intent of the phrase ['immediate vicinity'] is clear enough, Article 7 fails to deliver a clear-cut, objective test by which to judge whether certain islands are close enough to a mainland in order to be considered in its immediate vicinity.[47]

Reisman and Westerman are of the view that Article 7(1) introduces three cumulative tests as follows:

1. There must be a number of islands that are spatially related to each other so as to create a 'fringe';
2. The islands must be distributed 'along' the coast; and
3. There is a relational element between the islands and coast in terms of their proximity.

They are of the view that each of these elements must be established cumulatively in order to meet the geographical test.[48]

Islands play a critical role in how States have interpreted and applied Article 7 in their drawing of straight baselines. While international courts and tribunals and leading publicists take a conservative positon, there are examples of expansive interpretations of Article 7 in state practice. Some States, such as the US, actively resist excessive straight baseline claims and lodge diplomatic protests or ignore claims they consider to be inconsistent with the LOSC. However, it can generally be observed that many States remain silent on this matter with the effect that gradually more expansive island-related straight baseline claims are being tolerated.[49] Finally, it needs to be recalled that as artificial islands do not possess the status of islands, they have no impact upon the drawing of straight baselines.

III. Historic Waters

Claims to historic waters may encompass waters adjacent to an island or which may enclose islands and waters adjacent to a continental State. However, the

[47] Prescott and Schofield (n 3) 147.

[48] Reisman and Westerman, *Straight Baselines in International Maritime Boundary Delimitation* (n 16) 82–83; see also the discussion in S Kopela, *Dependent Archipelagos in the Law of the Sea* (Martinus Nijhoff 2013) 56–63.

[49] See a review of relevant state practice in this area in International Law Association, 'Baselines under the International Law of the Sea' (Final Report, Sydney Conference, 2018).

LOSC does not expressly deal with historic waters. The related concept of 'historic title' is referred to in the case of the delimitation of the territorial sea in Article 15, and in Article 298 where reference is made to 'historic bays and titles' which under certain conditions are exempted from compulsory dispute settlement under Part XV. Consistently with the LOSC,[50] the law on historic claims in the law of the sea is therefore considered under general international law. In this respect the ICJ has observed that general international law 'does not provide for a single "regime" for "historic waters" or "historic bays", but only for a particular régime for each of the concrete, recognized cases of "historic waters" or "historic bays"'. In the *Fisheries Case* the ICJ commented generally with respect to historic waters that: 'By "historic waters" are usually meant waters which are treated as internal waters but which would not have that character were it not for the existence of an historic title.'[51]

The most authoritative study on historic waters, and which remains of contemporary relevance,[52] is a 1962 study on the *Juridical Regime of Historic waters including historic bays* prepared by the United Nations Secretariat (UN Study) at the request of the ILC. The UN study concluded with respect to historic waters that:

> In determining whether or not a title to 'historic waters' exists, there are three factors which have to be taken into consideration, namely,
>
> (i) The authority exercised over the area by the State claiming it as 'historic waters';
> (ii) The continuity of such exercise of authority;
> (iii) The attitude of foreign States.[53]

Each criterion was then separately developed as follows:

> First, effective exercise of sovereignty over the area by the claiming State is a necessary requirement for title to the area as 'historic waters' of that State. Secondly, such exercise of sovereignty must have continued during a considerable time so as to have developed into a usage. Thirdly, the attitude of foreign States to the activities of the claiming State in the area must have been such that it can be characterized as an attitude of general toleration.[54]

These criteria continued to be accepted by publicists,[55] international courts and tribunals,[56] and also generally in state practice, though the US positon is that

[50] See Preamble, operative paragraph 8, *LOSC* which states '*Affirming* that matters not regulated by this Convention continue to be governed by the rules and principles of general international law.'

[51] *Fisheries Case* (n 8) 130.

[52] *South China Sea* (n 41) 94–95 [222].

[53] International Law Commission, 'Juridical Regime of Historic waters including historic bays – Study prepared by the Secretariat' in *Yearbook of the International Law Commission*, vol 2 (1962) UN Doc A/CN.4/143, 25 [185] (*UN Study*).

[54] ibid 25 [186].

[55] See eg O'Connell (n 16) 427–35; Pharand (n 5) 105; CR Symmons, *Historic waters and historic rights in the law of the sea: a modern reappraisal* (2nd edn, Brill Nijhoff 2019) 184–85 (*Historic waters and historic rights*).

[56] *South China Sea* (n 41) 113 [265].

'an actual showing of acquiescence by foreign states in such a claim is required, as opposed to a mere absence of opposition'.[57] In *South China Sea* the Tribunal generally commented on the international law regarding historic claims, including historic title and historic waters, and observed as follows:

> The term 'historic rights' is general in nature and can describe any rights that a State may possess that would normally arise under the general rules of international law, absent particular historical circumstances. Historic rights may include sovereignty, but may equally include more limited rights, such as fishing rights or rights of access, that fall well short of a claim of sovereignty. 'Historic title', in contrast, is used specifically to refer to historic sovereignty to land or maritime areas. 'Historic waters' is simply a term for historic title over maritime areas, typically exercised either as a claim to internal waters or as a claim to the territorial sea.[58]

Setting aside claims to an island based on some form of historic title or historic claim which fall within the international law of territoriality,[59] the waters adjacent to islands may be claimed as historic waters and so fall within the remit of this area of general international law.

There are three possible categories of historic waters claims in the waters adjacent to an island, subject to meeting the criteria noted above. The first is where waters adjacent to an island are the subject of an historic waters claim. In this respect, the fact that the claim is to waters adjacent to an island is no different than in the case of waters adjacent to a continental State.[60] The second is where islands adjacent to a mainland are encompassed within an historic waters claim, thereby including all of the waters between the mainland and the offshore islands. An equivalent claim was assessed by the ICJ in *Fisheries*,[61] where the legitimacy of the Norwegian claim was upheld as it related to the waters between the Norwegian mainland and the adjacent outer islands of the *skjærgaard*.[62] The third is where the waters between and adjacent to a cluster of islands, including archipelagos, are subject to such a claim. In this respect, claims of historic waters between and adjacent to such islands have in many instances now been enveloped within archipelagic State claims.[63] A similar position exists with respect to traditional or artisanal fishing rights. In *South China Sea* there was a reluctance to recognise such rights on the basis that the LOSC prevalled with respect to EEZ fishing entitlements.[64]

[57] Roach and Smith (n 27) 35.

[58] *South China Sea* (n 41) 96 [225].

[59] See discussion in Chapter 3 of this volume.

[60] An example that has been given is Sri Lanka and the Gulf of Manaar; see Symmons, *Historic Waters and Historic Rights* (n 55) 93.

[61] *Fisheries Case* (n 8) 130–31; also see the general analysis and discussion of this question in the *UN Study*.

[62] See the discussion in Symmons, *Historic Waters and Historic Rights* (n 55) 92.

[63] CR Symmons, *Historic Waters in the Law of the Sea: A Modern Re-Appraisal* (Martinus Nijhoff 2008) 295.

[64] *South China Sea* (n 41) 312–15 [799]–[803]; cf *Eritrea v Yemen* which *South China Sea* did not endorse on this point: 314 [803].

What is clear, however, on the basis of both state practice and the decisions of international courts and tribunals, is that historic waters claims are exceptional and may be only made under strict conditions.[65]

Canada has sought to make an historic waters claim with respect to the islands of the Canadian Arctic Archipelago situated to the north of the Canadian mainland. This claim was partly reflected in the 1970 Arctic Waters Pollution Prevention Act,[66] which established strict marine pollution provisions for vessels seeking to pass through the Northwest Passage and related waters, and the 1985 declaration of straight baselines around the islands of the Canadian Arctic Archipelago so as to enclose the waters as internal waters of Canada. Pharand has exhaustively assessed the Canadian claim – which can best be described as a mixed claim to the islands and waters between the islands and the mainland – which pre-dates Canadian Confederation (1876) and includes British actions dating back to 1576.[67] Setting aside British and Canadian claims to the islands, Pharand is of the view that upon applying the accepted criteria, Canada cannot succeed in making out a claim establishing that the waters of the Canadian Arctic Archipelago are historic internal waters.[68] This view is shared by the US, with its earliest recorded protest being in 1906.[69]

In *South China Sea* the Tribunal had occasion to consider the legitimacy of China's so-called 'nine-dash line', which is a series of nine dashes drawn on maps of the South China Sea encompassing the islands and waters within the sea, including those that make up the Paracel island group and Spratly island group. The Tribunal assessed the extent of the 'nine-dash line' and considered whether it could be characterised in a manner consistent with the LOSC or general international law. In that regard it was observed that:

> the scope of a claim to historic rights depends upon the scope of the acts that are carried out as the exercise of the claimed right. Evidence that either the Philippines or China had historically made use of the islands of the South China Sea would, at most, support a claim to historic rights to those islands. Evidence of use giving rise to historic rights with respect to the islands, however, would not establish historic rights to the waters beyond the territorial sea. The converse is also true: historic usage of waters of the South China Sea cannot lead to rights with respect to the islands there. The two domains are distinct.[70]

[65] Pharand (n 5) 94; see also *Continental Shelf (Tunisia v Libya Arab Jamahiriya)* (Dissenting Opinion of Judge Oda) [1982] ICJ Reps 18, 210 observing that 'the concept of historic waters may be claimed only where strict adherence to the geographical conditions required for internal waters (such as bays, straight baselines) might lead to a somewhat inequitable result because of the longstanding exercise of powers by the coastal State concerned.'

[66] Arctic Waters Pollution Prevention Act 1970 (Canada).

[67] Pharand (n 5) 113–25.

[68] ibid 125.

[69] Roach and Smith (n 27) 37.

[70] *South China Sea* (n 41) 113 [266].

In this regard, the Tribunal sought to emphasise the distinction between the international law of territoriality, upon which certain historic factors may be relevant for the purposes of asserting a territorial claim over an island, and historic factors as they may relate to the waters adjacent to that island.

With respect to China's activities within the 'nine-dash line', the Tribunal observed that these amounted to nothing more than the exercise of the high seas freedom of navigation and the freedom of fishing and in particular there was no evidence to suggest that China had sought to historically regulate or control fishing in the area beyond the territorial sea.[71] The Tribunal concluded that there was no basis to find that China had any historic rights to the living and non-living resources of the South China Sea within the EEZ and continental shelf of other coastal States,[72] and observed that the LOSC 'does not include any express provisions preserving or protecting historic rights that are at variance with the Convention'.[73] However, the Tribunal sought to emphasise that its determination on this aspect of the Award did not comment in any way on any of China's historic claims to the islands of the South China Sea.[74] The recent analysis and review in *South China Sea* of historic claims to waters adjacent to islands reinforces that such claims are exceptional under general international law. As such, unless such claims are currently recognised or have a longstanding historical background accompanied by acquiescence or acceptance by other States new claims are most unlikely to be recognised.[75]

IV. Bays

Straight or 'closing lines' may also be drawn across bays creating internal waters on the landward side of the baseline, and from which maritime claims can then be asserted into the adjacent seas. The law of the sea recognises two types of bays. The first are juridical bays, which are bays that meet certain geographic criteria set down in LOSC, Article 10. The second category are so-called 'historic bays'. Both types of bays have relevance for islands that are located with them.

[71] ibid 114–15 [270].
[72] ibid.
[73] ibid 103 [246].
[74] ibid 115 [272]; on this aspect of the Award see also analysis in SD Murphy, *International Law Relating to Islands* (Brill/Nijhoff 2017) 150–59; Chinese Society of International Law, 'The South China Sea Arbitration Awards: A Critical Study' (2018) 17(2) *Chinese Journal of International Law* 207, 427–539.
[75] This view is shared by Symmons, *Historic Waters and Historic Rights* (n 55) 430.

A. Juridical Bays

Article 10 provides for the drawing of straight baselines within a juridical bay. As bays shared by two or more States are excluded from the rule,[76] Article 10 only includes single State bays. Article 10(2) defines a juridical bay, providing some general guidance as to size and indentation from the coast. A semi-circle test is applied whose diameter is a line drawn across the mouth of the bay. The line is determined from the low-water mark of the natural entrance points of the bay. Determining the entrance points of a bay may not always be straightforward due to the coastal geography.[77] Different outcomes arise if the distance between the natural entrance points is less than or greater than 24 nm. If less than 24 nm, then a closing line is drawn across those entrance points and the waters on the landward side of the line are considered internal waters. If greater than 24 nm then a straight baseline of 24 nm shall be drawn within the limits of the bay. In this regard a special rule applies to bays within which islands are located across the mouth of the bay, so as to create more than one mouth or entrance point. In that instance, the semi-circle is drawn on a line which is the sum total of the lengths of lines across the different mouths of the bay.[78] The effect of this rule is to neutralise the impact of the islands and ensures the semi-circle test is not distorted by islands located across the mouth of the bay. Likewise, islands that are located within the bay are to be taken as part of the water area of the indentation for the purposes of applying the semi-circle test.[79]

The state practice with respect to islands and LOSC Article 10 bay closing lines is variable and in some instances contentious. Grenada and Mauritius are examples of coastal States whose proclaimed juridical bays satisfy the requirements of Article 10.[80] In the case of the UK, the Territorial Sea (Baselines) Order 2014 proclaims certain baselines adjacent to the UK, Channel Islands and Isle of Man and specifically endorses the application of Article 10.[81] However, there are a number of instances of state practice which exceed the provisions of Article 10 and the rules concerning bays more generally which have been the subject of protest. Examples include Libya's claims with respect to the Gulf of Sidra,[82] Argentina's

[76] LOSC (n 1) art 10(1); Westerman asserts this provision was 'necessary in order to prevent large bodies of water such as the Mediterranean or Baltic seas from technically becoming juridical bays under Article 7': GS Westerman, *The Juridical Bay* (Oxford University Press 1987) 79.

[77] SN Nandan and S Rosenne (eds), *United Nations Convention on the Law of the Sea 1982: A Commentary*, vol 2 (Martinus Nijhoff 1993) 117.

[78] LOSC (n 1) art 10(3).

[79] ibid.

[80] See, eg, Department of State (US), *Mauritius* (n 29) 1, 6 – with the exception of Mathurn Bay, the six bay closing lines put forward by Mauritius in the 2005 Regulations to the Maritime Zones Act 2005 satisfy the 'semi-circle test' and do not rely upon closing lines in excess of 24 nm. Grenada's 28 bays equally satisfy both requirements: Department of State (US), *Grenada: Archipelagic and Other Maritime Claims and Boundaries (Limits in the Sea No 135)* (Department of State 2014) 1, 3.

[81] The Territorial Sea (Baselines) Order 2014 (Order No 1353) (UK) 'Explanatory Note'.

[82] Roach and Smith (n 27) 46–47, 129.

straight baselines across the mouths of the San Jorge and San Matias gulfs,[83] and closing lines drawn across bays by Mauritania,[84] Sudan[85] and Costa Rica.[86] The US has also objected to the use of straight baselines to delimit waters off the mainland coast of Portugal and the Azores on the grounds that the baselines relied upon 'do not enclose juridical bays or lie in localities which meet the legal requirement that the coastline is deeply indented and cut into.'[87] Straight baselines drawn by Gabon in excess of 24 nm between Pointe Ngombe and Cap Lopes have also been questioned.[88]

There is relatively little jurisprudence on the application of Article 10 of the LOSC, though the ICJ in the *Land, Island and Maritime Frontier Dispute* case determined that its provisions 'might be found to express general customary law.'[89] The case provided some relevant statements on the legal status and effect of the closing line used to delimit the Gulf of Fonseca, which is a tri-State bay shared by El Salvador, Honduras, and Nicaragua, within which there are located a number of islands including Isla del Tigre (Tiger Island) and Meanguera del Golfo. The closing lines of the Gulf of Fonseca are drawn from Punta Amapala (on the coast of El Salvador) to Punta Cosigüina (in Nicaragua).[90] As the Gulf of Fonseca extends from the coast of one State to that of another, the Gulf does not satisfy the test for a juridical bay.[91] However the ICJ concurred with the generally accepted conclusion that the Gulf of Fonseca is an historic bay.[92]

B. Historic Bays

Article 10 of the LOSC does not apply to so-called 'historic bays'[93] and accordingly the rules of general international law, as reflected in customary international law, apply to such bays. Historic bays and waters have been the subject of comment by a number of international courts and tribunals, most recently in *South China Sea*

[83] ibid 46–47, 129.

[84] ibid 130.

[85] ibid.

[86] Department of State (US), *Straight Baselines Claim: Costa Rica (Limits in the Seas No 111)* (Department of State 1990) 1, 7 citing the Text of US Protest Note to Costa Rica, 18 December 1989.

[87] Department of State (US), *United States Responses to Excessive National Maritime Claims (Limits in the Seas No 112)* (Department of State 1992) 1, 32 quoting a diplomatic note transmitted by the American Embassy at Lisbon, based on instructions found in 1986 State telegram 266998.

[88] DA Colston and RW Smith, *International Maritime Boundaries*, vol 5 (Martinus Nijhoff 2005) 3687.

[89] *Land, Maritime and Island Frontier Dispute (El Salvador v Honduras: Nicaragua intervening)* (Judgment) [1992] ICJ Reps 351, 588 (*Land, Maritime and Island Frontier Dispute*). See also RR Churchill and AV Lowe, *The Law of the Sea* (3rd edn, Manchester University Press 1999) 42.

[90] *Land, Maritime and Island Frontier Dispute* (n 89) 588.

[91] ibid.

[92] ibid.

[93] LOSC (n 1) art 10(6).

where it was observed that 'The concept of a historic bay is well understood in international law'.[94] This characterisation extends to those bays which do not meet the criteria of juridical bays, but which historically have been treated as internal waters. There exists a body of historic and contemporary state practice to that effect which includes both continental States and island States, of which Great Britain was at the forefront as this area of law evolved during the nineteenth century.[95]

A number of factors will be relevant to identifying historic bays within islands. Longstanding state practice, including relevant decrees, laws, statutes and regulations that have considered the waters of the bay to be the equivalent of internal waters will be critical. A formal claim as to the historic status of the bay is also necessary. Such a claim would need to be one that has been publicised in a manner that other States will have knowledge and awareness of. Likewise, some level of recognition of the historic status of the waters of the bay by other States will be important. This could extend to recognising the historic rights of the coastal State to regulate fishing within the bay, or accepting baselines drawn across the bay for the purposes of a maritime boundary delimitation. Symmons lists historic bay claims by the Dominican Republic, the Philippines, Sri Lanka, and the UK.[96] Historic bays within islands are more than likely to be found in longstanding island States and also on islands that historically had governmental procedures in place enabling the exercise of sovereignty over such waters. An historic bay is therefore unlikely to be found in sparsely settled, remote islands. Vanuatu, an archipelagic State, makes provision in its Maritime Zones Act for the declaration of an historic title over a bay but to date no such claim has been made.[97] While there is an established body of law and state practice with respect to claims to historic bays, the claims of both continental States and island States have been subject to challenge. The US has protested claims to historic bays and historic waters by a number of coastal States.[98] US protests against historic bay claims have been made against island States including the Dominican Republic,[99] and Sri Lanka.[100] Mauritius, which also has claimed archipelagic State status, has drawn a 1.97 nm long historic

[94] *South China Sea* (n 41) 86 [205].

[95] See generally, O'Connell (n 16) ch 9.

[96] Symmons, *Historic Waters and Historic Rights* (n 55) 437–40 lists 'alleged historic bays' as reflected in post-World War II state practice, and the analysis of publicists, located in Argentina, Australia, Bulgaria, Canada, Cambodia, China, Dominican Republic, Egypt, France, Netherlands, Norway, Portugal, Guatemala, Italy, Kenya, Libya, Panama, Philippines, Russia, Slovenia, Sri Lanka, Sweden, Thailand, Tunisia, UK, Ukraine, US, Vietnam, and former French Equatorial Africa.

[97] Maritime Zones Act No 6 of 2010 (Vanuatu) s 7(3).

[98] Roach and Smith (n 27) 36–56.

[99] ibid 37, with respect to the Escocesa and Santo Domingo Bays, in which the UK joined the US in also expressing its views that these were not historic bays; see Department of State (US), *Dominican Republic: Archipelagic and other Maritime Claims and Boundaries (Limits in the Seas No 130)* (Department of State 2014) Annex IV.

[100] Roach and Smith (n 27) 38 with respect to Palk Bay; cf LFE Goldie, 'Historic Bays in International Law – An Impressionistic Overview' (1984) 11 *Syracuse Journal of International Law and Commerce* 211, 224–25.

bay closing line across Mathurin Bay on the island of Rodrigues. This claim, apparently not made until 2005, is considered by the US Department of State to not meet the criteria for an historic bay of 'acquiescence by foreign States of "open, effective, long term, and continuous exercise of authority over the body of water"'.[101]

V. Internal Waters

An island, whether it be part of a continental State or an island State, may also have internal waters as a result of the drawing of Article 7 straight baselines. This is made clear in Article 8 which makes no distinction between islands and other landmasses that are located 'on the landward side of the baseline of the territorial sea'. An exception exists with respect to archipelagic States where waters on the landward side of the territorial sea baseline are considered archipelagic waters. Nevertheless, it is possible for archipelagic States to have internal waters as a result of the drawing of closing lines consistent with Articles 9, 10 and 11 in the mouths of rivers, across bays and ports.[102] The internal waters of an island may arise from the drawing of Article 7 straight baselines as a result of the nature of the coastline, an adjacent fringe of islands, a river mouth, an historic or juridical bay, or a port. Accordingly, full sovereignty can be exercised over those internal waters in precisely the same manner as the internal waters of a mainland. Larger island States that have drawn Article 7 straight baselines have bodies of internal waters that are located on the landward side of those baselines, including Iceland, Ireland, Japan,[103] Madagascar, and the UK. Smaller island States including Cyprus, Malta, Nauru, and Samoa have also drawn straight baselines and thus have bodies of internal waters.

VI. Territorial Sea and Contiguous Zone

The sovereignty of a coastal State includes the area known as the territorial sea, which encompasses the water column, sea-bed, subsoil and the air space over that sea.[104] This sovereignty is part of the inherent right of all coastal States and it flows from the territorial entitlements of the State. The only distinction that applies is that which exists between an island (including juridical rocks), and low-tide elevations. Low-tide elevations situated beyond the breadth of the territorial sea

[101] Department of State (US), *Mauritius* (n 29) 6.

[102] See discussion in Chapter 5 section VII.B of this volume.

[103] See 'Deposit by Japan of charts and lists of geographical coordinates of points, pursuant to article 16, paragraph 2 of the Convention' (18 March 2008) UN Doc M.Z.N.61.2008.LOS, www.un.org/Depts/los/LEGISLATIONANDTREATIES/PDFFILES/mzn_s/mzn61.pdf.

[104] LOSC (n 1) art 2(1).

have no territorial sea of their own.[105] Low-tide elevations that are situated at a distance not exceeding the breadth of the territorial sea from the mainland or an island, may be used as a basepoint for the drawing of straight baselines from which the territorial sea is then measured.[106] As noted above, artificial islands do not generate their own territorial sea.[107] A naturally-formed island that has been the subject of land reclamation remains, however, a juridical island from which a territorial sea can legitimately be claimed.

A coastal State has an entitlement to establish a territorial sea that extends up to 12 nm from the baselines[108] and accordingly most coastal States seek to proclaim a territorial sea of 12 nm. However, there is no *requirement* that a 12 nm territorial sea be proclaimed, nor is there a requirement that a coastal State should have a uniform territorial sea of the same breadth around its coast. In this respect, it is notable that some coastal States have adopted variable breadths for territorial seas proclaimed from islands. In the 1978 Torres Strait Treaty between Australia and Papua New Guinea (PNG) provision is made for a fixed territorial sea breadth for 15 Australian islands located in the Torres Strait.[109] This allowance was made because the islands were to the north of a median line negotiated between the parties through the Torres Strait and by limiting the territorial sea entitlements of the islands it was possible to limit what would otherwise have been a distorting impact created by those Australian islands within an area of PNG sea-bed and fisheries jurisdiction. One of the islands in question, Pearce Cay, is located very close to the median line that runs through the Strait. An allowance is made for that island's territorial sea that is to the south of the median line and within an area of predominantly Australian fisheries and sea-bed jurisdiction.[110] When Australia extended its territorial sea from three to 12 nm in 1990, one consequence was that Pearce Cay was limited to a three nm territorial sea to the north (as per the Torres Strait Treaty) while to the south it generated a 12 nm territorial sea.[111]

This differential treatment of the territorial sea entitlement of certain islands is not exceptional. In the case of Japan, a territorial sea of less than 12 nm has

[105] ibid art 13(2).
[106] ibid art 13(1).
[107] ibid art 60(8).
[108] ibid art 3.
[109] Treaty between Australia and the Independent State of Papua New Guinea concerning Sovereignty and Maritime Boundaries in the area between the two Countries, including the area known as Torres Strait and Related Matters (Australia–Papua New Guinea) (adopted 18 December 1978, entered into force 15 February 1985) [1985] ATS 4 (Torres Strait Treaty) art 3(2) which provides: 'The territorial seas of the islands specified in sub-paragraph 1(a) of Article 2 of this Treaty shall not extend beyond three miles from the baselines from which the breadth of the territorial sea around each island is measured. Those territorial seas shall not be enlarged or reduced, even if there were to be any change in the configuration of a coastline or a different result from any further survey.'
[110] ibid art 3(3).
[111] See the discussion in BR Opeskin and DR Rothwell, 'Australia's Territorial Sea: International and Federal Implications of its Extension to 12 Miles' (1991) 22 *Ocean Development and International Law* 395, 399–401.

been proclaimed around some islands to ensure that the adjacent waters are not enclosed within the territorial sea so as to retain high seas corridors within certain straits.[112] The UK has also previously claimed a territorial sea of three nm around some islands that constitute British Overseas Territories, and a 12 nm territorial sea over other islands, including Great Britain.[113]

A coastal State is entitled to proclaim a contiguous zone that may not extend beyond 24 nm. The zone is contiguous to the territorial sea within which the coastal State can exercise enforcement jurisdiction with respect to customs, fiscal, immigration and sanitary matters.[114] To that end the coastal State can engage in enforcement of its laws and regulations with respect to any breaches that occur within the territorial sea and seek to punish such violations of its laws, or prevent infringement of its laws and regulations with respect to vessels entering its contiguous zone and navigating towards the territorial sea. Article 121(2) makes clear that islands can possess a contiguous zone consistently with the LOSC provisions 'applicable to other land territory'. As the contiguous zone is not a resources zone and does not confer any greater entitlements beyond the 12 nm territorial sea than law enforcement and prevention, a coastal State can, consistently with the LOSC, claim both a territorial sea and contiguous zone from a juridical rock. Where a coastal State previously considered a maritime feature to be a juridical island, and then conceded the feature to be a juridical rock, claims to an EEZ (or Fisheries Zone equivalent) and continental shelf would need to be abandoned.[115]

VII. Continental Shelf

The continental shelf was the first dedicated maritime zone focussed on resource sovereignty, and its significance for islands has grown as the regime developed through the 1945 Truman Proclamation, to the 1958 Convention on the Continental Shelf, and finally to the LOSC. Article 76 makes clear that the continental shelf of a coastal State comprises the sea-bed and subsoil extending to a

[112] See Department of State (US), *Straight Baseline and Territorial Sea Claims: Japan (Limits in the Seas No 120)* (Department of State 1998) 13, where it was observed with respect to the Japanese position regarding the Eastern and Western Channels of the Tsushima Strait, Osumi Strait, La Perouse Strait (Soya Strait) and Tsugaru Strait that: 'Japan did not wish to have the transit passage regime apply to five international straits situated adjacent to its coasts. By defining a narrow territorial sea less than 12 miles in these straits, Japan has maintained a channel of high seas through which all ships and aircraft could exercise high seas navigation and overflight freedoms.'; see also the detailed analysis that appears at 14–15.

[113] Roach and Smith (n 27) 138.

[114] LOSC (n 1) art 33(1).

[115] See the UK position with respect to Rockall discussed in R Churchill, 'United Kingdom: Accession to the UN Convention on the Law of the Sea' (1998) 13 *International Journal of Marine and Coastal Law* 263; and discussion in Chapter 1 section II.B of this volume.

minimum distance of 200 nm, or, where the continental margin permits, beyond that distance to a limit determined by a variety of factors based on geology and geomorphology. Coastal State continental shelf claims beyond 200 nm are based on the recommendations of the CLCS.[116] The effect of Article 76 is that all coastal States enjoy a minimum 200 nm continental shelf, which is to be distinguished from the 1958 Convention on the Continental Shelf which did not provide the same level of certainty for all States.[117] Article 76 LOSC does not make any distinction regarding the land from which a continental shelf extends, only referring to the existence of a 'coastal State'.[118] Artificial islands do not enjoy an entitlement to a continental shelf,[119] though they may be located within the continental shelf of the coastal State which has constructed the artificial island.[120]

The entitlement of coastal States to proclaim a continental shelf from offshore islands has been well recognised in state practice. It is reflected in numerous claims to a LOSC Article 76 juridical continental shelf of 200 nm, and in maritime boundary delimitations where the continental shelf entitlements of such islands are recognised.[121] The maritime domain may be a critical factor that reflects upon the continental shelf entitlement of an island. Singapore, for example, enjoys only a narrow continental shelf because of its geographic circumstances, where immediately to the north Malaysia is located across the Straits of Johor, while to the south across the Singapore Strait is Indonesia. Likewise, Sri Lanka's continental shelf is constrained by its geographic proximity to India located to the northwest across the Palk Strait. A similar position exists for Cyprus, which is constrained to the north and northeast by the Turkish and Lebanese coasts. The Australian islands of Boigu, Dauan, and Saibai, located immediately to the south of PNG in the Torres Strait, have no continental shelf entitlement under the 1978 Torres Strait Treaty because of their small size and location immediately offshore the PNG coast.[122]

The significance of islands for the purposes of continental shelf entitlements was highlighted once CLCS submissions under Article 76 procedures began in 2001. As part of this process coastal States were required to submit data supporting their claim to a continental shelf beyond 200 nm to the CLCS, with details of the submission made available via publication of an Executive Summary on the website of the United Nations Division of Ocean Affairs and the Law of the Sea. The transparency of CLCS submissions provided an opportunity for other States to comment through published communications to the Secretary-General of the United Nations.

[116] LOSC (n 1) art 76(8).
[117] Convention on the Continental Shelf (adopted 29 April 1958, entered into force 10 June 1964) 499 UNTS 311, art 1.
[118] LOSC (n 1) art 76(1).
[119] ibid art 60(8).
[120] ibid art 80.
[121] See discussion in Chapter 8 of this volume.
[122] Torres Strait Treaty (n 109) art 4.

Two comments can be made with respect to these processes. The first is that coastal States have sought to take advantage of their entitlement, consistent with Articles 76 and 121, to proclaim continental shelves beyond 200 nm from islands. Australia's practice here is prominent given that it has proclaimed a continental shelf beyond 200 nm offshore very large islands such as Tasmania,[123] and smaller islands such as Heard Island, Macquarie Island, and Norfolk Island. Of these three latter islands, only Norfolk Island has a permanent population – of 1,748 persons.[124] Nevertheless, as Australian sovereignty over these islands is uncontested and no other States have raised issues as to Australia's capacity to proclaim a continental shelf offshore these islands, Australia did so in 2012.[125] Other States to assert continental shelf claims consistent with LOSC Article 76 based on juridical islands include Mauritius, the Seychelles,[126] and the Philippines – an archipelagic State.[127] New Zealand has also received CLCS recommendations in the case of the remote and uninhabited Campbell and Auckland Islands in the Southern Ocean.[128]

The second observation is that some CLCS submissions involving islands were the subject of diplomatic protest with respect to territorial disputes over the islands. If a State is not the territorial sovereign over an island then it follows that it is not the coastal State entitled to proclaim a continental shelf offshore that island. Consistently with Rule 46 and Annex I of the CLCS Rules of Procedure,[129] the Commission may elect to not consider a submission relating to disputed land territory. Accordingly, for example, the CLCS did not consider that part of the original 2009 Argentine submission relating to the Falkland Islands, South Georgia and the South Sandwich Islands following a communication received from the

[123] Tasmania is a separate state under the Constitution of the Commonwealth of Australia, having all of the rights and entitlements of an Australian state with a 2021 population of 528,000.

[124] Department of Infrastructure, Regional Government and Cities (Government of Australia), 'Norfolk Island' www.infrastructure.gov.au/territories-regions-cities/territories/norfolk-island, based on Australian Bureau of Statistics 2016 data.

[125] 'Deposit by Australia pursuant to Article 76, paragraph 9, and 84 of the Convention, of relevant information, including geodetic data, permanently describing the outer limits of its continental shelf' (9 November 2012) UN Doc M.Z.N. 92.2012.LOS.

[126] 'Deposit by Mauritius and Seychelles of a list of geographical coordinates, pursuant to article 84, paragraph 2, of the Convention' (8 November 2012) UN Doc M.Z.N. 91.2012.LOS www.un.org/Depts/los/LEGISLATIONANDTREATIES/PDFFILES/mzn_s/mzn91ef.pdf.

[127] 'Deposit by the Philippines, pursuant to article 76, paragraph 9, of the Convention, of a chart and relevant information, including geodetic data, permanently describing the outer limits of its continental shelf' (17 July 2012) UN Doc M.Z.N. 88.2012.LOS, www.un.org/Depts/los/LEGISLATIONANDTREATIES/PDFFILES/mzn_s/mzn88ef.pdf.

[128] Commission on the Limits of the Continental Shelf 'Statement by the Chairman of the Commission on the Limits of the Continental Shelf on the progress of work in the Commission' CLCS/60 (26 September 2008) [8]–[11]; see discussion of the New Zealand maritime claims from these islands in J Mossop, 'The South China Sea Arbitration and New Zealand's Maritime Claims' (2017) 15 *New Zealand Journal of Public and International Law* 265.

[129] Commission on the Limits of the Continental Shelf, 'Rules of Procedure of the Commission on the Limits of the Continental Shelf' (17 April 2008) UN Doc CLCS/Rev/40.1, https://documents-dds-ny.un.org/doc/UNDOC/GEN/N08/309/23/PDF/N0830923.pdf?OpenElement.

UK indicating that it asserted sovereignty over these islands.[130] As to the status of an island under Article 121, the CLCS was also faced with a number of diplomatic communications lodged by China and the Republic of Korea with respect to Japan's CLCS submission regarding the entitlement of Okinotorishima[131] to generate a continental shelf. The position taken by the Commission on this matter was to note the diplomatic communications that had been received and to take no action on this aspect of the Japanese submission until such time as the 'matters referred to in the *notes verbales* had been resolved.'[132] The CLCS handed down recommendations to Japan with respect to other aspects of its CLCS submission but not in the case of Okinotorishima. Island territorial disputes are therefore a common aspect of diplomatic communications that have become an aspect of CLCS processes, which has effectively neutralised the capacity of certain islands to generate an extended continental shelf consistently with the LOSC.

VIII. Exclusive Economic Zone

While the recognition accorded to the continental shelf was a significant twentieth-century development in the law of the sea, the eventual recognition accorded to the EEZ during LOSC negotiations in the 1970s was perhaps more significant for island States and islands more generally. The continental shelf was a regime that developed States especially were able to take advantage of due to their economic and technological capability.[133] The EEZ, on the other hand, was an entitlement – equitably enjoyed by all States – to a 200 nm maritime zone. The configuration of the adjacent maritime area was therefore irrelevant and the only LOSC factor that needed to be taken into account was whether the land in question was a juridical island or a juridical rock.

The importance of the EEZ to island States was highlighted in disputes between Iceland and the UK in the 1960s and 1970s over Fisheries Zones.[134]

[130] See Commission on the Limits of the Continental Shelf, 'Summary of Recommendations of the Commission on the Limits of the Continental Shelf in regard to the submission made by Argentina on 21 April 2009' (21 August 2015; approved by the CLCS 11 March 2016) [11], www.un.org/Depts/los/clcs_new/submissions_files/arg25_09/2016_03_11_COM_SUMREC_ARG.pdf; see the UK Communication, Note 84/09 (6 August 2009), www.un.org/Depts/los/clcs_new/submissions_files/arg25_09/clcs_45_2009_los_gbr.pdf.

[131] See China Communication, Note CML/2/2009 (6 February 2009) www.un.org/depts/los/clcs_new/submissions_files/jpn08/chn_6feb09_e.pdf, and Republic of Korea Communication, Note MUN/046/09 (27 February 2009) www.un.org/depts/los/clcs_new/submissions_files/jpn08/kor_27feb09.pdf.

[132] See Commission on the Limits of the Continental Shelf, 'Summary of Recommendations of the Commission on the Limits of the Continental Shelf in regard to the submission made by Japan on 12 November 2008' (12 August 2011, approved by the CLCS 19 April 2012) [20] http://www.un.org/depts/los/clcs_new/submissions_files/jpn08/com_sumrec_jpn_fin.pdf.

[133] Convention on the Continental Shelf (n 117) art 1.

[134] See 'Regulations concerning the Fishery Limits off Iceland' (30 June 1958) proclaiming a 12 nm limit; and a 14 July 1971 policy statement of the Government of Iceland announcing the intention to declare a 50 nm zone from 1 September 1972: discussed in *Fisheries Jurisdiction (United Kingdom v Iceland)* (Merits) [1974] ICJ Reps 3, 12–13 [23]–[27] (*Fisheries Jurisdiction*).

In those disputes, which became known as the 'Cod Wars',[135] UK fishing vessels were potentially subject to exclusion from a 50 nm Icelandic Fishing Zone. The UK challenged the legitimacy of Iceland's actions before the ICJ and was successful in that the Court found Iceland could not unilaterally exclude the UK fishers who had 'established rights' within the area. Iceland, nevertheless, did enjoy a '[p]referential share to the extent of the special dependence of its people upon the fisheries in the seas around its coasts for their livelihood and economic development'.[136] In this respect, the ICJ accepted the concept of preferential rights for those States which had an exceptional dependence upon coastal fisheries,[137] though in doing so no priority was given to island States as such. Nevertheless, it is noteworthy that this pivotal case dealing with rights of access to fish stocks was between two island States.

Island States and continental States that possess juridical islands are entitled to an EEZ. This gives to islands some important entitlements under the law of the sea. First, all island States and communities that occupy islands enjoy a 200 nm EEZ entitlement ensuring that island peoples enjoy sovereign rights for the purposes of exploring and exploiting, and conserving and managing the natural resources of the EEZ, whether living or non-living.[138] This 200 nm EEZ entitlement has proven to be critical for several island States, especially those in the South Pacific and in parts of the Indian Ocean and Caribbean Sea.[139] Second, island coastal States in particular are able to exercise EEZ jurisdiction by enacting laws and regulations to protect and preserve the marine environment.[140] Entitlements bestowed upon States to protect waters adjacent to islands by way of marine parks,[141] marine sanctuaries,[142] marine exclusion zones,[143] pollution prevention zones,[144] and other forms of protected areas has been significant for many island communities and has allowed them to not only environmentally

[135] S Steinsson, 'Do liberal ties pacify? A study of the Cod Wars' (2018) 53 *Cooperation and Conflict* 339.

[136] *Fisheries Jurisdiction* (n 134) 34 [79].

[137] ibid 26 [58].

[138] LOSC (n 1) art 56 (1)(a).

[139] With respect to the South Pacific, see M Tsamenyi (ed), *Evaluation of the implications of the United Nations Convention on the Law of the Sea for SPREP activities* (South Pacific Regional Environment Programme 1996).

[140] LOSC (n 1) art 56(1)(b)(iii).

[141] See details on the Northwestern Hawaiian Islands Marine National Monument; discussed in DK Sproat and AF Gross, 'The NW. Hawaiian Islands Marine National Monument' (Spring 2008) 22 *Natural Resources & Environment* 57.

[142] See Department of Conservation (New Zealand), 'Auckland Islands Marine Mammal Sanctuary' www.doc.govt.nz/nature/habitats/marine/other-marine-protection/auckland-islands/.

[143] See measures adopted by New Zealand with respect to the Three Kings Islands area, Maritime New Zealand (New Zealand), 'Safety zones and precautionary areas', www.maritimenz.govt.nz/commercial/environment/offshore-industry/safety-zones.asp.

[144] Sri Lanka has a declared 'Pollution Prevention Zone' that is conterminous with its EEZ: Presidential Proclamation of 15 January 1977 in pursuance of Maritime Zones Law No 22 of 1 September 1976 (Sri Lanka).

manage those waters but also to preserve their natural features.[145] Given the rich marine biodiversity found adjacent to many islands, and particularly island States located in tropical waters, this is an important entitlement under the law of the sea which has flow-on consequences for their economy by way of tourism.

While the EEZ regime confers upon coastal States significant resource sovereignty and jurisdiction, these entitlements are not exhaustive, and Article 62 emphasises optimum utilisation of the living resources and contemplates access rights for the nationals of other States.[146] These entitlements can be particularly significant in congested maritime spaces where there are large populations and a history of fishers from many adjacent States within a region or sub-region accessing certain waters. From an island perspective, this has been a particular issue in the Mediterranean Sea, Caribbean Sea, and parts of Southeast Asia.[147] In this respect, Article 62(3) is of significance as it provides that a coastal State with surplus stocks is to give particular weight to providing access to fishers from developing States and those 'whose nationals have habitually fished in the zone or which have made substantial efforts in research and identification of stocks.'[148] While not strictly an example of an Article 62(3) agreement for access to surplus fish stocks, Australia and Indonesia in 1974 concluded by way of a Memorandum of Understanding access rights for traditional Indonesian fishers in the Australian Fishing Zone.[149] Those rights were particularly granted for the purposes of access to the Australian territories of Ashmore Reef and Cartier Island, which are approximately 300 nm northwest off the Australian coast in the Indian Ocean. The purpose of this arrangement was to permit access by traditional Indonesian fishers to continue their customary practices and target species such as trepang, trochus, abalone and sponges. Ashmore Reef and Cartier Island are both uninhabited and

[145] In the case of the Southwest Pacific, the Convention for the Protection of the Natural Resources and Environment of the South Pacific Region (adopted 24 November 1986, entered into force 22 August 1990) [1990] ATS 31, art 14 provides inter alia mechanisms for state parties to take the following action within their EEZ: 'The Parties shall, individually or jointly, take all appropriate measures to protect and preserve rare or fragile ecosystems and depleted, threatened or endangered flora and fauna as well as their habitat in the Convention Area. To this end, the Parties shall, as appropriate, establish protected areas, such as parks and reserves, and prohibit or regulate any activity likely to have adverse effects on the species, ecosystems or biological processes that such areas are designed to protect.'

[146] LOSC (n 1) art 62(1), (4).

[147] This is reflected in some of the issues faced by island States such as Malta and Cyprus (Mediterranean), the small island States of the Caribbean, and island/archipelagic States in Southeast Asia, such as Indonesia and the Philippines, in dealing with regional fishing disputes, including the actions of distant water fisheries; see discussion in I Papanicolopulu, 'The Mediterranean Sea' in DR Rothwell et al (eds), *The Oxford Handbook of the Law of the Sea* (Oxford University Press 2015) 604, 621; D Freestone and C Schofield, 'The Caribbean Sea and the Gulf of Mexico' in DR Rothwell et al (eds), *The Oxford Handbook of the Law of the Sea* (Oxford University Press 2015) 672, 684, 691.

[148] LOSC (n 1) art 62(3).

[149] 1974 Memorandum of Understanding between the Government of Australia and the Government of the Republic of Indonesia regarding the Operations of Indonesian Traditional Fishermen in the areas of the Australian Exclusive Fishing Zone and Continental Shelf, reproduced in (1978) 8 *Australian Year Book of International Law* 259–60.

now are declared marine reserves under Australian law, subject to the ongoing access right of the Indonesian fishers.

The proximity of islands adjacent to the coast of a foreign State within a relatively narrow sea has also resulted in some innovative solutions to fishing zones that over time are now reflected in EEZ arrangements. In the 1978 Torres Strait Treaty between Australia and PNG the parties needed to agree a sea-bed and fisheries boundary in circumstances where three Australian islands lay just offshore the PNG coast, potentially having a significant distorting impact on the direction of the boundary. Ultimately, it was agreed that the 'Fisheries Jurisdiction' line, which has now become the EEZ boundary, would divert from a median line so as to encompass the northern Australian islands in the strait.[150] However, recognising the importance of the strait's waters to the indigenous peoples of Australia and PNG for the purposes of movement, fishing, and other related cultural activities, a 'Protected Zone' was declared in the central area of the strait allowing for free movement, traditional fishing, traditional customary rights, and protection of the marine environment.[151] Similarly, in the case of the maritime boundary between Newfoundland (Canada) and St Pierre and Miquelon (France) in the northwest Atlantic, a long and narrow EEZ corridor exists for the two French islands that reflects the unique maritime domain.[152]

IX. Conclusions

Islands enjoy the same maritime entitlements as continental States with the only exception being juridical rocks – a form of juridical island – and artificial islands. As such the maritime entitlements of juridical islands, whether they are a part of a continental State, archipelagic State, or an island State, are a critical attribute under international law. In some instances, where an island is distant from other landmasses, the island may generate vast maritime zones entirely consistent with the LOSC which may in turn confer upon the island significant economic, political, social and strategic status. Whilst the maritime entitlements of islands should be unremarkable given the development of the law of the sea and the historical significance of island States such as the UK, it has only been following the conclusion of the LOSC, in tandem with the emergence of many new island States in the Pacific Ocean, Indian Ocean, and the Caribbean Sea, that the importance of maritime entitlements to islands has been better understood. For many island States – whether they be singular islands, multiple islands, or archipelagic States – LOSC maritime entitlements have radically changed the composition of the State

[150] Torres Strait Treaty (n 109) art 4; see also S Kaye, 'Jurisdictional Patchwork: Law of the Sea and Native Title Issues in the Torres Strait' (2001) 2 *Melbourne Journal of International Law* 381.

[151] Torres Strait Treaty arts 10–13.

[152] See the discussion in Chapter 8 section III.B of this volume.

to include both a land and a maritime dimension. However, that process is not settled. As the CLCS continues its consideration of continental shelf claims beyond 200 nm and maritime claims and associated maritime boundaries are resolved, the extent of the maritime entitlements of islands will become clearer. The work of the CLCS remains ongoing. Each CLCS recommendation concerning islands is part of an ongoing process of the resolution of islands and maritime entitlements. This is important for islands and international law.

8

Islands and Maritime Boundaries

I. Introduction

Maritime boundary delimitation has been an international law phenomenon over the past century.[1] As maritime claims gradually gained acceptance in customary international law little attention was initially given to the need to develop maritime boundary delimitation practice.[2] This was predominantly because the territorial sea was the only accepted maritime zone in customary international law, and even allowing for the lack of precision as to the limits of that zone, there were few instances where a territorial sea entitlement of two States would overlap if a three nm claim were made. This was certainly the case for States with opposite coastlines. Only those States in very close proximity to each other across narrow seas or straits were concerned about the need to delimit maritime boundaries. With respect to adjacent States, there was an appreciation that territorial sea claims extending from their adjoining coasts would eventually result in the need for agreed boundaries beyond the terminus of their land boundary. However, little priority was given to the settlement of this issue, partly because of a lack of precision as to not only the breadth of the territorial sea but also the level of control a coastal State could exercise within those waters. Significance is therefore rightly attached to the 1909 *Grisbådarna* arbitration between Norway and Sweden,[3] which is the first recorded settlement of a territorial sea maritime boundary. Some initial consideration of maritime boundary delimitation methodology took place at the time of the 1930 Hague Codification conference,[4] but no substantive agreement was reached at the time.

A significant change occurred in state practice with the first claims made to a continental shelf following the 1945 Truman Proclamation.[5] While the outer

[1] See generally the collected studies in V Prescott and C Schofield, *The Maritime Political Boundaries of the World* (2nd edn, Martinus Nijhoff 2005); and JI Charney et al (eds), *International Maritime Boundaries* vols I–VIII (Martinus Nijhoff/Brill 1993–2021).

[2] See some of this historical analysis in RP Anand, *Origin and Development of the Law of the Sea* (Martinus Nijohff 1982); T Treves, 'Historical Development of the Law of the Sea' in DR Rothwell et al (eds), *Oxford Handbook of the Law of the Sea* (Oxford University Press 2015) 1.

[3] *Grisbådarna Arbitration* (*Norway v Sweden*) (1910) 4 *American Journal of International Law* 226.

[4] See S Whittemore Boggs, 'Delimitation of the Territorial Sea' (1930) 24 *American Journal of International Law* 541 discussing US proposals that were put forward.

[5] President of the United States of America, *Policy of the United States with respect to the Natural Resources of the Subsoil and Seabed of the Continental Shelf, US Presidential Proclamation No 2667* (28 September 1945) (Truman Proclamation).

limit of the continental shelf was not clearly defined at that time, there was an appreciation that continental shelf claims could be asserted from not only a mainland of a continental State but also from the islands that composed that State. Part of this reasoning was that islands, just like a continent, also possessed a continental shelf, though the extent could be more variable.[6] There was also an early appreciation that islands could be located in such a way as to impact upon the continental shelf entitlements of mainland States. Some of the academic and practitioner discourse in the 1940s and 1950s reflected an understanding that islands would need to be taken into account in maritime boundary delimitation.[7] When the International Law Commission considered these issues between 1949 and 1956 there was an appreciation of the dynamic created by islands for maritime boundary delimitation, though no specific rule was recommended. This remained the position at the 1958 First United Nations Conference on the Law of the Sea which resulted in agreement being reached on the Convention on the Territorial Sea and Contiguous Zone,[8] and the Convention on the Continental Shelf.[9] Both instruments dealt with maritime boundary delimitation, but neither made precise reference to the impact of islands on those processes. This was the approach used during the Third United Nations Conference on the Law of the Sea resulting in adoption of the 1982 United Nations Convention on the Law of the Sea (LOSC).[10] The international law with respect to maritime boundary delimitation therefore makes no direct reference to islands; however, as will be discussed throughout this chapter, there is considerable state practice in this area and international courts and tribunals have given the impact of islands on maritime boundaries great consideration.[11]

Before commencing this discussion it is important to make clear the precise circumstances that fall within the analysis. First, it needs to be observed that, while the principal focus of attention is Article 121 juridical islands, there is also a need to take into account Article 121 juridical rocks. Both features enjoy maritime entitlements and those generated from an island can be equated with a mainland; however, a rock generates only a territorial sea.[12] Nevertheless, juridical rocks that

[6] In this respect it is notable that the Truman Proclamation, ibid, refers to the entitlement of the US to claim a continental shelf over an area 'contiguous to the coasts of the United States as appertaining to the United States', which was capable of extending to the continental shelf adjacent to the Hawaiian islands, to Long Island, and to the Florida Keys.

[7] S Whittemore Boggs, 'Delimitation of Seaward Areas under National Jurisdiction' (1951) 45 *American Journal of International Law* 240, giving multiple island examples.

[8] Convention on the Territorial Sea and Contiguous Zone (adopted 29 April 1958, entered into force 10 September 1964) 516 UNTS 206.

[9] Convention on the Continental Shelf (adopted 29 April 1958, entered into force 10 June 1964) 499 UNTS 311.

[10] United Nations Convention on the Law of the Sea (adopted 10 December 1982, entered into force 16 November 1994) 1833 UNTS 397 (LOSC).

[11] For one of the earlier assessments of this issue, see *Continental Shelf (Libyan Arab Jamahiriya v Malta)* (Judgment) [1985] ICJ Reps 13 (*Libya v Malta*).

[12] Rocks can also generate a contiguous zone, though there is minimal state practice with respect to the delimitation of contiguous zone maritime boundaries.

enjoy a territorial sea may have an impact on how a maritime boundary may be delimited, especially in very congested maritime space.[13] Second, it is possible to characterise how States engaged in maritime boundary delimitation need to take into account islands and rocks in multiple different ways. That is as between:

1. Two mainland States where islands are located in the relevant maritime zone;
2. A mainland State and an island State, including an archipelagic State; and,
3. Two island States, including archipelagic States.

In each one of these scenarios the islands in question may be of varying size and be close to a mainland, a geographic archipelago, a cluster of islands, or may be distant from a mainland. A great variety of geographic circumstances may therefore be at play. What follows will be an initial overview of maritime boundary delimitation, followed by consideration of the relevant decisions of international courts and tribunals, and state practice. Comments will then be made as to the impact of islands on maritime boundary delimitation.

II. Overview of Maritime Boundary Delimitation[14]

Determining the contemporary principles of maritime boundary delimitation is made difficult by the imprecise terminology used in the LOSC. While there is considerable jurisprudence in the field, the legal basis (in either treaty law or custom) upon which those judgments have been delivered has also been variable. Cases have been determined on the basis of customary international law, the 1958 Geneva Conventions, the LOSC, or a mixture of both custom and treaty law. During this time the jurisprudence has evolved, but so too has the international law of the sea, as there has been a gradual transition from the Geneva Conventions to the LOSC. International courts and tribunals have throughout this time been in search of objective criteria to apply in maritime boundary delimitation.[15] In light of their collective jurisprudence, state practice, and the delimitation methods laid down in LOSC Articles 15 (territorial sea), 74 (exclusive economic zone) and 83 (continental shelf), it is now possible to identify with reasonable clarity the key elements of contemporary maritime boundary delimitation. Islands create very

[13] See discussion of the status of Middle Rocks, in *Sovereignty over Pedra Branca/Pulau Batu Puteh, Middle Rocks and South Ledge* (*Malaysia v Singapore*) (Judgment) [2008] ICJ Reps 12, 99 [288]–[290].

[14] For more detailed analysis on this topic see Y Tanaka, *Predictability and Flexibility in the Law of Maritime Delimitation* (2nd edn, Hart Publishing 2019); and M Lando, *Maritime Delimitation as a Judicial Process* (Cambridge University Press 2019). T Cottier, *Equitable Principles of Maritime Boundary Delimitation: The Quest for Distributive Justice in International Law* (Cambridge University Press 2015).

[15] *Arbitration between Barbados and Trinidad and Tobago* (11 April 2006) PCA Case 2004-02 70 [230] (*Caribbean Sea*).

particular dynamics in this process, but for the time being the focus is on the key principles.

A. Delimitation Methodology

The International Court of Justice (ICJ) first began to identify different stages of the delimitation process in the *Libya v Malta Continental Shelf* case,[16] and since that time the approach has gradually become more refined. In its more recent judgments, the Court has referred to a 'methodology' to be applied in maritime boundary delimitation, and this represents a significant advance in the jurisprudence. Because of the difference in the language of Article 15 and Articles 74 and 83, there are variations in the approach taken with respect to a territorial sea delimitation and that for an EEZ or continental shelf delimitation. However, since adoption of the LOSC there has been a strong tendency to emphasise the importance of an equidistance or median line in respect of all three zones.

(i) Territorial Sea

In the 2007 *Nicaragua v Honduras* case the ICJ considered a methodology to be applied to an Article 15 territorial sea boundary.[17] The Court observed that '[t]he methods governing territorial sea delimitations have needed to be, and are, more clearly articulated in international law than those used for the other, more functional maritime areas'.[18] First, consideration should be given to the drawing of a provisional equidistance line.[19] Secondly, if this proves impossible because of certain features on the coastline or within the area of delimitation, an equidistance line may not be appropriate due to special circumstances.[20] Thirdly, the Court may consider alternative methods of delimitation proposed by the parties or elect to apply its own methods. Finally, there will also be a need to take into account relevant coasts which will include reference to the geographical configuration of the coastline and, when the territorial sea of adjacent States is being delimited, the geomorphological features of the area adjacent to the endpoint of a land boundary.[21]

[16] *Libya v Malta* (n 11) 13 [60].

[17] *Territorial and Maritime Dispute between Nicaragua and Honduras in the Caribbean Sea (Nicaragua v Honduras)* (Merits) [2007] ICJ Reps 659 (*Nicaragua v Honduras*).

[18] ibid 740 [269].

[19] ibid 740 [268].

[20] ibid 745 [281]. In *Maritime Delimitation and Territorial Questions between Qatar and Bahrain (Qatar v Bahrain)* (Merits) [2001] ICJ Reps 40, 94 [176] (*Qatar v Bahrain*) the Court observed that: 'The most logical and widely practised approach is first to draw provisionally an equidistance line and then to consider whether that line must be adjusted in the light of the existence of special circumstances.'

[21] ibid 748 [292]; this would be an especially important factor in instances where a river mouth is part of the land boundary.

(ii) EEZ, Continental Shelf and Single Maritime Boundaries

In the 2009 *Black Sea* case between Romania and Ukraine,[22] the Court for the first time referred generically to a 'delimitation methodology' that could be applied in cases dealing with the delimitation of the EEZ, continental shelf, or a single maritime boundary line.[23] This approach involves three stages. The first is the establishment of a provisional delimitation line which in the case of adjacent coasts will be an equidistance line, and in the case of opposite coasts a median line,[24] unless there are compelling reasons which make such a line unsuitable. The second stage is a consideration as to whether there are any factors which call for an adjustment of the provisional line in order to achieve an equitable result.[25] Finally, and after having made any adjustments to the provisional line as a result of the second stage, the Court will seek to verify that the line does not lead to an inequitable result 'by reason of any marked disproportion between the ratio of the respective coastal lengths and the ratio between the relevant maritime area of each State by reference to the delimitation line'.[26] This process thereby ensures that there is no great disproportionality between the division of the maritime area under delimitation and the relevant coastal lengths. A crucial element of this methodology is the determination of the 'relevant area', which the Court has referred to as a 'legal concept'.[27] This area will depend upon the configuration of the relevant coasts within their geographical context and a consideration of the seaward projections of those coasts which will differ depending on whether a territorial sea or much longer maritime boundary is being delimited, and the interests of any third States.[28] Likewise, different considerations will apply in the case of convex and concave coastlines, significant indentations such as gulfs, and when islands are within the area of delimitation.[29] The determination of the relevant area is crucial for the application of proportionality, which is undertaken at the third stage of the delimitation process.[30] Accordingly, a court will need to make a determination as to the relevant area under consideration prior to commencing the delimitation.[31]

[22] *Maritime Delimitation in the Black Sea (Romania v Ukraine)* (Judgment) [2009] ICJ Reps 61 (*Black Sea*).
[23] ibid 101–103 [115]–[122].
[24] ibid 101 [116].
[25] ibid 101–103 [120].
[26] ibid 103 [122].
[27] ibid 99–100 [110].
[28] *Nicaragua v Honduras* (n 17) 738–39 [262].
[29] *Black Sea* (n 22) 99–100 [110].
[30] ibid.
[31] *Delimitation of the maritime boundary in the Bay of Bengal (Bangladesh v Myanmar)* (Judgment) [2012] ITLOS Rep 4 [240] (*Bangladesh v Myanmar*) adopted the ICJ's 'three-stage' approach; likewise endorsed and followed in *Delimitation of the Maritime Boundary in the Atlantic Ocean (Ghana v Côte d'Ivoire)* (Judgment) [2017] ITLOS Rep 4, 103 [360].

B. Equitable Solution/Equitable Result

The adoption of LOSC Articles 74 and 83 ushered in a new era in maritime boundary delimitation with respect to the longest and most significant of the boundaries coastal States delimit. Nevertheless, as was observed in the 1999 *Eritrea v Yemen Arbitration*, although Articles 74 and 83 were 'designed to decide as little as possible', it was clear that 'both Articles envisage an equitable result'.[32] The ICJ in *Continental Shelf (Tunisia v Libyan Arab Jamahiriya)* gave initial guidance as to how this may be achieved, emphasising the importance of taking into account the relevant circumstances of the case.[33] This approach has been followed in subsequent decisions and is illustrated by consideration given to a wide range of relevant geographical factors in order to ensure they are taken into account in the final delimitation lines. However, there are constraints in seeking to achieve an equitable result, and, as was noted in the *Caribbean Sea* case, legal principle needs to be accounted for 'in particular in respect of the factors that may be taken into account', including that of the decided cases.[34] A common method used to achieve an equitable result/solution is an adjustment to the maritime boundary after the second stage of the delimitation process in order to ensure proportionality.[35]

C. Equidistance and Median Lines

Equidistance and median lines may be utilised in the case of territorial sea delimitations consistent with Article 15, subject to special circumstances, or the parties reaching agreement on another method. Likewise, notwithstanding some different approaches taken by courts and tribunals as to the relevance of an equidistance/median line,[36] there remain contemporary examples where an equidistance/median line has been applied as a provisional line, only to have been modified or adjusted in order to achieve an equitable solution.[37] This approach was endorsed by the ICJ as the first stage of a boundary delimitation in the 2009 *Black Sea* decision.[38] In some instances, as occurred in the

[32] *Award of the Arbitral Tribunal in the second stage of the proceedings between Eritrea and Yemen (Maritime Delimitation) (Eritrea v Yemen)* (17 December 1999) 22 RIAA 355 [116] (*Eritrea and Yemen – Maritime Delimitation*).

[33] *Continental Shelf (Tunisia v Libyan Arab Jamahiriya)* (Judgment) [1982] ICJ Reps 18, 60–61 [72].

[34] *Caribbean Sea* (n 15) 74 [243]; see also the discussion in B Kwiatkowska, 'The 2006 Barbados/Trinidad and Tobago Award: A Landmark in Compulsory Jurisdiction and Equitable Maritime Boundary Delimitation' (2007) 22 *International Journal of Marine and Coastal Law* 7, 38–43.

[35] *Black Sea* (n 22) 103 [122]; *Libya v Malta* (n 11) 51 [71].

[36] *Delimitation of the Maritime Boundary in the Gulf of Maine Area (Canada v United States)* (Judgment) [1984] ICJ Reps 246, 297 [107].

[37] *Caribbean Sea* (n 15) 106 [350]; *Qatar v Bahrain* (n 20) 111 [230].

[38] *Black Sea* (n 22) 101 [116], where it was also observed that: 'No legal consequences flow from the use of the terms "median line" and "equidistance line" since the method of delimitation is the same for both.'

Cameroon v Nigeria case,[39] or the *Guyana and Suriname Arbitration*,[40] a conclusion may even be reached that an equidistance line represents an equitable result and that no circumstances exist which require modification of the line. There is also significant state practice to the effect that where maritime boundaries have been settled by agreement, States have relied upon a partial equidistance line, modified equidistance line, or in some cases a line drawn only by reference to equidistance.[41]

D. Relevant and Special Circumstances

A feature of the law of maritime boundary delimitation has been the ongoing reference to 'special circumstances' as factors to be taken into account in the delimitation process. While now only expressly referred to in LOSC Article 15, there is extensive jurisprudence by international courts and tribunals referring to the impact of special circumstances or equivalent factors upon the placement of a maritime boundary. The factors which may be taken into account are extensive and predominantly geographical, and there is some limited scope for consideration to be given to historical factors which extends to relevant practice by the parties. The ICJ has observed that 'special circumstances are those circumstances which might modify the result produced by an unqualified application of the equidistance principle. … This concept can be described as a fact necessary to be taken into account in the delimitation process.'[42] Islands have traditionally been one special circumstance which the courts have been prepared to consider because of the impact they may have upon the direction of a maritime boundary, and the need to take into account the maritime zones the islands generate consistent with LOSC Article 121. Any pre-existing boundaries which extend into the maritime area under consideration, whether they be colonial or contemporary boundaries, will also have relevance.[43] Likewise, any pre-existing exercise of sovereign rights or jurisdiction will be relevant, such as the issuance of fishing licences.[44] The Court

[39] *Land and Maritime Boundary between Cameroon and Nigeria (Cameroon v Nigeria: Equatorial Guinea intervening)* (Judgment) [2002] ICJ Reps 303, 448 [306] (*Cameroon v Nigeria*).

[40] *Guyana and Suriname* (Award) (17 September 2007) PCA Case 2004-04, 127 [392], at https://pca-cpa.org/en/cases/9/.

[41] An example can be found in the Treaty between the Government of Australia and the Government of New Zealand Establishing Certain Exclusive Economic Zone Boundaries and Continental Shelf Boundaries (adopted 25 July 2004, entered into force 25 January 2006) [2006] ATS 4, in which the Australian government's 'National Interest Analysis' associated with this treaty makes direct reference to the use of equidistance: [2004] ATNIA 8.

[42] *Maritime Delimitation in the Area between Greenland and Jan Mayen (Denmark v Norway)* (Judgment) [1993] ICJ Reps 38, 62 [55] (*Jan Mayen*).

[43] *Black Sea* (n 22) 78–89 [43]–[76]; *Maritime Dispute (Peru v Chile)* (Judgment) [2014] ICJ Reps 3, 66 [183].

[44] A factor considered in the *Grisbådarna Arbitration* (n 3) 233–34.

has also indicated that the legitimate security considerations of the parties may be a factor in adjusting a provisional delimitation line.[45]

In recent cases international courts and tribunals have begun to refer to the concept of 'relevant circumstances'. In the 2006 *Barbados v Trinidad and Tobago Arbitration* (*Caribbean Sea*) the tribunal noted that: 'The identification of the relevant circumstances becomes accordingly a necessary step in determining the approach to delimitation'[46] and this refers to an identification of the maritime domain, particularly geographical features such as the length and configurations of the respective coastlines. Likewise, in the *Black Sea* case, the ICJ referred to identification of the 'relevant maritime area' as being an essential aspect of the delimitation process.[47] This step encompasses not only a physical identification of the outer limits of the area under delimitation but also relevant circumstances within that area which may be important in the delimitation process. Accordingly, the length of the relevant coastal fronts, their general direction and configuration, and associated coastal and geographical features such as islands, reefs, atolls, bays and peninsulas will need to be identified.[48] Whether 'relevant circumstances' are then considered to be 'special circumstances' that need to be accounted for in the delimitation process will become a matter for determination.

III. Decisions of International Courts and Tribunals

A brief review will now be undertaken of some of the prominent decisions of international courts and tribunals applying principles of maritime boundary delimitation in instances where islands were a prominent feature. Particular attention will be given to the more contemporary decisions in this area which have applied the LOSC. However, not all instances involving islands and maritime boundary delimitations have given islands any particular prominence. This was the case in the *Timor Sea Conciliation* between Australia and Timor-Leste where notwithstanding that Timor-Leste is the eastern portion of the island of Timor, its status as an island State did not figure prominently in the conciliation.[49] This highlights that the significance of islands in maritime boundary delimitations will depend on the geographic circumstances, as is demonstrated below in some of the relevant cases.

[45] *Libya v Malta* (n 11) 42 [51]; *Black Sea* (n 22) 127–28 [202]–[204]; *Territorial and Maritime Dispute (Nicaragua v Colombia)* (Merits) [2012] ICJ Reps 624, [222] (*Nicaragua v Colombia*). See further MD Evans, *Relevant Circumstances and Maritime Delimitation* (Oxford University Press 1989) 172–78.

[46] *Caribbean Sea* (n 15) 71 [233].

[47] *Black Sea* (n 22) 98–100 [106]–[114].

[48] *Cameroon v Nigeria* (n 39) 442 [290]; *Nicaragua v Honduras* (n 17) 701–27 [132]–[227].

[49] *In the Matter of the Maritime Boundary between Timor-Leste and Australia* (Award) (9 May 2018) PCA Case No 2016-10 (*Timor Sea Conciliation*); which resulted in finalisation of the Treaty between Australia and the Democratic Republic of Timor-Leste Establishing Their Maritime Boundaries in the Timor Sea (adopted 6 March 2018, entry into force 30 August 2019) [2019] ATS 16.

A. *Anglo-French Arbitration* (1977)

In the 1977 *Anglo-French Arbitration*[50] a tribunal was asked to determine the continental shelf maritime boundary between France and the United Kingdom (UK) in the vicinity of the English Channel. The relevant portions of the English Channel under review included an area south-east of the Isle of Wight (UK), passing to the south-west out into Atlantic Ocean proper between the Scilly Isles (UK), and the island of Ushant (France) which lay 14.1 miles from the French mainland. The most significant island features in this maritime area were four main groups of islands and associated maritime features composing the Channel Islands (UK), of which the main islands were populated, ranged in various sizes, and were in some instances as close as 6.6 nm from the French coast.[51] The Tribunal determined that the Channel Islands were 'territorial and political units which have their own separate existence'.[52] Notwithstanding the distinctive political status of the islands, a main boundary was drawn through the English Channel which effectively disregarded the Channel Islands. An additional boundary was, however, drawn partially around the Channel Islands, giving the UK a 12 nm continental shelf entitlement with the remaining seabed allocated to France.[53] The effect was to enclave the Channel Islands due to their close proximity to the French coast.[54] The Scilly Isles were considered to have a disproportionate impact on the direction of the maritime boundary and so were given 'half-effect'.[55] The Isle of Wight and Ushant, on the other hand, were given full effect in the drawing of an equidistance line boundary.[56]

B. *Canada v France Arbitration (St Pierre and Miquelon)* (1992)

In the 1992 arbitration between Canada and France with respect to the islands of St Pierre and Miquelon,[57] the Tribunal was faced with a maritime delimitation involving two relatively small French islands located off Canada's Atlantic coast and the Canadian island province of Newfoundland. Miquelon, the larger of the two French islands, is located 27 nm from Newfoundland.[58] Given the very significant

[50] *Case Concerning Delimitation of the Continental Shelf Between the United Kingdom and the French Republic* (1979) 18 ILM 397 (*Anglo-French Arbitration*).

[51] ibid 23 [6].

[52] ibid 89 [184]. For more details as to the status of the Channel Islands (Jersey, and Guernsey), see Chapter 4 section IV.G of this volume.

[53] ibid, 95–97 [201]–[203].

[54] JI Charney and LM Alexander (eds), *International Maritime Boundaries*, vol 2 (Martinus Njihoff 1993) 1740 (*IMB II*).

[55] ibid 1740.

[56] ibid 1741.

[57] *Case Concerning the Delimitation of Maritime Areas between Canada and the French Republic* (10 June 1992) 21 RIAA 265, (1992) 31 ILM 1149 (*St Pierre and Miquelon*).

[58] ibid 1160 [22].

difference in the size between Newfoundland (111,390km^2), and St Pierre and Miquelon (242km^2), it was observed that there existed a 'marked disparity' in the relevant coastal lengths.[59] Two sectors were decided upon for the relevant boundaries. In the western sector, to achieve a 'reasonable and equitable solution', St Pierre and Miquelon were granted a 12 nm territorial sea and an additional 12 nm for an EEZ, which could also be utilised for the purposes of a dual contiguous zone.[60] A Canadian request to enclave the islands was specifically denied.[61] In the southern sector a full 200 nm long projection of St Pierre and Miquelon was considered appropriate by way of a corridor 10.5 nm wide,[62] subject only to taking into account the relevant entitlements generated from Newfoundland.[63]

C. *Jan Mayen (Denmark v Norway)* (1993)

In the *Jan Mayen* case between Denmark and Norway,[64] the ICJ was asked to determine the maritime boundaries between Greenland (Denmark) and Jan Mayen (Norway). The case is notable given Greenland is the largest island in the world, and Jan Mayen is a very small island.[65] The population disparity was also (at the time) very significant with Greenland having a population of 55,000 residents and Jan Mayen reported to have 25 'technical and other staff'.[66] The disparity of the coastal lengths bordering the relevant maritime area was equally significant, being up to 1:9.2 in favour of Greenland on one calculation.[67] To ensure an equitable delimitation, it was considered that the relative disproportionality of the coastal lengths needed to be taken into account in this instance[68] with the consequence that a median line was shifted closer to Jan Mayen due to it being a special circumstance.[69] Denmark did make reference to LOSC Article 121 in its submissions before the Court but ultimately this did not prove to be persuasive in terms of how Jan Mayen was viewed. The limited nature of the Jan Mayen population and socio-economic factors were not taken into account in the drawing of the boundary.[70] A median line boundary was drawn, which in view of the facts noted

[59] ibid 1162 [33]; in which the coastal lengths were respectively Canada – 455.6 nm and France – 29.85 nm, resulting in a ratio of 15.3 (Canada) to 1 (France).

[60] ibid 1170 [69].

[61] ibid 1169 [68].

[62] ibid 1170 [70].

[63] See discussion in E Livingstone, 'A Tale of Two Islands: An Analysis of the Court of Arbitration's Decision in the Canada–France Maritime Boundary Dispute' (1994) 3 *Dalhousie Journal of Legal Studies* 1.

[64] *Jan Mayen* (n 42).

[65] The respective sizes of the land areas are: Greenland – 2,166,086 km^2, and Jan Mayen – 377 km^2: Central Intelligence Agency (US), *The World Factbook*, www.cia.gov/the-world-factbook/countries/.

[66] *Jan Mayen* (n 42) 46 [15].

[67] ibid 65 [61].

[68] ibid 67 [65].

[69] ibid 69 [69].

[70] ibid 73 [80].

above resulted in the line being drawn closer to Jan Mayen than to Greenland.[71] Taking into account differential positions with respect to the continental shelf and fishing zones, additional allowances were made for fishing rights for both States in the relevant maritime area.[72]

D. *Eritrea v Yemen Arbitral Award (Second Phase)* (1999)

In the 1999 *Eritrea v Yemen Arbitral Award (Second Phase)* case,[73] an arbitral tribunal was called upon to make determinations with respect to the maritime boundary between islands and some associated maritime features between Eritrea and Yemen in the Red Sea. The first phase of the case had settled territorial disputes with respect to the islands and associated features.[74] The Tribunal had a complex set of factual circumstances and was called upon to consider groups or subgroups of islands, some of which were geographic archipelagos. Based on the outcome of the First Phase of the proceedings, the key island groups were the Mohabbakah islands and the Haycocks (Eritrea), and the Zuqar–Hanish group of islands, the Jabal al-Tayr and the Zubayr group of islands (Yemen).[75] Grappling with the application of LOSC Articles 74 and 83 and achieving an equitable result, the Tribunal observed:

> This requirement of an equitable result directly raises the question of the effect to be allowed to mid-sea islands which, by virtue of their mid-sea position, and if allowed full effect, can … obviously produce a disproportionate effect – or indeed a reasonable and proportionate effect – all depending on their size, importance and like consideration in the general geographical context.[76]

A median line based upon LOSC Article 15 was endorsed.[77] Adjustments were then made to that line as a result of 'complications' arising from the actual location of some of the features. A unique aspect of this delimitation is the way in which the Tribunal sought to also take account of the baselines that could legitimately be drawn between the islands, which allowed for the fact the parties had been unable to proclaim such baselines in the wake of the First Phase decision.[78] An additional factor was the rejection by the Tribunal of the drawing of enclaves, and a clear preference for ensuring that all relevant features generated a minimum entitlement to

[71] ibid 77 [87].
[72] ibid 79–81 [90]–[93].
[73] *Eritrea and Yemen – Maritime Delimitation* (n 32).
[74] *Award of the Arbitral Tribunal in the first stage of the proceedings between Eritrea and Yemen (Territorial Sovereignty and Scope of the Dispute) (Eritrea v Yemen)* (9 October 1998) 22 RIAA 209; see Chapter 3 section III.B.(ii) of this volume for discussion of the territorial issues.
[75] ibid 326–27 [508] (Zuqar–Hanish group); 329 [524] (Jabal al-Tayr and the Zubayr group of islands).
[76] *Eritrea and Yemen – Maritime Delimitation* (n 32) 362 [117].
[77] ibid 366 [133].
[78] ibid 367 [142], 369 [151].

a territorial sea.[79] Likewise, the impact of special circumstances or historic title on the boundary was rejected.[80] Notwithstanding the considerable challenges faced by the Tribunal due to the complex geography of the region arising from the multiple islands, a proportionality test was applied. This resulted in coastal fronts of Yemen/Eritrea of 1:1.31 and water area ratio (following the delimitation) of Yemen/Eritrea of 1:1.09 which were considered acceptable.[81]

E. *Qatar v Bahrain* (2001)

In the 2001 *Maritime Delimitation and Territorial Questions between Qatar and Bahrain* case (Qatar v Bahrain),[82] the ICJ considered sovereignty over a number of land and associated island features, and the maritime boundary between Qatar and Bahrain in the Arab/Persian Gulf. The Court was first asked to adjudge sovereignty with respect to the Hawar Islands, and the associated Janan Islands, which are adjacent to the main islands of Bahrain.[83] Having found in favour of Bahrain with respect to the Hawar Islands,[84] and Qatar with respect to the Janan Islands,[85] the Court then turned to the maritime delimitation issues.[86] Resolution of these issues was complicated by Bahrain's claim to be a de facto archipelagic State,[87] and the associated issue of whether there existed a fringe of islands for the purposes of drawing straight baselines consistently with LOSC Article 7.[88] The Court elected to draw a single maritime boundary which was divided into several segments, allowing for account to be taken of relevant coastal features and the islands in the Gulf. A single maritime boundary was drawn based upon 'adjusted equidistance'.[89] Consideration was given to whether special circumstances existed justifying an adjustment of the equidistance line. The very small island of Qit'at Jaradah (Bahrain) was considered to fall into this category. It was uninhabited and without any vegetation, and located mid-way between the Qatar peninsula and the Bahraini coast. On the basis that taking into account this feature would have a disproportionate effect, it was considered a special circumstance and ignored for the purposes of the direction of the boundary.[90]

[79] ibid 370 [155].
[80] ibid 371 [158].
[81] ibid 373 [168].
[82] *Qatar v Bahrain* (n 20).
[83] ibid 53 [35].
[84] ibid 80–82, 85 [127]–[135], [146]–[148].
[85] ibid 90–91 [165].
[86] ibid 91 [167], which were determined on the basis of customary international law as, at the time, Bahrain had ratified the LOSC, while Qatar was a signatory.
[87] ibid 96 [181]; see discussion in Chapter 5 section VI.B of this volume.
[88] ibid 103 [211]–[213].
[89] ibid 115 [249].
[90] ibid 104–9 [219].

F. *Cameroon v Nigeria* (2002)

In *Land and Maritime Boundary between Cameroon and Nigeria*[91] the ICJ was asked to determine the maritime boundary between the two States in the Gulf of Guinea. While neither State had any prominent islands which impacted upon the delimitation, Bioko Island (Equatorial Guinea) was located within the Gulf offshore Cameroon. Various submissions were made to the Court as to the impact Bioko Island would have upon the delimitation of the relevant maritime boundary, and analogies were made to the situation of the Channel Islands in the *Anglo-French Arbitration*.[92] The Court noted that 'islands have sometimes been taken into account as a relevant circumstance in delimitation when such islands lay within the zone to be delimited and fell under the sovereignty of one of the parties'.[93] Nevertheless, as Bioko Island fell under the sovereignty of Equatorial Guinea any maritime delimitation issues regarding that island were for resolution by Cameroon and Equatorial Guinea and did not impact upon the Cameroon and Nigeria delimitation.[94]

G. *Caribbean Sea* (2006)

In the 2006 *Arbitration between Barbados and Trinidad and Tobago* (Caribbean Sea) case, a LOSC Annex VII Arbitral Tribunal was asked to determine the continental shelf and EEZ maritime boundary between the two Caribbean States. Trinidad and Tobago comprises two principal islands and a number of much smaller associated islands located off the South American coast in the Caribbean Sea. It is a declared archipelagic State.[95] Barbados is a single island State, also in the Caribbean Sea, and is located 116 nm northeast of Tobago.[96] This case is therefore important as it deals with maritime boundary delimitation between two island States, one of which is an archipelagic State. The approach of the Tribunal was to accept it was dealing with opposite States, and proceeded to divide the relevant areas into a western and an eastern section. In the western section a provisionally drawn equidistance line was assessed against arguments made by the parties with respect to a range of matters, none of which directly related to islands or their status as island States. As such the equidistance line was confirmed.[97] The eastern section was not found to raise any distinctive geographic issues from the western section,[98] and an equidistance line was adopted.[99]

[91] *Cameroon v Nigeria* (n 39).
[92] ibid 434 [274]. *Anglo-French Arbitration* (n 50).
[93] ibid 466 [299].
[94] ibid 466 [299].
[95] *Caribbean Sea* (n 15) 9 [42], [44].
[96] ibid 9 [43].
[97] ibid 84 [271].
[98] ibid 96 [313].
[99] ibid 98 [319].

H. *Nicaragua v Honduras* (2007)

In the *Case Concerning the Territorial and Maritime Dispute between Nicaragua and Honduras in the Caribbean Sea*,[100] the ICJ was asked to determine land and maritime issues between the two States, including the maritime boundary in the Caribbean Sea. Four of the islands were found to be Honduran – Bobel Cay, Savanna Cay, Port Royal Cay and South Cay – with undisputed Edinburgh Cay remaining with Nicaragua.[101] With respect to the maritime boundaries, delimitation of the islands was principally addressed under LOSC Article 15, with both parties in general agreement that all of the five offshore islands would generate a 12 nm territorial sea.[102] A provisional equidistance line was drawn in the vicinity of the islands, and the view was taken that there were no special circumstances that justified modification of that line.[103] The maritime boundary was accordingly drawn to reflect the respective entitlements of the islands, resulting in a diversion of the general direction of the maritime boundary from the coast so as to take into account the entitlements of the islands.

I. *Black Sea* (2009)

In the *Black Sea case* the ICJ considered the maritime boundary between Ukraine and Romania in the Black Sea. The case, as noted above, is significant for the way in which the Court developed and advanced the jurisprudence with respect to maritime boundary delimitation methodology. A critical feature in the maritime area was Serpents' Island, a Ukrainian island 20 nm from the coast and only 0.17 km^2 in size.[104] The issue for the Court was to determine the impact the island had upon the direction of the maritime boundary. An existing agreement between the parties had dealt with the territorial sea boundary adjacent to the island,[105] but now the Court was being asked to assess the EEZ and continental shelf boundary generally within the Black Sea. The view of the Court was that Serpents' Island could not be considered as part of the relevant coast, because 'the consequence would be a judicial refashioning of geography, which neither the law nor practice of maritime delimitation authorizes.'[106] The ultimate position was that Serpents' Island should have no effect on the delimitation and that the existing maritime boundary arrangements made with respect to the island would remain and not be disturbed by the Court's judgment with respect to the EEZ and continental shelf

[100] *Nicaragua v Honduras* (n 17).
[101] ibid 727 [227].
[102] ibid 751 [300].
[103] ibid 752 [304].
[104] *Black Sea* (n 22) 70 [16].
[105] ibid 74 [28].
[106] ibid 110 [149].

boundaries. The island therefore had no impact on the provisional equidistance line the Court had drawn in this instance.[107]

J. *Nicaragua v Colombia* (2012)

In the *Nicaragua v Colombia* case[108] the ICJ was confronted by the existence of multiple small offshore maritime features, ranging from islands to low-tide elevations. The existence of these multiple features created particular challenges for the delimitation of the maritime boundary, especially as the Colombian islands were relatively small as against the coastal front of Nicaragua facing the Caribbean Sea. In approaching this task the Court applied the *Black Sea* case delimitation methodology.[109] Importantly, in the context of the relevant maritime area, the Court emphasised that in applying this methodology the provisional delimitation line would take into account the parties' territories, including island territories, using methods that were 'geometrically objective and appropriate for the geography of the area.'[110] The construction of the provisional median line immediately raised the issue of the weight to be accorded to the offshore Nicaraguan and Colombian islands in the relevant maritime area. The Court included the offshore Nicaraguan islands in the construction of the base points from which Nicaragua's EEZ and continental shelf entitlements were to be determined.[111] The Colombian coast was confined to the islands within the area of overlapping entitlements, and the entire coastlines of those islands were considered, though the smaller cays were not.[112] The total lengths of the relevant coasts were 65 km (Colombia) and 531 km (Nicaragua) with a ratio of 1:8.2 in favour of Nicaragua.[113] The Court was, however, more selective when it came to determining the impact of the Colombian islands upon the provisional median line. It was adjudged that Quitasueño would not contribute to the provisional median line on the grounds that '[w]hen placing base points on very small maritime features would distort the relevant geography, it is appropriate to disregard them in the construction of a provisional median line.'[114] Similar considerations were applied to Serrana and Low Cay, so that the Colombian base points were limited to four islands and cays in the region.[115]

[107] ibid 123 [187]–[188]; for a 2021 application by the ICJ of the Black Sea delimitation methodology in a case in which islands were involved, see *Maritime Delimitation in the Indian Ocean (Somalia v Kenya)* [2021] ICJ Reps 40 [111].
[108] *Nicaragua v Colombia* (n 45).
[109] *Black Sea* (n 22) 101–3 [115]–[120].
[110] *Nicaragua v Colombia* (n 45) 695 [191].
[111] ibid 678 [145], 698–99 [201].
[112] ibid 679–80 [151].
[113] ibid 680 [153].
[114] ibid 699 [202].
[115] ibid 699 [202]–[203]; for a recent assessment of base points drawn from islands and their impact on maritime boundary delimitation, see *Maritime Delimitation in the Indian Ocean (Somalia v Kenya)* (n 107) (Separate Opinion of Judge Yusuf) 5 [18].

In taking account of relevant circumstances, the Court considered whether, if the Colombian islands were granted their full entitlements to an EEZ and continental shelf, Nicaragua's EEZ and continental shelf rights offshore its mainland coast and islands would be 'cut-off' by as much as three-quarters of the area into which the coast projects. Noting that this 'cut-off' effect would be created by a few small islands which were many nautical miles apart, the Court concluded that the islands should not be treated as though they were a continuous mainland coast stretching for over 100 nm and accordingly determined that this was a factor for consideration in determining whether the provisional boundary line should be adjusted to produce an equitable result.[116] It was also observed that Colombia's entitlements should also be maintained, and that likewise there was no consequential cut-off applied in the case of the Colombian islands.[117] The Court then proceeded to draw a line that connected up the western limits of the maritime entitlements of the principal Colombian islands, from which straight lines were then drawn so as to connect the EEZ and continental shelves of these islands east into the Caribbean Sea, thereby ensuring respect for the maritime entitlements of these islands.[118] As to the other two Colombian maritime features located to the north of this line – Quitasueño and Serrana – the Court concluded that both were entitled to generate only a 12 nm territorial sea, with the effect that both were enclaved within an area of Nicaraguan EEZ and continental shelf.[119]

K. *Bangladesh v Myanmar* (2012)

In the *Delimitation of the maritime boundary in the Bay of Bengal (Bangladesh v Myanmar)* case,[120] the International Tribunal for the Law of the Sea (ITLOS) was called upon to determine a maritime boundary in the Bay of Bengal. As Bangladesh and Myanmar were adjacent States, the only significant island that needed to be taken into account was St Martin's Island (Bangladesh) located adjacent to the Bangladesh/Myanmar land boundary terminus and eight km from the coast.[121] With respect to general principles in this area, ITLOS observed that:

> neither case law nor State practice indicates that there is a general rule concerning the effect to be given to islands in maritime delimitation. It depends on the particular circumstances of each case. The Tribunal also observes that the effect to be given to islands in delimitation may differ, depending on whether the delimitation concerns the

[116] ibid 703–4 [215].
[117] ibid 704 [216].
[118] ibid 710–11 [237].
[119] ibid 714–15 [238].
[120] *Bangladesh v Myanmar* (n 31).
[121] ibid 47 [149]. Another island that was referred to in the ITLOS decision but not taken into account in the delimitation was Oyster Island; ibid (Dissenting Opinion of Judge Lucky) 239 [5].

> territorial sea or other maritime areas beyond it. Both the nature of the rights of the coastal State and their seaward extent may be relevant in this regard.[122]

For the purposes of the territorial sea boundary, the view of ITLOS was that there were no compelling reasons to treat St. Martin's Island as a special circumstance consistent with LOSC Article 15.[123] With respect to the EEZ and continental shelf boundary, the Tribunal was of the view that St. Martin's Island was a feature that could be given effect but that in this instance to do so would have a distorting impact upon the delimitation of the boundary. Accordingly the island was not considered a relevant circumstance with respect to those boundaries.[124]

L. *Bangladesh v India* (2014)

In *Bay of Bengal Maritime Boundary Delimitation (Bangladesh v India)*,[125] a LOSC Annex VII Arbitral Tribunal was asked to determine the maritime boundary between Bangladesh and India in the Bay of Bengal. The boundary extended from the land terminus between the two States at the head of the Bay and included the territorial sea, EEZ and continental shelf. An initial issue was the determination of relevant territorial sea baselines within the Bay of Bengal land terminus area, and the Tribunal gave consideration to the status of a number of islands and low-tide elevations for those purposes.[126] Other than these small coastal islands that form part of the Bengal Delta, the other most significant islands were the Andaman Islands (India), located in the southern sector of the Bay of Bengal, which were taken into account for the purposes of measuring the relevant Indian coastline.[127] Ultimately, the delimitation of the maritime boundary proceeded on the basis that the relevant islands did not have a significant impact upon the direction of the boundary.

IV. State Practice

A review of state practice with respect to maritime boundary delimitation presents different perspectives to an assessment of the decisions of international courts and tribunals. In delimiting their maritime boundaries States seek to interpret the relevant provisions of the LOSC, and previously the Geneva Conventions, to

[122] ibid 46 [147]–[148].
[123] ibid 47 [152].
[124] ibid 86 [318]–[319].
[125] *In the Matter of the Bay of Bengal Maritime Boundary Arbitration (Bangladesh v India)* (Award) (7 July 2014) PCA Case No 2010-16 (*Bangladesh v India*).
[126] ibid 73–74 [260]–[264]. Neither State sought to use St. Martin's Island as a basepoint for delimitation purposes, ibid 105 [367].
[127] ibid 87–88 [303]–[305].

their advantage. However, state practice ultimately reflects a diplomatic outcome in which a maritime boundary treaty is negotiated. The law of the sea provides the framework for that approach and median/equidistance lines have played a critical role in those processes. A delimitation methodology, as that term has been adopted by international courts and tribunals, is not readily apparent. This, however, is reflective of how maritime boundary delimitation negotiations are conducted. Often it is only the outcome of that delimitation – as reflected in the negotiated treaty and the drawn boundary – that is available for analysis and review.

Another observation that can be made with respect to state practice in this area is that, as noted above, there is a considerable diversity in the geographic circumstances in which an island may be involved in a maritime boundary delimitation. The islands may not be a significant factor in the delimitation because of their location. In the Johor Strait Malaysia/Singapore maritime boundary the territorial sea within the strait is delimited. The islands of Singapore that directly face Malaysia on the Malay Peninsula are all taken into account and accorded an entitlement to a territorial sea;[128] however, the islands had no relevance to the delimitation, as a deep-water channel was selected as the basis for the boundary.[129] Likewise in the Australia/France Southern Ocean maritime boundary between the sub-Antarctic islands of Heard and McDonald Islands (Australia) and Kerguelen (France), a simple equidistance line is utilised to delimit a fishing zone and continental shelf.[130] As these islands were remote, of relatively similar size, had no permanent populations, and were far distant from any other land that could impinge on how the boundaries were drawn, an equidistance line approach was appropriate.

The analysis that follows below seeks to draw out instances in state practice where islands have had a significant impact on maritime boundary delimitation. The survey is not comprehensive as not all instances of state practice are noteworthy.[131] A regional or oceans focus has also been adopted for convenience.

[128] The Singaporean islands are the main island of Singapore, Pulau Ubin, and Pulau Tekong.

[129] Agreement between the Government of Malaysia and the Government of the Republic of Singapore to Delimit precisely the Territorial Waters Boundary in Accordance with the Straits Settlement and Johor Territorial Waters Agreement (adopted 7 August 1995, entered into force 7 August 1995); reproduced in JI Charney and LM Alexander (eds), *International Maritime Boundaries*, vol 3 (Martinus Nijhoff 1998) 2351 (*IMB III*); see analysis in ibid 2345.

[130] Agreement on Maritime Delimitation between the Government of Australia and the Government of the French Republic (adopted 4 January 1982, entered into force 10 January 1983) [1983] ATS 10, art 2.

[131] A more exhaustive study can be found in Prescott and Schofield (n 1); with respect to East and Southeast Asia, see SP Kim, *Maritime delimitation and interim arrangements in North East Asia* (Martinus Nijhoff 2004), and C Schofield, 'An incomplete maritime map: progress and challenges in the delimitation of maritime boundaries in South East Asia' in DR Rothwell and D Letts (eds), *Law of the Sea in South East Asia: Environmental, Navigational and Security Challenges* (Routledge 2020) 33.

A. Arctic Ocean

The Arctic Ocean is distinctive in that it contains large continental land masses, the largest island in the world (Greenland), and a mix of other islands including geographic archipelagos. In some instances, maritime boundaries which have involved islands have given little weight to their presence, such as the Russia/US Bering Strait maritime boundary,[132] and the Canada/Denmark Davis Strait maritime boundary.[133] The Davis Strait boundary is especially distinctive as the delimitation in the strait is discontinued either side of Hans Island to circumvent the territorial dispute over the island.[134] The maritime boundaries relating to Greenland are of especial interest due to its dominant size, effectively equating it to a continental mainland. In the Greenland (Denmark)/Iceland maritime boundary in the Denmark Strait,[135] the only additional relevant islands were Kolbeinsey (Iceland) and Grimsey (Iceland). Different views existed between Denmark and Iceland as to the status of these features, especially Kolbeinsey which Denmark considered to be a juridical rock.[136] Ultimately, Kolbeinsey was given diminished effect in the final boundary and Grimsey full effect. In that regard it should be noted that Kolbeinsey is 60 nm from Iceland and had a potential distorting impact on the boundary compared to Grimsey which is 22 nm from the Icelandic coast.[137] The boundary between Greenland (Denmark) and Svalbard (Norway) in Fram Strait is essentially an equidistance line.[138] Account is taken of Tobias Ø (Denmark),[139] an island 70 km east of the northern Greenland coast that was reportedly not

[132] The Agreement between the United States of America and the Union of the Soviet Socialist Republics on the Maritime Boundary, with Annex (adopted 1 June 1990, in force provisionally) 29 ILM 941; see discussion in JI Charney and LM Alexander, *International Maritime Boundaries*, vol 1 (Martinus Nijhoff 1993) 447 (*IMB I*).

[133] Agreement between the Government of the Kingdom of Denmark and the Government of Canada relating to the Delimitation of the Continental Shelf between Greenland and Canada (adopted 17 December 1973, entered into force 13 March 1974) 950 UNTS 147; see discussion in *IMB I* (n 132) 371.

[134] *IMB I* (n 132) 372; see discussion in Chapter 3 section V.F of this volume.

[135] Agreement between the Government of the Kingdom of Denmark along with the Local Government of Greenland on the one hand and the Government of the Republic of Iceland on the other hand on the Delimitation of the Continental Shelf and Fishery Zone in the Area between Greenland and Iceland (adopted 11 November 1997, entered into force 27 May 1998) (1999) 39 *Law of the Sea Bulletin* 35.

[136] For background on Kolbeinsey, see T Jacobsen and I Stone, 'Kolbeinsey: Iceland's Arctic island' (2006) 42(2) *Polar Record* 167.

[137] See discussion in JI Charney and RW Smith, *International Maritime Boundaries*, vol 4 (Martinus Nijhoff 2002) 2946–47 (*IMB IV*).

[138] Agreement between the Government of the Kingdom of Norway on the one hand, and the Government of the Kingdom of Denmark together with the Home Rule Government of Greenland on the other hand, concerning the Delimitation of the Continental Shelf and the Fisheries Zone in the Area between Greenland and Svalbard (adopted 20 February 2006, in force 2 June 2006) 2738 UNTS No I-42887.

[139] See discussion in DA Colson and RW Smith, *International Maritime Boundaries*, vol 6 (Martinus Nijhoff 2011) 4523 (*IMB VI*).

discovered until 1993 because it was covered by snow and ice for much of the year.[140] In 2006 a set of Agreed Minutes were reached between the Faroe Islands (Denmark), Iceland, and Norway (including Jan Mayen) with respect to projected continental shelf boundaries between the three States.[141] The Agreed Minutes sought to reflect delimitation of the respective anticipated overlapping continental shelf entitlements beyond 200 nm based on recommendations of the Commission on the Limits of the Continental Shelf with respect to three island groups – Faroe Islands, Iceland, Jan Mayen – and the Norwegian mainland coast (which is the subject of straight baselines along the Norwegian offshore islands (*skjaergard*)). All three States have now made Commission submissions. Notwithstanding the significant differences in the land areas of the islands and Norwegian mainland coast, the proposed boundary is based on equidistance.[142]

B. Northern Europe

The most complex set of maritime boundaries involving islands in Northern Europe are those found in the Baltic Sea where there are numerous States, a number of which gained independence following the dissolution of the former USSR, and multiple small islands including features properly classified as geographic archipelagos. Numerous maritime boundaries needed to be negotiated in this region where the LOSC maritime entitlements of islands were to be taken into account. The Estonia/Latvia boundary predominantly is drawn in the Gulf of Riga before extending into the open waters of the Baltic.[143] The relevant islands in the Gulf are Estonian, and most are either large in size or are located close to the Estonian mainland coast. An exception is Ruhnu Island (Estonia), 11.36 km^2 in size, with historically a small population, located in the centre of the Gulf of Riga not far offshore from the land boundary terminus of the two States. The island was granted only a 12 nm entitlement to the south so as to not unduly distort the boundary to the disadvantage of Latvia.[144] A triparty agreement between Estonia, Latvia and Sweden in the Baltic Sea gives little prominence to islands in the region.[145] The related Estonia/Sweden maritime boundary in the Baltic Sea

[140] O Bennike et al, 'Tuppiap Qeqertaa (Tobias Island): a newly discovered island off northeast Greenland' (2006) 42(4) *Polar Record* 309.

[141] Agreed Minutes on the Delimitation of the Continental Shelf beyond 200 Nautical Miles between the Faroe Islands, Iceland and Norway in the Southern Part of the Banana Hole of the Northeast Atlantic (20 September 2006) www.regjeringen.no/en/dokumenter/Agreed-Minutes/id446839/.

[142] *IMB VI* (n 139) 4532; the relevant land areas are the Faroes (1,397 km^2), Jan Mayen (380 km^2), and Iceland (103,000 km^2).

[143] Agreement between the Government of the Republic of Estonia and the Government of the Republic of Latvia on the Maritime Delimitation in the Gulf of Riga, the Strait of Irbe and the Baltic Sea (adopted 12 July 1996, entered into force 10 October 1996) *IMB IV* (n 137) 3014.

[144] See analysis in *IMB IV* (n 137) 2995, 3005–6.

[145] Agreement between the government of the Republic of Estonia, the government of the Republic of Latvia and the government of the kingdom of Sweden on the common maritime boundary point in the

needed to take into account significant offshore islands of both States,[146] in particular Saaremaa and Hiiumaa (Estonia) and Gotland and Gotska Sandön (Sweden). These islands had featured in the previous Sweden/USSR boundary delimitation in this part of the Baltic Sea and the Swedish islands had effectively been given 75 per cent effect.[147] A similar approach was adopted in the 1998 Estonia/Sweden Agreement.[148] The Estonia/Finland boundary in the Gulf of Finland and Baltic Sea takes into account numerous islands.[149] The boundary gives full effect to the relevant islands and is based upon an equidistance line.[150] A critical issue at the western terminus of the boundary is the weight to be accorded to the Bogskär island group (Finland) which was left unresolved.[151] The Bogskär islands were also relevant in the Finland/Sweden maritime boundary in the northern Baltic and Åland Sea.[152] In this boundary, five straight segments were selected for a single maritime boundary of 94.5 nm which runs between the Åland Islands (Finland) and the Swedish mainland into the Baltic Sea. The boundary takes into account multiple factors, including the 1921 agreement on the status of the Åland Islands, and existing fishing zones.[153] The precise weight given to the Bogskär islands is unclear, other than to observe they have been granted some maritime entitlement. Finally the Denmark (Faroe Islands)/UK maritime boundary in the vicinity of the Faroe Islands, the Shetland Islands (UK), Orkney Islands (UK) and mainland of Scotland is notable for the different island groups and configurations that needed to be taken into account.[154] Negotiations over this boundary were complex because

Baltic Sea (adopted 30 April 1997, entered in force 20 February 1998) reproduced in *IMB IV* (n 137) 3056, with analysis at ibid 3041.

[146] Agreement between the government of the Republic of Estonia and the government of the Kingdom of Sweden on the delimitation of the maritime zones in the Baltic Sea (adopted 2 November 1998, entered in force 26 July 2000) 2474 UNTS 55.

[147] See Agreement between the Government of the Kingdom of Sweden and the Government of the Union of Soviet Socialist Republics on the Delimitation of the Continental Shelf and the Swedish Fishing Zone and the Soviet Economic Zone in the Baltic Sea (adopted 18 April 1988, entered in force 22 June 1988) (1988) 27 ILM 295; see analysis in *IMB II* (n 54) 2061–62.

[148] See analysis in *IMB IV* (n 137) 3096–97.

[149] Agreement between the Republic of Estonia and the Republic of Finland on the boundaries of the maritime zones in the Gulf of Finland and the Northern Baltic Sea (adopted 18 October 1996, in force 7 January 1997) reproduced in *IMB IV* (n 137) 3038.

[150] See analysis in *IMB IV* (n 137) 3019.

[151] See comment in *IMB IV* (n 137), 3028–29. These islands have been described as 'two uninhabited rocks with a total area of 4–5 sq. km': *IMB III* (n 129) 2543.

[152] Agreement between Finland and Sweden Concerning the Delimitation in the Åland Sea and the Northern Part of the Baltic Sea of the Finnish Continental Shelf and Fishing Zone and the Swedish Economic Zone (adopted 2 June 1994, entered into force 30 July 1995) 1887 UNTS 229.

[153] See discussion in *IMB II* (n 54) 2539; see also the earlier Agreement between Finland and Sweden Concerning the Delimitation of the Continental Shelf in the Gulf of Bothnia, The Åland Sea and the Northernmost Part of the Baltic Sea (adopted 29 September 1972, entered into force 15 January 1973), ibid 1954; and in Department of State (US), *Limits in the Seas No 71* (16 June 1976) www.state.gov/wp-content/uploads/2019/11/LIS-71.pdf.

[154] Agreement between the Government of the Kingdom of Denmark together with the Home Government of the Faroe Islands on the one hand and the Government of the United Kingdom of Great Britain and Northern Ireland on the other hand relating to the Maritime Delimitation in the area between the Faroe Islands and the United Kingdom (adopted 18 May 1999, entered into force 21 July 1999) (1999) UKTS No 76.

of previous issues with respect to fishing zones claimed by the two States, and the Faroe Islands' dependence on fishing entitlements in that part of the North Sea. Notwithstanding that background, essentially the boundary is based on an equidistance line in which full effect is predominantly given to the relevant large and small islands within the delimited area. In that regard the reliance placed by both States upon the baselines with respect to the islands was significant for finalisation of an equidistance line boundary in the agreement.[155]

C. Caribbean

The Caribbean is an area where there are many small islands, a mix of large and small continental States, island States, and archipelagic States. In some instances the delimitations have been relatively simple, such as those in the case of Cuba/Jamaica where there were no significant islands in the relevant maritime space between the two States and as such an equidistance line was adopted.[156] Likewise the UK and United States also adopted an equidistance line in two maritime boundaries in the case first of the British Virgin Islands (UK)/Puerto Rico and US Virgin Islands (US),[157] and secondly Anguilla (UK)/US Virgin Islands (US).[158] Notable aspects of these boundaries are that with respect to the British Virgin Islands/Puerto Rico and US Virgin Islands, the US was prepared to negotiate a single boundary that jointly applied to two geographically proximate US territories and where Puerto Rico is significantly larger than the other relevant islands.[159] The Anguilla/US Virgin Islands boundary is notable as it is only 1.34 nm in length.[160] The 2001 Honduras/Cayman Islands (UK) boundary involves a continental Latin American State with relevant offshore islands, and very small UK islands in the central Caribbean.[161] Two small Honduran islands needed to be taken into account: Swan Islands located 122 nm off the Honduran continental

[155] See discussion in *IMB IV* (n 137) 2955.

[156] Agreement between the Government of Jamaica and the Government of the Republic of Cuba on the Delimitation of the Maritime Boundary between the two States (adopted 18 February 1994, entered into force 18 July 1995) reproduced in *IMB III* (n 129) 2214; and analysis at ibid 2205.

[157] Treaty Between the Government of the United States of America and the Government of Great Britain and Northern Ireland on the Delimitation in the Caribbean of a Maritime Boundary Relating to Puerto Rico/US Virgin Islands and the British Virgin Islands (adopted 5 November 1993, entered into force 1 June 1995) (1995) UKTS No 77.

[158] Treaty Between the Government of the United States of America and the Government of Great Britain and Northern Ireland on the Delimitation in the Caribbean of a Maritime Boundary Relating to the US Virgin Islands and Anguilla (adopted 5 November 1993, entered 1 June 1995) (1995) UKTS No 71.

[159] See analysis in *IMB III* (n 129) 2161.

[160] See analysis in ibid 2171.

[161] Treaty between the Government of the United Kingdom of Great Britain and Northern Ireland and the Government of the Republic of Honduras concerning the Delimitation of the Maritime Areas between the Cayman Islands and the Republic of Honduras (adopted 4 December 2001, entered into force 1 March 2002) (2002) UKTS No 25.

coast with an area of 3.9 km^2, and Cayo Gorda with an area of 0.007 km^2. Of the three Cayman Islands (Grand Cayman, Little Cayman, and Cayman Brac), only the largest – Grand Cayman – was taken into account.[162] A simplified equidistance and median line was adopted, described as a 'pragmatic line' that sought to take into account the impact of the islands and the differential coastal fronts.[163]

D. Africa

In Africa some of the most prominent maritime boundaries involving islands are to be found in the Gulf of Guinea where there are a number of inhabited islands, including the archipelagic State of Sao Tome and Principe. Two sets of boundaries involving Equatorial Guinea are of interest due to that State comprising mainland African territory, and four offshore islands in the Gulf of Guinea, including the capital Malabo on the island of Bioko. The 2000 partial delimitation of the maritime boundary between Nigeria and Equatorial Guinea gives full effect to Bioko but also sought to take into account existing oil and gas concessions in the Gulf.[164] The boundary predominantly reflects mutual interests in the Gulf rather than undue reliance upon an equidistance line.[165] More complex geography in the Gulf of Guinea is reflected in the negotiated boundaries between Equatorial Guinea and São Tomé and Principe where multiple islands of both States and Equatorial Guinea's African mainland needed to be taken into accounted. In a 1999 treaty[166] two sectors were drawn reflecting the north-eastern facing islands and mainland, and the south-western facing islands. In both instances an equidistance line was utilised and the islands of both States were given full effect, including Annobon (Equatorial Guinea) which lies to the south of Sao Tome and Principe in the south-western sector.[167] The 2001 Gabon/Sao Tome and Principe boundary in the Gulf is less complex and no islands belonging to Gabon had a significant impact upon utilisation of a traditional equidistance line.[168] In the case of Nigeria/Sao Tome and Principe a permanent maritime boundary has not been delimited, but in 2001 agreement was reached on a joint development zone within

[162] See analysis in DA Colson and RW Smith, *International Maritime Boundaries*, vol 5 (Martinus Nijhoff 2005) 3564 (*IMB V*).

[163] ibid 3568.

[164] Treaty Regarding Delimitation of the Maritime Boundary between the Federal Republic of Nigeria and the Republic of Equatorial Guinea Concerning Their Maritime Boundary (adopted 23 September 2000, entered into force 3 April 2002) www.un.org/Depts/los/LEGISLATIONANDTREATIES/PDFFILES/TREATIES/NGA-GNQ2000MB.PDF.

[165] See analysis in *IMB IV* (n 137) 2657.

[166] Treaty Regarding Delimitation of the Maritime Boundary between the Republic of Equatorial Guinea and the Democratic Republic of Sao Tome and Principe (adopted 26 June 1999, in force provisionally) reproduced in *IMB IV* (n 137) 2654.

[167] See discussion in *IMB IV* (n 137) 2647.

[168] Agreement on the Delimitation of the Maritime Border between The Gabonese Republic and the Democratic Republic of Sao Tome and Principe (adopted 26 April 2001) www.un.org/Depts/los/LEGISLATIONANDTREATIES/PDFFILES/TREATIES/GAB-STP2001MB.PDF; *IMB V* (n 162) 3691; and analysis in ibid 3683.

the relevant area of the Gulf of Guinea.[169] This reflected the significant oil concessions each State had in the Gulf, and ongoing maritime boundary delimitations with neighbours such as Cameroon and the need to eventually take into account Bioko Island (Equatorial Guinea).[170]

E. Indian Ocean

In the Indian Ocean, a number of maritime boundaries have been negotiated between continental States, archipelagic States, and island States in which islands have played a prominent role. One of the most prominent Indian Ocean boundaries is that between Australia and Indonesia.[171] A 1997 treaty sought to settle a number of outstanding fisheries/EEZ and seabed/continental shelf maritime boundary issues between the two countries from a far eastern sector in the Arafura Sea, through the Timor Sea and into the Indian Ocean. In the Indian Ocean, a feature is the small inhabited Australian islands of Christmas Island and Cocos (Keeling) Islands, and the uninhabited Ashmore and Cartier Islands (Australia). All are distant from the Australian coast and relatively close to the Indonesian archipelago.[172] Australia's small islands were recognised as LOSC juridical islands with full entitlements; nevertheless, concessions were made vis-à-vis the Indonesian archipelago and the Australian islands were not given full effect.[173] In the southwest Indian Ocean a number of boundaries have been concluded in which islands have been prominent. These include boundaries between Gloriso Islands (France)/Seychelles,[174] Réunion (France)/Mauritius,[175] Réunion (France)/Madagascar,[176] and Mauritius/Seychelles.[177] However, in all

[169] Treaty between the Federal Republic of Nigeria and the Democratic Republic of Sao Tome and Principe on the Joint Development of Petroleum and other Resources in Respect of Areas of the Exclusive Economic Zone of the Two States (adopted 21 February 2001, entered into force 2003) reproduced in *IMB V* (n 162) 3649.

[170] See analysis in *IMB V* (n 162) 3638.

[171] Treaty between the Government of Australia and the Government of the Republic of Indonesia establishing an Exclusive Economic Zone Boundary and Certain Seabed Boundaries (adopted 14 March 1997, not yet in force) [1997] ATNIF 4 (Australia–Indonesia Treaty).

[172] Christmas Island is 186 nm from the coast of Java (Indonesia).

[173] See Australia–Indonesia Treaty (n 171); see analysis in *IMB II* (n 54) 2705–6.

[174] Agreement between the Government of the French Republic and the Government of the Republic of Seychelles Concerning the Delimitation of the Maritime Boundary of the Exclusive Economic Zone and the Continental Shelf of France and Seychelles (adopted 19 February 2001, entered in force 19 February 2001) 2162 UNTS 28.

[175] Convention between the Government of the French Republic and the Government of Mauritius on the Delimitation of the French and Mauritian Economic Zones between the Islands of Reunion and Mauritius (adopted 2 April 1980, entered into force 2 April 1980) reproduced in *IMB II* (n 54) 1360.

[176] Accord between the Government of the French Republic and the Government of the Republic of Madagascar dealing with the delimitation of maritime spaces situated between La Réunion and Madagascar (adopted 14 April 2005, entered into force 18 June 2007) 2624 UNTS 17.

[177] Agreement between the Government of the Republic of Mauritius and the Government of the Republic of Seychelles On the Delimitation of the Exclusive Economic Zone between the Two States, (adopted 29 July 2008, entered in force 19 November 2008) *IMB VI* (n 139) 4398.

instances equidistance or modified equidistance lines were utilised. A number of factors were at play here. These included the distance between the islands, such that no single islands of any of the States were especially proximate to each other so as to have a distorting impact on the boundary. Even in the case of the Réunion (France)/Madagascar boundary, where there is a significant disparity in the size of the islands,[178] the agreement has been described as 'short and uncomplicated'.[179]

F. Pacific Ocean

Like the Caribbean, the Pacific Ocean is characterised by a large number of small island States, including archipelagic States, overseas territories of large metropolitan States, and significant continental States. This has created an interesting legal and political dynamic for negotiated maritime boundary treaties. The Papua New Guinea (PNG)/Solomon Islands maritime boundary is one of the few examples of a negotiated treaty between two archipelagic States; however, the archipelagic baselines of the two States did not have a significant impact on the direction of the boundary. The boundary, which is approximately 1,000 nm in length, is a modified equidistant line and encompasses the territorial sea, continental shelf and EEZ/fishing zones.[180] A prominent feature of the boundary is that the large island of Bougainville (PNG) abuts small islands of the Solomon Islands in the Bougainville Strait. All of the relevant island features, which are inhabited, are given their full entitlements.[181] The Federated States of Micronesia (FSM) and the Marshall Islands (an archipelagic State) settled their maritime boundaries in 2006.[182] The boundary seeks to take into account the maritime entitlements of Ebon, Namdrik, Ujae and Ujelang (Marshall Islands) and Kosrae, Pingelap, Mokil, Pohnpei and Pakin (FSM). The boundary can predominantly be described as based on an equidistant line involving small distant islands.[183] One of the most innovative maritime boundaries in the region is that between Australia and PNG in the Torres Strait and related

[178] Madagascar has a size of 592,800 km^2, and La Réunion has a size of 2,512 km^2 and Madagascar is thus 235 times as large as La Réunion: *IMB VI* (n 139) 4407.

[179] *IMB VI* (n 139) 4409.

[180] Treaty between the Independent States of Papua New Guinea and Solomon Islands Concerning Sovereignty, Maritime and Seabed Boundaries between the Two Countries, and Cooperation on Related Matters (adopted 25 January 1989, not yet in force).

[181] See analysis in *IMB III* (n 129) 2323; and JRV Prescott, 'The Papua New Guinea–Solomon Islands Maritime Boundary' (1994) 11 *Ocean Yearbook* 179.

[182] Treaty between the Federated States of Micronesia and the Republic of the Marshall Islands Concerning Maritime Boundaries and Cooperation on Related Matters (adopted 5 July 2006, entered in force 24 July 2015) UN Registration No 54649.

[183] *IMB VI* (n 139) 4316; see also Department of State (US), *Republic of the Marshall Islands: Archipelagic and other Maritime Claims and Boundaries' (Limits in the Seas No 145)* (Department of State 2020) www.state.gov/wp-content/uploads/2020/02/LIS-145-Marshall-Islands.pdf.

areas.[184] A major challenge in drawing the boundary was that while the northern tip of Australia and the PNG mainland are at some distance, the Torres Strait has many very small Australia islands, some of which are immediately south of the PNG coastline. The approach taken was to determine differential boundaries for the seabed (continental shelf), which effectively is a median line through the Torres Strait, while a fishing zone (EEZ) boundary recognises the legitimate entitlements of the multiple small Australian islands that are located to the north of the sea-bed boundary line. Another feature of the treaty is that some of the Australian islands located north of the sea-bed boundary line only enjoy a three nm territorial sea, while Australian islands to the south of the line have a 12 nm territorial sea.[185] The Australia/New Zealand maritime boundary in the Tasman Sea between a continental and an island State, features allowances for Tasman Sea islands.[186] In particular the entitlements of Norfolk Island and Lord Howe Island (Australia) and Three Kings Island (New Zealand) in the central Tasman Sea, and Macquarie Island (Australia) and the Campbell and Auckland Islands (New Zealand) in the southern Tasman Sea had to be accounted for. Another distinctive feature of the boundaries is how both States sought to take into account their anticipated entitlements to an extended continental shelf consistently with LOSC Article 76.[187] The boundary is predominantly based on an equidistance line, yet Australia acknowledged that:

> Not all of the boundary, however, runs along the equidistance line. Where an isolated island of one country lies close to the much longer coastline of another country, it is consistent with international law and practice for the boundary to be located closer to the isolated island. This particularly affects Lord Howe and Norfolk Islands, the latter of which lies closer to New Zealand than to Australia.[188]

V. Impact of Islands on Maritime Boundary Delimitation[189]

Islands can have a significant impact on maritime boundary delimitation; however, it is not possible to prescribe a clear set of 'rules'. Each geographic and political

[184] Treaty between Australia and the Independent State of Papua New Guinea concerning Sovereignty and Maritime Boundaries in the area between the two Countries, including the area known as Torres Strait, and Related Matters (adopted 18 December 1978, entered into force 15 February 1985) [1985] ATS 4 (Torres Strait Treaty).

[185] ibid art 3; the Treaty also uniquely provides for a Torres Strait Protected Zone, which encompasses the Australian and PNG islands scattered throughout the strait and facilities the movement of peoples and respect for customary rights within the region: ibid arts 10, 11.

[186] Treaty between the Government of Australia and the Government of New Zealand Establishing Certain Exclusive Economic Zone Boundaries and Continental Shelf Boundaries (adopted 25 July 2004, entry into force 25 January 2006) [2006] ATS 4.

[187] See analysis of this boundary in *IMB V* (n 162) 3759.

[188] Treaty between the Government of Australia and the Government of New Zealand Establishing Certain Exclusive Economic Zone Boundaries and Continental Shelf Boundaries [2004] ATNIA 8 [18].

[189] See the analysis in V Prescott and G Triggs, 'Islands and Rocks and their Role in Maritime Delimitation' in *IMB V* (n 162) 3245; see also DE Karl, 'Islands and the Delimitation of the Continental Shelf: A Framework for Analysis' (1977) 71 *American Journal of International Law* 642.

situation raises its own distinctive set of issues which the ICJ recognised in *Libya v Malta* when it observed:

> In the view of the Court, it is not a question of an 'island State' having some sort of special status in relation to continental shelf rights … It is simply that Malta being independent, the relationship of its coasts with the coasts of its neighbours is different from what it would be if it were a part of the territory of one of them. In other words, it might well be that the sea boundaries in this region would be different if the islands of Malta did not constitute an independent State, but formed a part of the territory of one of the surrounding countries. This aspect of the matter is related not solely to the circumstances of Malta being a group of islands, and an independent State, but also to the position of the islands in the wider geographical context, particularly their position in a semi-enclosed sea.[190]

Nevertheless, there do remain some core fundamental criteria to be taken into account. The first factor is the distinction between a LOSC juridical island and juridical rock. An island, that enjoys all of the law of sea entitlements of a mainland, will be more difficult to discount and give less weight to than a rock. Islands will also in most instances have a permanent population, which in some instances can be very significant. It follows that not only will they have an economic life of their own, but that can also be substantively reflected in multiple different types of economic activity extending from land-based activities but also marine industries such as fishing and offshore oil and gas fields. The second factor is the political status of the island.[191] If the island is the principal territory of a State, or is encompassed within the baselines of an archipelagic State, it will inevitably be given much more weight and prominence in boundary delimitation than an island or islands that are distant from a metropolitan territory. This distinction can be seen by the manner in which Sao Tome and Principe has been able to settle maritime boundaries in the Gulf of Guinea, how boundaries have been settled in the Caribbean, and the boundary between PNG and the Solomon Islands in the Pacific. Politically distinctive, but nonetheless distant islands from the mainland such as the UK Channel Islands were treated differently in the *Anglo-French Arbitration*.

With those two fundamental criteria established, what other factors can be identified as being applied and taken into account? Proximity to the coastline of the other State is clearly a critical factor, especially in the case of small islands. Whereas the Channel Islands were given diminished effect in the *Anglo-French Arbitration*, a different approach was adopted with respect to small Australian islands close to the PNG coast in the Torres Strait Treaty. A distinguishing feature between the two is the number of Australian islands scattered throughout the strait, which extend from the north-eastern tip of Australia to the very edge of

[190] *Libya v Malta* (n 11) 42 [53].
[191] On this point see D Bowett, 'Islands, Rocks, Reefs and Low-Tide Elevations in Maritime Boundary Delimitations' in *IMB I* (n 132) 131, 132.

mainland PNG. Decisions taken to enclave islands, or to reduce their maritime entitlements, often arise in instances where the islands will have a significant distorting impact on the direction of the maritime boundary, as was the case with Ruhnu Island in the Gulf of Riga. That the islands are very small, are sparsely populated or have historically had no permanent settlement can be a related factor, as occurred in *Qatar v Bahrain*. What can be identified from both the cases and state practice is that islands may have no impact on the direction of the boundary and effectively not be taken into account (*Black Sea; Bangladesh v Myanmar*), may be subject to a partial or full enclave (*Anglo-French Arbitration*; *Nicaragua v Colombia*; *St Pierre and Miquelon*), or may be given something approaching half or discounted effect (Greenland/Iceland; Torres Strait). There remain, however, an overwhelming number of instances where islands have been given full effect and maritime boundaries have been delimited on the basis of equidistance/median lines (Greenland/Svalbard; Faroe Islands; Cuba/Jamaica; Nigeria/Equatorial Guinea).

Caution needs to be exercised in suggesting general rules. However, where distant islands, island States, and archipelagic States are the subject of maritime boundary delimitation a median/equidistance line approach will often be utilised. This is especially reflected in state practice in the Arctic and Indian Oceans. When applying a delimitation methodology, an international court or tribunal will likewise favour an equidistance line and only adjust that line due to special circumstances such as the need to maintain proportionality based on coastal lengths (*Jan Mayen*). In that respect, maritime boundary delimitation between island States or island territories can be no different than that which takes place between mainland States, especially if the delimitation does not involve the interests of third States. In delimitations involving Greenland, it has effectively been dealt with as if it were a continental mainland because of its size. While Greenland's coastal front outweighs the opposite coastal fronts of Iceland, Jan Mayen, and Svalbard, no distinctive weight has been given to it as an island. In this respect, the maritime domain within which the islands are located will also be important. Islands in remote oceans and seas, which are more thinly populated, do not result in as heavily contested or complex maritime boundary arrangements as when islands are found in more temperate areas with larger populations. In these latter instances, there is much more potential for historical (Estonia/Finland; Finland/Sweden) and economic factors (Nigeria/Sao Tome and Principe) to come into play. Archipelagic State baselines will certainly be taken into account in delimitation of maritime boundaries, subject to the State's status being recognised (*Qatar v Bahrain*). There is also some distinction in the state practice and decisions between territorial sea delimitations (*Nicaragua v Honduras*; Bering Strait), where giving effect to islands in most instances will not have a significant distorting impact on the boundary, and EEZ/continental shelf boundaries, where giving full effect to small islands can significantly impact a boundary.

VI. Conclusions

The practice of maritime boundary delimitation has existed for a century and only gained significant momentum post-1945. Some of the early examples of state practice and decisions by international courts and tribunals appear rudimentary in a contemporary light. Nevertheless that practice has developed and evolved, consistently with the law of the sea, to place an emphasis upon the need to ensure an equitable result. That is the key criteria under the LOSC and the ICJ's delimitation methodology has been promoted to attain that outcome. While this is also a driver in state practice, States have the capacity to make concessions and 'discounts' in their maritime boundary negotiations in ways that are not available to international courts and tribunals. The political dynamic at play between the States engaged in a maritime boundary negotiation should also not be overlooked. Islands clearly have a major impact on maritime boundary delimitation. They can be the subjects of delimitation as island States, or they can be the objects of delimitation, especially in the context of islands of a metropolitan State. At all times a critical factor is that islands generate legitimate entitlements to maritime zones under the LOSC, and those entitlements, when they overlap with entitlements generated from other islands or a mainland, are subject to maritime boundary delimitation. There is no formula to that process. There is an agreed delimitation methodology and there is considerable state practice, however, as this chapter has highlighted, islands can become a factor in maritime boundary delimitation in many different and unpredictable ways.

9

Islands and Human Rights

I. Introduction

A feature of the twentieth century was the comprehensive development of international human rights law, and while some initial developments took place prior to 1945, the creation of the United Nations (UN) was the catalyst for the international human rights regime that exists in the twenty-first century. The Charter of the United Nations (UN Charter)[1] was the initial centrepiece, followed first by the 1948 Universal Declaration of Human Rights (UDHR),[2] then by the two 1966 International Covenants on Civil and Political Rights (ICCPR)[3] and Economic, Social and Cultural Rights (ICESCR).[4] In combination with the 1965 International Convention on the Elimination of All Forms of Racial Discrimination (ICERD),[5] these were the legal foundation of the modern UN human rights system. These human rights instruments did not have a specific focus on islands, but rather the rights of people both individually and collectively. In this respect, the development of international human rights law provided a basis for the protection of the interests of every individual person, no matter where they were located, and also for groups of peoples. Accordingly, the recognition in UDHR Article 2 of individual rights and freedoms with respect to matters such as race, colour, sex, language, and religion, was importantly clarified such that no distinction was to be made:

> on the basis of the political, jurisdictional or international status of the country or territory to which a person belongs, whether it be independent, trust, non-self-governing or under any other limitation of sovereignty.[6]

[1] Charter of the United Nations (adopted 26 June 1945, entered into force 24 October 1945) 1 UNTS xvi (UN Charter).

[2] Universal Declaration of Human Rights (adopted 10 December 1948) UNGA Res 217 A(III) (UDHR).

[3] International Covenant on Civil and Political Rights (adopted 16 December 1966, entered into force 23 March 1976) 999 UNTS 171.

[4] International Covenant on Economic, Social and Cultural Rights (adopted 16 December 1966, entered into force 3 January 1976) 993 UNTS 3.

[5] International Convention on the Elimination of All Forms of Racial Discrimination (adopted 21 December 1965, entered into force 4 January 1969) 660 UNTS 1.

[6] UDHR (n 2) art 2; for some discussion of the background to the finalisation of the text of art 2, see J Morsink, *The Universal Declaration of Human Rights: Origins, Drafting and Intent* (University of Pennsylvania Press 1999) 96–101.

Given the status in 1945 of many islands as territories under colonial control or which were the home of peoples that were ethnically and historically distinct from metropolitan powers,[7] it is the right of self-determination in the UN Charter[8] and associated human rights instruments that was, and remains, one of the most important human rights recognised for the peoples of islands.

Since 1945 a number of other important human rights have emerged that reflect an evolution in the thinking about rights and particularly the challenges faced by island peoples. These include matters such as health, food security, environmental impact and climate change and the potential loss of statehood. This chapter will initially assess these challenges faced by islands, before undertaking a review of the right of self-determination for island peoples. Consideration will also be given to the status of 'Small Island Developing States' and the way in which this group of States is considered within the United Nations, along with parallel processes that recognise the distinctive status of certain island communities at regional and sub-regional levels. The significance for islands of the connection between human rights, climate change, and sea-level rise is discussed in more detail in Chapter 10.

II. Human Rights Treaties and Islands[9]

The emergence of international human rights since 1945 can be principally traced through the development of the UN human rights instruments noted above, the interpretation and application of human rights by UN institutions, including the UN human rights treaty bodies, and the implementation of human rights through relevant domestic laws and statutes. Regional human rights frameworks, especially in Europe, are also relevant given the number of European States with overseas island territories. In this respect there are multiple and varying state practices giving effect to international human rights in islands, and distinctions can be made between island States, islands that are part of metropolitan States, and external island territories that while part of a State are considerably distant from the metropolitan territory. It is with respect to the last two categories that it needs to be recalled that international human rights instruments permit for some variation in how States parties accept their human rights treaty obligations and ultimately apply them within their territory.

[7] A Aust, 'Treaties, Territorial Application' in R Wolfrum (ed), *Max Planck Encyclopedia of Public International Law* (online edn, Oxford University Press 2006) [B2] observes with respect to metropolitan territory that 'Territory thus comprises the metropolitan territory of a State and any other territory under its sovereignty. Non-metropolitan territories … are today generally called overseas territories. … Whether territory of a State is metropolitan or overseas is a matter for the constitution of the State, though "metropolitan" usually comprises only the mainland and nearby islands'.

[8] UN Charter (n 1) art 1(2), referring to self-determination as one of the purposes of the United Nations; see also art 55.

[9] In addition to the discussion below, also see WW Boyer, *America's Virgin Islands: A History of Human Rights and Wrongs* (2nd edn, Carolina Academic Press 2010).

While treaties may make clear the extent of their territorial scope, such that they include islands and overseas territories,[10] this is rarely the case with multilateral human rights treaties where the general rules of treaty law apply. In this respect, Article 29 of the 1969 Vienna Convention on the Law of Treaties[11] provides that 'Unless a different intention appears from the treaty or is otherwise established, a treaty is binding upon each party in respect of its entire territory.' Aust describes this as providing a flexible rule, which allows a State to express its position in various ways.[12] The options include:

- lodging a declaration upon signature or ratification of a treaty;
- lodging an interpretative statement making clear that the State, in becoming a party, will extend the treaty to various territories or exclude its application to those territories; or
- lodging a reservation such that the whole treaty or particular articles of a treaty are excluded from certain territories.[13]

The manner in which these issues have been addressed in the context of the ICCPR demonstrates the potentially far-reaching implications for the application of human rights. Article 2(1) of the ICCPR indicates that for each State party, the Covenant extends to 'all individuals within its territory and subject to its jurisdiction'. This raises issues as to the extent of a State's territory, but does not distinguish between the status of that territory and whether it is an overseas or non-self-governing territory (NSGT).[14] Article 50 also contains a so-called 'federal clause' making clear that the Covenant applies 'to all parts of federal States without any limitations or exceptions.' However, while this provision had clear implications for the islands within federations such as Australia, Canada and Malaysia, this guarantee did not apply in the case of metropolitan States with diverse island territories. Nevertheless, the nexus of territory and jurisdiction would be broad

[10] See the 1980 Convention on the Conservation of Antarctic Marine Living Resources (adopted 20 May 1980, entered into force 7 April 1982) 1329 UNTS 47, where art I outlines the area of application of the Convention, thereby including Southern Ocean islands (including external and overseas territories) of Australia, France, New Zealand, South Africa, and the UK in addition to islands immediately adjacent to the Antarctic coast.

[11] Vienna Convention on the Law of Treaties (adopted 23 May 1969, entered into force 27 January 1980) 1155 UNTS 331 (VCLT).

[12] A Aust, *Modern Treaty Law and Practice* (3rd edn, Cambridge University Press 2013) 179 (*Modern Treaty Law*).

[13] As to the potential for a reservation to be made, or for the practice of States to 'exclude' the application of a multilateral treaty to their overseas territories, the ILC Special Rapporteur has suggested that this practice amounts to a reservation; however this interpretation has been subject to critique; see International Law Commission, 'Reservations to treaties: Titles and texts of draft guidelines of the Guide to Practice adopted by the Drafting Committee of the fiftieth session' (31 July 1998) UN Doc A/CN.4/L.563 [1.1.3]–[1.1.4]; and discussion in Aust, *Modern Treaty Law* (n 12) 183.

[14] See the general discussion on this point in M Nowak, *UN Covenant on Civil and Political Rights CCPR Commentary* (2nd edn, NP Engel 2005) 41–42; and S Joseph and M Castan, *The International Covenant on Civil and Political Rights: Cases, Materials and Commentary* (3rd edn, Oxford University Press 2013) 92–112.

enough to extend to the wide range of island territories that exist under international law which have a relationship with a metropolitan power, and subject to the exceptions noted below this is reflected in practice.

The United Kingdom has certain longstanding practices relating to which parts of its Overseas Territories are included when it ratifies a treaty.[15] Upon becoming a party to the ICCPR the UK made declarations[16] which sought to exempt or modify the application of certain parts of the Covenant to Jersey, Hong Kong, Montserrat, the Turks and Caicos Islands, the British Virgin Islands, the Cayman Islands, the Falkland Islands, the Gilbert Islands, the Pitcairn Islands Group, St Helena and Dependencies, and Tuvalu.[17] The Netherlands also sought to make reservations to the ICCPR with respect to its overseas island territories of the Netherlands Antilles, which over time have been adjusted as the status of those territories changed.[18]

Denmark also has in place a number of territorial exclusions with respect to certain human rights treaties as they apply to Greenland and the Faroe Islands, many of which have now been withdrawn. These included exclusion of the ICERD from the Faroe Islands until withdrawn in 1972 following the adoption of legislation to give effect to the Convention on the islands,[19] and the exclusion of the Optional Protocol to the Convention against Torture and Other Cruel, Inhuman or Degrading Treatment or Punishment[20] with respect to the Faroe Islands until withdrawn in 2005.[21] The Convention on the Rights of the Child (CRC)[22] was excluded from application to Greenland and the Faroe Islands until the reservation

[15] See the discussion in Aust, *Modern Treaty Law* (n 12) 184.

[16] Note that there is no express provision in the ICCPR dealing with the making of declarations or reservations, but the general rules of treaty law as found in VCLT (n 11) arts 19–23 do apply and this is reflected in ICCPR state practice; see the discussion in Nowak (n 14) XVIII; and generally Joseph and Castan (n 14) 885-923.

[17] See details of the UK position at United Nations Treaty Collection, 'International Covenant on Civil and Political Rights', treaties.un.org/doc/db/survey/humanrightsconvs/Chapt_IV_4/reservations/UK.pdf; for some discussion of the application of international human rights instruments in the British Overseas Territories see P Clegg and P Gold, 'The UK Overseas Territories: a decade of progress and prosperity?' (2011) 49 *Commonwealth & Comparative Politics* 115; for a discussion of the particular issues that arise for the UK in the application of treaties to the Crown Dependencies of the Isle of Man and those that make up the Channel Islands, see Aust, *Modern Treaty Law* (n 12) 185–96.

[18] See details at United Nations Treaty Collection, 'International Covenant on Civil and Political Rights', https://treaties.un.org/Pages/ViewDetails.aspx?src=TREATY&mtdsg_no=IV-4&chapter=4&clang=_en#EndDec; the engagement of the Netherlands in the protection of human rights in the Antilles has been the subject of critique; see HM Smith-Cannoy and CA Smith, 'Human Trafficking and International Cheap Talk: The Dutch Government and the Island Territories' (2012) 11 *Journal of Human Rights* 51.

[19] See the text of the original Danish Declaration at 820 UNTS 457; relevant legislation having been adopted in the Faroe Islands on 1 November 1972.

[20] Optional Protocol to the Convention against Torture and Other Cruel, Inhuman or Degrading Treatment or Punishment (signed 18 December 2002, entered into force 22 June 2006) 2375 UNTS 237.

[21] See details at United Nations Treaty Collection, 'Optional Protocol to the Convention against Torture and Other Cruel, Inhuman or Degrading Treatment or Punishment', https://treaties.un.org/Pages/ViewDetails.aspx?src=TREATY&mtdsg_no=IV-9-b&chapter=4&clang=_en.

[22] Convention on the Rights of the Child (adopted 20 November 1989, entered into force 2 September 1990) 1577 UNTS 3.

was withdrawn in 1993.[23] Denmark also had a similar exclusion with respect to two of the CRC Optional Protocols[24] until they were withdrawn with respect to both territories in 2004 and 2016.[25] However, Denmark retains a territorial exclusion with respect to the CRC Optional Protocol on a communications procedure with respect to both the Faroe Islands and Greenland.[26] Territorial exclusions have also been made by New Zealand with respect to the Cook Islands and the Convention on the Elimination on All Forms of Discrimination Against Women,[27] and Tokelau and the Optional Protocol to the Convention on the Rights of Persons with Disabilities.[28]

The territorial application of human rights obligations to islands has also been relevant in European law, where Article 56 of the European Convention on Human Rights relevantly provides:

> Territorial application
>
> 1. Any State may at the time of its ratification or at any time thereafter declare … that the present Convention shall, subject to paragraph 4 of this Article, extend to all or any of the territories for whose international relations it is responsible.
>
> ….

[23] See details at United Nations Treaty Collection, 'Convention on the Rights of the Child', https://treaties.un.org/Pages/ViewDetails.aspx?src=TREATY&mtdsg_no=IV-11&chapter=4&clang=_en#8.

[24] Optional Protocol to the Convention on the Rights of the Child on the involvement of children in armed conflict (adopted 25 May 2000, entered into force 12 February 2002) 2173 UNTS 222; Optional Protocol to the Convention on the Rights of the Child on the sale of children, child prostitution and child pornography (adopted 25 May 2000, entered into force 18 January 2002) 2171 UNTS 227.

[25] See details at United Nations Treaty Collection, 'Optional Protocol to the Convention on the Rights of the Child on the involvement of children in armed conflict', https://treaties.un.org/Pages/ViewDetails.aspx?src=TREATY&mtdsg_no=IV-11-b&chapter=4&clang=_en#4; and United Nations Treaty Collection, 'Optional Protocol to the Convention on the Rights of the Child on the sale of children, child prostitution and child pornography', https://treaties.un.org/Pages/ViewDetails.aspx?src=TREATY&mtdsg_no=IV-11-c&chapter=4&clang=_en.

[26] Optional Protocol to the Convention on the Rights of the Child on a communications procedure, (adopted 19 December 2011, entered into force 14 April 2014) UNTS No 2753; see details at United Nations Treaty Collection, 'Optional Protocol to the Convention on the Rights of the Child on a communications procedure', https://treaties.un.org/pages/ViewDetails.aspx?src=TREATY&mtdsg_no=IV-11-d&chapter=4&clang=_en#1.

[27] Convention on the Elimination of All Forms of Discrimination against Women (adopted 18 December 1979, entered into force 3 September 1981) 1239 UNTS 13; see details at United Nations Treaty Collection, 'Convention on the Elimination of All Forms of Discrimination against Women', https://treaties.un.org/Pages/ViewDetails.aspx?src=TREATY&mtdsg_no=IV-8&chapter=4&clang=_en#EndDec – with respect to arts 2(f), 5(a); over the history of the Convention New Zealand has made a number of reservations with respect to the application of particular articles to the Cook Islands and Niue; nevertheless New Zealand's instrument of ratification indicated that in accordance with the special relationships which exist between New Zealand and the Cook Islands and between New Zealand and Niue, there had been consultations regarding the Convention between the Government of New Zealand and the Government of the Cook Islands and between the Government of New Zealand and the Government of Niue; that the Government of the Cook Islands, which has exclusive competence to implement treaties in the Cook Islands, has requested that the Convention should extend to the Cook Islands; that the Government of Niue which has exclusive competence to implement treaties in Niue, has requested that the Convention should extend to Niue, and that accordingly the Convention applied also to the Cook Islands and Niue.

[28] Optional Protocol to the Convention on the Rights of Persons with Disabilities (adopted 13 December 2006, entered into force 3 May 2008) 2518 UNTS 283; see details at United Nations Treaty Collection, 'Optional Protocol to the Convention on the Rights of Persons with Disabilities', https://treaties.un.org/Pages/ViewDetails.aspx?src=TREATY&mtdsg_no=IV-15-a&chapter=4&clang=_en.

3. The provisions of this Convention shall be applied in such territories with due regard, however, to local requirements.
4. Any State which has made a declaration … may at any time thereafter declare on behalf of one or more of the territories to which the declaration relates that it accepts the competence of the Court to receive applications from individuals, non-governmental organisations or groups of individuals as provided by Article 34 of the Convention.[29]

In this respect France's instrument of ratification indicated that the Convention applies to all French overseas territories,[30] while the Netherlands has made various declarations with respect to the Netherlands Antilles islands which have reflected the changing status of Aruba.[31] The UK has also made declarations extending the Convention to the Sovereign Base Areas of Akrotiri and Dhekelia in Cyprus, being territory for whose international relations the UK is responsible.[32] Specific provision has been made by the UK from time to time for the application of the Convention to the UK Crown Dependencies (Bailiwick of Jersey, Bailiwick of Guernsey and the Isle of Man) and UK Overseas Territories, and for the competence of the European Court of Human Rights over human rights complaints originating from those islands.[33]

The territorial application of human rights treaties to islands that are overseas or external territories of metropolitan States has raised a number of important foundational issues with respect to the reach of those treaties into the islands. Much also depends upon the extent of the municipal legal regime that has been developed, including the level of self-government exercised by an island territory and the general support for and promotion of human rights within the metropolitan State itself.[34]

III. Human Rights Issues and Islands

As island territories gradually gained independence post-1945, and the status of islands as NSGTs and overseas territories came under the spotlight as the UN human rights regime developed, there has been a greater appreciation of the distinctive human rights issues faced by islands. Foremost amongst these has been

[29] Convention for the Protection of Human Rights and Fundamental Freedoms (as amended) (adopted 4 November 1950, entered into force 3 September 1953) 213 UNTS 221.

[30] Council of Europe, 'Reservations and Declarations for Treaty No 005 – Convention for the Protection of Human Rights and Fundamental Freedoms', www.coe.int/en/web/conventions/full-list?module=treaty-detail&treatynum=005.

[31] ibid.

[32] ibid.

[33] ibid.

[34] See the discussion of the case of Norfolk Island (Australia) in H Irving, 'Autonomies of Scale' in Y Ghai and S Woodman (eds), *Practising Self-Government: A Comparative Study of Autonomous Regions* (Cambridge University Press 2013) 200.

the realisation of the right to self-determination and an appreciation that this right may take many forms, ranging from full independence in the case of Singapore, to continued association with a metropolitan State as in the case of the Cook Islands. While there has been considerable progress in this regard, and many island territories that were formerly under colonial domination have gained independence since 1945, a number of island territories continue to seek self-determination, as discussed in more detail below.

Other than self-determination, the enjoyment of international human rights standards in islands varies considerably with multiple factors at play, including culture, economics, geography, history, and politics. In this respect, while there are exceptionally high levels of endorsement of international human rights treaties, the level of respect for the international treaty obligations arsing under those instruments is variable. However, these issues are not unique to islands. In this respect, it is noteworthy that in its *2021 World Report*, Human Rights Watch only reported on 10 island States.[35] This should not be seen as suggesting that island States, especially small island States, are not worthy of distinctive human rights analysis but rather may be a result of the significance of much larger scale human rights concerns elsewhere in the world and the relatively small scale of the populations of island States and territories.[36] Some critical human rights issues have arisen in a number of island States and their associated territories in recent decades, including in Fiji,[37] Indonesia,[38] the Philippines,[39] the Solomon Islands,[40] and Sri Lanka.[41] The human rights concerns have ranged from internal armed conflict, the enforcement of harsh internal security standards, and military intervention in democratic processes, extrajudicial killings, and corruption within police and security forces. Some of these issues are reflected in a 2021 investigation commenced by the International Criminal Court prosecutor into the situation in the Philippines from 2011–19 and alleged international crimes associated with the

[35] Human Rights Watch, *World Report 2021* (2021), www.hrw.org/sites/default/files/media_2021/01/2021_hrw_world_report.pdf; those being Cuba, Haiti, Indonesia, Japan, Maldives, PNG, Philippines, Singapore, Sri Lanka, and the UK.

[36] This is also reflected by the way in which various NGOs conduct their human rights surveys, including the composition of indexes that seek to rank compliance with respect to certain human rights; see eg I Vásquez and T Porčnik, *Human Freedom Index* (Cato Institute 2018) which provides only limited assessment with respect to island States in the Caribbean and the Pacific.

[37] See VP Nanda, 'Ethnic Conflict in Fiji and International Human Rights Law' (1992) 25 *Cornell International Law Journal* 565.

[38] See H Juwana, 'Human Rights in Indonesia' (2006) 4 *Indonesian Journal of International Law* 27.

[39] See R Weissman, '"Development" and the Denial of Human Rights in Ramos's Philippines' (1994) 7 *Harvard Human Rights Journal* 251.

[40] See TT Kabutaulaka, 'Solomon Islands' (2004) 16 *The Contemporary Pacific* 393; the security situation arising from the collapse of state institutions and the threat to human rights in the Solomon Islands was so great that in 2003 the Regional Assistance Mission to the Solomon Islands (RAMSI) was created to restore stability and security, see E Wainwright, 'Responding to state failure – the case of Australia and Solomon Islands' (2003) 57 *Australian Journal of International Affairs* 485.

[41] See R Hoole, 'Sri Lanka: Ethnic Strife, Fratricide, and the Peace vs. Human Rights Dilemma' (2009) 1 *Journal of Human Rights Practice* 120.

so-called 'war on drugs'.[42] The US Department of State also assessed in 2021 significant ongoing human rights concerns in island States such as the Comoros, Cuba, the Dominican Republic, Haiti, Indonesia, Jamaica, Papua New Guinea (PNG), the Philippines, and Sri Lanka.[43]

In addition to fundamental human rights issues facing islands and islanders, which at a general level are no different to those of continental lands, there is an increasing awareness of some distinctive human rights issues that islands face. Increasingly these issues are associated with the impacts of climate change and include matters such as food security, health,[44] and the loss of environment.[45] In recent years there has been increased awareness not only of the general impacts of climate change, but of its particular health and human security impacts upon islands.[46] A heavy reliance by some island States, especially small islands, on fish for food creates vulnerabilities in case of fish-stock collapse. Islands also do not have the land capacity for a wide range of agricultural products and conditions are not always suitable for livestock, which in turn results in a degree of reliance upon imported foods. Even when there are significant agricultural crops, such as sugar cane, the impact of climate change and severe weather events can make crops vulnerable.[47] Connell, for example, has argued that:

> Food security has worsened in Pacific islands in the past 50 years despite numerous regional and international organisations, and national development plans, promoting policies and programmes designed to encourage greater self-sufficiency in food production and consumption, and more adequate food security, mainly by encouraging improved local production but with few positive outcomes.[48]

Major weather events in recent years have had a significant impact upon agriculture in parts of the Pacific and Caribbean, which have highlighted island vulnerabilities with respect to food security and the consequential impacts upon human rights.[49] Even islands such as Puerto Rico have been impacted by these

[42] International Criminal Court, 'Situation in the Philippines: ICC Pre-Trial Chamber I authorises the opening of an investigation' (15 September 2021) www.icc-cpi.int/Pages/item.aspx?name=PR1610.

[43] See Department of State (US), *2020 Country Reports on Human Rights Practices* (Department of State 2021) www.state.gov/reports/2020-country-reports-on-human-rights-practices/.

[44] The link between health, food security and climate change is commented on in J Barnett, 'Dangerous climate change in the Pacific Islands: food production and food security' (2011) 11 *Regional Environmental Change* 229.

[45] See generally EG Hanna and L McIver, 'Small Island States – Canaries in the Coal Mine of Climate Change and Health' in Colin D. Butler (ed), *Climate Change and Global Health* (CABI 2014) 181–92.

[46] See L Nurhidayah, 'Sea-Level Rise (SLR) and Its Implication on Human Security and Human Rights in Indonesia: A Legal Analysis' in R Djalante, J Jupesta, and E Aldrian (eds), *Climate Change Research, Policy and Actions in Indonesia* (Springer 2020) 33; N Lewis, 'Islands in a Sea of Change: Climate Change, Health and Human Security in Small Island States' in HJS Fernando, Z Klaić and JL McCulley (eds), *National Security and Human Health Implications of Climate Change* (Springer 2012) 13–24.

[47] See Barnett (n 43); cf MG Allen, 'Framing food security in the Pacific Islands: empirical evidence from an island in the Western Pacific' (2015) 15 *Regional Environmental Change* 1341.

[48] J Connell, 'Food security in the island Pacific: Is Micronesia as far away as ever?' (2015) 15 *Regional Environmental Change* 1299.

[49] The UN Office for the Coordination of Humanitarian Affairs reported in 2017 that: 'The 2017 hurricane season has caused unprecedented levels of destruction across the Caribbean. It has devastated the

weather events, which not only raised issues with respect to its natural disaster response, but also health and food security on the island which is 900 miles distant from the US east coast.[50] The link between the particular vulnerabilities of islands, especially small islands, and climate change as a result of the impacts of sea-level rise,[51] severe weather events, and crop failures has placed a spotlight on adaptation and the capacity of island communities to respond to these challenges.[52] As a result, there is now a much more expansive view of how human rights are viewed in island communities, which goes beyond traditional conceptions of human rights as advanced in the UN system and now includes a range of matters that impact upon human security, some of which are unique to islands.[53]

IV. Self-Determination[54]

The rights of island peoples have a long history in international law that predates the UN Charter, as highlighted by the Åland Islands in the early 1920s,[55] followed by multiple examples of islands engaged in or seeking self-determination from 1945 onwards, a number of which are associated with UN Charter

lives of millions of people, and left hundreds of thousands of people homeless and displaced': United Nations Office for the Coordination of Humanitarian Affairs, 'Hurricane Season 2017', www.unocha.org/hurricane-season-2017.

[50] AR Hernández and L McGinley, 'Harvard study estimates thousands died in Puerto Rico because of Hurricane Maria', *The Washington Post* (Washington, 29 May 2018) www.washingtonpost.com/national/harvard-study-estimates-thousands-died-in-puerto-rico-due-to-hurricane-maria/2018/05/29/1a82503a-6070-11e8-a4a4-c070ef53f315_story.html?noredirect=on&utm_term=.7cd86d265e3d.

[51] See discussion in Chapter 10 of this volume.

[52] See eg BK Sovacool, 'Perceptions of climate change risks and resilient island planning in the Maldives' (2012) 17 *Mitigation and Adaptation Strategies for Climate Change* 731.

[53] An example is the Pacific Climate Change Migration and Human Security (PCCM-HS) programme, which commenced in 2020 with support from the International Organization for Migration as the lead agency, Economic and Social Commission for Asia and the Pacific, International Labour Organization, the Office for the High Commissioner for Human Rights, the Platform on Disaster Displacement, and Pacific Islands Forum Secretariat, with funding from the Trust Fund for Human Security and the New Zealand Aid Programme: 'Pacific Climate Change Migration and Human Security (PCCM-HS) programme', www.unescap.org/announcement/pacific-climate-change-migration-and-human-security-pccm-hs#.

[54] There is a voluminous literature on this topic; see eg C Tomuschat (ed), *Modern Law of Self-Determination* (Martinus Nijhoff 1993); A Cassese, *Self-determination of peoples: a legal reappraisal* (Cambridge University Press 1995); J Castellino, *International Law and Self-Determination* (Martinus Nijhoff 2000); AF Bayefsky (ed), *Self-Determination in International Law: Quebec and Lessons Learned* (Kluwer Law International 2000); R McCorquodale (ed), *Self-Determination in International Law* (Ashgate 2000); and K Knop, *Diversity and Self-Determination in International Law* (Cambridge University Press 2002).

[55] 'Report of the International Committee of Jurists entrusted by the Council of the League of Nations with the task of giving an advisory opinion upon the legal aspects of the Aaland Islands question' [October 1920] *League of Nations Official Journal* 3; see contemporary discussion at that time in PM Brown, 'The Aaland Islands Question' (1921) 15 *American Journal of International Law* 268, 268–72; CN Gregory, 'The Neutralization of the Aaland Islands' (1923) 17 *American Journal of International Law* 63.

Chapter XII processes.[56] The criteria for the identification of what might be called 'self-determination' territories have historically included those that were under the UN Charter Chapters IX and XII mandate and trusteeship system, Chapter XI NSGTs, and certain territories where the principle of self-determination had been adopted as the criterion for the settlement of a dispute.[57] Islands, or parts of islands, that have enjoyed or have sought self-determination have predominantly fallen under the first two categories. Highlighting the significance of the *Namibia Advisory Opinion*, where the ICJ observed that 'the subsequent development of international law in regard to non-self-governing territories … made the principle of self-determination applicable to all of them',[58] Crawford noted in 2006 that the 'principle of self-determination is firmly established in international law, in particular in relation to territories of colonial type.'[59] The principle was clearly endorsed by the Court in 1995 in *East Timor* where, even when exercising its discretion and declining to adjudge the case brought by Portugal, it was observed that the East Timorese enjoyed a right of self-determination.[60] More recently in the 2019 *Chagos Archipelago* Advisory Opinion the Court declared self-determination to be a 'fundamental human right.'[61]

Island territories, both prior to and since the adoption of the UN Charter, have been prominent in self-determination discourse, and in that regard the fact they constitute distinct geographical areas as opposed to being territories situated within a continental landmass has been important. Islands subject to claims of self-determination are also more likely to be the home of a recognisable group of people.[62] Islands have also had a long history of settlement and colonisation, and the peoples of distant island territories are often culturally and ethnically distinct

[56] See eg discussion in RS Clark, 'Self-Determination and Free Association-Should the United Nations Terminate the Pacific Islands Trust' (1980) 21 *Harvard International Law Journal* 1; N Hirayasu, 'The Process of Self-Determination and Micronesia's Future Political Status under International Law' (1987) 9 *University of Hawaii Law Review* 487; P Ruffatto, 'U.S. Action in Micronesia as a Norm of Customary International Law: The Effectuation of the Right to Self-Determination for Guam and Other Non-Self-Governing Territories' (1993) 2 *Pacific Rim Law and Policy Journal* 377; JM Van Dyke, C Di Amore-Siah and GW Berkley-Coats, "Self-Determination for Non self-Governing Peoples and for Indigenous Peoples: The Cases of Guam and Hawai'i' (1996) 18 *University of Hawai'i Law Review* 623.

[57] J Crawford, *The Creation of States in International Law* (2nd edn, Clarendon Press 2006) 116–17.

[58] *Legal Consequences for States of the Continued Presence of South Africa in Namibia (South West Africa) notwithstanding Security Council Resolution 276 (1970)* (Advisory Opinion) [1971] ICJ Reps 16, 31.

[59] Crawford (n 57) 122.

[60] *Case Concerning East Timor (Portugal v Australia)* (Judgment) [1995] ICJ Reps 90, 105–6; see the discussion by Knop (n 54) 190–211, and GJ Simpson, 'Judging the East Timor Dispute: Self-Determination at the International Court of Justice' (1994) 17 *Hastings International and Comparative Law Review* 323.

[61] *Legal Consequences of the Separation of the Chagos Archipelago from Mauritius in 1965* (Advisory Opinion) [2019] ICJ Reps 95, 131 [144] (*Chagos Advisory Opinion*).

[62] J Summers, *Peoples and International Law: How Nationalism and Self-Determination Shape a Contemporary Law of Nations* (Martinus Nijhoff 2007) 322 who observes that 'The working assumption behind colonial self-determination is that a non-self-governing, trust or mandate territory equates to a people.'

from the metropolitan States.[63] Though, as has occurred in the case of French island overseas territories such as Mayotte and New Caledonia, there may remain a strong connection with a distant metropolitan State.[64]

A significant issue, however, for islands is the *form* of self-determination that they may seek given their geographic size, population, economy, and isolation.[65] In this respect, islands that could be considered micro-States, face some very particular challenges.[66] Self-determination can take many forms[67] and in addition to an island moving towards full statehood, other forms of self-determination can be enjoyed through ongoing dependency with a metropolitan State, which may include an island State such as New Zealand.[68] In this respect, Crawford has observed that 'the question of the ambit of self-determination, [and] the territories to which it applies, has arguably remained as much a matter of politics as law.'[69] This can certainly be seen in the way in which politics has played a critical role in acts of self-determination for certain islands such as East Timor/Timor-Leste, and remains a critical ongoing issue for other islands such as Greenland (Denmark), New Caledonia (France), and Puerto Rico (US).[70] What follows below is an analysis of some of the more prominent island territories engaged in various processes of self-determination: the Chagos Archipelago, New Caledonia, Bougainville, the Faroe Islands and Greenland.[71]

[63] This is not to suggest that overseas territories have not been influenced by the culture of the metropolitan State, as is the case of the Falkland Islands (UK), and New Caledonia (France), and Norfolk Island (Australia).

[64] In the case of Mayotte, see the discussion in M Pomerance, *Self-Determination in Law and Practice: The New Doctrine in the United Nations* (Martinus Nijhoff 1982) 30–31.

[65] The issue of isolation for the island is a particular issue in the Indian Ocean and Pacific Oceans, which is to be contrasted with the situation of small island States in the Caribbean.

[66] J Duursma, *Fragmentation and the international relations of Micro-States: Self-determination and statehood* (Cambridge University Press 1996) 430–33; this has been a longstanding issue of debate in the Pacific, see RA Herr, 'Microstate Sovereignty in the South Pacific: Is Small Practical?' (1988) 10 *Contemporary Southeast Asia* 182.

[67] See *Chagos Advisory Opinion* (n 61) 131 [144] where the Court observed that: 'The Court is conscious that the right to self-determination, as a fundamental human right, has a broad scope of application.' Also see *Western Sahara* (Advisory Opinion) [1975] ICJ Reps 36 [71] where it was observed that the 'right of self-determination leaves the General Assembly a measure of discretion with respect to the forms and procedures by which that right is to be realized'; and as outlined in United Nations General Assembly (UNGA) Resolution 1514 (VX) 'Declaration on the Granting of Independence to Colonial Countries and Peoples' (14 December 1960) UN Doc A/RES/1514 (VX) discussed in Chapter 4 section III.B of this volume.

[68] For an economic assessment of these relationships and the distinction between dependent and independent islands, see JL McElroy and CE Parry, 'The long-term propensity for political affiliation in island microstates' (2012) 50 *Commonwealth and Comparative Politics* 403–21.

[69] Crawford (n 57) 115.

[70] Special Committee on Decolonization (UN), 'Special Committee on Decolonization Approves Text Calling upon United States to Promote Puerto Rico's Self-Determination, Eventual Independence' (18 June 2021) UN Doc GA/COL/3346.

[71] Other islands are engaged in a variety of political processes regarding their futures. One of the more prominent examples is the Indonesian province of West Papua, see discussion in M Janki, 'West Papua and the Right to Self-Determination under International Law' (2010) 34 *West Indian Law Journal* 1; S Heathcote, 'Secession, self-determination and territorial disagreements: Sovereignty claims in the contemporary South Pacific' (2021) 34 *Leiden Journal of International Law* 653, 656–59, who also notes secessionist movements in Kiribati, the Solomon Islands, and Vanuatu, ibid, 662–65.

A. Chagos Archipelago

One of the most prominent island territories subject to self-determination debate in the past decade has been the Chagos Archipelago, administered by the UK. The archipelago, located in the Indian Ocean, was occupied by the Dutch from 1638 to 1710, followed by a short period of French administration. Under the terms of the 1814 Treaty of Paris the islands were then ceded to the UK who administered the archipelago as a dependency of the colony of Mauritius.[72] As Mauritius moved towards eventual independence in 1968, the UK in 1965 created the British Indian Ocean Territory (BIOT) comprising the Chagos Archipelago, which was detached from Mauritius, and the Aldabra, Farquhar and Desroches Islands that were detached from the Seychelles.[73] Over a two-year period commencing in 1964, the UK was also engaged in discussions with the US over building military facilities in the Chagos Archipelago and these talks concluded in 1966 with an agreement that paved the way for the building of a US military facility on the island of Diego Garcia in the archipelago.[74] These developments were the subject of consideration by the UN, with the General Assembly adopting two resolutions in 1965 and 1966, expressing concern regarding the violation of the territorial integrity of Mauritius and actions that were incompatible with the UN Charter.[75] Between 1967 and 1973 the entire population of the archipelago was forcibly removed or prevented from returning to the islands.[76] In the years that followed questions were raised as to the legality of these processes within the Organisation of African Unity,[77] and before UK and European courts.[78] In 2015 an Annex VII Arbitral Tribunal constituted under the 1982 United Nations Convention on the Law of the Sea (LOSC)[79] considered certain matters raised by Mauritius relating to a marine protected area proclaimed by the UK in the vicinity of the Chagos Archipelago. Self-determination was raised by Mauritius, but not conclusively addressed in the

[72] This historical account is drawn from *Chagos Advisory Opinion* (n 61) 107 [27]–[28].

[73] ibid 108 [33]; see British Indian Ocean Territory Order 1965 (SI 1965/1920) (UK).

[74] For background to this development, and the significance of the US military facility, see D Vine, *Island of Shame: The Secret History of the U.S. Military Base on Diego Garcia* (Princeton University Press 2011).

[75] See UNGA Res 2066 (XX) 'Question of Mauritius' (16 December 1965) UN Doc A/RES/2066 (XX); and UNGA Res 2232 (XXI) 'Question of American Samoa, Antigua, Bahamas, Bermuda, British Virgin Islands, Cayman Islands, Cocos (Keeling) Islands, Dominica, Gilbert and Ellice Islands, Grenada, Guam, Mauritius, Montserrat, New Hebrides, Niue, Pitcairn, St. Helena, St. Kitts-Nevis-Anguilla, St. Lucia, St. Vincent, Seychelles, Solomon Islands, Tokelau Islands, Turks and Caicos Islands and United States Virgin Islands' (20 December 1966) UN Doc A/RES/2232 (XXI).

[76] *Chagos Advisory Opinion* (n 61) 110 [43]; on this point and related aspects of the history of the archipelago during this period, see S Evers and M Kooy (eds), *Eviction from the Chagos Islands: Displacement and Struggle for Identity Against Two World Powers* (Brill 2011).

[77] Organisation of African Unity Resolution 99 (XVII) (1980); Decision AHG/Dec.159 (XXXVI (2000); see also Africa Union Decision 331 (2010).

[78] See generally S Allen, *The Chagos Islanders and International Law* (Hart Publishing 2014) ch 1, 2.

[79] United Nations Convention on the Law of the Sea (adopted 10 December 1982, entered into force 16 November 1994) 1833 UNTS 397.

award in which the Tribunal indicated it had no jurisdiction to resolve a sovereignty dispute.[80]

In 2019, following the adoption of a UN General Assembly Resolution requesting an Advisory Opinion,[81] the ICJ handed down its opinion on a number of matters relating to the Chagos Archipelago. By a majority of 13 votes to one, the Court determined that the 1968 process of decolonisation of Mauritius had not been lawfully completed following the separation of the Chagos Archipelago, that the UK was under an obligation to bring to an end its administration of the Chagos Archipelago as rapidly as possible, and that member States are under an obligation to cooperate with the UN to complete the decolonisation of Mauritius.[82] In the view of the Court, the UK was 'under an obligation to bring an end to its administration of the Chagos Archipelago as rapidly as possible, thereby enabling Mauritius to complete the decolonization of its territory in a manner consistent with the right of peoples to self-determination.'[83] As a follow up to the Court's Advisory Opinion, the UN General Assembly in 2019 adopted Resolution 73/295 in which it called upon the UK to withdraw from the Chagos Archipelago within six months in order to permit Mauritius to complete the process of decolonisation, and that the UK's continued administration of the archipelago was a wrongful act.[84] The UK did not take any action in response to that resolution.[85]

The status of the Chagos Archipeago also came before the International Tribunal for the Law of the Sea (ITLOS) in a maritime boundary dispute between Mauritius and the Maldives.[86] In a 2021 preliminary objections ruling, the ITLOS Special Chamber was of the view that the ICJ Advisory Opinion had legal effect and that:

> the process of decolonization of Mauritius was not lawfully completed when that country acceded to independence in 1968, following the separation of the Chagos Archipelago, and that the United Kingdom is under an obligation to bring to an end its administration of the Chagos Archipelago as rapidly as possible.[87]

Self-determination for the Chagossians remains an ongoing issue.[88]

[80] *In the Matter of the Chagos Marine Protected Area Arbitration before an Arbitral Tribunal under Annex VII of the 1982 United Nations Convention on the Law of the Sea (Mauritius v United Kingdom)* (Award) (18 March 2015) PCA Case No 011-03; cf Dissenting and Concurring Opinion, Judge Kateka and Judge Wolfrum, 18–20 [70]–[77].

[81] UNGA Res 71/292 (22 June 2017) UN Doc A/RES/71/292.

[82] *Chagos Advisory Opinion* (n 61) 140 [183].

[83] ibid 139 [178].

[84] UNGA Resolution 73/295 'Advisory opinion of the International Court of Justice on the legal consequences of the separation of the Chagos Archipelago from Mauritius in 1965' (22 May 2019) UN Doc A/RES/73/295, adopted 116–6 with 56 abstentions; see O Bowcott and J Borger, 'UK suffers crushing defeat in UN vote on Chagos Islands', *The Guardian* (London, 23 May 2019) www.theguardian.com/world/2019/may/22/uk-suffers-crushing-defeat-un-vote-chagos-islands.

[85] BBC News, 'Chagos Islands dispute: UK misses deadline to return control' (22 November 2019), at www.bbc.com/news/uk-50511847.

[86] *Dispute concerning delimitation of the maritime boundary between Mauritius and Maldives in the Indian Ocean between Mauritius and the Maldives* (Preliminary Objections Judgment) (28 January 2021) ITLOS Reports 2020–21, to be published.

[87] ibid 62 [205].

[88] S Allen, 'Self-Determination, The Chagos Advisory Opinion and the Chagossians' (2020) 69 *International and Comparative Law Quarterly* 203; V Kattan, 'The Chagos Advisory Opinion and the

B. New Caledonia

New Caledonia comprises a collection of islands in the South Pacific including the largest island, Grande Terre, and the smaller Loyalty Islands, Bélop Archipelago, Isle of Pines, and the Huon Islands. Grande Terre was discovered and named as New Caledonia by the English explorer Captain James Cook in 1774, but it was France that annexed the islands in 1853, and they were made a French overseas territory in 1946. The current status of the islands is that they are a 'sui generis community within the French Republic governed under part XIII of the Constitution'[89] and fall within the responsibility of the French Minister for Overseas Territories. A 54-member Congress is drawn from elected members of three provincial assemblies that reflect various geographic regions. France remains an Administering Power in New Caledonia and is represented by a High Commissioner, consistently with the status of the islands as a NSGT. As such, New Caledonia has remained under the remit of the UNGA Special Political and Decolonization Committee and there is an ongoing acknowledgement that the peoples of New Caledonia enjoy a right of self-determination.[90]

In the 1970s an independence movement emerged in New Caledonia, and after a period of political troubles, including violent confrontations between 1984 and 1988 that resulted in approximately 80 deaths, the Matignon and Nouméa Accords were concluded in 1988. These were designed to ease tensions and to provide a pathway towards the eventual transferral of sovereign power to the Government of New Caledonia.[91] As part of this process, a referendum was held in New Caledonia on 4 November 2018, with the question being: 'Do you want New Caledonia to accede to full sovereignty and become independent?' The outcome was a vote of 56.7 per cent saying No, and 43.3 per cent saying Yes.[92] However, France agreed to a three-stage process with further votes in 2020 and 2021. The 2020 referendum returned a majority 'No' vote of 53 per cent.[93] A final vote took place in December

Law of Self-Determination' (2020) 10 *Asian Journal of International Law* 12; J Reynolds, 'Decolonising the Chagos Islands?' [2018–19] *Nigerian Yearbook of International Law* 455.

[89] Special Committee on the Situation with regard to the Implementation of the Declaration on the Granting of Independence to Colonial Countries and Peoples, 'New Caledonia: Working paper prepared by the Secretariat' (22 February 2017) UN Doc A/AC.109/2017/11, [1].

[90] See eg UNGA Res 71/119 'Question of New Caledonia' (28 December 2016) UN Doc A/RES/71/119.

[91] Special Committee on the Situation with regard to the Implementation of the Declaration on the Granting of Independence to Colonial Countries and Peoples, 'New Caledonia: Working paper prepared by the Secretariat' (22 February 2017) UN Doc A/AC.109/2017/11, [4]–[5] see detailed discussion in N Maclellan, 'The Noumea accord and Decolonisation in New Caledonia' (1999) 34(3) *The Journal of Pacific History* 245; DA Chappell, 'The Noumea Accord: Decolonization without Independence in New Caledonia?' (1999) 72 *Pacific Affairs* 373.

[92] S Dziedzic and P Srinivasan, 'New Caledonia narrowly rejects independence from France in historic referendum', *ABC News* (online, 5 November 2018) www.abc.net.au/news/2018-11-05/new-caledonia-rejects-independence-from-france/10464248; see analysis in D Fisher, *New Caledonia's Independence Referendum: Local and Regional Implications* (Lowy Institute 2019) 9–10, www.lowyinstitute.org/publications/new-caledonia-s-independence-referendum-local-and-regional-implications.

[93] State Services in New Caledonia, 'Speech proclaiming the results of the consultation of October 4, 2020' (5 October 2020), www.nouvelle-caledonie.gouv.fr/Politiques-publiques/Elections/Elections-2020/REFERENDUM-2020/Discours/Discours-de-proclamation-des-resultats-de-la-consultation-du-4-octobre-2020.

2021 with an overwhelming 96 per cent voting 'No'; however, turnout was very low due to the COVID-19 pandemic, raising issues as to the legitimacy of the vote and next steps.[94]

The issue remains under General Assembly review.[95]

C. Bougainville

Bougainville is another prominent Southwest Pacific territory engaged in self-determination processes. Papua New Guinea (PNG) gained independence from Australia in 1975 which resulted in the finalisation of PNG territory, including the island of Bougainville which lies at the eastern edge of the archipelago. Bougainville enjoys rich reserves of copper and significant mining was undertaken there during the 1970s–1980s. During this period an independence movement developed resulting in violent unrest from 1988–97.[96] In 2001, PNG agreed to recognise the Autonomous Bougainville Government (ABG) under the terms of a peace agreement reflected in the PNG Constitution.[97] Certain levels of autonomy were granted to the ABG and mechanisms were put in place for an eventual independence referendum.[98] This occurred in 2019 resulting in 97 per cent support for independence.[99] Since that time ongoing PNG and ABG negotiations have been taking place as to the next steps in Bougainville's move towards independence. These negotiations are expected to extend into the late 2020s.[100] However, as Heathcote has observed:

> In the case of Bougainville, even if cast in terms of self-determination, independence rests on PNG's consent, pursuant to the procedures agreed to in a peace agreement

[94] D Robie, 'New Caledonia votes to stay with France, but it's a hollow victory that will only ratchet up tensions', *The Conversation* (online, 13 December 2021) https://theconversation.com/new-caledonia-votes-to-stay-with-france-but-its-a-hollow-victory-that-will-only-ratchet-up-tensions-173646. Even if the people of New Caledonia were to support independence as an exercise of the right of self-determination, there remains discussion as to what form that may take; see J Fraenkel, 'Introduction: The Long-run Impact of New Caledonia's Noumea Accord' (2019) 54 *The Journal of Pacific History* 199, who comments that 'A future partnership with France is now the preferred option of a least some in the pro-independence leadership'.

[95] See UNGA Res 73/115 'Question of New Caledonia' (19 December 2018) UN Doc A/RES/73/115; UNGA Res 74/106 'Question of New Caledonia' (13 December 2019) UN Doc A/RES/74/106; UNGA Res 75/115 'Question of New Caledonia' (10 December 2020) UN Doc A/RES/75/115; UNGA Res 76/98 'Question of New Caledonia' (9 December 2021) UN Doc A/RES/76/98.

[96] See discussion in AJ Regan, 'Causes and Courses of the Bougainville Conflict' (1998) 33 *Journal of Pacific History* 269; this was not the first occasion that an independence movement had arisen in Bougainville; see Heathcote (n 71) 660–61.

[97] Constitution of the Independent State of Papua New Guinea (1975), pt XIV Bougainville Government and Bougainville Referendum.

[98] ibid ss 338–343.

[99] N Whiting, 'Bougainville votes overwhelmingly for independence from Papua New Guinea in landmark referendum', *ABC News* (online, 11 December 2019) www.abc.net.au/news/2019-12-11/bougainville-independence-referendum-result/11787434.

[100] J McDonald, 'Bougainville Inches Closer to Independence', *The Diplomat* (online, 19 July 2021) https://thediplomat.com/2021/07/bougainville-inches-closer-to-independence/.

between the parties, PNG having exercised on behalf of Bougainville and the rest of the former colonial territory, its right to self-determination in 1975 when PNG became independent. The so-called 'one shot' (at independence) rule thus comes into play, which on a traditional analysis bars further legal entitlement to self-determination.[101]

D. Faroe Islands and Greenland

The Faroe Islands and Greenland are a part of the Danish realm and are located in the North Atlantic, with Greenland adjacent to North America. The circumstances of the two sets of islands are different, but both raise important issues with respect to self-determination. The Faroe Islands, comprising 18 islands of which one is uninhabited, are located midway between Scotland and Iceland adjoining the Norwegian Sea. Historically the islands have been connected politically with modern-day Denmark since the fourteenth century and were Denmark's most northerly province and recognised as part of the Danish Realm from the first Danish Constitution in 1849. However, there was a sense that Denmark was a type of colonial power, no doubt due to the physical distance between Copenhagen and the islands.[102] During World War II when Denmark was under German occupation, the Faroe Islands were occupied by the British. During this period the Faroe Islands enjoyed a degree of independence with the result that at the end of the war the political status of the islands could not revert to that which had applied previously.[103] There was a surge of support for independence in the immediate post-war period during which time a referendum was held in 1946, and in 1948 Home Rule was granted under the 1948 Act of Home Rule for the Faroe Islands.[104]

Greenland is the world's largest island and has an indigenous Inuit population. The island was first reached by European Viking explorers in the tenth century and was subject to Danish colonisation in the eighteenth century. The status of Greenland was the subject of contest in the nineteenth and early twentieth century between Denmark and Norway, and in 1933 the Permanent Court of International Justice resolved this in favour of Denmark in the *Legal Status of Eastern Greenland* case.[105] Greenland's status as effectively a Danish colony was disturbed during World War II when, with Denmark under German occupation, and Greenland located strategically for the purposes of the Allied war effort, part of the island came under US control. At the end of the war, while control reverted to Denmark, like the Faroe Islands, circumstances for Greenland had changed. With the recognition of

[101] Heathcote (n 71) 656.

[102] JA Jensen, 'The Position of Greenland and the Faroe Islands Within the Danish Realm' (2003) 9 *European Public Law* 170, 171.

[103] ibid.

[104] ibid; for more background to this development see JF West, *Faroe: The Emergence of a Nation* (C Hurst 1972) 185–97.

[105] *Legal Status of Eastern Greenland Case (Denmark v Norway)* [1933] PCIJ Reps, Ser A/B No 53.

the rights of people to self-determination, Denmark came under some pressure with respect to its position concerning Greenland. In 1953 Greenland was made a part of the Danish Realm, with the result that representation was gained in the Danish Parliament, and in 1979 this was followed by Home Rule similarly to the Faroe Islands.[106]

The effect of Home Rule for these islands has been that the respective Acts:

> establish that the authorities in the two home rule areas shall consist of a democratically elected local Parliament and a local government subject to the rules of parliamentarism. However, what distinguishes the home rule arrangements from other forms of local government in Denmark is, in particular, the fact that a number of subject areas have been handed over to regulation by the Faroese (Greenlandic) authorities in the sense that these authorities have both legislative and administrative authority within these areas. The decisions of the local Parliaments in these areas are called home rule Acts and have the same legal effect as ordinary Danish Acts.[107]

Legislation enacted by the Danish Parliament, which specifically applies to either the Faroe Islands or Greenland, makes clear that consultations have taken place with the respective Faroese and Greenlandic parliaments.[108]

The case for self-determination for the Faroe Islands and Greenland is well understood;[109] Denmark has not contested that status. As observed by Jensen in 2003, there is 'no doubt that the inhabitants of both the Faroe Islands and Greenland consider themselves as separate peoples. Everything therefore points to recognizing both populations as separate peoples that have the right to self-determination'.[110] In recent years the debate regarding self-determination for these islands has intensified.[111] In the case of the Faroe Islands, the 2005 Takeover Act of the Faroe Islands resulted in more responsibility being vested in the Faroese public authorities – excepting foreign, security and defence policy, and foreign exchange and monetary policy.[112] The complementary 2005 Foreign Policy Act conferred upon the Faroe Islands capacity to: 'negotiate and conclude agreements under international law with foreign states and international organisations, including administrative agreements, which relate entirely to subject matters under the jurisdiction of the Authorities of the Faroes.'[113] These constitutional

[106] Jensen (n 102) 171–72.
[107] ibid 173.
[108] ibid.
[109] F Harhoff, 'The Status of Indigenous Peoples under International Law: Greenland and the Right to Self-Determination' (1995) 32 *Canadian Yearbook of International Law* 243–57; M Ackrén, 'The Faroe Islands: Options for Independence' (2006) 1 *Island Studies Journal* 223–38.
[110] Jensen (n 102) 177.
[111] See eg R Adler-Nissen, 'The Faroe Islands: Independence dreams, globalist separatism and the Europeanization of postcolonial home rule' (2014) 49 *Cooperation and Conflict* 55; DC Cambou, 'Disentangling the conundrum of self-determination and its implications in Greenland' (2020) 56 *Polar Record* E3.
[112] Takeover Act of the Faroe Islands 2005 (Denmark) s 1(2).
[113] Foreign Policy Act of the Faroe Islands 2005 (Denmark) s 1(1).

and political developments are significant and have resulted in the Faroe Islands acquiring levels of autonomy equivalent to other island States that are self-governing but remain in free association with a larger State, such as the Cook Islands and New Zealand.[114] In Greenland, the adoption in 2009 of the Self-Government Act has provided for additional levels of autonomy.[115] There are options which it can seek to pursue in coming years that may see the adoption of an outcome similar to that in the Faroe Islands, or may eventually see Greenland become independent.[116]

V. Small Island Developing States

An important development in the contemporary international system has been the recognition of the distinctive status of 'Small Island Developing States' (SIDS) within the UN. Initially, much of this focus related to questions of sustainable development; however, over time the impacts of climate change have also been highlighted which in turn has raised the human rights vulnerabilities of these island States.[117] The circumstances of SIDS were first recognised at the 1992 United Nations Conference on Environment and Development (UNCED) which adopted the 1992 Rio Declaration on Environment and Development, and Agenda 21,[118] of which Chapter 17 directly addressed 'Sustainable development of small islands'.[119] The basis for action with respect to SIDS was as follows:

> Small island developing States, and islands supporting small communities are a special case both for environment and development. They are ecologically fragile and vulnerable. Their small size, limited resources, geographic dispersion and isolation from markets, place them at a disadvantage economically and prevent economies of scale. For small island developing States the ocean and coastal environment is of strategic importance and constitutes a valuable development resource.[120]

[114] See discussion in Chapter 4 section IV.C.

[115] M Ackrén and U Jakobsen, 'Greenland as a self-governing sub-national territory in international relations: past, current and future perspectives' (2015) 51 *Polar Record* 404–12; and for a review of those processes see M Ackrén, 'Referendums in Greenland – From Home Rule to Self-Government' (2019) 19 *Fédéralisme Régionalisme* https://popups.uliege.be/1374-3864/index.php?id=1892.

[116] A Grydehøj, 'Unravelling economic dependence and independence in relation to island sovereignty: The case of Kalaallit Nunaat (Greenland)' (2020) 15 *Island Studies Journal* 89; Cambou (n 111).

[117] See F Ghina, 'Sustainable Development in Small Island Developing States' (2003) 5 *Environment, Development and Sustainability* 139; C Betzold, 'Adapting to climate change in small island developing states' (2015) 133(3) *Climate Change* 481; these issues are also considered in Chapter 10 of this volume.

[118] United Nations Conference on Environment and Development, 'Agenda 21, Rio Declaration' (United Nations 1992) sustainabledevelopment.un.org/content/documents/Agenda21.pdf (Agenda 21).

[119] ibid ch 17, paras 17.1, 17.123–17.136.

[120] ibid para 17.123.

Building upon this foundation and upon Agenda 21's goals and objectives, the SIDS have been able to politically organise themselves within the UN system to form the Alliance of Small Island States (AOSIS) which includes 39 members (see Table 9.1).[121] Within this group, three regions are represented: the Caribbean; the Pacific; and Africa, Indian Ocean, and South China Sea (AIS). The special interests of these States are advanced by the UN Secretary-General's High Representative for the Least Developed Countries, Landlocked Developing Countries and Small Island Developing States (UN-OHRLLS).[122] The role of the UN-OHRLLS is to assist the UN Secretary-General in facilitating the implementation of the UN programme of action in relation to this group of States, and by providing associated support for the UN Economic and Social Council and the UN General Assembly in these matters.[123]

Table 9.1

Alliance of Small Island States
Antigua and Barbuda, Bahamas, Barbados, Belize, Cabo Verde, Comoros, Cook Islands, Cuba, Dominica, Dominican Republic, Federated States of Micronesia, Fiji, Grenada, Guinea Bissau, Guyana, Haiti, Jamaica, Kiribati, Maldives, Marshall Islands, Mauritius, Nauru, Niue, Palau, Papua New Guinea, St. Kitts and Nevis, St. Lucia, St. Vincent and the Grenadines, Samoa, São Tomé and Príncipe, Seychelles, Singapore, Solomon Islands, Suriname, Timor-Leste, Tonga, Trinidad and Tobago, Tuvalu, Vanuatu
Source: Alliance of Small Island States, 'Membership', www.aosis.org/about/member-states/.

The UN focus on SIDS has centred on matters such as oceans and seas, sustainable development, education, and cooperation. Landmark outcomes from those processes have included the 1994 Programme of Action for the Sustainable Development of Small Island Developing States, concluded in Barbados,[124] and the follow-up 2005 Mauritius Strategy for the Further Implementation of the Programme of Action for the Sustainable Development of Small Island Developing States,[125]

[121] For discussion see K Mooney, 'Alliance of Small Island States' in SG Philander (ed), *Encyclopedia of Global Warming and Climate Change* (Sage 2008) 26–27; for some background to this development see L Briguglio, 'The Global Involvement of Small Island Developing States' in S Page (ed), *Regions and development: politics, security, and economics* (Frank Cass 2000) 241.

[122] The UN-OHRLLS defines for its purposes SIDS as 'remote from world markets and suffer from climate change and fragile natural environments': High Representative for the Least Developed Countries, Landlocked Developing Countries and Small Island Developing States (UN), 'What we do', at https://www.un.org/ohrlls/content/what-we-dohttp://unohrlls.org/about-un-ohrlls/what-we-do/.

[123] ibid.

[124] UNGA, 'Programme of Action for the Sustainable Development of Small Island Developing States' (October 1994) UN Doc A/CONF.167/9, www.un.org/esa/dsd/dsd_aofw_sids/sids_pdfs/BPOA.pdf; discussed in MD Griffith, 'Reflections on the implementation of the Programme of Action on the Sustainable Development of Small Island Developing States (SIDS)' (1995) 29 *Ocean & Coastal Management* 139.

[125] UNGA, 'Mauritius Strategy for the Further Implementation of the Programme of Action for the Sustainable Development of Small Island Developing States' (21 August 2006) UN Doc A/61/277, www.un.org/ga/search/view_doc.asp?symbol=A/61/277&Lang=E.

which has now evolved into the 2014 SIDS Accelerated Modalities of Action (SAMOA) Pathway, adopted in Apia, Samoa.[126] Unsurprisingly there have been differential levels of implementation in the priority areas of the SAMOA Pathway,[127] and there remains an ongoing challenge with respect to monitoring and follow-up. The impacts of climate change are also gaining increased attention for these States, and robust views are being presented at global conferences and meetings including at the 2021 Glasgow COP26 climate summit.[128] The COVID-19 pandemic has also had significant impacts for SIDS, extending from health and welfare of the community, through human rights, to a range of economic impacts including border closures resulting in a downturn in foreign tourism.[129]

A related development, albeit one that has taken place outside of the UN, has been the emergence of the 'Archipelagic and Islands States Forum' that was originally proposed by Indonesia in 2017.[130] The forum met for the first time in 2018,[131] and issued a declaration with a focus on sustainable use of ocean resources and innovative financing mechanisms on climate actions.[132] A subsequent forum meeting took place in 2019 and the group remains active in advancing matters of mutual interest to archipelagic and island States.[133]

There also exist a number of regional and sub-regional organisations of which the small island States are eligible to become members, including the Caribbean Community (CARICOM), the Pacific Islands Forum (PIF), and the Indian Ocean Commission. Each of these bodies has a particular focus on distinctive regional

[126] UNGA, 'SIDS Accelerated Modalities of Action (SAMOA) Pathway' (14 November 2014) UN Doc A/RES/69/15, www.un.org/ga/search/view_doc.asp?symbol=A/RES/69/15&Lang=E.

[127] See UNGA Res 74/217 'Follow-up to and implementation of the SIDS Accelerated Modalities of Action (SAMOA) Pathway and the Mauritius Strategy for the Further Implementation of the Programme of Action for the Sustainable Development of Small Island Developing States' (19 December 2019) UN Doc A/RES/74/217.

[128] See Statement by The Honourable Bruce Bilimon, Minister of Health and Human Services, The Republic of the Marshall Islands on Behalf of Pacific SIDS (COP26, Glasgow, United Kingdom 9 November 2021) https://unfccc.int/sites/default/files/resource/SIDS_MARSHALL_ISLANDS_cop26cmp16cma3_HLS_EN.pdf; and D Hoad, 'The 2015 Paris Climate Agreement: outcomes and their impacts on small island states' (2016) 11 *Island Studies Journal* 315.

[129] UN-OHRLLS (UN), 'State of the Least Developed Countries 2021. Building back better in response to COVID-19', www.un.org/ldc5/sites/www.un.org.ldc5/files/stateldc_2021.pdf.

[130] LB Pandjaitan, 'Statement to The United Nations Ocean Conference to Support the Implementation of Sustainable Development Goal 14' (6 June 2017) https://sustainabledevelopment.un.org/content/documents/23849indonesia.pdf.

[131] Delegates attended from Cuba, Comoro Island, Cyprus, Fiji, Guinea Bissau, Indonesia, Jamaica, Madagascar, New Zealand, PNG, Saint Kitts and Nevis, Sri Lanka, Seychelles, Singapore, Solomon Islands, Suriname, Timor-Leste and the UK.

[132] UNDP Indonesia, 'Archipelagic and island states ministers reach a milestone with declaration on sustainable ocean, climate actions' (Press Release, 1 November 2018) www.id.undp.org/content/indonesia/en/home/presscenter/pressreleases/2018/9/archipelagic-and-island-states-ministers-reach-a-milestone-with-.html.

[133] The November 2019 forum declaration identified the four main areas of cooperation as: 1) climate change mitigation, adaptation, and disaster management; 2) economic challenges and opportunities which consist of blue economy, responsible and sustainable fisheries and aquaculture, economic growth and creation of decent working opportunities; 3) marine plastic debris; and 4) good maritime governance: Archipelagic and Island States Forum, www.aisforum.org/.

issues, which not only reflects geography, but also the culture, history and political society that connects the members. The PIF is perhaps the most advanced of these groups in terms of a consideration of human rights issues, with the 2015 Denarau Declaration on Human Rights and Good Governance adopted by members of parliament from Fiji, Kiribati, the Marshall Islands, Nauru, Niue, Palau, Samoa, the Solomon Islands, Tuvalu, Tonga, and Vanuatu, being an important step in regional processes recognising the vital role of Parliament and parliamentarians to respect, fulfil, protect and promote the inherent rights of all people in the Pacific.[134] Nevertheless, a 2016 report identified variations in the acceptance of human rights instruments within the Pacific and challenges in their implementation at a national level, concluding that: 'The implementation process, however, must be a priority to ensure that international human rights commitments are translated into real actions in each Pacific state.'[135] The combined impacts of climate change and COVID-19 have seen the PIF focus more attention on regional resilience to address these challenges which have a significant human rights dimension. The PIF 'Pacific Resilience Facility' seeks to respond to this challenge by establishing a regional financing facility with a goal of US$1.5 billion particularly targeted to supporting those 'exposed to climate change and disaster risks, particularly women and girls, children, the elderly and people with disabilities'.[136]

VI. Conclusions

The human rights project has been one of the most significant global and societal movements across the last century and is closely connected with the UN, the UDHR, and associated global and regional mechanisms. Islands and islanders were not a specific focus for human rights, but it is striking that early in the twentieth century distinctive island issues were identified in the case of the Åland Islands. One hundred years later, in the 2020s, the situation of the Chagos Archipelago is attracting considerable international legal attention in various fora. While islands and human rights have not throughout the past century been a principal focus of international human rights discourse, they have gradually become a focal point. There are a number of reasons for this. First, the UN Charter and its associated UN human rights treaty bodies and agencies put into place frameworks, mechanisms and processes whereby human rights could be realised by island communities. At one level this was simply reflected through the adoption of the UDHR, ICCPR,

[134] Denarau 2015 Declaration on Human Rights and Good Governance (adopted 30 January 2015 at Denarau, Fiji) http://www.parliament.gov.to/~parliam1/images/news/Denarau_2015_Declaration.pdf.

[135] Pacific Community (SPC) and UN Office of the High Commissioner for Human Rights (UNOHCHR), *Human Rights in the Pacific: A situational analysis* (Quality Print 2016) 5; see also a 2020 assessment with respect to business and human rights in the Pacific: Office of the United Nations High Commissioner for Human Rights (UN), '1st UN Pacific Forum on Business and Human Rights' (1–2 December 2020) www.ohchr.org/EN/Issues/Business/Pages/2020UN-pacific-forum.aspx.

[136] Pacific Islands Forum, 'The Pacific Resilience Facility', www.forumsec.org/prf/.

ICESCR, and ICERD. However these were universal rights and applied to metropolitan territories, island territories, and newly emerging island States. This put governments on notice that newly independent island States were to aspire to meeting global international human rights norms and standards, and that colonial powers were likewise to meet these same standards for their overseas island territories no matter what particular form they took. Second, the recognition of the right of self-determination likewise applies equally to all peoples. That right has been exercised in various high-level settings around the world and in many different forms. As that right has been exercised over time, it is striking that in the 2020s some of the highest profile remaining examples of self-determination – Chagos Archipelago, Greenland, New Caledonia – are island territories. Third, there has also been an increased attention and understanding of some of the specific human rights issues that confront islands. The public administration challenges of realising human rights in some island territories have always been well understood, especially in those that are remote. The SIDS movement has sought to address some of those challenges and has been successful in raising increased global awareness of some of distinctive island human rights issues. The COVID-19 pandemic has further highlighted the vulnerabilities and human rights challenges facing certain island communities. Finally, the human rights of all island States and islanders are facing challenges caused by climate change and sea-level rise. Those threats may prove to be existential. The international law issues are outlined in the following chapter.

10

Islands and Sea-Level Rise

I. Introduction

A modern phenomenon for all States and for international law is climate change. There has been a growing appreciation of this issue over the past three decades, highlighted by the adoption in 1992 of the United Nations Framework Convention on Climate Change (UNFCCC)[1] and its successor instruments, the 1997 Kyoto Protocol and the 2015 Paris Agreement.[2] As highlighted across the six Assessment Reports issued by the Intergovernmental Panel on Climate Change (IPCC) since 1990, climate change is having multiple impacts ranging from warming of the atmosphere and oceans, to desertification, melting of the ice caps and glaciers, species disturbance and loss, and an increase in large-scale weather events such as cyclones and hurricanes.[3] Many of these impacts have significant consequences for islands and include sea-level rise (SLR) and associated salt water inundation, crop failures, environmental damage and impact from storm surges, and fish-stock migration. From the perspective of islands and international law much of the focus has been on oceans and the law of the sea;[4] however, other dimensions such as territoriality, human rights, and human security are equally as important.[5]

The specific issue of islands and SLR has also fallen within the remit of the International Law Commission (ILC), which in 2019 established an open-ended Study Group on 'Sea-level rise and International Law'.[6] In 2018 the ILC observed that:

> more than 70 States are or are likely to be directly affected by sea-level rise, a group which represents more than one third of the States of the international community. …

[1] United Nations Framework Convention on Climate Change (adopted 9 May 1992, entered into force 21 March 1994) 1771 UNTS 107.

[2] Kyoto Protocol to the United Nations Framework Convention on Climate Change (adopted 11 December 1997, entered into force 16 February 2005) 2303 UNTS 214; Paris Agreement (adopted 12 December 2015, entered into force 4 November 2016) UN Reg No 54113.

[3] See generally Intergovernmental Panel on Climate Change 'Synthesis Report of the Sixth Assessment Report' (IPCC, 2021) www.ipcc.ch/ar6-syr/.

[4] See K Scott, 'Climate change and the law of the sea in the Asia Pacific' in DR Rothwell and D Letts (eds), *Law of the Sea in South East Asia: Environmental, Navigational and Security Challenges* (Routledge 2020) 94; T Stephens, 'Warming Waters and Souring Seas: Climate Change and Ocean Acidification' in DR Rothwell et al (eds), *The Oxford Handbook of the Law of the Sea* (Oxford University Press 2015) 777.

[5] See eg M Gerrard and G Wannier (eds), *Threatened island nations: legal implications of rising seas and a changing climate* (Cambridge University Press 2013).

[6] International Law Commission, 'Sea-level rise in relation to international law: First issues paper by Bogdan Aurescu and Nilüfer Oral, Co-Chairs of the Study Group on sea-level rise in relation to international law' (28 February 2020) UN Doc A/CN.4/740, 1 [1]–[4].

> Another quite large number of States is likely to be indirectly affected (for instance, by the displacement of people or the lack of access to resources). Sea-level rise has become a global phenomenon and thus creates global problems, impacting on the international community as a whole.[7]

Since 2012 the International Law Association (ILA) has also generally had these matters under consideration in various forms.[8] The questions associated with SLR and islands are also now on the political agenda of specially affected States. The Pacific Islands Forum (PIF) has been considering these issues since 2010, and in August 2021 the 18 members adopted the 'Declaration on Preserving Maritime Zones in the face of Climate Change-Related Sea-Level Rise'.[9] The September 2021 Leaders' Declaration of the Association of Small Island States (AOSIS) echoed the PIF Declaration in its call for baseline stability under the 1982 United Nations Convention on the Law of the Sea (LOSC).[10] These initiatives have some significant implications for how island States in particular view the impact of SLR for the law of the sea and the LOSC.

This chapter addresses these issues by reflecting on many of the international legal challenges that SLR poses for islands, and revisits some of the analysis from earlier chapters. Given the evolving understanding of these issues and increasing attention that is being given to this general topic by the ILC, the discussion will remain at a preliminary level, albeit one that scopes out some of the principal international legal challenges posed by SLR for islands.

II. Climate Science

In 2020 the ILC was very clear that 'Sea-level rise is a fact that is currently happening.'[11] Growing attention has been given to this phenomenon within the scientific

[7] International Law Commission, 'Report of the International Law Commission, Seventieth session' (30 April–1 June and 2 July–10 August 2018) UN Doc A/73/10, annex B [1].

[8] See International Law Association, 'International Law and Sea-Level Rise' (Report, Sydney Conference, 2018) www.ila-hq.org/images/ILA/DraftReports/DraftReport_SeaLevelRise.pdf; International Law Association, 'International Law and Sea-Level Rise' (Interim Report, Johannesburg Conference, 2016), ila.vettoreweb.com/Storage/Download.aspx?DbStorageId=936&StorageFileGuid=6bc111aa-af31-4e3d-84bc-c77223adfdf8.

[9] Pacific Islands Forum, 'Declaration on Preserving Maritime Zones in the Face of Climate Change-Related Sea-Level Rise' (6 August 2021) www.forumsec.org/2021/08/11/declaration-on-preserving-maritime-zones-in-the-face-of-climate-change-related-sea-level-rise/ (PIF Declaration); see also consideration of these issues within the Caribbean Community: CARICOM, 'Secretary-General's Remarks – CARICOM Senior Officials (Fisheries, Law of the Sea and Marine Conservation) Briefing on Proposed Collaboration with the Cloudburst Foundation' (22 April 2021) caricom.org/secretary-generals-remarks-caricom-senior-officials-fisheries-law-of-the-sea-and-marine-conservation-briefing-on-proposed-collaboration-with-the-cloudburst-foundation/.

[10] United Nations Convention on the Law of the Sea, (adopted 10 December 1982, entered into force 16 November 1994) 1833 UNTS 397 (LOSC); see Association of Small Island States, 'Launch Of The Alliance Of Small Island States Leaders' Declaration' (22 September 2021) www.aosis.org/launch-of-the-alliance-of-small-island-states-leaders-declaration/ (AOSIS Declaration).

[11] International Law Commission, 'Sea-level rise in relation to international law' (n 6) 80 [219].

community, and especially the IPCC. The 2019 *IPCC Special Report on the Ocean and Cryosphere in a Changing Climate* specifically focusses in chapter 4 on SLR implications for low-lying islands, coasts and communities.[12] The key points arising from this IPCC assessment are that global mean sea level is rising, with melting glaciers and ice sheets the major contributors.[13] Additional drivers include thermal expansion, land water storage, subsidence, ocean dynamics, and geodynamics. When all are combined, relative sea-level changes impacting on mean sea level can result in extreme sea-level events.[14] SLR can vary regionally by +/– 30 per cent due to variable thermal expansion, ocean dynamics, and land ice loss.[15] The IPCC's 2019 assessment observes that increases in SLR from 1–2 mm per year in the past century have gradually risen to 3–4 mm per year, with projected increases to 4–9 mm per year extending to 10–20 mm per year by the end of the century.[16] It was observed that 'The combined effect of mean and extreme sea levels results in events which are rare in the historical context … occurring yearly at some locations by the middle of this century under all emission scenarios.'[17] Extreme weather events such as cyclones and hurricanes, resulting in king tides and storm surges add to the impact of SLR for coastal communities and islands.[18] The combined impacts of SLR and climate change may make some islands uninhabitable, either because crops fail, drinking water is no longer potable, or because the physical size of the island decreases to the extent that it can no longer sustain a population.[19]

Research published in 2021 framed around the Paris Agreement assumptions of limiting global warming to 1.5 to 2°C reinforce some of the IPCC's 2019 assessments.[20] Estimates have been made that by 2100 approximately 50 per cent of over 7000 locations will experience what are currently 100-year extreme-sea-level events, at least once a year even under a 1.5°C warming model.[21] Areas identified as being particularly susceptible to these impacts include parts of the southern hemisphere and the subtropics including Hawaii and the Caribbean.[22]

[12] M Oppenheimer et al, 'Sea Level Rise and Implications for Low-Lying Islands, Coasts and Communities' in H Pörtner et al (eds), *IPCC Special Report on the Ocean and Cryosphere in a Changing Climate* (IPCC 2019) ch 4, 321 (IPCC 2019 Report).

[13] ibid 323.

[14] ibid Figure 4.1, 326; see also G Milne et al, 'Identifying the causes of sea-level change' (2009) 2 *Nature Geoscience* 471.

[15] IPCC 2019 Report (n 12) 326.

[16] ibid 327.

[17] ibid 327.

[18] 'Moving Story: Pacific countries face more complex problems than sinking', *The Economist* (7 August 2021) 20–21 ('Moving Story'); A Vaughan, 'Hurricane Ida was almost certainly made worse by climate change', *New Scientist* (31 August 2021) www.newscientist.com/article/2288675-hurricane-ida-was-almost-certainly-made-worse-by-climate-change/.

[19] C Storlazzi, 'Most atolls will be uninhabitable by the mid-21st century because of sea-level rise exacerbating wave-driven flooding' (2018) 4 *Science Advances* eaap9741; *The Economist*, 'Moving Story' (n 18) 20.

[20] C Tebaldi et al, 'Extreme sea levels at different global warming levels' (2021) 11 *Nature Climate Change* 746.

[21] ibid; for other projections see E Kirezci et al, 'Projections of global-scale extreme sea levels and resulting episodic coastal flooding over the 21st Century' (2020) 10 *Scientific Reports* 11629.

[22] C Tebaldi et al (n 20).

The evidence associated with SLR appears compelling. It is notable that expert bodies as diverse as the ILC and IPCC are giving considerable attention to the issue. The challenges are formidable. As the IPCC observed in 2019:

> At the century scale and without adaptation, the vast majority of low-lying islands, coasts and communities face substantial risk from these coastal hazards, whether they are urban or rural, continental or island, at any latitude, and irrespective of their level of development.[23]

With that background, some of the specific questions arising for international law will now be considered.

III. Islands and Artificial Islands[24]

The issues arising with respect to islands, SLR and international law commence with their characterisation. The definition of an island under LOSC Article 121 is well settled with an essential attribute being that the land is above water at high tide. An area of land that is not above water at high tide is a LOSC Article 13 low-tide elevation (LTE). The first issue that therefore arises with respect to the consequence of SLR is whether an island becomes so awash that it is no longer above water at high tide and becomes an LTE. Such an event would not be extraordinary and there are examples of where naturally formed islands do because of erosion become inundated with water at high tide and effectively become LTEs. This is especially the case with small recently formed volcanic islands, which due to their instability are prone to erosion by the sea.[25] There is also existing state practice in which attempts have been made to halt erosion of certain features so that their status does not become questionable, as has occurred with Okinotorishima (Japan) and Kolbeinsey Island (Iceland).[26] Low-lying islands, because of SLR, may therefore see their status converted from being an Article 121 island to an Article 13 LTE with consequential impacts upon the maritime entitlement of the feature.

The more significant consequence, especially from a law of the sea perspective, is a juridical island becoming a juridical rock because the feature is no longer capable of sustaining human habitation or an economic life of its own. This could arise from the loss of potable water, loss of agricultural land, seawater soil contamination, or diminution of habitable land. The temporal dynamics associated with the loss of these characteristics would also need to be taken into account. Outward migration from the island and abandonment of any form of settlement and associated activity may be an indicator of the island's changed status. Technological

[23] IPCC 2019 Report (n 12) 328.

[24] See also generally S Kaye, 'The Law of the Sea Convention and Sea Level Rise after the *South China Sea Arbitration*' (2017) 93 *International Law Studies* 423.

[25] S Plank et al, 'The short life of the volcanic island New Late'iki (Tonga) analyzed by multi-sensor remote sensing data' (2020) 10 *Scientific Reports* 22293.

[26] International Law Commission, 'Sea-level rise in relation to international law' (n 6) 78 [215].

mitigation strategies, and especially the potential to undertake land reclamation in response to SLR and inundation, would also need to be taken into account. As the Arbitral Tribunal in *South China Sea* discounted the significance of size in distinguishing between a juridical island and juridical rock,[27] that would not be a decisive factor in determining whether an island's juridical status was altered.

Given the precedent that has been set by island reclamation and artificial island-building activities in the South China Sea, it must be anticipated that some States will engage in these activities in response to SLR. The ILC anticipates a rise in land reclamation in response to SLR,[28] and land reclamation on islands is already well-established. Singapore, for example, is engaging in coastal protection measures including 'engineered solutions such as building sea walls and dykes, and are complemented by nature-based solutions such as active mangrove restoration' which may cost as much as SGD 100 billion over the next 50–100 years.[29] The building of artificial islands in response to SLR is an option for a coastal State fearful of losing habitable land, and especially in the case of small island States. An example of such a response is that of the Maldives, where the artificial island – Hulhumalé – has been constructed next to the capital Malé, at 2.1 m above sea level to allow for future SLR.[30] However, as was highlighted in *South China Sea*, issues will arise with the application of the 'natural state doctrine' and distinguishing between rocks, reefs, shoals and other small maritime features, and artificial islands constructed upon those features.[31]

IV. Status and Territoriality[32]

International law has long accommodated the growth and loss of territory which may arise under a variety of circumstances, including from natural events such as accretion.[33] While international law assumes the continuity of States, statehood may be extinguished under a number of circumstances and a State may no

[27] *In the Matter of the South China Sea Arbitration before an Arbitral Tribunal constituted under Annex VII of the 1982 United Nations Convention on the Law of the Sea (Philippines v China)* (Merits) (12 July 2016) 227 [538] (*South China Sea*).

[28] International Law Commission, 'Sea-level rise in relation to international law' (n 6) 76 [211].

[29] Government of Singapore, 'Response of the Republic of Singapore to the International Law Commission's request on the topic "Sea-Level Rise in relation to International Law"' (*International Law Commission*, 5 February 2020) https://legal.un.org/ilc/sessions/72/pdfs/english/slr_singapore.pdf [7].

[30] Government of Maldives, 'Information and examples of State practice on "Sea-level rise in relation to international law" A submission by the Republic of Maldives' (*International Law Commission*, 31 December 2019) https://legal.un.org/ilc/sessions/72/pdfs/english/slr_maldives.pdf 8.

[31] *South China Sea* (n 27) 214–15 [511]; see also I Saunders, 'The limits of the natural state doctrine: Rocks, islands, and artificial islands in a changing world' in DR Rothwell and D Letts (eds), *Law of the Sea in South East Asia: Environmental, Navigational and Security Challenges* (Routledge 2020) 118.

[32] See generally on this topic S Lee and L Bautista, 'Climate Change and Sea Level Rise: Nature of the State and of State Extinction' in R Barnes and R Long (eds), *Frontiers in International Environmental Law: Oceans and Climate Challenges – Essays in Honour of David Freestone* (Brill 2021) 194; B Johnstone, 'The unprecedented "sinking island" phenomenon: The legal challenges on statehood caused by rising sea level' (2019) 23 *New Zealand Journal of Environmental Law* 97.

[33] R Anand, 'Accretion' in R Wolfrum (ed), *Max Planck Encyclopedia of Public International Law* (online edn, Oxford University Press 2006).

longer exist and enjoy sovereignty over territory.[34] While territorial loss for an existing State is not exceptional, territorial loss from projections associated with SLR would be exceptional and have a very particular impact upon island States and islands. This could extend from the complete loss of all State territory, to territory becoming uninhabitable, and to the loss of specific islands or parts of islands. Traditional international law places a heavy emphasis upon territory being an essential State attribute,[35] and Crawford has observed 'Evidently, States are territorial entities.'[36] This minimal requirement can be met by very small areas of land, as in the case of the Holy See (Vatican) with 0.44 km^2 of land.[37] Therefore, that a State is physically diminished due to SLR does not impair one of the essential legal attributes of the State. The State can continue to exist and be recognised as such, albeit with reduced territorial entitlements. The most significant issues arise in the case of where the territory of a State becomes uninhabitable as a result of SLR and the inhabitants elect to abandon the territory,[38] or exceptionally the territory completely disappears.[39] In some instances peoples may be able to internally migrate to other islands within the State, but in other instances this may not be practical. Ultimately this raises the prospect of whether international law absolutely demands the existence of territory for a State, or whether it may be possible for a de-territorialised State to exist.[40]

The impact of SLR upon island States and the real prospect of de-territorialisation to the point that the territory of the State disappears may trigger reconsideration of the centrality of territory to continuing statehood.[41] There is an historical example of a legal entity that once possessed title over land and which still retains international legal personality. The Sovereign Military Order of Malta possessed territory over islands in the case of Rhodes (1310–1528) and then Malta (1530–1798). Control over those territories was lost, yet the Order still functions and is recognised as possessing international legal personality, though not at the level of a State.[42] In the digital age this could even extend to data or virtual territories.[43] In the case of islands, this particularly highlights whether a State facing

[34] Eight examples of State extinction from 1945–2005 are listed in J Crawford, *The Creation of States in International Law* (2nd edn, Clarendon Press 2006) 716.

[35] Montevideo Convention on Rights and Duties of States (adopted 26 December 1933, entered into force 26 December 1934) 165 LNTS 19, art 1.

[36] Crawford (n 34) 46.

[37] Central Intelligence Agency (US), 'Holy See (Vatican)' (*The World Factbook*) www.cia.gov/the-world-factbook/countries/holy-see-vatican-city.

[38] Here a distinction needs to be drawn between abandonment of a territorial claim and abandoning land that is no longer fit for habitation: D Wong, 'Sovereignty Sunk? The Position of "Sinking States" at International Law' (2013) 14 *Melbourne Journal of International Law* 1, 13–16.

[39] R Rayfuse, 'International Law and Disappearing States – Maritime Zones and the Criteria for Statehood' (2011) 41 *Environmental Policy and Law* 281.

[40] V Bílková, 'A State Without Territory' [2016] *Netherlands Yearbook of International Law* 19.

[41] C Ryngaert, 'Territory in the Law of Jurisdiction: Imagine Alternatives' [2016] *Netherlands Yearbook of International Law* 49, 65–68.

[42] Bílková (n 40) 32; Crawford (n 34) 231–33.

[43] F Johns, 'Data Territories: Changing Architectures of Association in International Law' [2016] *Netherlands Yearbook of International Law* 107.

the prospect of de-territorialisation could seek to build artificial islands within its existing territorial sea to which the population could relocate if the natural islands become uninhabitable. The actions of the Maldives in building the artificial island of Hulhumalé are an indicator that some island States are pursuing that option. This may, in turn, raise future questions as to the status of such artificial islands if much of the existing land in the Maldives is lost to SLR.

V. Archipelagic States[44]

The LOSC archipelagic State regime centres around the capacity of island States to draw straight archipelagic baselines and become a juridical archipelago. The LOSC in Article 47 outlines the strict criteria under which those baselines are to be drawn and the reliance placed upon the capacity of the State to utilise the outermost islands, drying reefs, and LTEs for that purpose.[45] Any diminution in the ability of an existing archipelagic State to be able to rely upon those maritime features would raise questions as to whether archipelagic baselines should be redrawn. Archipelagic baselines have been previously redrawn, as occurred when Timor-Leste gained independence in 2002, thereby necessitating a modification of Indonesia's archipelagic baselines.[46] However there does not appear to have been any instance to date where existing straight archipelagic baselines have been redrawn as a consequence of SLR.

The two principal matters that arise for archipelagic States are the potential redrawing of their straight archipelagic baselines, and the loss of their maritime entitlements. The Maldives has expressed its concerns about these challenges, highlighting not only the impact upon baselines, but also that the loss of land from SLR would impact upon the LOSC Article 47 area of water to area of land ratio.[47] The phenomenon of SLR for archipelagos has highlighted the issue of whether straight archipelagic baselines should be ambulatory or fixed, bearing in mind the debates that have existed as to whether an archipelagic State must declare that status and also the need to deposit charts with the United Nations (UN) showing its baselines.[48] Antigua and Barbuda has argued, in the context of the impact of SLR upon its archipelagic baselines, that 'Ambulatory baselines would redouble

[44] See also D Freestone and C Schofield, 'Sea Level Rise and Archipelagic States: A Preliminary Risk Assessment' (2021) 35 *Ocean Yearbook Online* 340; A Abdulla, 'Sea level rise, statehood and artificial islands for environmentally displaced persons under international law: Future of the Maldives' (2020) 4 *International Journal of Social Research and Innovation* 1; HT Nguyen, 'Sea-Level Rise and the Law of the Sea in the Western Pacific Region' (2020) 13 *Journal of East Asia and International Law* 121.

[45] LOSC (n 10) art 47 (1),(4).

[46] See discussion in Chapter 5 of this volume.

[47] Government of Maldives, 'Information and examples of State practice on 'Sea-level rise in relation to international law' A submission by the Republic of Maldives' (*International Law Commission*, 31 December 2019) https://legal.un.org/ilc/sessions/72/pdfs/english/slr_maldives.pdf, 14–15; Stephens (n 4) 790–91.

[48] LOSC (n 10) art 47(9).

those adverse consequences by causing, at the very least, a significant shrinking of Antigua and Barbuda's maritime zones or even an unravelling of its archipelagic baselines' and has indicated its support for fixed archipelagic baselines.[49] These issues are also relevant for island territories that may be considering their future as independent archipelagic States. Territories such as Bougainville, New Caledonia, and Tokelau may all seek to gain independence in the future and look to become recognised archipelagic States. The impact of SLR upon their existing islands and reefs will have consequences for their being able to meet the LOSC archipelagic State criteria.

Another consequence of SLR for an archipelagic State is that it may refocus attention on the construction of artificial islands. An archipelagic State is able to legitimately construct artificial islands within its archipelagic waters and its adjoining maritime zones in the same manner as a coastal State. However, there would be additional incentives for an archipelagic State to construct artificial islands to both support its population and to mitigate against the impact of SLR upon its archipelagic State status. Construction by the Maldives of the artificial island Hulhumalé, within its existing straight archipelagic baselines, is illustrative of this response. This in turn would raise questions as to whether lawfully constructed artificial islands may be taken into account in the drawing, or redrawing of straight archipelagic baselines, and whether they can be equated with land for the purposes of the LOSC Article 47 water-to-land ratio. It will also give added urgency to land reclamation, and raise issues that were highlighted in *South China Sea* as to when a rock, reef or an LTE becomes an artificial island.[50] This issue has been highlighted by the ILC, which posed the question generally with respect to islands as follows:

> The question is to what degree can the status of an island entitled to the entire panoply of maritime entitlements be conserved through artificial means and still maintain its character of being 'naturally formed' as per paragraph 1 of article 121 of the Convention and international law.[51]

VI. Maritime Entitlements and Maritime Boundaries[52]

The effects of SLR for islands and their maritime entitlements commence with the diminution of the land territory from which a maritime claim is asserted. This can range from minor impacts upon baselines to reductions in the size of the

[49] Government of Antigua and Barbuda, 'Antigua and Barbuda's submission on the effects of sea-level rise on the law of the sea' (*International Law Commission*, 14 September 2021) https://legal.un.org/ilc/sessions/72/pdfs/english/slr_antigua_barbuda.pdf, 6 [29], 7 [41]–[45].

[50] See discussion in Chapter 2 of this volume.

[51] International Law Commission, 'Sea-level rise in relation to international law' (n 6) 77 [212].

[52] See also C Schofield and D Freestone, 'Islands Awash Amidst Rising Seas: Sea Level Rise and Insular Status under the Law of the Sea' (2019) 34 *International Journal of Marine and Coastal Law* 391.

land territory with flow-on implications for the coastline. The most immediate impact of SLR will be upon baselines and the relevant LOSC rules with respect to the normal baselines (Article 5), reefs (Article 6), straight baselines (Article 7), mouths of rivers (Article 9), bays (Article 10), LTEs (Article 13) and, as noted above, archipelagic baselines.[53] The low-water line is the most susceptible to SLR, and is the foundation for the baseline rules in Articles 5 and 6. This line has been recognised as ambulatory, and as such is subject to variation.[54] However, the impact of SLR will potentially result in much greater variations to the low-water line, raising questions for how coastal States are to respond given the expectation that the low-water line be marked on official charts.[55] Straight baselines and their variants rely upon natural features for the drawing of the baseline to and from the coast, a number of which will also be susceptible to the impact of SLR. Smaller islands that are relied upon as basepoints for Article 7(1) straight baselines may diminish in size. The impact of this phenomenon may be de minimis, but that would be less so if islands composing a fringe were to disappear such that straight baselines could no longer be drawn in that coastal vicinity. More probable is that small islands impacted by SLR may eventually become LTEs and could still be utilised for the purposes of drawing straight baselines. Likewise, there are issues that arise with respect to dependent archipelagos and the capacity to draw straight baselines either from a continental coast or from the coast of adjacent islands.

Recalling that all maritime entitlements are asserted from the baselines, of whichever form, the issue that arises is the impact SLR would have upon the features from which maritime entitlements are asserted. A juridical island may become a juridical rock as a result of SLR and no longer enjoy a LOSC Article 121(3) entitlement to an EEZ or continental shelf. Likewise, a juridical rock may become an LTE, and have no maritime entitlement other than when it is used for the purposes of drawing a territorial sea baseline. Isolated juridical rocks that become LTEs as a result of SLR would therefore have no maritime entitlement and result in a considerable diminution of maritime entitlement for the coastal State.[56] This consequently raises questions with respect to maritime boundaries.

[53] Early discussions on this issue can be found in AHA Soons, 'The Effects of a Rising Sea Level on Maritime Limits and Boundaries' (1990) 37 *Netherlands International Law Review* 207; DD Caron, 'When Law Makes Climate Change Worse: Rethinking the Law of Baselines in Light of Rising Sea Level' (1990) 17 *Ecology Law Quarterly* 621; for more recent analysis, see C Armstrong and J Corbett, 'Climate Change, Sea Level Rise, and Maritime Baselines: Responding to the Plight of Low-Lying Atoll States' (2021) 21 *Global Environmental Politics* 89; K Purcell, *Geographical Change and the Law of the Sea* (Oxford 2020).

[54] International Law Commission, 'Sea-level rise in relation to international law' (n 6) 41 [104]; International Law Association, 'Report of the Committee on Baselines under the International Law of the Sea' (2012) 31; Purcell (n 53) 44–48.

[55] LOSC (n 6) arts 5 and 6; J Roach and R Smith, *Excessive Maritime Claims* (3rd edn, Martinus Nijhoff 2012) 70.

[56] C Schofield, *The Regime of Islands Reframed: Developments in the Definition of Islands under the International Law of the Sea* (Brill 2019) 9: calculating that a 'mere' juridical rock would generate a territorial sea of 452 nm^2.

The impact of SLR for maritime boundaries is not confined only to island States or archipelagic States, but also extends to continental States, given the number of States which in some way place reliance upon straight baselines or the maritime entitlements of islands or rocks for the purposes of determining their maritime boundaries. Three potential scenarios arise:

1. Where a juridical island or juridical rock impacted by SLR is the basis for a settled maritime boundary;
2. Where there are ongoing negotiations for settlement of a maritime boundary in which SLR dynamics have become a consideration; and
3. Where maritime boundaries are not yet under negotiation but which will involve islands that may be subject to SLR.

As to the first scenario, there again may be de minimis implications which the affected States may elect to overlook. However, in alternate scenarios there will be other interests that will need to be taken into account. This will especially arise in the case of overlapping EEZ and continental shelf maritime boundaries where distant islands have been relied upon for the purposes of extending a maritime entitlement. If a juridical island becomes a juridical rock or even an LTE due to SLR, the outer limit of an EEZ or continental shelf maritime entitlement may be radically impacted such that there is now an area of high seas and deep seabed in an area of the ocean previously considered to be under State jurisdiction and resource sovereignty. Such a scenario would engage the interests of the international community, including the International Seabed Authority.

The potential unravelling of well entrenched maritime boundaries due to SLR would impact on the certainty and stability of the maritime order and international law in general. One response as reflected in state practice is to fix baselines from which maritime entitlements have been asserted and which in turn are the basis for maritime boundaries.[57] Likewise, there is state practice and support for fixed outer limits of maritime boundaries which would not be disturbed as a result of SLR.[58]

The issue arising from these proposals is that they are to the benefit of the relevant coastal States, but not necessarily to the benefit of the international community. States currently engaged in maritime boundary delimitation and that are sensitised to SLR are at least able to buttress any agreement against its impacts. Fixing the outer coordinates of a settled maritime boundary with precision will be of assistance. Treaty law is also of relevance, especially the Vienna Convention on the Law of Treaties[59] and the application of the Article 62 fundamental change of circumstances rule. The impact of SLR upon a settled maritime boundary may well

[57] International Law Commission, 'Sea-level rise in relation to international law' (n 6) 30 [83], 34 [89], 41 [104], references to state practice from the Maldives, 30 [84], Papua New Guinea 34 [89].

[58] ibid 48 [125] referencing the position of the United Kingdom, and United States; see also Stephens (n 4).

[59] Vienna Convention on the Law of Treaties (VCLT) (adopted 23 May 1969, entered into force 27 January 1980) 1155 UNTS 331.

constitute a fundamental change of circumstances which would justify termination of a boundary treaty, especially if a juridical island or juridical rock no longer exists. However, Article 62(2)(a) exempts a boundary treaty from application of the rule. Uncertainty has existed as to whether the exemption applies to only land, or both land and maritime boundaries. In 1978 the International Court of Justice in the *Aegean Sea Continental Shelf* case suggested that the Vienna Convention rule did not apply in the case of maritime boundaries,[60] and the ILC endorsed this view in its 2020 study.[61] Likewise, in 2014 the LOSC Annex VII Arbitral Tribunal in the *Bay of Bengal Maritime Boundary* arbitration emphasised the importance of stability in maritime boundary delimitation, making direct reference to the impact of climate change.[62] Those States which have set aside maritime boundary delimitation until some point in the future will be well advised to take into account SLR and its impact on islands within their maritime domain.[63]

VII. Human Rights[64]

The human rights implications of SLR for island communities are significant,[65] many of which directly flow on from the issues noted above. The loss of territory and potentially statehood for people that compose a State is critical to their human rights and extend across a whole range of social, political, economic and cultural rights under international human rights law.[66] Indigenous island communities will be particularly impacted by SLR, especially in the Pacific, raising specific matters with respect to the rights of indigenous peoples.[67] Islands that have either been lost to SLR or become uninhabitable will result in internal displacement within island States as peoples relocate from one island to another.[68] This will in turn raise issues with respect to population density on remaining islands, which themselves may be impacted by the effects of SLR. Human security on islands and island

[60] *Aegean Sea Continental Shelf (Greece v Turkey)* (Judgment) [1978] ICJ Reps 3, 36–37 [85].

[61] International Law Commission, 'Sea-level rise in relation to international law' (n 6) 46 [119].

[62] *Bay of Bengal Maritime Boundary Arbitration (Bangladesh v India)* (Award) (7 July 2014) PCA Case No 2010-16, 63 [216]–[217].

[63] See comment by International Law Commission, 'Sea-level rise in relation to international law' (n 6) 53 [139].

[64] See also generally ME Hauer et al, 'Sea-level rise and human migration' (2020) 1 *Nature Reviews Earth & Environment* 28–39.

[65] J McAdam and E Ferris, 'Planned Relocations in the Context of Climate Change: Unpacking the Legal and Conceptual Issues' (2015) 4 *Cambridge Journal of International and Comparative Law* 137.

[66] International Covenant on Civil and Political Rights (adopted 19 December 1966, entered into force 23 March 1976) 999 UNTS 172; International Covenant on Economic, Social and Cultural Rights, (adopted 16 December 1966, entered into force 3 January 1976) 999 UNTS 3.

[67] UN Declaration on the Rights of Indigenous Peoples (adopted 13 September 2007) UN Doc. A/RES/61/295.

[68] See Committee on International Law and Sea Level Rise (International Law Association), 'Sydney Declaration of Principles on the Protection of Persons Displaced in the Context of Sea Level Rise', (Declaration, Sydney Conference 2018) www.ila-hq.org/index.php/committees.

States impacted by SLR will therefore be threatened. In the most extreme of cases, there is the prospect of the loss of statehood arising from de-territorialisation. If an island State effectively loses international legal personality, and the peoples of that State are not given status elsewhere, they are at risk of becoming stateless.[69] The loss of citizenship arising from the dissolution of a State because it no longer exists due to SLR and persons becoming stateless as a result, has profound implications for the civil, political, and socio-economic human rights of the affected populations.[70] Peoples facing displacement would be compelled to migrate, but without the protection of the Refugee Convention[71] as they would not be refugees or persons capable of claiming asylum.[72] In response to predicted SLR impacts, Kiribati purchased land in Fiji in 2014 to effectively provide Kiribati citizens with a place of refuge if their islands became uninhabitable.[73] The effective migration of a people from one State to another in addition to creating complex political and social issues,[74] raises novel international law questions, especially any obligations that are owed by the 'host' State in this situation. Recognition of the importance of these matters, with specific reference to SLR, in the 2018 Global Compact for Migration[75] was an important awareness-raising exercise, but more action will need to be taken to clarify international legal rights and responsibilities. The phenomena of SLR for islands more generally raises issues with respect to human security and the ability of peoples to continue to live on lands they have traditionally inhabited.

VIII. Conclusions

The effects of SLR for islands are real and there is increasing attention being given to the international legal challenges that are arising, and will arise in the future for

[69] See Convention relating to the Status of Stateless Persons (adopted 28 September 1954, entered into force 6 June 1960) 360 UNTS 117.

[70] J McAdam, '"Disappearing States", Statelessness and the Boundaries of International Law' in J McAdam (ed), *Climate Change and Displacement: Multidisciplinary Perspectives* (Oxford University Press 2010) 105.

[71] Convention relating to the Status of Refugees (adopted 28 July 1951, entered into force 22 April 1954) 189 UNTS 150.

[72] J McAdam, *Climate Change, Forced Migration and International Law* (Cambridge University Press 2012) 39, who argues with respect to the Convention and refugee law that 'Though there are some circumstances in which it will be applicable, it is, by and large, an inappropriate normative framework for responding to the needs of those forced to move on account of environmental or climate change impacts. Nevertheless, refugee law has some useful standards to offer any new protection-oriented instrument, such as the assessment of potential, future harm.'

[73] E Hermann and W Kempf, 'Climate Change and the Imagining of Migration: Emerging Discourses on Kiribati's Land Purchase in Fiji' (2017) 29 *The Contemporary Pacific* 231; 'Moving Story' (n 18) 20–21.

[74] E Piguet, 'Climatic Statelessness: Risk Assessment and Policy Options' (2019) 45(4) *Population and Development Review* 865.

[75] UNGA, 'Global Compact for Safe, Orderly and Regular Migration' UNGA Res 73/195 (19 December 2018) A/RES/73/195 [21(h)].

islands. It would appear that all islands will to varying degrees be impacted by SLR. Greenland, the largest recognised island with aspirations for eventual independence from Denmark, is being assailed by other impacts of climate change which may radically transform its polar ice cap and landscape.[76] Ice melt associated with the Greenland ice cap will also have significant SLR implications globally.[77] An accumulation of climate-related events in various parts of the world give an added urgency to considering and addressing SLR issues and their impacts upon islands.

Politically, groups of States are seeking to make their position clear on some of the key international legal questions noted above. The 2021 PIF Declaration may in time come to represent a milestone in how States clarified their position with respect to baselines, maritime boundaries and SLR. The Declaration clearly states that the LOSC does not create an 'affirmative obligation' to keep baselines and the limits of maritime zones under review, that maintenance of existing maritime zones notwithstanding climate change and SLR accords with the LOSC, and that once maritime zones have been established and notified to the UN Secretary-General those zones will be maintained without any review or update of baselines notwithstanding 'physical changes connected to climate change-related sea-level rise.'[78] That the Forum includes a diverse group of States ranging from G20 member States, to archipelagic States, to small-island developing States is significant. The 2021 AOSIS Declaration, which includes an even larger group of States, endorses a similar approach to the PIF Declaration.[79] In sum, a total of 44 PIF and AOSIS members in 2021 supported a new approach towards LOSC baseline and maritime boundary stability in response to SLR.

The maintenance of existing baselines and maritime boundaries has become a focal point for the international law discourse and this is reflected in the 2020 ILC Study Group report and the ILC work plan on this issue. There will inevitably be competing views on these questions within the international community. That there was no active consideration given to the issues associated with SLR and the law of the sea during LOSC negotiations presents an opportunity for a contemporary resolution of the question without the legacy of past debates being determinative. Based on comments made in the UN and submissions to the ILC, there would appear to be growing support for this position.[80] That powerful coastal

[76] V Sankaran, 'First recorded rainfall on Greenland's ice sheet peak leads to widespread melt' *Independent* (21 August 2021).

[77] A Aschwanden et al, 'Contribution of the Greenland Ice Sheet to sea level over the next millennium' (2019) 5(6) *Science Advances* eaav9396.

[78] PIF Declaration (n 9).

[79] AOSIS Declaration (n 10), which relevantly states: '41. *Affirm* that there is no obligation under the United Nations Convention on the Law of the Sea to keep baselines and outer limits of maritime zones under review nor to update charts or lists of geographical coordinates once deposited with the Secretary-General of the United Nations, and that such maritime zones and the rights and entitlements that flow from them shall continue to apply without reduction, notwithstanding any physical changes connected to climate change-related sea-level rise.'

[80] See generally International Law Commission, 'Sea-level rise in relation to international law' (n 6) 34 [89].

and maritime States appear open to a resolution of these challenges posed by SLR with an approach that supports stability and certainty with respect to baselines and maritime boundaries is important.[81]

The current focus on law of the sea issues is understandable given how groups such as the PIF and AOSIS have sought to give it prominence. There will no doubt be legal solutions found which gain political endorsement; however, ultimately these will only be short-term international law responses to SLR. The longer-term questions associated with principles of statehood and the human rights of island peoples impacted by SLR will remain after law of the sea issues have been settled. This will be the bigger challenge for international law.

[81] See United States of America, 'Comments of the United States Regarding Sea-Level Rise in Relation to the Law of the Sea' (*International Law Commission*, 14 February 2020), https://legal.un.org/ilc/sessions/72/pdfs/english/slr_us.pdf, 2 where it is stated: 'The United States recognizes that sea-level rise may lead to increases in inundation and coastal erosion, which may result in changes to baselines and the corresponding limits of a coastal State's maritime zones. In this regard, the United States supports efforts to protect States' maritime zones in a manner that is consistent with the rights and obligations of other States. Such efforts could include physical measures for coastal reinforcement, such as the construction of seawalls, and coastal ecosystem protection and restoration. The United States also supports States' negotiation and conclusion of maritime boundary agreements, as well as the delineation and publication of the limits of their maritime zones in accordance with international law as reflected in the Convention.'

11

A Regime of Islands?

I. Introduction

Is there a regime of islands in international law? This is the central question posed in this concluding chapter. The question is prompted by Part VIII 'Regime of Islands' of the 1982 United Nations Convention on the Law of the Sea (LOSC),[1] which includes a single provision: Article 121 'Régime of islands'. The LOSC does not define a regime, so to explore this question there is a need to initially define a regime under international law. This in itself is challenging, as the topic has generated considerable debate in recent decades.[2] A preliminary definition for this analysis suffices at present. Young suggests that: 'regimes are sets of norms, decision-making procedures and organisations coalescing around functional issue-areas and dominated by particular modes of behaviour, assumptions and biases.'[3] It also needs to be acknowledged that the term 'regime' is one that has longstanding usage in a law of the sea context and has been utilised by diverse communities ranging from the United Nations (UN),[4] the International Court of Justice (ICJ),[5] LOSC Annex VII Arbitral Tribunals,[6] the International Law Commission (ILC),[7] to scholars.[8]

[1] United Nations Convention on the Law of the Sea (adopted 10 December 1982, entered into force 16 November 1994) 1833 UNTS 397 (LOSC).

[2] RO Keohane, 'International Relations and International Law: Two Optics' (1997) 38 *Harvard International Law Journal* 487; A Slaughter, A Tulumello and S Wood, 'International Law and International Relations Theory: A New Generation of Interdisciplinary Scholarship' (1998) 92 *American Journal of International Law* 367; M Koskenniemi, 'The Fate of Public International Law: Between Technique and Politics' (2007) 70 *Modern Law Review* 1.

[3] MA Young, 'Introduction: The Productive Friction between Regimes' in MA Young (ed), *Regime Interaction in International Law: Facing Fragmentation* (Cambridge University Press 2012) 1, 11.

[4] See eg United Nations Conference on the Law of the Sea, 'Volume IV: Second Committee (High Seas: General Regime)' (Geneva, 24 February – 27 April 1958); United Nations, 'Juridical Regime of Historic Waters, Including Historic Bays' 143 (9 March 1962) UN Doc A/CN.4/.

[5] *Continental Shelf (Tunisia v Libyan Arab Jamahiriya)* (Judgment) [1982] ICJ Reps 18, 73–74 [100] discussing the regime of historic waters, historic bays, and continental shelf.

[6] *In the Matter of the South China Sea Arbitration before an Arbitral Tribunal constituted under Annex VII of the 1982 United Nations Convention on the Law of the Sea (Philippines v China)* (Merits) (12 July 2016) PCA Case 2013-19 (*South China Sea*), 113 [269], 132 [309] where there is discussion of an international legal regime for the oceans, the territorial sea, and the continental shelf.

[7] It is notable that the ILC in its formal 'Analytical Guide to the Work of the International Law Commission' only directly refers to regimes in the context of the law of the sea with respect to the 'regime of the high seas', at https://legal.un.org/ilc/guide/8_1.shtml, the 'regime of the territorial sea', at

To begin this review it is necessary to assess how 'regime' is used in Part VIII and Article 121, and whether there exists a LOSC regime as understood in international law or some other form of international law set of norms and rules. While the use of the term regime is not unique to Article 121, and it is found elsewhere referencing a regime of internal waters (Article 7), regime of passage through straits (Articles 34, 35, 233), regime of innocent passage (Article 45), regime of archipelagic sea lanes passage (Article 49), specific legal regime of the exclusive economic zone (Article 55), and international regime of the Area (Articles 154, 155), it is only used in the title to Part VIII. This suggests that the regime in Part VIII and Article 121 differs from other aspects of the LOSC.[9] But is this really the case? As previous chapters have illustrated, the LOSC also specifically addresses islands in the context of reefs (Article 6), straight baselines (Article 7), bays (Article 10), low-tide elevations (Article 13), right of transit passage (Article 38), Archipelagic States (Part IV), and artificial islands (Articles 60, 80 and 87). The commentaries on Part VIII make reference to the significance given to the question of islands and the law of the sea, observing for example that 'In giving special attention to the regime for islands, the Convention reflects the importance of islands in the delimitation of maritime space',[10] but other than noting the diplomatic history of how the 'regime of islands' evolved there is little consideration of its particular significance.[11] Given the importance of other parts of the LOSC for islands, especially Part IV Archipelagic States, which in sum is the most comprehensive set of provisions in the Convention relating to islands and the most significant for those island States which enjoy those entitlements, the Part VIII Regime of Islands is not as far-reaching as its title would suggest. Its focus is exclusively on islands from a law of the sea perspective, and no attempt is made to consider broader island issues in general international law.[12] The most exhaustive decision by any court or tribunal to date on Article 121 occurred in *South China Sea*; however, no effort was made in that decision to fully assess the meaning of a regime of islands.[13]

https://legal.un.org/ilc/guide/8_2.shtml, and the 'Juridical régime of historic waters, including historic bays', at https://legal.un.org/ilc/guide/8_4.shtml.

[8] See LJ Bouchez, *The Regime of Bays in International Law* (AW Sythoff 1964); M Gorina-Ysern, *An International Regime for Marine Scientific Research* (Brill 2004); E Egede, *Africa and the Deep Seabed Regime: Politics and International Law of the Common Heritage of Mankind* (Springer 2011).

[9] The LOSC negotiating history highlights how the term 'regime of islands' prevailed throughout the negotiations; see eg Algeria, Dahomey, Guinea, Ivory Coast, Liberia, Madagascar, Mali, Mauritania, Morocco, Sierra Leone, Sudan, Tunisia, Upper Volta and Zambia, 'Draft Articles on the Regime of Islands, Draft Art. 3,' UN Doc A/CONF.62/C.2/L.62/Rev.1 (27 August 1974); Romania, 'Draft Articles on Definition of and Regime Applicable to Islets and Islands Similar to Islets,' UN Doc A/CONF.62/C.2/L.53 (12 August 1974).

[10] SN Nanden and S Rosenne (eds), *United Nations Convention on the Law of the Sea: A Commentary* vol III (Martinus Nijhoff 1995) 321.

[11] S Talmon, 'Part VIII Regime of Islands' in A Proelss (ed), *United Nations Convention on the Law of the Sea: A Commentary* (CH Beck 2017) 858–80; see also Nanden and Rosenne (n 10) 321–39.

[12] Talmon (n 11) 859.

[13] *South China Sea* (n 6) 175 [387] where the tribunal only observed that Part VIII and Article 121 'presents a definition, a general rule, and an exception to that general rule.'

It can therefore be concluded that Part VIII and Article 121 do not create anything approaching the fulsome regime that Young suggests should exist. How then can Part VIII and Article 121 be characterised? As discussed in Chapter one, Article 121 is critical to understanding the juridical status of an island and the distinction between a juridical island and juridical rock. Article 121 also makes clear the maritime entitlements of those features, which in turn have significance for coastal State maritime entitlements and consequences for maritime boundary delimitation. Nevertheless, while Part VIII and Article 121 are central to understanding how islands are characterised under the LOSC, as noted throughout this work there are many other LOSC provisions that refer to islands in different contexts, especially Part IV and Archipelagic States. To understand whether there is a regime of islands in international law it is necessary to go beyond the LOSC.

II. Regimes, Islands and International Law

While some of the early literature on the study of islands and international law place an emphasis upon the legal regime of islands, little attention is given to what a regime is for the purposes of international law.[14] To begin it can be observed that the ICJ has referred to the general existence of regimes in international law,[15] and has also specifically discussed regimes in the context of the LOSC and Part VIII.[16] However, there has been little detailed elaboration by the Court on the precise content and scope of what an international law regime may be, other than within the particular context of a matter before the Court.

International law has concerned itself with self-contained regimes,[17] and objective regimes.[18] The first is the most relevant to the current analysis and in

[14] See eg DW Bowett, *The Legal Regime of Islands in International Law* (Oceana 1979); K Jayaraman, *Legal Regime of Islands* (Marwah Publications 1982).

[15] *United States Diplomatic and Consular Staff in Tehran (United States of America v Iran)* (Judgment) [1980] ICJ Reps 3, 40 [86] where the Court observed that: 'The rules of diplomatic law, in short, constitute a self-contained régime which, on the one hand, lays down the receiving State's obligations regarding the facilities, privileges and immunities to be accorded to diplomatic missions and, on the other, foresees their possible abuse by members of the mission and specifies the means at the disposal of the receiving State to counter any such abuse.'

[16] With respect to the LOSC, see the discussion in *Territorial and Maritime Dispute between Nicaragua and Honduras in the Caribbean Sea (Nicaragua v Honduras)* (Judgment) [2007] ICJ Reps 659, 674 [139].

[17] See B Simma, 'Self-contained regimes' (1985) 16 *Netherlands Yearbook of International Law* 111–36; D McRae, 'The Relationship between International Economic Law and Public International Law: The Role of Self-Contained Regimes' (2019) 11 *Indian Journal of International Economic Law* 1.

[18] CF de Casadevante Romani, 'Objective Regime' in R Wolfrum (ed), *Max Planck Encyclopedia of Public International Law* (online edn, Oxford University Press 2021); and see discussion in B Simma, 'The Antarctic Treaty as a Treaty Providing for an Objective Regime' (1986) 19 *Cornell International Law Journal* 189; R Rayfuse, 'The United Nations Agreement on Straddling and Highly Migratory

2006 the ILC gave specific consideration to self-contained regimes, in which it noted its previous analysis of this phenomenon in the context of the international law of state responsibility.[19] Considering self-contained regimes as a form of *lex specialis*, the ILC observed that such special regimes 'often have their own institutions to administer the relevant rules'.[20] Three types were identified:

1. Where sometimes violation of a particular group of (primary) rules is accompanied by a special set of (secondary) rules concerning breach and reactions to breach;
2. Where a special regime is formed by a set of special rules, including rights and obligations, relating to a special subject matter; and
3. Where sometimes all the rules and principles that regulate a certain problem area are collected together so as to express a 'special regime'.[21]

With respect to this final category, the ILC observed that: 'Expressions such as "law of the sea", "humanitarian law", "human rights law", "environmental law" and "trade law", etc. give expression to some such regimes. For interpretative purposes, such regimes may often be considered in their entirety.'[22] As Young has observed, these definitions of 'self-contained' or 'special regimes' contain differing assumptions,[23] and bundle together both the international law and international relations scholarship in the field.[24]

Of particular interest to this analysis is how the ILC viewed the self-contained regime of the Kiel Canal (Germany)[25] and the impact of the Treaty of Versailles.[26] In the *S.S. Wimbledon*[27] case before the Permanent Court of International Justice issues were raised with respect to the specific sets of international law rules

Fish Stocks as an Objective Regime: A Case of Wishful Thinking' (1999) 20 *Australian Year Book of International Law* 253.

[19] International Law Commission, 'Articles on Responsibility of States for Internationally Wrongful Acts', reprinted in J Crawford, *The International Law Commission's articles on state responsibility: introduction, text, and commentaries* (Cambridge University Press 2002).

[20] Study Group of the International Law Commission, 'Fragmentation of International Law: Difficulties arising from the Diversification and Expansion of International Law' (18 July 2006) UN Doc A/CN.4/L.702, 11 [14(11)].

[21] Ibid 11–12 [14(12)].

[22] ibid 12 [14(12)].

[23] Young (n 3) 5.

[24] The foundational definition of a regime in international relations scholarship was posed by Krasner as 'sets of implicit or explicit principles, norms, rules and decision-making procedures around which actors' expectations converge in a given area of international relations': S Krasner, 'Structural causes and regime consequences: regimes as intervening variables' (1982) 26 *International Organization* 185, 186; also see S Krasner (ed), *International Regimes* (Cornell University Press 1983).

[25] Report of the Study Group of the International Law Commission, 'Fragmentation of International Law: Difficulties arising from the Diversification and Expansion of International Law' 58th Session (1 May – 9 June, 3 July – 11 August 2006) UN Doc A/CN.4/L.682, 65–68 [123]–[129] (ILC 2006 Report).

[26] Treaty of Peace between the Allied and Associated Powers and Germany, and Protocol (adopted 28 June 1919, entered into force 10 January 1920) 225 CTS 188 (Treaty of Versailles).

[27] *Case of the S.S. 'Wimbledon'* (1923) PCIJ Rep Series A No 1, 15.

established for the Kiel Canal post-World War I and the interaction of those rules alongside general international law.[28] The Court commented that those rules:

> differ on more than one point from those to which other internal navigable waterways of the [German] Empire are subjected … the Kiel Canal is open to the war vessels and transit traffic of all nations at peace with Germany, whereas free access to the other German navigable waterways … is limited to the Allied and Associated Powers alone … The provisions of the Kiel Canal in the Treaty of Versailles are therefore self-contained.[29]

The ILC observed that this was an example of a special regime that may arise from a single treaty, several treaties, or a treaty and non-treaty developments such as customary international law.[30]

Young, however, urges caution with adopting a broad definition of regimes, and has written:

> notions of 'regimes' obscure the generality of international law and may distort our understanding about the overall international legal system. It makes the use of metaphors in the regime literature – such as 'ships', 'islands', 'arenas' and 'platforms' – seem rather imprudent.[31]

Care therefore needs to be exercised not to assert too liberally that there exists a regime of islands in international law. What then is the evidence that such a regime may exist independently of the LOSC?

III. Fragments of a Regime of Islands

At the core of any regime of islands is the definition of what is an island, of which the starting point is LOSC Article 121. That provides a base-level understanding of what constitutes a natural island. This study has also focussed on artificial islands, and the LOSC does not provide a clear definition of such islands other than, by default, that they are not naturally-formed Article 121 juridical islands. A broad category of islands under international law extends from a fully entitled Article 121 juridical island, to Article 121 juridical rocks, to a range of additional features that may be either islands or rocks such as atolls, banks, ledges, reefs, sandbanks, sandbars, and shoals, and ends with artificial islands. As highlighted in *South China Sea*, there is also the hybrid category of juridical rocks, reefs, and other associated maritime features that, as a result of land reclamation and associated construction works, become artificial islands. Exactly when that conversion from a natural state into an artificial state takes place, is unclear. What can be

[28] ILC 2006 Report (n 25) 66–67 [126]–[127].
[29] *Case of the S.S. 'Wimbledon'* (n 27) 23–24.
[30] International Law Commission (n 20) 12 [14(12)].
[31] Young (n 3) 10.

observed is that this is a distinctive aspect of islands and international law, as there is no equivalent inquiry into the characterisation of the mainland of a continental State as a result of land reclamation.

Islands also include archipelagos and dependent archipelagos, of which the first category is the most significant because of the distinctive LOSC entitlements they enjoy under Part IV. At one level an archipelagic State when viewed through a law of the sea lens is just another coastal State which has special rules for the drawing of baselines and is bound to respect the navigational rights and freedoms of foreign vessels within its archipelagic waters. Otherwise, an archipelagic State enjoys the same maritime entitlements as other coastal States. There are two important qualifiers to be able to enjoy these entitlements. The first is that the State must meet the Part IV criteria and there have been instances where States claiming de jure or de facto archipelagic status have had their claims denied.[32] The second is that the entitlement is framed upon the existence of a State. Here the LOSC blends with general international law. Caution needs to be exercised in this type of analysis, as the law of the sea is almost exclusively framed around the rights of States – coastal, flag, port, land-locked, geographically-disadvantaged – but none have such a distinctive set of rights as archipelagic States. This in turn leads to a consideration of the existence of States under general international law.

The general international law rules with respect to the existence of States are founded upon the 1933 Montevideo Convention[33] and they continue to be applied when new States emerge into the international system. There is nothing particular about those general international law rules as they apply to islands, though they have been applied to many island States in the post-War era. The existence of territory is a critical dimension for the emergence of any State. Some island States have very small territories, but the same phenomenon exists with very small continental States such as the Holy See (Vatican). There is nothing therefore that is very distinctive about islands and statehood, other than to observe that a majority of the remaining non-self-governing territories under the UN Charter are islands. One central aspect of general international law relating to islands and the Montevideo Convention is the existence of defined territory. Disputes with respect to territory are not exceptional to islands; however, they have become more common in recent decades. The general international law, developed primarily by the ICJ, with respect to territoriality has a distinctive jurisprudence as it relates to islands, but the general principles are ones that apply to both disputed continental and island territory. There may be a trend of

[32] *South China Sea* (n 6) 236 [573]; *Maritime Delimitation and Territorial Questions between Qatar and Bahrain (Qatar v Bahrain)* (Merits) [2001] ICJ Reps 40, 103 [213].

[33] Montevideo Convention on the Rights and Duties of States (1933) 165 LNTS 19.

more island territorial disputes arising because of their maritime entitlements, but that has not had a direct impact on the application of the relevant international law principles being applied to resolve those disputes. Nevertheless, it can be observed that many of the most contentious unresolved territorial disputes are those that exist with respect to islands.

Sea-level rise (SLR) is a natural phenomenon which, as discussed in Chapter ten, is impacting on all States, but especially islands and island States. This has raised the issue of territorial loss as a result of SLR which may make islands, including island States, uninhabitable. The prospect of so-called de-territorialisation is of particular concern to small island States, including archipelagic States. This has in turn raised academic debate as to whether it may be possible for virtual States to exist.[34] While these discussions are at a very preliminary stage, and it is notable that the ILC is assessing SLR and international law, this is a phenomenon that will have disproportional impact upon islands. Any future resolution of this issue under general international law will be applicable to islands.

This in turn leads to a consideration of islands and human rights, of which the impact of SLR is part of the modern discourse. The international law of human rights has not made any general provisions for islands, though there has been a developing discourse with respect to the particular issues confronting small-island developing States. Greater attention has been given to self-determination for islanders and this is an international legal phenomenon that has grown in momentum in the post-War era. Initially, self-determination was closely aligned with aspects of decolonisation and significant advances have been made in the UN era. However, in the twenty-first century it is notable that many of the remaining territories eligible for decolonisation, and territories that are engaged in debates with respect to their eventual self-determination, are islands. This extends from the very largest of islands in the case of Greenland (Denmark) to much smaller island territories such as Bougainville (Papua New Guinea) and Tokelau (New Zealand). The significance of islands, self-determination, human rights, and territoriality for international law was highlighted by the ICJ in the *Chagos Archipelago* Advisory Opinion,[35] in which the central issues remain unresolved. The international human rights issues with respect to islands and islanders are therefore becoming more distinctive over time, and these are especially being highlighted by the critical climate-change issues that islands are facing with respect to SLR.

[34] F Johns, 'Data Territories: Changing Architectures of Association in International Law' [2016] *Netherlands Yearbook of International Law* 107; J Everard, *Virtual States: The Internet and the boundaries of the nation-state* (Routledge 2000); and more generally on the significance of geography in this context, D Bethlehem, 'The End of Geography: The Changing Nature of the International System and the Challenge to International Law' (2014) 25 *European Journal of International Law* 9.

[35] *Legal Consequences of the Separation of the Chagos Archipelago from Mauritius in 1965*, Advisory Opinion [2019] ICJ Reps 95.

IV. A Future Regime of Islands

On the basis of the criteria set by the ILC, it is difficult to argue that there exists a distinctive self-contained regime in international law with respect to islands. Nevertheless, the ILC did observe that:

> The establishment of a special regime in the wider sense (*S.S. Wimbledon*, any interlinked sets of rules, both primary and secondary) would also normally take place by treaty or several treaties (e.g. the WTO 'covered treaties'). However, it may also occur that a set of treaty provisions develops over time, without conscious decision by States parties, perhaps through the activity of an implementing organ, into a regime with its own rules of regime-administration, modification and termination. … The widest of special regimes – denominations such as 'international criminal law', 'humanitarian law', 'trade law', 'environmental law' and so on – emerge from the informal activity of lawyers, diplomats, pressure groups, more through shifts in legal culture and in response to practical needs of specialization than as conscious acts of regime-creation. Such notions mirror the functional diversification of the international society or, more prosaically, the activities of particular caucuses seeking to articulate or strengthen preferences and orientations that seem not to have received sufficient attention under the general law. The application of special 'principles' by specialized implementation organs is a visible feature of such regimes.[36]

There is clearly a developing foundation for a special regime of islands. That regime has a firm basis in the LOSC where Part VIII – Article 121 is at its core. There are multiple additional pillars to that developing special LOSC regime, including Part IV – archipelagic States, and the practices that have developed with respect to straight baselines, dependent archipelagos, maritime entitlements, and maritime boundaries. Those core provisions which are already reflected in the LOSC are in the process of being supplemented by island States in response to SLR. The 2021 Pacific Islands Forum Declaration[37] seeking to affirm existing settled maritime boundaries in the face of SLR is an important addition to the growing regime. Importantly, every State signatory to the Declaration bar one is an island State, and the single continental State – Australia – has significant island territories that will also be impacted by SLR. The less detailed, but complementary, 2021 Association of Small Island States Declaration, includes an even larger group of States.[38] This LOSC foundation for the developing regime is one that may in time include additional pillars with respect to islands and distinctive issues of territoriality such as virtual territories in response to the impact of SLR, and may have implications for how statehood is viewed if island States are de-territorialised. The impact of

[36] ILC 2006 Report (n 25) 84–85 [157]–[158].

[37] Pacific Islands Forum, 'Declaration on Preserving Maritime Zones in the Face of Climate Change-Related Sea-Level Rise' (6 August 2021) www.forumsec.org/2021/08/11/declaration-on-preserving-maritime-zones-in-the-face-of-climate-change-related-sea-level-rise/.

[38] Association of Small Island States, 'Launch Of The Alliance Of Small Island States Leaders' Declaration' (22 September 2021) www.aosis.org/launch-of-the-alliance-of-small-island-states-leaders-declaration/.

climate change and SLR for islands may in time force a complete rethink of territoriality and international law, and have implications for how artificial islands are viewed under the LOSC as a legitimate response to peoples losing their homelands and cultures to SLR. That this human rights dimension of SLR also raises particular issues with respect to the rights of indigenous peoples will give additional impetus to any developing *lex specialis*.

A LOSC regime of islands does not currently exist in ways that would satisfy the ILC, and yet the term regime has been liberally applied throughout the history of the law of the sea and within the LOSC. There is compelling evidence of a developing regime of islands that, while having a foundation in the law of the sea, is much more comprehensive. The various strands of that regime are capable of identification and distinctive elements clearly exist. The test will be whether they continue to gain momentum. What is apparent, however, is that international law has entered an age of islands. Never before have islands demanded such attention from international law. They are in the global legal spotlight in multiple different contexts and international law is continuing to develop around them.

APPENDIX 1

Current Status of former and current islands
Chapter XI Non-Self-Governing Territories and Chapter XII Trust Territories[1]

Territory	Current Status	UN Status	Admin Power/ Authority	UNGA Res	Comments
American Samoa	NSGT 1946; UST	NSGT	US	2069 (XX); 49/47; 52/71	Unorganized, unincorporated US territory
Anguilla	NSGT 1946; BOT	NSGT	UK	52/77	Seceded from St Kitts and Nevis 1967
Bahamas	IS 1973	FTNSGT	UK	3051 (XXVIII)	
Barbados	IS 1966	FTNSGT	UK	2175 (XXI)	
Bermuda	NSGT 1946; BOT	NSGT	UK	3289 (XXIX); 52/77	Independence rejected 1995
British Solomon Islands[2]	IS 1978	NSGT	UK	33/1	Now Solomon Islands
British Virgin Islands	BOT	NSGT	UK	52/77	Part of Leeward Islands; separate colony in 1956
Brunei	IS 1984	FTNSGT	UK	3159C (XXVIII); 39/1	Declined to join Federation of Malaysia (1963)
Cape Verde Archipelago	IS 1975	FTNSGT	Portugal	3363 (XXX)	Independence as Cape Verde, now Cabo Verde

(continued)

[1] Hong Kong is not included, as its landmass is dominated by the mainland which is part of continental Asia.
[2] Part of the Western Pacific High Commission Territories.

(Continued)

Territory	Current Status	UN Status	Admin Power/ Authority	UNGA Res	Comments
Cayman Islands	BOT	NSGT	UK	52/77	
Comoro Archipelago	IS 1975	NSGT	France	3385 (XXX)	Independence as the Comoros
Cocos (Keeling Islands)	Australian External Territory	FTNSGT	Australia	39/30	Transferred from Straits Settlement in 1955
Cook Islands	FA with New Zealand	FTNSGT	New Zealand	2064 (XX)	Home Rule since 1965
Cyprus	IS 1960	FTNSGT	UK	1489 (XV); 37/253	
Dominica	IS 1978	FTNSGT	UK	2422C (XXIII); 2707 (XXV); 33/107	FA under West Indies Act 1967
Falkland (Malvinas) Islands	BOT	NSGT	UK	2065 (XX); 43/25; 51/407	Subject to claim by Argentina
Fiji	IS 1970	FTNSGT	UK	1951 (XVIII); 2068 (XX): 2622 (XXV)	
French Polynesia	FOT	NSGT	France	52/71	
Gilbert and Ellice Island Colony[3]	IS Tuvalu (Ellice Island) (1978) IS Kiribati (Gilbert Island) (1979)	NSGT	UK	55/1; 54/1	
Greenland	Int: Denmark	FTNSGT	Denmark	849 (IX)	Home Rule since 1979
Grenada	IS 1974	FTNSGT	UK	3204 (XXIX)	FA under West Indies Act 1967

(continued)

[3] Part of the Western Pacific High Commission Territories.

(Continued)

Territory	Current Status	UN Status	Admin Power/ Authority	UNGA Res	Comments
Guam	UST	NSGT	US	2069 (XX); 52/77; 49/46	Organized; unincorporated US territory
Hawaii	Int: US	FTNSGT	US	149 (XIV)	US State from 1959
Jamaica	IS 1962	FTNSGT	UK	1750 (XV)	
Leeward Islands	IS: Antigua and Barbuda (1981); St Kitts and Nevis (1983); BOT: Anguilla (1967)/ British Virgin Islands (1956)	NSGT	UK	38/18; 39/11; 52/77	Initial FA under West Indies Act 1967 (UK)
Macau	Int: China	FTNSGT	Portugal	No Res	China resumed sovereignty 1999
Madagascar	IS 1960	FTNSGT	France	1478 (XV)	Independence as Malagassy Republic, now Madagascar
Malayan Union	IS: Malaya (1957)/ Malaysia (1963)	FTNSGT	UK	1134 (XI)	Includes Sabah and Sarawak in Borneo
Malta	IS 1964	FTNSGT	UK	1950 (XVIII)	
Mauritius	IS 1968	FTNSGT	UK	2232 (XXI)	Four islands detached from Mauritius to form the British Indian Ocean Territory (BIOT)[4]

(continued)

[4] The BIOT comprises a total of 58 islands with no permanent population, excepting Diego Garcia which has a military base.

(Continued)

Territory	Current Status	UN Status	Admin Power/ Authority	UNGA Res	Comments
Mayotte	FOT	FTNSGT	France	48/18	Part of the Comoro Archipelago but remained a FOT after Comoros independence
Montserrat	BOT	NSGT	UK	52/77	Part of Leeward Islands; rejected FA 1967
Nauru	IS 1968	FTNSGT	Australia	140 (II); 2347 (XXII)	
Netherlands Antilles	FA as Aruba, and Curacao with Netherlands	FTNSGT	Netherlands	945 (X)	Aruba (1986) and Curaçao (2010) are constituent 'countries' of the Netherlands
Netherlands Indies	IS: Indonesia (1950)	FTNSGT	Netherlands	448 (V); 491 (VI); 1752 (XVI)	West New Guinea ceded to Indonesia (1962); UN referendum supporting association (1969)
New Caledonia	FOT	NSGT	France	A/Res/42/7; 49/45; 57/136	Referenda – 2018; 2020; 2021
New Guinea	IS: Papua New Guinea (1975)	FTNSGT	Australia	63 (I); 3284 (XXIX)	Joined in union with FTNSGT of Papua
New Hebrides	IS: Vanuatu (1980)	FTNSGT	UK	3290 (XXIX); 36/1	Originally a condominium
Niue	FA with New Zealand	FTNSGT	New Zealand	3285 (XXIX)	
North Borneo (Sabah)	IS: Malaysia	FTNSGT	UK	No Res	Joined Federation of Malaysia

(continued)

(Continued)

Territory	Current Status	UN Status	Admin Power/ Authority	UNGA Res	Comments
Pacific Islands	IS: Federated States of Micronesia (1986); Marshall Islands (1986); Palau (1994)	FTNSGT	US	2183 (LIII); UNSC Res 683; 956	Federated States of Micronesia, Marshall Islands and Palau in FA as independent States with US; Commonwealth of Northern Mariana Islands (CNMI) has US Commonwealth status since 1975
Papua	IS: Papua New Guinea (1975)	FTNSGT	Australia	3284 (XXIX)	Joined in union with FTNSGT of New Guinea
Pitcairn Is	BOT	NSGT	UK	52/77	Formerly part of Western Pacific High Commission Territories
Portuguese Timor	IS: Timor-Leste (2002)	FTNSGT	Portugal	3485 (XXX)	Occupied by Indonesia: 1975–99
Puerto Rico	FA with US	FTNSGT	US	748 (VIII)	Commonwealth status
Reunion	FOT	FTNSGT	France		DROM status (1974)
São Tomé Principe	IS: São Tomé and Principe (1975)	FTNSGT	Portugal	3364 (XXX)	
Sarawak	IS: Malaysia	FTNSGT	UK	No Res	Claimed by North Borneo; joined Federation of Malaysia
Seychelles	IS 1976	FTNSGT	UK	3287 (XXIX)	
Singapore	IS 1965	FTNSGT	UK	2019 (XX)	Became part of Federation of Malaysia 1963

(continued)

(Continued)

Territory	Current Status	UN Status	Admin Power/ Authority	UNGA Res	Comments
St Helena	BOT	NSGT	UK	52/77	Crown Colony since 1834
St Lucia	IS 1979	FTNSGT	UK	34/1	FA under West Indies Act 1967
St Pierre and Miquelon	FOT	FTNSGT	France		Self-governing territorial overseas collectivity of France (OCT) status
St Vincent	IS: St Vincent and the Grenadines (1979)	FTNSGT	UK	35/1	FA under West Indies Act 1967
Tokelau	NSGT 1946	NSGT	New Zealand	66 (1); 52/77; 49/47; 59/133	Referendums on self-determination in 2006 and 2007 defeated
Trinidad and Tobago	IS 1962	FTNSGT	UK	1751 (XVII)	
Turks and Caicos Islands	BOT	NSGT	UK	52/77	Dependency of Jamaica (1874–1959); UK colony with Bahamas (1962–73)
US Virgin Islands	UST	NSGT	US	2069 (XX); 52/77; 49/46	Organized, unincorporated US territory
Western Samoa	IS: 1962	FTNSGT	New Zealand	63 (I); 1926 (XVI)	Name changed to Samoa in 1997

Key: Admin Power – Administering Power; BOT – British Overseas Territory; ET – External Territory; FA – Free Association; FOT – French Overseas Territory; FTNSGT – former Trust and Non-Self-Governing Territory; Int – Integration; IS – Independent State; NSGT – Non-Self Governing Territory; UST – United States Territory.

BIBLIOGRAPHY

Abdulla A, 'Sea level rise, statehood and artificial islands for environmentally displaced persons under international law: Future of the Maldives' (2020) 4 *International Journal of Social Research and Innovation* 1.

Ackrén M, 'Referendums in Greenland – From Home Rule to Self-Government' (2019) 19 *Fédéralisme Régionalisme*.

—— 'The Faroe Islands: Options for Independence' (2006) 1 *Island Studies Journal* 223.

Ackrén M and Jakobsen U, 'Greenland as a self-governing sub-national territory in international relations: past, current and future perspectives' (2015) 51 *Polar Record* 404.

Adler-Nissen R, 'The Faroe Islands: Independence dreams, globalist separatism and the Europeanization of postcolonial home rule' (2014) 49 *Cooperation and Conflict* 55.

Aldrich R and Connell J, *The Last Colonies* (Cambridge University Press 1998).

Allaby M, *A Dictionary of Geology and Earth Sciences* (5th edn, Oxford University Press 2020).

Allen MG, 'Framing food security in the Pacific Islands: empirical evidence from an island in the Western Pacific' (2015) 15 Regional Environmental Change 1341.

Allen S, 'Self-Determination, The Chagos Advisory Opinion and the Chagossians' (2020) 69 *International and Comparative Law Quarterly* 203.

—— *The Chagos Islanders and International Law* (Hart Publishing 2014).

Amerasinghe CF, 'The Problem of Archipelagoes in the International Law of the Sea' (1974) 23 *International and Comparative Law Quarterly* 539.

Anand RP, 'Accretion' in Wolfrum R (ed), *Max Planck Encyclopedia of Public International Law* (online edn, Oxford University Press 2006).

—— *Origin and Development of the Law of the Sea* (Martinus Nijhoff 1983).

Anderson D, 'Some Aspects of the Regime of Islands in the Law of the Sea' (2017) 32 *International Journal of Marine and Coastal Law* 316.

Anyanova E, 'Delimitation of the Aegean Sea' (2013) 3 *International Journal of Public Law and Policy* 210.

Arellano Rodriguez VE, 'The Legal Status of Mid-Ocean Archipelagos of Mainland States under International Law: The Case of the Galapagos' (2017) 6(2) *UCL Journal of Law and Jurisprudence* 71.

Armstrong C and Corbett J, 'Climate Change, Sea Level Rise, and Maritime Baselines: Responding to the Plight of Low-Lying Atoll States' (2021) 21 *Global Environmental Politics* 89.

Asada M, 'Senkaku/Diaoyu Islands' in Wolfrum R (ed), *Max Planck Encyclopedia of International Law* (online edn, Oxford University Press 2007).

Aschwanden A et al, 'Contribution of the Greenland Ice Sheet to sea level over the next millennium' (19 June 2019) 5 *Science Advances* eaav9396.

Asia Maritime Transparency Initiative, 'Occupation and Island Building' (2021) https://amti.csis.org/island-tracker/.

Association of Small Island States, 'Launch Of The Alliance Of Small Island States Leaders' Declaration' (22 September 2021), www.aosis.org/launch-of-the-alliance-of-small-island-states-leaders-declaration/.

Association of Southeast Asian Nations, 'Declaration on the Conduct of the Parties in the South China Sea (4 November 2002)', https://asean.org/declaration-on-the-conduct-of-parties-in-the-south-china-sea-2/.

Aung Myoe M, 'Myanmar's maritime challenges and priorities' in Ho J and Bateman S (ed), *Maritime Challenges and Priorities in Asia* (Routledge 2012) 83.

Aust A, 'Treaties, Territorial Application' in Wolfrum R (ed), *Max Planck Encyclopedia of Public International Law* (online edn, Oxford University Press 2006).

—— *Modern Treaty Law and Practice* (3rd edn, Cambridge University Press 2013).

Australian Government Great Barrier Reef Marine Park Authority, 'Reef Facts', www.gbrmpa.gov.au/the-reef/reef-facts.

Balkin R, 'The Role of the International Maritime Organization in the Settlement of International Disputes' in Rothwell DR and Bateman S (eds), *Navigational Rights and Freedoms and the New Law of the Sea* (Martinus Nijhoff 2000) 293.

Barnett J, 'Dangerous climate change in the Pacific Islands: food production and food security' (2011) 11 *Regional Environmental Change* 229.

Barron N, 'Archipelagos and Archipelagic States under UNCLOS III: No Special Treatment for Hawaii' (1981) 4 *Hastings International and Comparative Law Review* 509.

Batongbacal JL, 'Barely Skimming the Surface: Archipelagic Sea Lanes Navigation and the IMO' in Oude Elferink AG and Rothwell DR (eds), *Oceans Management in the 21st Century: Institutional Frameworks and Responses* (Martinus Nijhoff 2004) 49.

Baumert K and Melchior B, 'The Practice of Archipelagic States: A Study of Studies' (2015) 46 *Ocean Development and International Law* 60.

Bayefsky AF (ed), *Self-Determination in International Law: Quebec and Lessons Learned* (Kluwer Law International 2000).

BBC News, 'Chagos Islands dispute: UK misses deadline to return control' (22 November 2019), www.bbc.co.uk/news/uk-50511847.

—— 'Denmark to build "first energy island" in North Sea' (4 February 2021), www.bbc.com/news/world-europe-55931873.

Beckman R, 'Case between Malaysia and Singapore concerning sovereignty over Pedra Branca/Pulau Batu Puteh, Middle Rocks and South Ledge' (2008) 14 *Asian Yearbook of International Law* 273.

Bekker P, 'The World Court Awards Sovereignty Over Several Islands in the Caribbean Sea to Colombia and Fixes a Single Maritime Boundary between Colombia and Nicaragua' (15 January 2013) 17(3) *ASIL Insights*.

Bennike O et al, 'Tuppiap Qeqertaa (Tobias Island): a newly discovered island off northeast Greenland' (2006) 42 (223) *Polar Record* 309.

Bethlehem D, 'The End of Geography: The Changing Nature of the International System and the Challenge to International Law' (2014) 25 *European Journal of International Law* 9.

Betzold C, 'Adapting to climate change in small island developing states' (2015) 133(3) *Climate Change* 481.

Bílková V, 'A State Without Territory' [2016] *Netherlands Yearbook of International Law* 19.

Bouchez LJ, *The Regime of Bays in International Law* (AW Sythoff 1964).

Bowcott O and Borger J, 'UK suffers crushing defeat in UN vote on Chagos Islands' *The Guardian* (London, 23 May 2019).

Bowett DW, *The Legal Regime of Islands in International Law* (Oceana 1979).

Boyce DG, *The Falklands War* (Palgrave Macmillan 2005).

Boyer WW, *America's Virgin Islands: A History of Human Rights and Wrongs* (2nd edn, Carolina Academic Press 2010).

Briguglio L, 'The Global Involvement of Small Island Developing States' in Page S (ed), *Regions and development: politics, security, and economics* (Frank Cass 2000) 241.

Brown ED, 'Maritime Zones: A Survey of Claims' in Churchill R, Simmonds KR and Welch J (eds), *New Directions in the Law of the Sea*, vol 3 (British Institute of International and Comparative Law 1973).

Brown PM, 'The Aaland Islands Question' (1921) 15 *American Journal of International Law* 268.

Bruijn JR, 'Between Batavia and the Cape: Shipping Patterns of the Dutch East India Company' (1980) 11 *Journal of Southeast Asian Studies* 251.

Burmester H, 'Island Outposts of Australia' in Bateman WSG and Ward MW (eds), *Australia's Offshore Maritime Interests* (Centre for Maritime Studies 1985) 54.

Burrett T, 'Great expectations: Domestic Politics and the Russo–Japanese Northern Territories Dispute' in Kingston J (ed), *Critical Issues in Contemporary Japan* (2nd edn, Routledge 2019) 158.

Butcher JG, 'Becoming an Archipelagic State: The Juanda Declaration of 1957 and the "Struggle" to gain International Recognition of the Archipelagic Principle' in Cribb R and Ford M (eds), *Indonesia beyond the Water's Edge* (Institute of Southeast Asian Studies 2009).
Byers M, *International Law and the Arctic* (Cambridge University Press 2013).
Byrne D, 'Time on the Waterline: Coastal Reclamations and Seawalls in Sydney and Japan' (2018) 5 *Journal of Contemporary Archaeology* 53.
Cambou DC, 'Disentangling the conundrum of self-determination and its implications in Greenland' (2020) 56 *Polar Record* E3.
Caribbean Community: CARICOM, 'Secretary-General's Remarks – CARICOM Senior Officials (Fisheries, Law of the Sea and Marine Conservation) Briefing on Proposed Collaboration with the Cloudburst Foundation' (22 April 2021), caricom.org/secretary-generals-remarks-caricom-senior-officials-fisheries-law-of-the-sea-and-marine-conservation-briefing-on-proposed-collaboration-with-the-cloudburst-foundation/.
Caron DD, 'When Law Makes Climate Change Worse: Rethinking the Law of Baselines in Light of Rising Sea Level' (1990) 17 *Ecology Law Quarterly* 621.
Cassese A, *Self-determination of peoples: a legal reappraisal* (Cambridge University Press 1995).
Castellino J, *International Law and Self-Determination* (Martinus Nijhoff 2000).
Castles AC, 'International Law and Australia's Overseas Territories' in O'Connell DP (ed), *International Law in Australia* (Law Book Co 1966).
Central Intelligence Agency (US), 'Australia', *The World Factbook*, www.cia.gov/the-world-factbook/countries/australia/.
—— 'Bahrain', *The World Factbook*, www.cia.gov/the-world-factbook/countries/bahrain/.
—— 'French Southern and Antarctic Lands', *The World Factbook*, www.cia.gov/the-world-factbook/countries/french-southern-and-antarctic-lands/.
—— 'Greenland', *The World Factbook*, www.cia.gov/the-world-factbook/countries/greenland/.
—— 'Holy See (Vatican)', *The World Factbook*, www.cia.gov/the-world-factbook/countries/holy-see-vatican-city/.
—— 'Indonesia', *The World Factbook*, www.cia.gov/the-world-factbook/countries/indonesia/.
—— 'Niue', *The World Factbook*, www.cia.gov/the-world-factbook/countries/niue/.
—— 'Nauru', *The World Factbook*, www.cia.gov/the-world-factbook/countries/nauru/.
—— 'Northern Mariana Islands', *The World Factbook*, www.cia.gov/the-world-factbook/countries/northern-mariana-islands/.
—— 'Philippines', *The World Factbook*, www.cia.gov/the-world-factbook/countries/philippines/.
—— 'Puerto Rico', *The World Factbook*, www.cia.gov/the-world-factbook/countries/puerto-rico/.
—— 'Tuvalu', *The World Factbook*, www.cia.gov/the-world-factbook/countries/tuvalu/.
—— 'United States Pacific Wildlife Refuges', *The World Factbook*, www.cia.gov/the-world-factbook/countries/united-states-pacific-island-wildlife-refuges/.
Chanda N and Holloway N, 'Troubled Waters: Indonesia's Neighbours Consider Responses to Closure of Straits', *Far Eastern Economic Review* (10 November 1988).
Chappell, DA, 'The Noumea Accord: Decolonization without Independence in New Caledonia?' (1999) 72 *Pacific Affairs* 373.
Charney JI and Alexander LM (eds), *International Maritime Boundaries*, vol 1 (Martinus Nijhoff 1993).
—— *International Maritime Boundaries*, vol 2 (Martinus Njihoff 1993).
—— *International Maritime Boundaries*, vol 3 (Martinus Nijhoff 1998).
Charney JI and Smith RW, *International Maritime Boundaries*, vol 4 (Martinus Nijhoff, 2002).
Chee SY et al, 'Land reclamation and artificial islands: Walking the tightrope between development and conservation' (2017) 12 *Global Ecology and Conservation* 80.
Chinese Society of International Law, 'The South China Sea Arbitration Awards: A Critical Study' (2018) 17 *Chinese Journal of International Law* 207.
Churchill R, 'United Kingdom: Accession to the UN Convention on the Law of the Sea' (1998) 13 *International Journal of Marine and Coastal Law* 263.
Churchill R and Ulfstein G, 'The Disputed Maritime Zones around Svalbard' in Nordquist M, Moore JN and Heidar TH (eds), *Changes in the Arctic Environment and the Law of the Sea* (Martinus Nijhof 2010) 551.

Churchill RR and Lowe AV, *The Law of the Sea* (3rd edn, Manchester University Press 1999).
Clark RS, 'Self-Determination and Free Association-Should the United Nations Terminate the Pacific Islands Trust' (1980) 21 *Harvard International Law Journal* 1.
Clegg P and Gold P, 'The UK Overseas Territories: a decade of progress and prosperity?' (2011) 49 *Commonwealth & Comparative Politics* 115.
Coll AR and Arend AC (eds), *The Falklands War: lessons for strategy, diplomacy, and international law* (Allen & Unwin 1985).
Colson DA, 'Sovereignty over Pulau Ligitan and Pulau Sipadan (Indonesia/Malaysia)' (2003) 97 *American Journal of International Law* 398.
Colson DA and Smith RW, *International Maritime Boundaries*, vol 5 (Martinus Nijhoff 2005).
—— *International Maritime Boundaries*, vol 6 (Martinus Nijhoff 2011).
Connell J, 'Food security in the island Pacific: Is Micronesia as far away as ever?' (2015) 15 *Regional Environmental Change* 1299.
Coquia JR, 'Maritime Boundary Problems in the South China Sea' (1990) 24 *University of British Columbia Law Review* 117.
Cordner LG, 'The Spratly Islands Dispute and the Law of the Sea' (1994) 25 *Ocean Development and International Law* 61.
Cottier T, *Equitable Principles of Maritime Boundary Delimitation: The Quest for Distributive Justice in International Law* (Cambridge University Press 2015).
Country Garden Pacificview, 'Forest City' www.forestcitycgpv.com.
Crawford J, 'The Right of Self-Determination in International Law: Its Development and Future' in Alston P (ed), *People's Rights* (Oxford University Press 2001) 7.
—— *Brownlie's Principles of Public International Law* (9th end Oxford University Press 2019).
—— *Chance, Order, Change: The Course of International Law* (Brill 2014).
—— *The Creation of States in International Law* (2nd edn, Clarendon Press 2006).
Dalay G, 'Turkey, Europe, and the Eastern Mediterranean: Charting a Way Out of the Current Deadlock' (*Policy Briefing* (Brookings Doha Center), January 2021).
Davenport T, 'Island-Building in the South China Sea: Legality and Limits' (2018) 8 *Asian Journal of International Law* 76.
Dawes PR and Tukiainen T, 'Hans Ø, celebrated island of Nares Strait between Greenland and Canada: from dog-sledge to satellite mapping' (2008) 15 *Geological Survey of Denmark and Greenland Bulletin* 77.
Dayant A, 'Not one, but two new points of tension for France in the Pacific' (*The Interpreter* (Lowy Institute), 19 March 2019).
de Casadevante Romani CF, 'Objective Regime' in Wolfrum R (ed), *Max Planck Encyclopedia of Public International Law* (online edn, Oxford University Press 2021).
Department of Conservation (New Zealand), 'Auckland Islands Marine Mammal Sanctuary' www.doc.govt.nz/nature/habitats/marine/other-marine-protection/auckland islands/.
Department of Foreign Affairs and Trade (Australia), 'Australia-Taiwan relationship' (23 May 2021).
Department of Infrastructure, Regional Government and Cities (Government of Australia), 'Norfolk Island', www.infrastructure.gov.au/territories-regions-cities/territories/norfolk-island.
Department of State (US), *2020 Country Reports on Human Rights Practices* (Department of State 2021).
—— *Antigua and Barbuda: Archipelagic and Other Maritime Claims and Boundaries (Limits in the Sea No 133)* (Department of State 2014).
—— *Bahamas: Archipelagic and Other Maritime Claims and Boundaries (Limits in the Sea No 125)* (Department of State 2014).
—— *Dominican Republic: Archipelagic and other Maritime Claims and Boundaries (Limits in the Seas No. 130)* (Department of State 2014).
—— *Ecuador Maritime Claims and Boundaries (Limits in the Seas No 147)* (Department of State 2020).
—— *Grenada: Archipelagic and Other Maritime Claims and Boundaries (Limits in the Sea No 135)* (Department of State 2014).
—— *Indonesia: Archipelagic and Other Maritime Claims and Boundaries (Limits in the Sea No 141)* (Department of State 2014).

—— *Jamaica's Maritime Claims and Boundaries (Limits in the Sea No 128)* (Department of State 2014).
—— *Limits in the Seas: No. 139 Tuvalu's Maritime Claims and Boundaries* (Department of State 2014).
—— *Mauritius: Archipelagic and Other Maritime Claims and Boundaries (Limits in the Sea No 140)* (Department of State 2014).
—— *Norway Maritime Claims and Boundaries (Limits in the Seas No 148)* (Department of State 2020).
—— *Philippines: Archipelagic and Other Maritime Claims and Boundaries (Limits in the Sea No 142)* (Department of State 2014) 3.
—— *Republic of the Marshall Islands: Archipelagic and other Maritime Claims and Boundaries' (Limits in the Seas No 145)* (Department of State 2020).
—— *Seychelles: Archipelagic and Other Maritime Claims and Boundaries (Limits in the Sea No 132)* (Department of State 2014).
—— *Solomon Islands: Archipelagic and other Maritime Claims and Boundaries (Limits in the Sea No 136)* (Department of State 2014).
—— *Spain Maritime Claims and Boundaries (Limits in the Seas No 149)* (Department of State 2020).
—— *Straight Baseline and Territorial Sea Claims: Japan (Limits in the Seas No 120)* (Department of State 1998).
—— *Straight Baselines Claim: Costa Rica (Limits in the Seas No 111)* (Department of State 1990).
—— *Straight Baselines: Chile (Limits in the Seas No 80)* (Department of State 1978).
—— *Straight Baselines: Cuba (Limits in the Seas No 76)* (Department of State 1977).
—— *Straight Baselines: Svalbard (Limits in the Seas No 39)* (Department of State 1972).
—— *Straight Baselines: Vietnam (Limits in the Seas No 99)* (Department of State 1983).
—— 'U.S. Relations with Taiwan' (24 May 2021),www.state.gov/u-s-relations-with-taiwan/.
—— *United States Responses to Excessive National Maritime Claims (Limits in the Seas No 112)* (Department of State 1992).
Doherty B, 'West Papua independence leaders declare 'government-in-waiting'' *The Guardian* (1 December 2020).
Dolven B et al, 'Chinese Land Reclamation in the South China Sea: Implications and Policy Options' (Document No R44072, Congressional Research Service 2015).
Dosenrode S, 'Spill-back: The Faroe Islands' Zigzag towards Independence' in Dosenrode S (ed), *Limits to Regional Integration* (Routledge 2015) 197.
Dubner, BH, *The Law of Territorial Waters of Mid-Ocean Archipelagos and Archipelagic States* (Martinus Nijhoff 1976).
Dupuy F and Dupuy P-M, 'A Legal Analysis of China's Historic Rights Claim in the South China Sea' (2013) 107 *American Journal of International Law* 124.
Duursma J, *Fragmentation and the international relations of micro-states: self-determination and statehood* (Cambridge University Press 1996).
Dziedzic S and Srinivasan P, 'New Caledonia narrowly rejects independence from France in historic referendum' *ABC News* (online, 5 November 2018).
Edwards R, 'Statement (Falkland Islands (Malvinas))', *Caribbean regional seminar on the implementation of the Third International Decade for the Eradication of Colonialism*: accelerating decolonization through renewed commitment and pragmatic measures, Saint George's, Grenada, 2–4 May 2019).
Egede E, *Africa and the Deep Seabed Regime: Politics and International Law of the Common Heritage of Mankind* (Springer 2011).
Elliott PD, 'The East Timor Dispute' (1978) 27 *International and Comparative Law Quarterly* 238.
Enghave SM, 'Energy island in the North Sea' (Danish Energy Agency), ens.dk/en/our-responsibilities/wind-power/energy-islands/energy-island-north-sea.
Eslami M and Sotoudehfar S, 'Iran–UAE Relations and Disputes Over the Sovereignty of Abu Musa and Tunbs,' in Leandro FJBS, Branco C, and Caba-Maria F (eds), *The Geopolitics of Iran* (Palgrave Macmillan 2021) 343.
Evans MD, *Relevant Circumstances and Maritime Delimitation* (Oxford University Press 1989).
Evensen J, 'Certain Legal Aspects Concerning the Delimitation of Territorial Waters of Archipelagos' in *United Nations Conference on the Law of the Sea: Official Records*, vol 1 (United Nations 1958) 289.
Everard J, *Virtual States: The Internet and the boundaries of the nation-state* (Routledge 2000).

Evers J (ed), 'Island', *National Geographic Resource Library* (2012) www.nationalgeographic.org/encyclopedia/island/.

Evers S and Kooy M (eds), *Eviction from the Chagos Islands: Displacement and Struggle for Identity Against Two World Powers* (Brill 2011).

Faroe Islands, 'The constitutional status of the Faroe Islands' (14 May 2018) https://www.faroeislands.fo/government-politics/constitutional-status/.

Fischer SR, *Islands: From Atlantis to Zanzibar* (Reaktion Books 2012).

Fisher D, *New Caledonia's Independence Referendum: Local and Regional Implications* (Lowy Institute 2019).

Foighel I, 'Home Rule in Greenland' (1979) 48 *Nordic Journal of International Law* 4.

Foreign Office (Great Britain), *Spitsbergen* (HM Stationery Office 1920).

Fraenkel J, 'Introduction: The Long-run Impact of New Caledonia's Noumea Accord' (2019) 54 *The Journal of Pacific History* 199.

Franckx E and Benatar M, 'Straight baselines around insular formations not constituting an archipelagic state' in Jenner CJ and Thuy TT (eds), *The South China Sea: A Crucible of Regional Cooperation or Conflict-making Sovereignty Claims?* (Cambridge University Press 2016) 186.

Freestone D and Schofield C, 'Sea Level Rise and Archipelagic States: A Preliminary Risk Assessment' (2021) 35 *Ocean Yearbook Online* 340.

—— 'The Caribbean Sea and the Gulf of Mexico' in Rothwell DR et al (eds), *The Oxford Handbook of the Law of the Sea* (Oxford University Press 2015) 672.

Frizzell S, 'Truce? Canada, Greenland, Denmark inch closer to settling decades-old spat over Hans Island', *CBC News* (28 May 2018).

Gaeth T, 'Coastal Reclamation in the 21st Century' (2020) 86 *Crit* 31.

Gerrard M and Wannier G (eds), *Threatened island nations: legal implications of rising seas and a changing climate* (Cambridge University Press 2013).

Ghina F, 'Sustainable Development in Small Island Developing States' (2003) 5 *Environment, Development and Sustainability* 139.

Glaser R, Haberzettl P, and Walsh RPD, 'Land reclamation in Singapore, Hong Kong and Macau' (1991) 24 *GeoJournal* 365.

Global Security, 'Tiran and Sanafir Islands' (7 March 2018), www.globalsecurity.org/military/world/war/tiran.htm.

Goebel J, *The Struggle for the Falkland Islands* (Yale University Press 1982).

Goldie LFE, 'Historic Bays in International Law – An Impressionistic Overview' (1984) 11 *Syracuse Journal of International Law and Commerce* 211.

Gorina-Ysern M, *An International Regime for Marine Scientific Research* (Brill 2004).

Grant TD, 'Defining Statehood: The Montevideo Convention and its Discontents' (1998–1999) 37 *Columbia Journal of Transnational Law* 403.

—— 'Micro States' in Wolfrum R (ed), *Max Planck Encyclopedia of Public International Law* (online edn, Oxford University Press 2013.

Greenwood C, 'Iraq's Invasion of Kuwait: Some Legal Issues' (1991) 47 *The World Today* 39.

Gregory CN, 'The Neutralization of the Aaland Islands' (1923) 17 *American Journal of International Law* 63.

Greig DW, 'Sovereignty and the Falkland Islands Crisis' (1983) 8 *Australian Year Book of International Law* 20.

Griffith MD, 'Reflections on the implementation of the Programme of Action on the Sustainable Development of Small Island Developing States (SIDS)' (1995) 29 *Ocean & Coastal Management* 139.

Grydehøj A, 'Island city formation and urban island studies' (2015) 47 *AREA* 429.

—— 'Unravelling economic dependence and independence in relation to island sovereignty: The case of Kalaallit Nunaat (Greenland)' (2020) 15 *Island Studies Journal* 89.

Gumrukcu T, 'North Cyprus leader backs two-state proposal for U.N. talks' *Reuters* (26 April 2021).

Gupta A, 'Upper Zakum Offshore Oil Field Development, Abu Dhabi' *Offshore Technology*, 5 August 2019.

Guymon CLD (ed), *Digest of United States Practice in International Law* (Department of State 2017) 2017–2021.

Haller-Trost R, *Historical legal claims: a study of disputed sovereignty over Pulau Batu Puteh (Pedra Branca)* (Maritime Briefing (International Boundaries Research Unit) 1993).

Hanna EG and McIver L, 'Small Island States – Canaries in the Coal Mine of Climate Change and Health' in Butler CD (ed), *Climate Change and Global Health* (CABI 2014) 181.

Hannikainen L, 'The Continued Validity of the Demilitarised and Neutralised Status of the Aland Islands' (1994) 54 *Zeitschrift für ausländisches öffentliches Recht und Völkerrecht* 614.

Harhoff F, 'The Status of Indigenous Peoples under International Law: Greenland and the Right to Self-Determination' (1995) 32 *Canadian Yearbook of International Law* 243.

Harris WL, 'Microstates in the United Nations: A Broader Purpose' (1970) 9 *Columbia Journal of Transnational Law* 23.

Hattenhauer C, 'Heligoland' in Wolfrum R (ed), *Max Planck Encyclopedia of International Law* (online edn, Oxford University Press 2013).

Hauer, ME et al, 'Sea-level rise and human migration' (2020) 1 *Nature Reviews Earth & Environment* 28.

Hayward P and Fleury C, 'Absolute waterfrontage: Road networked artificial islands and finger island canal estates on Australia's Gold Coast' (2016) 2 *Urban Island Studies* 25.

Heathcote S, 'Secession, self-determination and territorial disagreements: Sovereignty claims in the contemporary South Pacific' (2021) 34 *Leiden Journal of International Law* 653.

Heijmans AMJ, 'Artificial Islands and the law of Nations' (1974) 21 *Netherlands International Law Review* 139.

Herman LL, 'The Modern Concept of the Off-Lying Archipelago in International Law' (1985) 23 *Canadian Yearbook of International Law* 172.

Hermann E and Kempf W, 'Climate Change and the Imagining of Migration: Emerging Discourses on Kiribati's Land Purchase in Fiji' (2017) 29 *The Contemporary Pacific* 231.

Hernández AR and McGinley L, 'Harvard study estimates thousands died in Puerto Rico because of Hurricane Maria' *The Washington Post* (Washington, 29 May 2018).

Herr RA, 'Microstate Sovereignty in the South Pacific: Is Small Practical?' (1988) 10 *Contemporary Southeast Asia* 182.

Hirayasu N, 'The Process of Self-Determination and Micronesia's Future Political Status under International Law' (1987) 9 *University of Hawaii Law Review* 487.

Hoad D, 'The 2015 Paris Climate Agreement: outcomes and their impacts on small island states' (2016) 11 *Island Studies Journal* 315.

Hoadley JS, 'Indonesia's Annexation of East Timor: Political, Administrative, and Developmental Initiatives' (1977) *Southeast Asian Affairs* 133.

Hodgson RD and Alexander LM, *Towards an Objective Analysis of Special Circumstances: Bays, Rivers, Coastal and Oceanic Archipelagos and Atolls* (Occasional Paper No 13, Law of the Sea Institute, University of Rhode Island 1972) 45.

Holder J and Harrison C (eds), *Law and Geography* (Oxford University Press 2003).

Honniball AN, 'Singapore: Pedra Branca/Pulau Batu Puteh – Land Reclamation at Maritime Features Pending Maritime Delimitation' (2021) 6 *Asia-Pacific Journal of Ocean Law and Policy* 276.

Hoole R, 'Sri Lanka: Ethnic Strife, Fratricide, and the Peace vs. Human Rights Dilemma' (2009) 1 *Journal of Human Rights Practice* 120.

Horn LA, 'To Be or Not To Be: The Republic of Minerva-Nation Founding by Individuals' (1973) 12 *Columbia Journal of Transnational Law* 520.

Horne G, *The apocalypse of settler colonialism: the roots of slavery, white supremacy, and capitalism in 17th century North America and the Caribbean* (Monthly Review Press 2017).

Horner J, 'The Iraq-Kuwait Border dispute' (1992) 7 *Journal of Borderlands Studies* 1.

Housing Development Corporation, 'Hulhamalé: The City of Hope' (2016) https://hdc.com.mv/hulhumale/.

Hsieh L, 'The Legal Status of Taiwan in United State Courts' (2009) 6 (2) *Taiwan International Law Quarterly* 53–84.

Human Rights Watch, *World Report 2021* (2021).

Igarashi M, *Associated Statehood in International Law* (Kluwer Law International 2002).
Intergovernmental Panel on Climate Change 'Synthesis Report of the Sixth Assessment Report' (*IPCC*, 2021).
International Criminal Court, 'Situation in the Philippines: ICC Pre-Trial Chamber I authorises the opening of an investigation' (15 September 2021).
International Law Association, 'Baselines under the International Law of the Sea' (Final Report, Sydney Conference, 2018).
—— 'International Law and Sea-Level Rise' (Report, Sydney Conference, 2018).
—— 'International Law and Sea-Level Rise' (Interim Report, Johannesburg Conference, 2016).
—— 'Report of the Committee on Baselines under the International Law of the Sea' (2012).
International Law Commission (ILC), 'Sea-level rise in relation to international law: First issues paper by Bogdan Aurescu and Nilüfer Oral, Co-Chairs of the Study Group on sea-level rise in relation to international law' (28 February 2020) UN Doc A/CN.4/740.
—— 'Articles concerning the Law of the Sea with commentaries' in *Yearbook of the International Law Commission*, vol 2 (1956).
—— 'Articles on Responsibility of States for Internationally Wrongful Acts', reprinted in J Crawford, *The International Law Commission's articles on state responsibility: introduction, text, and commentaries* (Cambridge University Press 2002).
—— 'Commentary to the articles concerning the law of the sea' in *Yearbook of the International Law Commission*, vol 2 (1956) UN Doc A/CN.4/SER.A/1956/Add.l 265.
—— 'Regime of the Territorial Sea' reprinted in *Yearbook of the International Law Commission*, vol 2 (1952) UN Doc A/CN.4/53.
—— 'Regime of the Territorial Sea' reprinted in *Yearbook of the International Law Commission*, vol 2 (1954) UN Doc A/CN.4/77.
—— 'Report of the International Law Commission covering the work of the eighth session (23 April–4 July 1956)' in *Yearbook of the International Law Commission*, vol 2 (1956) UN Doc A/3159 253.
—— 'Report of the International Law Commission, Seventieth session' (30 April–1 June and 2 July–10 August 2018) UN Doc.A/73/10.
—— 'Reservations to treaties: Titles and texts of draft guidelines of the Guide to Practice adopted by the Drafting Committee of the fiftieth session' (31 July 1998) UN Doc. A/CN.4/L.563.
—— Report of the Study Group of the International Law Commission, 'Fragmentation of International Law: Difficulties arising from the Diversification and Expansion of International Law' (18 July 2006) UN Doc. A/CN.4/L.702 11 [14(11)].
Irving H, 'Autonomies of Scale' in Ghai Y and Woodman S (eds), *Practising Self-Government: A Comparative Study of Autonomous Regions* (Cambridge University Press 2013) 200.
Isaacus and the Editorial Committee, 'The Cook Islands' in Ntumy MA (ed), *South Pacific Islands Legal Systems* (University of Hawaii Press 1993).
Jacobsen T and Stone I, 'Kolbeinsey: Iceland's Arctic island' (2006) 42 *Polar Record* 167.
Jalinoosi A and Moradifar S, 'Analyzing the Consequences of the UAE Creating Artificial Islands in The Persian Gulf (Considering the Copenhagen School)' (2017) 1 *Journal of World Sociopolitical Studies* 281.
Janki M, 'West Papua and the Right to Self-Determination under International Law' (2010) 34 *West Indian Law Journal* 1.
Jayaraman K, *Legal Regime of Islands* (Marwah 1982).
Jayewardene HW, *The Regime of Islands in International Law* (Martinis Nijhoff 1990).
Jennings R and Watts A (eds), *Oppenheim's International Law: Volume 1 Peace* (9th edn, Longman 1992).
Jensen JA, 'The Position of Greenland and the Faroe Islands Within the Danish Realm' (2003) 9 *European Public Law* 170.
Jessup PC, *The Law of Territorial Waters and Maritime Jurisdiction* (GA Jennings 1927).
Jet Propulsion Laboratory, NASA, 'Hulhumale, Maldives' (22 January 2021), www.jpl.nasa.gov/images/hulhumale-maldives.

Jia BB, 'A Preliminary Study of the Problem of the Isle of Kolbeinsey' (1997) 66 *Nordic Journal of International Law* 301.

Johns F, 'Data Territories: Changing Architectures of Association in International Law' [2016] *Netherlands Yearbook of International Law* 107.

Johnson DHN, 'Artificial Islands' (1951) 4 (2) *International and Comparative Law Quarterly* 203.

—— 'The Minquiers and Ecrehos Case' (1954) 3 *International and Comparative Law Quarterly* 189.

Johnstone B, 'The unprecedented "sinking island" phenomenon: The legal challenges on statehood caused by rising sea level' (2019) 23 *New Zealand Journal of Environmental Law* 97.

Joseph S and Castan M, *The International Covenant on Civil and Political Rights: Cases, Materials and Commentary* (3rd edn, Oxford University Press 2013).

Joyner CC and Harden S, 'Small Is Dangerous: Micro States in a Macro World' (1985) 82 *American Political Science Review* 341.

Juwana H, 'Human Rights in Indonesia' (2006) 4 *Indonesian Journal of International Law* 27.

Kabutaulaka TT, 'Solomon Islands' (2004) 16 *The Contemporary Pacific* 393.

Karl DE, 'Islands and the Delimitation of the Continental Shelf: A Framework for Analysis' (1977) 71 *American Journal of International Law* 642.

Katalin Molnar A, *Timor Leste: politics, history, and culture* (Routledge 2010).

Kattan V, 'The Chagos Advisory Opinion and the Law of Self-Determination' (2020) 10 *Asian Journal of International Law* 12.

Kaye SB, 'Jurisdictional Patchwork: Law of the Sea and Native Title Issues in the Torres Strait' (2001) 2 *Melbourne Journal of International Law* 381.

—— 'The Law of the Sea Convention and Sea Level Rise after the *South China Sea Arbitration*' (2017) 93 *International Law Studies* 423.

—— 'The Torres Strait Islands: Constitutional and Sovereignty Questions Post-Mabo' (1994–1995) 18 *University of Queensland Law Journal* 38.

Kebaish KA, 'Tiran and Sanafir: A Historical and Constitutional Argument Opposing the Territorial Cession of the Tiran and Sanafir Islands to Saudi Arabia' (2019) 97 *Texas Law Review* 835.

Keohane RO, 'International Relations and International Law: Two Optics' (1997) 38 *Harvard International Law Journal* 487.

Kim SP, *Maritime delimitation and interim arrangements in North East Asia* (Martinus Nijhoff 2004).

Kirezci E et al, 'Projections of global-scale extreme sea levels and resulting episodic coastal flooding over the 21st Century' (2020) 10 *Scientific Reports* 11629.

Knop K, *Diversity and Self-Determination in International Law* (Cambridge University Press 2002).

Koh T and Lin J, 'The Land Reclamation Case: Thoughts and Reflections' (2006) 10 *Singapore Year Book of International Law* 1.

Kohl AW, 'China's Artificial Island Building Campaign in the South China Sea: Implications for the Reform of the United Nations Convention on the Law of the Sea' (2018) 122 *Dickinson Law Review* 917.

Kopela S, '2007 Archipelagic Legislation of the Dominican Republic: An Assessment' (2009) 24 *International Journal of Marine and Coastal Law* 501.

—— *Dependent Archipelagos in the Law of the Sea* (Martinus Nijhoff 2013).

Koskenniemi M, 'The Fate of Public International Law: Between Technique and Politics' (2007) 70 *Modern Law Review* 1.

Krasner S (ed), *International Regimes* (Cornell University Press 1983).

—— 'Structural causes and regime consequences: regimes as intervening variables' (1982) 26 *International Organization* 185.

Ku C, 'The Archipelagic States Concept and Regional Stability in Southeast Asia' (1991) 23 *Case Western Reserve Journal of International Law* 463.

Kusumaatmadja M, 'The Concept of the Indonesian Archipelago' (1982) 10 *Indonesian Quarterly* 12.

Kwiatkowska B, 'The 2006 Barbados/Trinidad and Tobago Award: A Landmark in Compulsory Jurisdiction and Equitable Maritime Boundary Delimitation' (2007) *22 International Journal of Marine and Coastal Law* 7.

—— 'The Archipelagic Regime in Practice – Making or Breaking International Law?' (1991) 6 *International Journal of Estuarine and Coastal Law* 1.

Kwiatkowska B and Agoes ER, *Archipelagic Waters Regime in the Light of the 1982 United Nations Law of the Sea Convention and State Practice* (ICLOS, UNPAD 1991).

Lando M, *Maritime Delimitation as a Judicial Process* (Cambridge University Press 2019).

Lathrop C, 'Sovereignty over Pedra Branca/Pulau Batu Puteh, Middle Rocks and South Ledge' (2008) 102 *American Journal of International Law* 828.

—— 'Territorial and Maritime Dispute Between Nicaragua and Honduras in the Caribbean Sea (Nicaragua v. Honduras)' (2008) 102 *American Journal of International Law* 113.

Lathrop CG, Roach JA, and Rothwell DR (eds), *Baselines under the International Law of the Sea: Reports of the International Law Association Committee on Baselines under the International Law of the Sea* (Brill 2018).

Lauterpacht H, *The Development of International Law by the International Court* (Stevens 1958).

Lay SH, Churchill R and Nordquist M (eds), *New Directions in the Law of the Sea*, vol 1 (Oceana Publications 1973).

Lee S, 'Dok Do/Takeshima Islands from a Korean Perspective' in Wolfrum R (ed), *Max Planck Encyclopedia of Public International Law* (online edn, Oxford University Press 2014).

—— 'The 1951 San Francisco Peace Treaty with Japan and the Territorial Disputes in East Asia' (2002) 11 *Pacific Rim Law and Policy Journal* 63.

Lee S and Bautista L, 'Climate Change and Sea Level Rise: Nature of the State and of State Extinction' in Barnes R and Long R (eds), *Frontiers in International Environmental Law: Oceans and Climate Challenges – Essays in Honour of David Freestone* (Brill 2021) 194.

Lee S and Lee HE (eds), *Dokdo: Historical Appraisal and International Justice* (Martinus Nijhoff 2011).

Leifer M, 'Indonesia and the Incorporation of East Timor' (1976) 32 *The World Today* 347.

Lewis N, 'Islands in a Sea of Change: Climate Change, Health and Human Security in Small Island States' in Fernando HJS, Klaić Z and McCulley JL (eds), *National Security and Human Health Implications of Climate Change* (Springer 2012) 13.

Lewis R, 'The Artificial Construction and Modification of Maritime Features: Piling Pelion on Ossa' (2021) 52 *Ocean Development and International Law* 239.

Lim I, 'Jurong Island' (*Singaporeinfopedia*, 1 March 2016) https://eresources.nlb.gov.sg/infopedia/articles/SIP_505_2004-12-17.html.

Livingstone E, 'A Tale of Two Islands: An Analysis of the Court of Arbitration's Decision in the Canada-France Maritime Boundary Dispute' (1994) 3 *Dalhousie Journal of Legal Studies* 1.

Loja MH, 'The Spratly Islands as a Single Unit Under International Law: A Commentary on the Final Award in Philippines/China Arbitration' (2016) 47 *Ocean Development and International Law* 309.

Lyon AHE, 'The Principality of Sealand, and Its Case for Sovereign Recognition' (2015) 29 *Emory International Law Review* 637.

MacDonald R St J, 'The Minquiers and Ecrehos Case' (1952–55) *McGill Law Journal* 277.

Maclellan N, 'The Noumea accord and Decolonisation in New Caledonia' (1999) 34(3) *The Journal of Pacific History* 245.

Maritime and Port Authority of Singapore, 'Development of Tuas Next-Generation Port Phase 2 begins' (4 July 2019).

Marques Antunes NS, 'The Eritrea-Yemen Arbitration: First Stage-The Law of Title to Territory Re-Averred' (1999) 48 *International and Comparative Law Quarterly* 362.

Martin I, *Self-Determination in East Timor: The United Nations, the Ballot, and International Intervention* (Lynne Rienner 2001).

Matsui Y, 'International Law of Territorial Acquisition and the Dispute over the Senkaku (Diaoyu) Islands' (1997) 40 *Japanese Annual of International Law* 3.

Mbengue MM, 'Non-Self-Governing Territories' in Wolfrum R (ed), *Max Planck Encyclopedia of Public International Law* (online edn, Oxford University Press 2013).

McAdam J, '"Disappearing States", Statelessness and the Boundaries of International Law' in McAdam J (ed), *Climate Change and Displacement: Multidisciplinary Perspectives* (Oxford University Press 2010) 105.

—— *Climate Change, Forced Migration and International Law* (Cambridge University Press 2012).
McAdam J and Ferris E, 'Planned Relocations in the Context of Climate Change: Unpacking the Legal and Conceptual Issues,' (2015) 4 *Cambridge Journal of International and Comparative Law* 137.
McCormack G, 'Much Ado over Small Islands: The Sino-Japan confrontation over Senkaku/Diaoyu' in Liao TF, Hara K, and Wiegand K (eds), *The China-Japan Border Dispute: Islands of Contention in Multidisciplinary Perspective* (Ashgate 2015).
McCorquodale R (ed), *Self-Determination in International Law* (Ashgate 2000).
McDonald J, 'Bougainville Inches Closer to Independence' *The Diplomat* (online, 19 July 2021).
McDorman TL, 'An International Law Perspective on Insular Features (Islands) and Low-tide Elevations in the South China Sea' (2017) 32 *International Journal of Marine and Coastal Law* 298.
—— *Salt Water Neighbors: International Ocean Law Relations between the United States and Canada* (Oxford University Press 2009).
McDougal MS and Burke WT, *The Public Order of the Oceans* (Yale University Press 1962).
McElroy JL and Parry CE, 'The long-term propensity for political affiliation in island microstates' (2012) 50 *Commonwealth and Comparative Politics* 403.
McKinnon JB, 'Arctic Baselines: A Litore Usque ad Litus' (1987) 66 *Canadian Bar Review* 790.
McMahon E, 'Australia, the Island Continent: How Contradictory Geography Shapes the National Imaginary' (2010) 13 *Space and Culture* 178.
McRae D, 'The Relationship between International Economic Law and Public International Law: The Role of Self-Contained Regimes' (2019) 11 *Indian Journal of International Economic Law* 1.
Menefee SP, 'Republics of the Reefs: Nation-Building on the Continental Shelf and in the World's Oceans' (1994) 25 *California Western International Law Journal* 81.
Merrills JG, 'Sovereignty over Pulau Ligitan and Pulau Sipadan (Indonesia v Malaysia), Merits, Judgment of 17 December 2002' (2003) 52 *International and Comparative Law Quarterly* 797.
Milne G et al 'Identifying the causes of sea-level change' (2009) 2 *Nature Geoscience* 471.
Ministry of Foreign Affairs and Trade (New Zealand), 'Cook Islands: Constitutional Status and International Personality' (May 2005).
—— 'International Treaty Making: Guidance for government agencies on practice and procedures for concluding international treaties and arrangements' (September 2020) www.mfat.govt.nz/assets/About-us-Corporate/Treaties-Model-instruments/International-Treaty-Making-Guide-2020.pdf.
—— 'Niue'. www.mfat.govt.nz/en/countries-and-regions/australia-and-pacific/niue/.
Ministry of Foreign Affairs (Republic of China (Taiwan)), 'Diplomatic Allies' (1 October 2021), https://en.mofa.gov.tw/AlliesIndex.aspx?n=1294&sms=1007.
Ministry of Foreign Affairs (Turkey), 'The Kardak Dispute' www.mfa.gov.tr/the-kardak-dispute.en.mfa.
Ministry of Foreign Affairs of Finland, 'The special status of the Aland Islands', um.fi/the-special-status-of-the-aland-islands.
Ministry of Justice (UK), 'Fact sheet on the UK's relationship with the Crown Dependencies'.
Molenaar EJ, *Coastal State Jurisdiction over Vessel-Source Pollution* (Kluwer Law International 1998).
Mooney K, 'Alliance of Small Island States' in Philander SG (ed), *Encyclopedia of Global Warming and Climate Change* (Sage 2008).
Moore JB, *History and Digest of the International Arbitrations to Which the United States Has Been a Party*, vol 1 (Government Printing Office 1898) 755.
Morsink J, *The Universal Declaration of Human Rights: Origins, Drafting and Intent* (University of Pennsylvania Press 1999).
Mosses M, 'Revisiting the Matthew and Hunter Islands Dispute in Light of the Recent Chagos Advisory Opinion and Some Other Relevant Cases: An Evaluation of Vanuatu's Claims relating to the Right to Self-Determination, Territorial Integrity, Unlawful Occupation and State Responsibility Under International Law' (2019) 66 *Netherlands International Law Review* 475.
Mossop J, 'The South China Sea Arbitration and New Zealand's Maritime Claims' (2017) 15 *New Zealand Journal of Public and International Law* 265.
Mrgudovic N, 'The French Overseas Territories in transition' in Clegg P and Killingray D (eds), *The non-independent territories of the Caribbean and the Pacific: continuity and change* (University of London, Institute of Commonwealth Studies 2012) 85.

Munavvar M, *Ocean States: Archipelagic Regimes in the Law of the Sea* (Martinus Nijhoff 1995).
Murphy SD, *International Law Relating to Islands* (Brill/Nijhoff 2017).
Nanda VP, 'Ethnic Conflict in Fiji and International Human Rights Law' (1992) 25 *Cornell International Law Journal* 565.
Nandan SN and Rosenne S (eds), *United Nations Convention on the Law of the Sea 1982: A Commentary*, vol 2/3 (Martinus Nijohff 1993/1995).
Neverova EV, 'The Southern Kuril Deadlock: effectiveness v. protest' (2019) 3 *Moscow Journal of International Law* 47.
Nguyen HT, 'Sea-Level Rise and the Law of the Sea in the Western Pacific Region' (2020) 13 *Journal of East Asia and International Law* 121.
Nordquist M, Lay SH and Simmonds KR (eds), *New Directions in the Law of the Sea*, vol 7 (Oceana Publications 1980).
Nossum JH, 'What Vietnam could gain from redrawing its baselines' (Winter 2001–2002) *IBRU Boundary and Security Bulletin* 97.
Novak G, 'Overseas Territories, Australia, France, Netherlands, New Zealand, United Kingdom, United States of American' in Wolfrum R (ed), *Max Planck Encyclopedia of Public International Law* (online edn, Oxford University Press 2017).
Nowak M, *UN Covenant on Civil and Political Rights CCPR Commentary* (2nd edn, NP Engel 2005).
Noyes JE, 'The Territorial Sea and Contiguous Zone' in Rothwell DR, Oude Elferink AG, Scott KN and Stephens T (eds), *The Oxford Handbook of the Law of the Sea* (Oxford University Press 2015) 91.
Nunn P, *Vanished Islands and Hidden Continents of the Pacific* (University of Hawaii Press 2008).
Nunn P et al, 'Classifying Pacific Islands' (2016) 3 *Geoscience Letters* 7.
Nurhidayah L, 'Sea-Level Rise (SLR) and Its Implication on Human Security and Human Rights in Indonesia: A Legal Analysis' in Djalante R, Jupesta J, and Aldrian E (eds), *Climate Change Research, Policy and Actions in Indonesia* (Springer 2020) 33.
Nyamekye K and Premdas RR, 'Papua New Guinea-Indonesian Relations over Irian Jaya' (1979) 19 *Asian Survey* 927.
O'Connell DP, 'Mid-Ocean Archipelagos in International Law' (1971) 45 *British Yearbook of International Law* 1.
—— 'The Condominium of the New Hebrides' (1968–1969) 43 *British Yearbook of International Law* 71.
—— *The International Law of the Sea*, vol 1 (Clarendon Press 1982).
O'Donnell T, Robinson D and Gillespie J (eds), *Legal Geography: Perspectives and Methods* (Routledge 2020).
Office of Insular Affairs, Department of the Interior (US), 'Commonwealth of the Northern Mariana Islands', www.doi.gov/oia/islands/cnmi.
—— 'Definitions of Insular Area Political Organizations', www.doi.gov/oia/islands/politicatypes.
—— 'Palmyra Atoll', www.doi.gov/oia/islands/palmyraatoll.
Office of the United Nations High Commissioner for Human Rights (UN), '1st UN Pacific Forum on Business and Human Rights' (1–2 December 2020), www.ohchr.org/EN/Issues/Business/Pages/2020UN-pacific-forum.aspx.
Opeskin BR and Rothwell DR, 'Australia's Territorial Sea: International and Federal Implications of its Extension to 12 Miles' (1991) 22 *Ocean Development and International Law* 395.
Oppenheimer M et al, 'Sea Level Rise and Implications for Low-Lying Islands, Coasts and Communities' in H Pörtner et al (eds), *IPCC Special Report on the Ocean and Cryosphere in a Changing Climate* (IPCC 2019) ch 4.
Oude Elferink AG, 'Artificial Islands, Installations and Structures' in Wolfrum R (ed), *Max Planck Encyclopedia of Public International Law* (online edn, Oxford University Press 2013).
—— 'Maritime Delimitation between the United Kingdom and Denmark/Faroe Islands' (1999) 14(4) *International Journal of Marine and Coastal Law* 541.
Oxman BH, 'Transit of Straits and Archipelagic Waters by Military Aircraft' (2000) 4 *Singapore Journal of International and Comparative Law* 377.

Pacific Community (SPC) and UN Office of the High Commissioner for Human Rights (UNOHCHR), *Human Rights in the Pacific: A situational analysis* (Quality Print 2016).

Palestini L, 'The *Territorial and Maritime Dispute* (*Nicaragua* v. *Colombia*): On Territorial Sovereignty and the International Court of Justice's "Failure to Rule" on the Geographical Scope of the Archipelago of San Andrés' (2016) 15 *The Law and Practice of International Courts and Tribunals* 56.

Palma MA, 'The Philippines as an Archipelagic and Maritime Nation: Interests, Challenges and Perspectives' (2009) *RSIS Working Paper* No 182.

Palmer S, 'The Turkish Republic of Northern Cyprus: Should the United States Recognize it as an Independent State' (1986) 4 *Boston University International Law Journal* 423.

Pandjaitan LB, 'Statement to The United Nations Ocean Conference to Support the Implementation of Sustainable Development Goal 14' (6 June 2017).

Papadakis N, *The International Legal Regime of Artificial Islands* (Sijthoff 1977).

Papanicolopulu I, 'The Mediterranean Sea' in Rothwell DR et al (eds), *The Oxford Handbook of the Law of the Sea* (Oxford University Press 2015) 604.

Parsons M, *The Falklands War* (Sutton 2000).

Pedersen T, 'The Svalbard Continental Shelf Controversy: Legal Disputes and Political Rivalries' (2006) 37 *Ocean Development and International Law* 339.

Perl R, *The Falkland Islands Dispute in International Law and Politics: A Documentary Sourcebook* (Oceana 1983).

Permanent Mission of the Republic of the Philippines to the United Nations 'Note Verbale No. 11-00494' (5 April 2011).

Permanent Mission of the Socialist Republic of Viet Nam to the United Nations 'Note Verbale No. 77/HC-2011' (3 May 2011).

Pharand D, 'The Arctic Waters and the Northwest Passage: A Final Revisit' (2007) 38 *Ocean Development and International Law* 3.

—— *Canada's Arctic Waters in International Law* (Cambridge University Press 1988).

Piguet E, 'Climatic Statelessness: Risk Assessment and Policy Options' (2019) 45(4) *Population and Development Review* 865.

Plank S et al, 'The Short Life of the Volcanic Island New Late'iki (Tonga) Analyzed by Multi-sensor Remote Sensing Data' (2020) 10 *Scientific Reports* 22293.

Pomerance M, *Self-Determination in Law and Practice: The New Doctrine in the United Nations* (Martinus Nijhoff 1982).

Prescott JRV, 'Straight and Archipelagic Baselines' in Blake G (ed), *Maritime Boundaries and Ocean Resources* (Croom Helm 1987).

Prescott V and Schofield C, *The Maritime Political Boundaries of the World* (2nd edn, Martinus Nijhoff 2005).

Prescott V and Triggs G, *International Frontiers and Boundaries* (Martinus Nijhoff 2008).

President of the United States of America, *Policy of the United States with respect to the Natural Resources of the Subsoil and Seabed of the Continental Shelf, US Presidential Proclamation No 2667* (28 September 1945).

Principe Gamboa F and Teodoro J, 'The role of archipelagic sea lanes in the Philippines' national security' (*Philippine Strategic Forum*, 30 November 2020).

Proelss A, 'Article 60 Artificial Islands, installations and structures in the exclusive economic zone' in Proelss A (ed), *United Nations Convention on the Law of the Sea: A Commentary* (CH Beck 2017) 464.

Purcell, K, *Geographical Change and the Law of the Sea* (Oxford University Press 2019).

Quillen AB, 'The "Kuril Islands" or the "Northern Territories": Who Owns Them? – Island Territorial Dispute Continues to Hinder Relations between Russia and Japan' (1993) 18 *North Carolina Journal of International Law and Commercial Regulation* 633.

Rajan HP, 'The Legal Regime of Archipelagos' (1986) 29 *German Yearbook of International Law* 137.

Ratner SR, 'Drawing a Better Line: *UTI Possidetis* and the Borders of New States' (1996) 90 *American Journal of International Law* 590.

Rayfuse R, 'International Law and Disappearing States – Maritime Zones and the Criteria for Statehood' (2011) 41 *Environmental Policy and Law* 281.

—— 'The United Nations Agreement on Straddling and Highly Migratory Fish Stocks as an Objective Regime: A Case of Wishful Thinking' (1999) 20 *Australian Year Book of International Law* 253.

Regan AJ, 'Causes and Courses of the Bougainville Conflict' (1998) 33 *Journal of Pacific History* 269.

Reisman WM and Westerman GS, *Straight Baselines in International Maritime Boundary Delimitation* (MacMillan 1992).

Report of the International Committee of Jurists entrusted by the Council of the League of Nations with the task of giving an advisory opinion upon the legal aspects of the Aaland Islands question [October 1920] *League of Nations Official Journal* 3.

Report of Second Committee: Territorial Sea' (Hague Conference, 10 April 1930) reproduced in S Nandan S and Rosenne S (eds), *United Nations Convention on the Law of the Sea: A Commentary* III (Martinus Nijhoff 1995).

Report of the Study Group of the International Law Commission, 'Fragmentation of International Law: Difficulties arising from the Diversification and Expansion of International Law' 58th Sess (1 May – 9 June, 3 July – 11 August 2006) UN Doc A/CN.4/L.682.

Reynolds J, 'Decolonising the Chagos Islands?' [2018–19] *Nigerian Yearbook of International Law* 455.

Rich TS, 'Does It Matter If Taiwan Loses Formal Recognition?' (*Australian Outlook*, 9 October 2019).

Riding T, 'Making Bombay Island: land reclamation and geographical conceptions of Bombay, 1661–1728' (2018) 59 *Journal of Historical Geography* 27.

Roach JA, 'Artificial islands in the South China Sea: the legal regime and implications of the Award' in Jayakumar S et al (eds), *The South China Sea Arbitration: The Legal Dimension* (Edward Elgar 2018) 205.

—— 'Offshore Archipelagos Enclosed by Straight Baselines: an Excessive Claim?' (2018) 49 *Ocean Development and International Law* 176.

Roach JA and Smith RW, *Excessive Maritime Claims* (3rd edn, Martinus Nijhoff 2012).

Rodríguez-Santiago E, 'The Evolution of Self-Determination of Peoples in International Law' in Tesón FR (ed), *The Theory of Self-Determination* (Cambridge University Press 2016) 201.

Rossi CR, 'A Unique International Problem: The Svalbard Treaty, Equal Enjoyment, and Terra Nullius: Lessons of Territorial Temptation from History' (2015) 15 *Washington University Global Studies Law Review* 93.

Rothwell DR, 'Arctic sovereignty and its legal significance for Canada' in Jensen LC and Hønneland G (eds), *Handbook of the Politics of the Arctic* (Edward Elgar 2015) 247.

—— 'The Indonesian Straits Incident: Transit or Archipelagic Sea Lanes Passage?' (1990) 14 *Marine Policy* 491.

—— *The Polar Regions and the Development of International Law* (Cambridge University Press 1996).

Rothwell DR and Stephens T, *The International Law of the Sea* (2nd edn, Bloomsbury 2016).

Rottman GL, *World War II Pacific island guide: a geo-military study* (Greenwood Press 2001).

Royle S and Brinklow L, 'Definitions and Typologies' in Baldacchino, G (ed), *The Routledge International Handbook of Island Studies: A World of Islands* (Routledge 2018) 3.

Ruffatto P, 'U.S. Action in Micronesia as a Norm of Customary International Law: The Effectuation of the Right to Self-Determination for Guam and Other Non-Self-Governing Territories' (1993) 2 *Pacific Rim Law and Policy Journal* 377.

Rumpf C, 'Comments on the Legal Status of Cyprus: Issues of Conflict and their Causes' in Giegerich T (ed), *The EU Accession of Cyprus-Key to the Political and Legal Solution of an 'Insoluble' Ethnic Conflict?* (Nomos 2005).

Ryngaert C, 'Territory in the Law of Jurisdiction: Imagine Alternatives' [2016] *Netherlands Yearbook of International Law* 49.

Sankaran V, 'First recorded rainfall on Greenland's ice sheet peak leads to widespread melt' *Independent* (21 August 2021).

Saunders I, 'The limits of the natural state doctrine: Rocks, islands, and artificial islands in a changing world' in Rothwell DR and Letts D (eds), *Law of the Sea in South East Asia: Environmental, Navigational and Security Challenges* (Routledge 2020) 118.

—— 'The South China Sea Award, Artificial Islands and Territory' (2016) 34 *Australian Year Book of International Law* 31.
Schmidtke RC, 'Artificial Islands of the Future: The Seasteading Movement and the International Legal Regimes Governing Seasteads in EEZs and on the High Seas' (2019) 21 *Asian-Pacific Law & Policy Journal* 1.
Schofield C, 'An incomplete maritime map: progress and challenges in the delimitation of maritime boundaries in South East Asia' in Rothwell DR and Letts D (eds), *Law of the Sea in South East Asia: Environmental, Navigational and Security Challenges* (Routledge 2020) 33.
—— 'Departures from the Coast: Trends in the Application of Territorial Sea Baselines under the Law of the Sea Convention' (2012) 27 *International Journal of Marine and Coastal Law* 723.
—— *The Regime of Islands Reframed: Developments in the Definition of Islands under the International Law of the Sea* (Brill 2019).
—— 'The Trouble with Islands: The Definition and Role of Islands and Rocks in Maritime Boundary Delimitation' in Van Dyke, JM and Hong, S-Y (eds), *Maritime boundary disputes, settlement processes, and the law of the sea* (Martinus Nijhoff 2009) 19.
Schofield C and Freestone D, 'Islands Awash Amidst Rising Seas: Sea Level Rise and Insular Status under the Law of the Sea' (2019) 34 *International Journal of Marine and Coastal Law* 391.
Schrijver NJ and Prislan V, 'Cases Concerning Sovereignty over Islands before the International Court of Justice and the Dokdo/Takeshima Issue' (2015) 46 *Ocean Development and International Law* 281.
Scott K, 'Climate change and the law of the sea in the Asia Pacific' in Rothwell DR and Letts D (eds), *Law of the Sea in South East Asia: Environmental, Navigational and Security Challenges* (Routledge 2020) 94.
Scovazzi T, 'Bays and Deeply Indented Coastlines: The Practice of South American States' (1995) 26(2) *Ocean Development and International Law* 161.
Seatrade Maritime News, 'Mumbai Port Trust to Build a new Container Terminal; Permission Granted by Maharashtra Coastal Zone Management' (11 May 2021) www.seatrade-maritime.com/ports-logistics/mumbai-port-build-new-container-terminal.
Selden M, 'Japanese territorial disputes with Korea and China: Small islets, enduring conflicts' in Kingston J (ed), *Critical Issues in Contemporary Japan* (2nd edn, Routledge 2019).
Sengupta D, Chen R, and Meadows ME, 'Building beyond land: An overview of coastal land reclamation in 16 global megacities' (2018) 90 *Applied Geography* 229.
Serdy A, 'Bringing Taiwan into the International Fisheries Fold: The Legal Personality of a Fishing Entity' (2005) 75 *British Yearbook of International Law* 183.
Shaw MN, *International Law* (8th edn, Cambridge University Press 2017).
—— *Title to Territory in Africa: International Legal Issues* (Oxford University Press 1985.
Shearer IA, *Starke's International Law* (11th edn Butterworths 1994).
Silverstein AL, 'Okinotorishima: Artificial Preservation of a Speck of Sovereignty' (1990) 16 *Brooklyn Journal of International Law* 409.
Simma B, 'Self-contained regimes' (1985) 16 *Netherlands Yearbook of International Law* 111.
—— 'The Antarctic Treaty as a Treaty Providing for an Objective Regime' (1986) 19 *Cornell International Law Journal* 189.
Simpson GJ, 'Judging the East Timor Dispute: Self-Determination at the International Court of Justice' (1994) 17 *Hastings International and Comparative Law Review* 323.
Slaughter A, Tulumello A and Wood S, 'International Law and International Relations Theory: A New Generation of Interdisciplinary Scholarship' (1998) 92 *American Journal of International Law* 367.
Smith JM, 'UNCLOS: China, India, and the United States Navigate an Unsettled Regime' (30 April 2021) 3608 *Asian Studies Center Backgrounder* 13.
Smith-Cannoy HM and Smith CA, 'Human Trafficking and International Cheap Talk: The Dutch Government and the Island Territories' (2012) 11 *Journal of Human Rights* 51.
Song L, 'The Curious History of the Minerva Reefs: Tracing the Origin of Tongan and Fijian Claims Over the Minerva Reefs' (2019) 54 *The Journal of Pacific History* 417.

Song YH, 'Okinotorishima: A "Rock" or an "Island"? Recent Maritime Boundary Controversy between Japan and Taiwan/China,' in Hong SY and van Dyke JM (eds), *Maritime Boundary Disputes, Settlement Processes, and the Law of the Sea* (Brill 2009) 145.

Soons AHA, 'Artificial Islands and Installations in International Law' (Occasional Paper No 22, Law of the Sea Institute, University of Rhode Island 1974).

—— 'The Effects of a Rising Sea Level on Maritime Limits and Boundaries' (1990) 37 *Netherlands International Law Review* 207.

Sovacool BK, 'Perceptions of climate change risks and resilient island planning in the Maldives' (2012) 17 *Mitigation and Adaptation Strategies for Climate Change* 731.

Special Committee on Decolonization (UN), 'Special Committee on Decolonization Approves Text Calling upon United States to Promote Puerto Rico's Self-Determination, Eventual Independence' (18 June 2021) UN Doc GA/COL/3346.

Special Committee on the Situation with regard to the Implementation of the Declaration on the Granting of Independence to Colonial Countries and Peoples, 'New Caledonia: Working paper prepared by the Secretariat' (22 February 2017) UN Doc A/AC.109/2017/11.

Sproat DK and Gross AF, 'The NW. Hawaiian Islands Marine National Monument' (Spring 2008) 22 *Natural Resources & Environment* 57.

Starke JG, 'The Acquisition of Title to Territory by Newly Emerged States' (1965–1966) 41 *British Yearbook of International Law* 411.

State Services in New Caledonia, 'Speech proclaiming the results of the consultation of October 4, 2020' (5 October 2020).

Statement By The Honourable Bruce Bilimon, Minister of Health and Human Services, The Republic of the Marshall Islands on Behalf of Pacific SIDS (COP26, Glasgow, United Kingdom 9 November 2021).

Steinsson S, 'Do liberal ties pacify? A study of the Cod Wars' (2018) 53 *Cooperation and Conflict* 339.

Stephen J and Menon A, 'Fluid territories: Rethinking state territorialisation in Palk Bay, South Asia' (2016) 70 *Norsk Geografisk Tidsskrift – Norwegian Journal of Geography* 263.

Stephens T, 'The Collateral Damage from China's 'Great Wall of Sand': The Environmental Dimensions of the *South China Sea Case*' (2016) 34 *Australian Year Book of International Law* 41.

—— 'Warming Waters and Souring Seas: Climate Change and Ocean Acidification' in Rothwell D et al (eds), *The Oxford Handbook of the Law of the Sea* (Oxford University Press 2015) 777.

Stevenson C, 'Hans Off: The Struggle for Hans Island and the Potential Ramifications for International Border Dispute Resolution' (2007) 30 *Boston College International and Comparative Law Review* 263.

Stolper TE, *China, Taiwan, and the offshore islands* (Sharpe 1985).

Storey IJ, 'Creeping Assertiveness: China, the Philippines and the South China Sea Dispute' (1999) 29 *Contemporary Southeast Asia* 95.

Storlazzi C, 'Most atolls will be uninhabitable by the mid-21st century because of sea-level rise exacerbating wave-driven flooding' (2018) 4 *Science Advances* eaap9741.

Stratford E (ed), *Island Geographies: Essays and Conversations* (Routledge 2017).

Subramanian S, 'How Singapore Is Creating More Land for Itself', *The New York Times* (20 April 2017), www.nytimes.com/2017/04/20/magazine/how-singapore-is-creating-more-land-for-itself.html.

Summers J, *Peoples and International Law: How Nationalism and Self-Determination Shape a Contemporary Law of Nations* (Martinus Nijhoff 2007).

Sweeney FS, 'Rocks v. Islands: Natural Tensions over Artificial Features in the South China Sea' (2017) 31 *Temple International & Comparative Law Journal* 599.

Syatauw JJG, *Some Newly Established Asian States and the Development of International Law* (Martinus Nijhoff 1961).

Symmons CR, *The Maritime Zones of Islands in International Law* (Martinus Nijhoff 1979).

—— 'Ireland and the Rockall Dispute: An Analysis of Recent Developments' (Spring 1998) *IBRU Boundary and Security Bulletin* 78.

—— *Historic waters and historic rights in the law of the sea: a modern reappraisal* (2nd edn Brill Nijhoff 2019).

Talmon S, 'Part VIII Regime of Islands', in Proelss A (ed), *United Nations Convention on the Law of the Sea: A Commentary* (CH Beck 2017) 858.
Tan ATH, *Security Perspectives of the Malay Archipelago* (Edward Elgar 2004).
Tanaka Y, *Predictability and Flexibility in the Law of Maritime Delimitation* (2nd edn, Hart 2019).
—— *The International Law of the Sea* (3rd edn, Cambridge University Press 2019).
—— *The South China Sea Arbitration: Toward an International Legal Order in the Oceans* (Hart Publishing 2019).
Tangsubkul P and Dzurek DJ, 'The Emerging Concept of Midocean Archipelagos' (1982) 3 *Ocean Yearbook* 386.
Tebaldi C et al, 'Extreme sea levels at different global warming levels' (2021) 11 *Nature Climate Change* 746.
The Economist, 'Moving Story: Pacific countries face more complex problems than sinking' (7 August 2021) www.economist.com/asia/2021/08/07/pacific-countries-face-more-complex-problems-than-sinking.
—— 'Pirates in South-East Asia: Malacca buccaneers' (27 June 2015) www.economist.com/asia/2015/06/25/malacca-buccaneers.
The State Council (PRC), 'China Adheres to the Position of Settling Through Negotiation the Relevant Disputes Between China and the Philippines in the South China Sea' (13 July 2016) english.www.gov.cn/state_council/ministries/2016/07/13/content_281475392503075.htm.
Tomuschat C (ed), *Modern Law of Self-Determination* (Martinus Nijhoff 1993).
Townend A, 'Tokelau's 2006 Referendum on Self-Government' (2007) 5 *New Zealand Journal of Public and International Law* 12.
Treves T, 'Historical Development of the Law of the Sea' in DR Rothwell et al (eds), *Oxford Handbook of the Law of the Sea* (Oxford University Press 2015) 1.
Trümpler K, 'Article 6 Reefs' in Proelss A (ed), *United Nations Convention on the Law of the Sea: A Commentary* (CH Beck/Hart/Nomos 2017) 60.
—— 'Article 7 Straight Baselines' in Proelss A (ed), *United Nations Convention on the Law of the Sea: A Commentary* (CH Beck 2017) 65.
Tsamenyi M (ed), *Evaluation of the implications of the United Nations Convention on the Law of the Sea for SPREP activities* (South Pacific Regional Environment Programme 1996).
Ulfstein G, *The Svalbard Treaty: From Terra Nullius to Norwegian Sovereignty* (Scandinavian University Press 1995).
United Nations, 'Deposit by the Republic of Indonesia of a list of geographical coordinates of points, pursuant to article 47, paragraph 9, of the Convention' (25 March 2009) UN Doc MZN67.2009.
—— 'Deposit by the Republic of the Philippines of a list of geographical coordinates of points, pursuant to article 47, paragraph 9, of the Convention' (21 April 2009) UN Doc MZN 69.2009.
—— 'Growth in United Nations Membership' (21 May 2021) www.un.org/en/about-us/growth-in-un-membership.
—— 'Juridical Regime of Historic Waters, Including Historic Bays' 143 (9 March 1962) UN Doc A/CN.4/.
—— *The Law of the Sea: Current Developments and State Practice* (1987).
—— 'The United Nations and Decolonization: Non-Self-Governing Territories'.
—— 'The United Nations and Decolonization: Non-Self-Governing Territories – Tokelau' www.un.org/dppa/decolonization/en/nsgt/tokelau.
—— 'The United Nations and Decolonization: Special Committee on Decolonization'.
UNDP Indonesia, 'Archipelagic and island states ministers reach a milestone with declaration on sustainable ocean, climate actions' (Press Release, 1 November 2018).
UNESCO, 'Rock Islands Southern Lagoon' (*World Heritage List*).
United Nations Conference on Environment and Development, 'Agenda 21, Rio Declaration' (United Nations 1992).
United Nations Conference on the Law of the Sea (Geneva, 24 February–27 April 1958) Volume IV: Second Committee (High Seas: General Regime).

United Nations Conference on the Law of the Sea, 'Certain Legal Aspects Concerning the Delimitation of the Territorial Waters of Archipelagos' vol 1 (Preparatory Document No 15, 27 November 1957) UN Doc. A/CONF.13/18, 290.

United Nations Division for Ocean Affairs and Law of the Sea 'Suspension of innocent passage' www.un.org/depts/los/convention_agreements/innocent_passages_suspension.htm#:~:text=Article%2025%2C%20paragraph%203%2C%20of,foreign%20ships%20if%20such%20suspension.

—— 'China – Communication received with respect to the submission of Malaysia, Commission on the Limits of Continental Shelf, CML/14/2019', 12 December 2019.

—— Office of Legal Affairs (UN) (2014) *Law of the Sea Bulletin* No 83.

United Nations Economic and Social Council Official Records, *The Principle of Self-Determination in Relation to Chapters XI, XIII and XIII of the Charter of the United Nations* (16 April 1952) 8th session UN Doc E/CN.4/662.

United Nations General Assembly Resolution 1514 (VX) (14 December 1960) UN Doc A/RES/1514(XV).

United Nations General Assembly, 'Global Compact for Safe, Orderly and Regular Migration' UNGA Res 73/195 (19 December 2018) A/RES/73/195.

United Nations Mission to Tokelau, *Report of the United Nations Mission to observe the October 2007 referendum on self-determination of Tokelau* (3 December 2007) UN Doc A/AC.109/2007/19.

United Nations Office for Ocean Affairs and the Law of the Sea, *Baselines: An Examination of the Relevant Provisions of the United Nations Convention on the Law of the Sea* (UN 1989).

—— *Baselines: An Examination of the Relevant Provisions of the United Nations Convention on the Law of the Sea* (United Nations 1989).

—— *The Law of the Sea: Archipelagic States* (United Nations 1990).

United Nations Office for the Coordination of Humanitarian Affairs, 'Hurricane Season 2017' www.unocha.org/hurricane-season-2017.

United States of America, 'Comments of the United States Regarding Sea-Level Rise in Relation to the Law of the Sea' (*International Law Commission*, 14 February 2020).

United States Geological Survey, 'EarthView – Expansion at the Port of Rotterdam', 22 December 2016, www.usgs.gov/news/earthview-expansion-port-rotterdam.

UN-OHRLLS (UN), 'State of the Least Developed Countries 2021. Building back better in response to COVID-19'.

Valencia MJ and Van Dyke JM, 'Vietnam's National Interests and the Law of the Sea' (1994) 25 *Ocean Development and International Law* 217.

Van Dyke JM, 'Addressing and Resolving the Dokdo Matter' in Lee S and Lee HE (eds), *Dokdo: Historical Appraisal and International Justice* (Martinus Nijhoff 2011) 29.

—— 'Aegean Sea' in Wolfrum R (ed), *Max Planck Encyclopedia of International Law* (online edn, Oxford University Press 2010).

—— 'An Analysis of the Aegean Disputes under International Law' (2005) 36 *Ocean Development and International Law* 63.

—— 'Legal Issues Related to Sovereignty over Dokdo and Its Maritime Boundary' (2007) 38 *Ocean Development and International Law* 157.

Van Dyke JM, Di Amore-Siah C and Berkley-Coats GW, "Self-Determination for Non Self-Governing Peoples and for Indigenous Peoples: The Cases of Guam and Hawai'i' (1996) 18 *University of Hawai'i Law Review* 623.

Vásquez I and Porčnik T, *Human Freedom Index* (Cato Institute 2018).

Vaughan A, 'Hurricane Ida was almost certainly made worse by climate change' *New Scientist* (31 August 2021).

Vine D, *Island of Shame: The Secret History of the U.S. Military Base on Diego Garcia* (Princeton University Press 2011).

Wainwright E, 'Responding to state failure – the case of Australia and Solomon Islands' (2003) 57 *Australian Journal of International Affairs* 485.

Waldock CHM, 'Disputed Sovereignty in the Falkland Islands Dependencies' (1948) 25 *British Year Book of International Law* 311.

Walker CW, 'Jurisdictional Problems Created by Artificial Islands' (1973) 10 *San Diego Law Review* 638.
Walker GK (ed), *Definitions for the Law of the Sea: Terms Not Defined by the 1982 Convention* (Martinus Nijhoff 2012).
Weissman R, '"Development" and the Denial of Human Rights in Ramos's Philippines' (1994) 7 *Harvard Human Rights Journal* 251.
West JF, *Faroe: The Emergence of a Nation* (C Hurst 1972).
Westerman GS, *The Juridical Bay* (Oxford University Press 1987) 79.
Whiteman MM, *Digest of International Law*, vol 4 (United States Department of State 1965).
Whiting N, 'Bougainville votes overwhelmingly for independence from Papua New Guinea in landmark referendum', *ABC News* (online, 11 December 2019).
Whittemore Boggs S, 'Delimitation of Seaward Areas under National Jurisdiction' (1951) 45 *American Journal of International Law* 240.
—— 'Delimitation of the Territorial Sea' (1930) 24 *American Journal of International Law* 541.
Whomersley C, 'Offshore Archipelagos Enclosed By Straight Baselines: A Reply to J. Ashley Roach' (2018) 49 *Ocean Development and International Law* 203.
Wiegand KE, 'Bahrain, Qatar, and the Hawar Islands: Resolution of a Gulf Territorial Dispute' (2012) 66 *The Middle East Journal* 78.
—— 'The South Korean–Japanese security relationship and the Dokdo/Takeshima islets dispute' (2015) 28 *The Pacific Review* 347.
Wisnomoerti N, 'Indonesia and the Law of the Sea' in Park C-H and Park JK (eds), *The Law of the Sea: Problems from the East Asian Perspective* (Law of the Sea Institute 1987).
Witular RA, 'Java Sea, Lombok Strait Becoming More Dangerous, Government Says', *The Jakarta Post* (3 August 2005).
Wong, 'Sovereignty Sunk? The Position of "Sinking States" at International Law' (2013) 14 *Melbourne Journal of International Law* 1.
Wouters J and Verhoeven S, 'Prescription' in Wolfrum R (ed), *Max Planck Encyclopedia of International Law* (online edn, Oxford University Press 2008).
Xue G, 'How Much Can a Rock Get? – A Reflection from the Okinotorishima Rocks' (2011) 13 *China Oceans Law Review* 1.
Young MA, 'Introduction: The Productive Friction between Regimes' in Young MA (ed), *Regime Interaction in International Law: Facing Fragmentation* (Cambridge University Press 2012) 1.
Zha D and Valencia MJ, 'Mischief Reef: Geopolitics and implications' (2001) 31 *Journal of Contemporary Asia* 86.
Zhang J, Su F, and Ding Z, 'Sea Reclamation Status of Countries around the South China Sea from 1975 to 2010' (2017) 9 *Sustainability* 878.
Zinberg Y, 'Kuril Islands' in Wolfrum R (ed) *Max Planck Encyclopedia of International Law* (online edn, Oxford University Press 2011).

INDEX

Aaland Islands, 1, 78–9, 99, 142, 145, 208, 225, 237
Alexander, LM, 144
American Institute of International Law, 103
Anguilla, 91, 93, 209, 262, 264
annexation, 60
Antigua and Barbuda, 17, 116, 127, 132, 235, 245–6, 264
Archipelagic and Islands States Forum, 236
archipelagic sea lanes passage (ASLP):
  archipelagic states' obligations, 137–8
  designation of sea lanes, 135–6, 138–40
  nature of right, 125, 133
  normal mode, 133–4
  overview, 133–40
  state practice, 138–40
  users' obligations, 136–7
  within archipelagic sea lanes, 134–5
archipelagic states
  see also dependent archipelagos
  baselines, 120–4, 247
  early legal developments, 103–4
  entitlements, 258
    archipelagic waters, 124–6
    baselines, 120–4, 247
    maritime zones, 124–6
    navigation and overflight, 130–40
    overview, 120–40
    state practice, 126–30
  forms, 102
  geography, 7
  Indonesian claims, 105–8
  international law, 101–3
  list, 116–18
  LOSC, 112–20, 162
    definition, 112–18
    entitlements, 120–40
    navigation and overflight, 130–40
    recognition, 119–20
    sea levels and, 245–6
  navigation rights
    ASLP, 125, 133–40
    innocent passage, 130–3
    overview, 130–40
  overview, 101–41
  Philippines claims, 105–6, 108–10
  sea-levels, 245–6
  UNCLOS I, 104–5, 107
  UNCLOS III, 106, 110–12
Argentina:
  bays, 175–6
  continental shelf, 182–3
  Malvinas *see* Falklands Islands
artificial islands:
  continental shelf and, 181
  definition, 19–37
  entitlements, 163
  exclusive economic zones, 23–9
  land reclamation, 33–5, 36, 179
  legal history, 21–2
  LOSC, 23–9, 36, 37
  overview, 19–37
  sea-levels (SLR), 242–3, 246
  South China Sea, 19, 27–9, 36
  Spratly Islands, 30–2, 35
  state practice
    contemporary practice, 29–33
    early practice, 22–3
  territorial sea and, 179
Aruba, 76, 222, 265
ASEAN, 73
Asia Maritime Transparency Initiative, 29–30
Association of Small Islands States (AOSIS), 2, 235, 240, 251, 252, 260
Australia:
  archipelagic states and, 102, 139
    Indonesia, 138
    LOSC negotiations, 107
    Philippines, 110, 129
  boundaries, 195, 205, 211, 212–13, 214–15
  continental shelf, 181, 182
  dependent archipelagos, 146
  EEZs, 185, 186
  Great Barrier Reef, 9
  human rights, 219
  island territories, 14, 18, 43, 58, 77
    acquisition, 61
    archipelagic states, 102

League of Nations mandates, 78
sea levels, 260
status, 92, 102
trust territories, 80
PNG and, 231
status, 41
Tasmania, 77, 87, 182
territorial sea, 179
aviation, 126, 130–40
Azores, 146, 176

Bahamas, 111, 112, 116, 123, 132, 235, 262, 267
Bahrain:
archipelagic state, 119–20, 120–1
baselines, 148, 150, 152, 168–9
boundaries, 199–200, 215
island territories, 58
Qatar v Bahrain, 50, 168–9, 199–200, 215
Bangladesh, 58, 203–4, 215
Barbados, 195, 200, 235, 262
baselines:
archipelagic states, 120–4, 247
dependent archipelagos, 146–53
entitlements, 163–70
Fisheries Case, 164–6
LOSC, 164–70
sea levels and, 247
straight baselines, 166–8
sea-level rise and, 247
straight baselines, 166–70
case law, 168–70
LOSC Article 7, 166–8
bays:
historic bays, 171, 176–8
juridical bays, 175–6
LOSC, 174–8
Belgium, 158
Belize, 235
Bermuda, 91, 93, 262
Borneo, 41, 50, 85, 102, 109, 113, 264, 265, 266
Bougainville, 43, 212, 231–2, 246, 259
boundaries:
case law, 195–204
Anglo-French Arbitration, 196, 214, 215
Bangladesh v India, 204
Bangladesh v Myanmar, 203–4, 215
Black Sea, 201–2, 215
Cameroon v Nigeria, 200
Caribbean Sea, 200
Eritrea v Yemen, 198–9
Jan Mayen, 197–8, 215
Nicaragua v Columbia, 202–3, 215
Nicaragua v Honduras, 201, 215
Qatar v Bahrain, 199–200, 215
St Pierre and Miquelon, 196–7, 215
delimitation, 190–5
case law, 195–204
continental shelf, 190, 192
EEZs, 192
equidistance, 193–4
equitable solution, 193
impact of islands on, 213–15
median lines, 193–4
methodology, 191–2
proportionality, 192, 199
relevant/special circumstances, 194–5
single maritime boundaries, 192
territorial sea, 190, 191
LOSC, 189–91, 194–5
Article 121, 189–90, 194
overview, 188–216
sea-level rise and, 246–9
state practice, 204–13, 248
Africa, 210–11
Arctic Ocean, 206–7
Caribbean, 209–10
Indian Ocean, 211–12
Northern Europe, 207–9
Pacific Ocean, 212–13
Bowett, D, 1
British Antartic Territory (BAT), 94
British Indian Ocean Territory, 93, 94, 228
British Solomon Islands, 262
British Virgin Islands, 91, 93, 209, 220, 262, 264
Brunei, 41, 85, 113, 123, 262
Bulgaria, 129
Burke, WT, 22

Cameroon, 194, 200
Canada:
boundaries, 196–7, 206–7
Canadian Arctic Achipelago, 58, 102, 154–5, 173
EEZs, 186
Hans Island (Tartupaluk) dispute, 69–70
historic waters, 173
human rights, 219
island territories, 77, 87, 102, 114
Northwest Passage, 163, 173
Canary Islands, 159–60
Cape Verde Archipelago, 112, 115, 116, 128, 132, 235, 262
CARICOM, 236–7

Cayman Islands, 91, 93, 209–10, 220, 263
cession, 60–1, 66
Chagos Archipelago:
human rights, 226, 237
ICJ case, 2, 229, 259
Mauritius/UK dispute, 39, 66–7, 228–9
recognition, 119
self-determination, 228–9, 238, 259
significance, 4
Channel Islands, 58, 96–7, 175, 196, 200, 214, 222
Chile: Pacific Coast, 155
China:
archipelagic baselines and, 149
archipelagic state status, 120
baselines, 149, 167
continental shelf, 183
island territories, 3, 77
dependent archipelagos, 156–7
maritime disputes, 17
Senkaku/Diaoyu Islands, 72
South China Sea see South China Sea
Svalbard and, 99
Taiwan and, 39, 42, 97
United States and, 156, 167
Chinese Society of International Law, 156–7
Churchill, R, 98–9
climate change
see also sea-level rise
COP26 climate summit, 2, 236
impact, 225, 260–1
international treaties, 239
new issue, 218
science, 240–2
small islands and, 237
Cocos (Keeling Islands), 61, 211, 263
Colombia:
boundaries, 202–3
ICJ case, 13, 18
Nicaragua v Colombia, 53–4, 202–3
colonialism, 76, 83, 226–7
see also decolonisation
Commission on the Limits of the Continental Shelf (CLCS), 18, 74, 156, 163, 181–3, 207
Comoros, 116, 132, 224, 235, 263, 265
Connell, J, 224
contiguous zones:
archipelagic states, 124
entitlements, 180
UNCLOS Article 121, 11, 180
continental shelf:
archipelagic states, 124
artificial islands, 26–7
boundaries, 190, 192
entitlements, 163, 180–3
sea levels and, 248
state practice, 188–9
UNCLOS Article 121, 11
Convention on the Continental Shelf (1958), 22, 23, 180–1, 189
Convention on the Rights of the Child (CRC), 220–1
Convention on the Territorial Sea and Contiguous Zone (1958), 10, 22, 105, 108, 121, 147, 164, 166
Cook, James, 230
Cook Islands, 76–7, 88, 89–90, 100, 221, 223, 234, 235, 263
Corfu, 1
Costa Rica, 176
COVID-19, 231, 236, 237, 238
Crawford, James, 55, 63, 81–2, 83, 88, 140, 226, 227, 244
Crete, 65, 77
Cuba:
archipelagic baselines, 149, 152
boundaries, 215
geography, 102
human rights, 224
status, 79, 122, 235
United States and, 167
Curaçao, 265
customary international law, 13, 34, 101, 110, 153–4, 156, 161, 162, 176, 188, 190
Cyprus, 67, 87, 94, 164, 178, 181, 222, 263

decolonisation, 39, 40, 59, 76, 85, 96, 100, 101, 229, 259
definition of islands:
artificial islands, 19–37
associated maritime features, 8–9
forms, 3
geography, 5–9
historical diplomacy, 9–10
international case law, 12–16
Annex VII arbitral tribunals, 15–16
ICJ, 12–14
ITLOS, 14–15
juridical classification, 9–18
LOSC Article 121, 5, 10–12, 242, 260
rocks, 8

South China Sea, 6, 15–16, 18, 243, 254, 257–8
state practice, 16–18
types, 7–8
Denarau Declaration on Human Rights (2015), 237
Denmark:
artificial islands, 32
Faroe Islands *see* Faroe Islands
Greenland *see* Greenland
Hans Island (Tartupaluk) dispute, 69–70
human rights: territorial scope, 220–1
island territories, 90–1
cession, 61
LOSC negotiations, 105
maritime boundaries, 34, 206–7, 208–9
Jan Mayen, 197–8
WWII German occupation, 232
dependent archipelagos:
baselines, 146–53, 158
archipelagic baselines, 152–3
coastal archipelagos, 149–51
flexible straight lines, 153
fringe of islands, 147–9
mid-ocean archipelagos, 151–2
state practice, 154–60
straight baselines, 146–52
entitlements, 153–4
examples, 142
forms, 145–6
geographical definition, 143–4
legal definition, 144–5
LOSC, 142–3, 160–1
baselines, 146–53, 158
definition, 144–5
entitlements, 153–4
overview, 142–61
political status, 145
state practice, 154–60, 161
Canada (Arctic), 154–5
Chile (Pacific Coast), 155
Myanmar (Myeik Kyunzu), 158
Norway (Svalbard), 98–9, 101, 142, 158–9
South China Sea, 156–7
Spain (Canary Islands), 159–60
Vietnam (Tho Chu Archipelago), 160
Diego Garcia, 66, 94, 228, 264n4
Djibouti, 149, 167
Dominica, 235, 263
Dominican Republic, 41, 79, 113, 116, 119, 128, 132, 141, 177, 224, 235
Dutch East India Company (VOC), 38, 44–5
East Timor, 43, 60, 83, 86, 102, 122, 226, 227
see also Timor Leste
economic life of their own: meaning, 16
Ecuador, 149, 157–8, 167
Egypt, 61
El Salvador: ***Land, Island and Maritime Frontier***, 48–9, 176
entitlements:
baselines *see* baselines
bays *see* bays
contiguous zone *see* contiguous zones
continental shelf *see* continental shelf
EEZs *see* exclusive economic zones
historic waters *see* historic waters
internal waters *see* internal waters
LOSC, 162–3
overview, 162–87
sea-level rise and, 246–9
territorial sea *see* territorial sea
environmental rights, 218, 224
Equatorial Guinea, 200, 210, 211, 215
Eritrea, 49–50, 56, 142, 168, 193, 198–9
Estonia, 168, 207–8, 215
European Convention on Human Rights (ECHR), 221–2
European Union, 158
Evensen, Jen, 104–5
exclusive economic zones (EEZs):
archipelagic states, 124
artificial islands, 23–9
boundaries, 190, 192
entitlements, 163, 183–6
historic waters, 172
importance, 183–4
LOSC, 11, 162
preferential rights, 184
sea levels and, 248
UNCLOS Article 121, 11

Falklands Islands:
1982 war, 39, 60, 69
Argentine/UK dispute, 68–9
continental shelf, 182–3
dependent archipelago, 145
significance, 4
status, 68, 76, 91, 92, 263
Faroe Islands:
boundaries, 207, 208–9, 215
dependent archipelago, 145, 157
human rights, 220
integration, 90–1
self-determination, 232–4

Ferse, SCA, 29
Fiji, 41, 110, 111, 112, 115, 127, 223, 235, 237, 250, 263
Finland:
Aaland Islands, 1, 79, 99, 142, 145
boundaries, 208, 215
Fitzmaurice, Gerald, 105
food security, 218, 224, 225
France:
boundaries
Anglo-French Arbitration, 196, 200, 214
Australia, 205
Indian Ocean, 211–12
St Pierre and Miquelon, 196–7, 215
Clipperton Island, 45–6
colonialism, 66, 68, 86, 98
human rights: territorial scope, 222
island territories, 3, 14, 17–18, 58, 71–2, 227
archipelagos, 114–15
categories, 92–3
LOSC negotiations: archipelagic states, 107
Minquiers and Ecrehos, 1, 12, 47–8, 56, 58, 62, 97
New Caledonia *see* New Caledonia
Reunion *see* Reunion
territorial disputes, 71–2
Vanuatu and, 43
François Report, 103–4
free association, 84–5, 88–90
French Polynesia, 92–3, 102, 263
fringe of islands, 144, 146–9, 151, 153, 155, 166–70, 178, 199

Gabon, 176, 210
Galapagos Islands, 157–8
Geneva Conventions, 22, 154, 162, 190, 204
geography: definition of islands and, 6–9
Germany:
Galapagos Islands and, 158
Heligoland islands, 61
Indonesia and, 138
Kiel Canal, 256–7
Versailles Treaty (1919), 78
WWII occupation of Denmark, 232
Gilbert and Ellice Island, 220, 263
Greece:
Galapagos Islands and, 158
island territories, 58, 77, 87
territorial disputes, 65–6, 67
Greenland:
boundaries, 197–8, 206–7, 215
Denmark and, 41
Eastern Greenland, 1, 46–7, 51, 55, 58, 64–5, 232
human rights, 220
ice melt, 251
integration, 90–1
Jan Mayen and, 12–13
self-determination, 100, 227, 232–4, 238, 259
significance, 4
size, 8
status, 41, 233, 263
Grenada, 116, 124, 127, 132, 175, 235, 263
Grenadines *see* **St Vincent and Grenadines**
Guam, 76, 91, 92, 94, 264
Guinea-Bissau, 142, 235
Guyana, 194, 235

Hague Codification Conference (1930), 9, 21, 103, 188
Haiti, 41, 79, 113, 224, 235
Hawaii, 77, 87, 102, 114, 142, 145, 241, 264
health rights, 218, 224
Heathcote, Sarah, 231–2
historic waters, 170–1
Hodgson, RD, 144
Honduras:
archipelagic baselines and, 149
boundaries, 191, 201, 209–10, 215
ICJ case, 13
Land, Island and Maritime Frontier, 48–9, 176
Nicaragua v Honduras, 51–2, 191, 201, 215
United States and, 167
Hong Kong, 33, 220
human habitation: meaning, 15, 16
human rights:
Denarau Declaration on Human Rights (2015), 237
growth of international law, 76, 217–18
indigenous people, 261
island issues, 222–34, 259
overview, 217–38
sea level rise and, 4, 249–50
self-determination *see* self-determination
treaties: territorial scope, 218–22
Human Rights Watch, 223

Iceland:
boundaries, 206, 207
Cod Wars, 184
exclusive economic zones, 183–4
internal waters, 178
island territories, 206, 242

LOSC negotiations, 105
maritime boundaries, 34
sea levels, 242
status, 79, 122
ICERD, 217, 220, 238
independent states: status, 85–7
India:
Bangladesh v India, 204
boundaries, 204
island territories, 61, 77
Indian Ocean Commission, 236–7
indigenous people, 15, 71, 78, 186, 232, 249, 261
Indonesia:
Archipelagic and Islands States Forum and, 236
archipelagic sea lanes: designation, 138–40
archipelagic state, 102, 113, 116
baselines, 121, 129
LOSC negotiations, 105–8, 110–12
state practice, 126–7
decolonisation, 101
Dutch colonialism, 38
East Timor and, 39, 41, 60, 86
EEZs, 185
human rights, 223, 224
innocent passage, 132
island territories: acquisition, 61
maritime boundaries, 41, 115, 123, 126, 211
maritime disputes, 104
Papua New Guinea and, 41
Pulau Litigan and Pulau Sipadan, 50–1, 122
recognition, 119
security issues, 132, 137, 138
statehood, 79
innocent passage: archipelagic states, 130–3
Institut de Droit International, 103
integration, 90–1
Intergovernmental Panel on Climate Change (IPCC), 239, 241, 242
internal waters:
archipelagic states, 105, 125–6, 127, 132, 143
artificial islands, 21, 22, 33
baselines, 147, 178
bays, 174, 175, 177
dependent archipelagos, 150, 151
historic waters, 171, 172, 173
Indonesia, 107
land reclamation, 36
Philippines, 110, 129
regime, 254
International Civil Aviation Organization (ICAO), 136, 139
International Committee of Jurists, 78–9
International Covenant on Civil and Political Rights (ICCPR), 217, 219–20, 237–8
International Covenant on Economic, Social and Cultural Rights (ICESCR), 217, 238
International Criminal Court, 223–4
International Law Association, 103, 150, 240
International Law Commission (ILC):
archipelagic baselines, 147
archipelagic states, 103–4, 111
artificial islands, 21–2
definition of island, 9–10, 246
Fisheries Case and, 164, 165
historic waters, 171
island regime, 260
land reclamation, 243
maritime boundaries, 189, 249
regime of islands and, 253
sea-levels and, 239–40, 242, 251, 259
state responsibility, 256–7
International Maritime Organization (IMO), 139, 140
Inuit, 232
Ireland, 41, 85, 122, 158, 178
islands: definition *see* **definition of islands**
Italy, 77, 149, 167

Jamaica, 117, 122–3, 209, 215, 224, 235, 264, 267
Jan Mayen, 12–13, 197–8, 207, 215
Japan:
archipelagic state, 102
baselines, 149, 152
LOSC negotiations, 107
artificial islands, 34
colonialism, 38
continental shelf, 183
internal waters, 178
island territories, 17, 77
League of Nations mandates, 78
sea levels, 242
Ryukyu islands, 142
status, 101, 122
territorial disputes, 67–8, 70–1
Senkaku/Diaoyu Islands, 72–3
territorial sea, 179–80
United States and, 167
Jayewardene, HW, 1
Jayraman, K, 1
Jennings, R, 84–5
Jensen, JA, 233

Kiribati, 117, 119, 128, 132, 235, 237, 250, 263
Kopela, S, 2
Korea *see* **North Korea; South Korea**
Kyoto Protocol (1997), 239

land reclamation:
artificial islands, 6, 20, 33–5, 36, 243, 257–8
juridical islands, 179
sea level rise and, 243
South China Sea, 19, 28–32, 37, 246
Latvia, 158, 168, 207
League of Nations:
emergence, 76
mandates, 77–9, 226
Leeward Islands, 262, 264, 265
Libya, 175, 191, 214
lighthouses, 9, 10, 22, 53, 56, 68, 123
LOSC
see also UNCLOS I; UNCLOS II; UNCLOS III
archipelagic states *see* archipelagic states
artificial islands, 19, 23–9, 36, 37
bays, 174–8
contiguous zones, 11, 180
continental shelf, 11, 180–3
definition of islands *see* definition of islands
dependent archipelagos *see* dependent archipelagos
entitlements *see* specific entitlements
exclusive economic zones, 183–6
historic waters, 171–4
independence, 85
internal waters, 178
land reclamation, 33
maritime boundaries *see* boundaries
regime of islands and, 253–5, 257–8, 260–1
territorial sea, 178–80

Macau, 264
McDougal, MS, 22
Madagascar, 122, 164, 178, 211–12, 264
Malayan Union, 264
Malaysia:
archipelagic state, 113
artificial islands, 32
boundaries, 41, 123, 126, 205
human rights, 219
independence, 85
land reclamation, 34–5
Pedra Branca/Pulau Betu Puteh, Middle Rocks and South Ledge, 52–3
Pulau Litigan and Pulau Sipadan, 50–1, 122
South China Sea Islands *see South China Sea*

Maldives, 32, 67, 117, 128, 229, 235, 243, 245, 246
Malta, 10, 178, 191, 214, 244, 264
Man, Isle of, 77, 96, 175, 222
maritime boundaries *see* **boundaries**
Marshall Islands, 81, 88, 89, 94, 102, 117, 119, 128, 141, 212, 235, 237, 266
Mauritania, 176
Mauritius:
archipelagic state, 117
baselines, 122, 167
bays, 175, 177–8
boundaries, 211
Chagos Archipelago *see* Chagos Archipelago
independence, 85
innocent passage, 132
internal waters, 127
LOSC negotiations, 110, 111
recognition, 119
status, 235, 264
United States and, 167
Mayotte, 93, 227, 265
Mexico, 17, 45–6, 149, 167
Micronesia, 80, 88, 89, 94, 102, 212, 235, 266
migration, 244, 250
Minquiers, 1, 12, 47–8, 56, 58, 62, 97
Monaco, 41
Montevideo Convention (1933): statehood criteria, 40–2, 86, 97, 258
Montserrat, 91, 93, 220, 265
Mumby, P, 29
Munavvar, M, 2
Murphy, SD, 1
Myanmar, 158, 203–4, 215

Namibia, 226
NATO, 65–6
Nauru, 8, 41, 78, 80, 86, 178, 235, 237, 265
navigation rights: archipelagic states, 130–40
Netherlands:
colonialism, 38, 66, 98
Galapagos Islands and, 158
human rights: territorial scope, 220, 222
Island of Palmas, 44–5, 55, 61, 62
island territories, 44–5, 51, 76
cession, 61
LOSC negotiations: archipelagic states, 107
Netherlands Antilles, 112, 220, 222, 265
Netherlands Indies, 265
New Caledonia:
connection to metropole, 227
dependent archipelago, 145

disputes, 43
French acquisition, 71–2
self-determination, 2, 100, 227, 230–1, 238, 246
status, 76, 92, 93, 230, 265
New Guinea, 78, 80, 113, 115, 119, 127, 265, 266
New Hebrides, 71, 86, 145, 265
New Zealand:
baselines, 152
boundaries, 213
continental shelf, 182
Cook Islands *see* Cook Islands
dependent archipelagos, 145
island territories, 76–7, 87–9, 259
League of Nations mandates, 78
trust territories, 80
LOSC negotiations, 107
status, 79, 122
Nicaragua:
boundaries, 191, 201, 202–3
Land, Island and Maritime Frontier, 48–9, 176
Nicaragua v Colombia, 13, 18, 53–4, 202–3
Nicaragua v Honduras, 13, 51–2, 191, 201, 215
Nigeria, 194, 200, 210, 215
Niue, 88, 89, 235, 237, 265
non-self governing territories:
free association, 84–5
French categories, 92–2
human rights, 219, 222–3
integration, 90–1
list, 262–7
self-determination, 82–3, 90
status, 81–5
UK categories, 93–4
UN list, 91–2, 100
US categories, 94–6
North Korea, 99
Northern Mariana Islands, 81, 88, 95, 266
Norway:
baselines, 164–6
boundaries, 206–7
Jan Mayen, 197–8, 207, 215
Svalbard (Spitsbergen), 206–7, 215
Eastern Greenland, 1, 46–7, 51, 55, 58, 64–5, 232
Fisheries Case, 164–6
Greenland and, 232
Grisbårdana arbitration, 188
island territories, 12, 114
maritime disputes, 104
Svalbard (Spitsbergen), 98–9, 101, 142, 158–9, 206–7, 215

O'Connell, DP, 107
Oman, 149, 167
Organisation of African Unity, 66, 228
Orkney Islands, 208–9
overflight:
archipelagic states, 125, 130–40
civil aviation rules, 136, 139

Pacific Islands, 78, 80, 89, 95, 96, 266
Pacific Islands Forum, 2, 236–7, 240, 251, 252, 260
Palau, 80, 88, 89, 95, 152, 235, 237, 266
Palmas, 1, 44–5, 55, 61, 62, 74
Papadakis, N, 1–2
Papua New Guinea:
archipelagic state, 112, 117
Bougainville *see* Bougainville
boundaries, 115, 123, 127–8, 212–13, 214–15
EEZs, 186
human rights, 224
independence, 80, 85, 231
Indonesia and, 41
recognition, 43
status, 113, 235, 266
territorial sea, 179
territoriality, 58
Paris Agreement (2015), 239, 241
Paris Treaty (1814), 66, 228
Paris Treaty (1898), 44, 61, 108
Pharand, D, 173
Philippines:
archipelagic state, 102, 117
baselines, 121, 126–7, 129
LOSC negotiations, 105–6, 108–12
sea lanes, 139, 140
bays, 177
decolonisation, 101
human rights, 223–4
LOSC negotiations, 105–6, 108–12, 110
maritime disputes, 104
number of islands, 41
security issues, 132, 137
South China Sea Islands *see South China Sea*
Spanish cession, 61, 108–9
statehood, 79
pirates, 137
Pitcairn, 91, 93, 100, 220, 266

Portugal:
archipelagic baselines and, 149
Azores, 146, 176
bays, 176
dependent archipelagos, 146
East Timor and, 83, 86, 101–2
United States and, 167
Prescott, JRV, 115, 149, 150, 163, 170
Puerto Rico, 76, 88, 95, 209, 224–5, 227, 266

Qatar:
baselines, 168–9
boundaries, 199–200, 215
Qatar v Bahrain, 50, 168–9, 199–200, 215

recognition of states: international law, 42–3
Refugee Convention, 250
regime of islands:
fragments, 257–9
future, 260–1
international case law, 255–7
LOSC, 253–5, 257–8, 260–1
overview, 253–61
Reisman, WM, 149, 170
Réunion, 77, 93, 211, 211–12, 266
Rhodes, 244
Rio Declaration (1992), 234
Rockall, 8, 17, 18
rocks:
boundaries, 189–90
definition of islands and, 8
UNCLOS and, 11, 12, 15, 16
Romania, 192, 201–2
Russia, 3, 41, 70–1, 206

Sabah, 85, 265
St Helena, 91, 93, 220, 267
St Kitts and Nevis, 17, 235, 262, 264
St Lucia, 17, 235, 267
St Pierre and Miquelon, 93, 100, 186, 196–7, 215, 267
St Vincent and Grenadines, 17, 117, 127, 235, 267
Samoa:
American Samoa, 91, 94, 209, 262
Denarau Declaration on Human Rights (2015), 237
independence (1962), 80
internal waters, 178
status, 235
Western Samoa, 78, 80, 267
San Francisco Peace Treaty (1951), 61, 68, 72, 73, 75
Sao Tomé and Principe, 115, 117, 210–11, 214, 215, 235, 266
Sarawak, 85, 264, 266
Saudi Arabia, 61
Schofield, C, 149, 150, 163, 170
sea-level rise (SLR)
see also climate change
2021 Declaration, 240, 251, 260
archipelagic states, 245–6
artificial islands, 242–3, 246
climate science, 240–2
entitlements and, 246–9
Glasgow COP26, 2, 236
human rights and, 249–50
impact, 225, 239, 260–1
islands, 242–3
land reclamation and, 33, 243, 246
LOSC, 251
maritime boundaries and, 246–9
migration, 250
overview, 239–52
significance, 4
status, territoriality and, 243–5, 259
self-determination:
Aaland Islands, 99
Bougainvile, 231–2, 259
Chagos Archipelago, 228–9, 238, 259
emergence, 259
Faroe Islands, 232–4
form, 227
Greenland, 232–4, 238, 259
human right, 225–7
New Caledonia, 230–1, 238
NSGTs, 82–3, 90
UN right, 76, 82–3, 90, 95, 218, 225–6, 259
Seychelles, 118, 119, 128, 132, 182, 211, 228, 235, 266
Shearer, IA, 64
Shetland Islands, 208–9
Singapore:
artificial islands, 20, 32
boundaries, 205
continental shelf, 181
independence, 223
island territories, 58–9
land reclamation, 33–4, 34–5, 243
Pedra Branca/Pulau Betu Puteh, Middle Rocks and South Ledge, 52–3
status, 235, 266
small island developing states, 218, 234–7

Solomon Islands, 43, 112, 118, 119, 128, 132, 212, 214, 223, 235, 237, 262
South China Sea:
archipelagic baselines, 129–30, 152–3
archipelagic states, 120, 141
artificial islands, 19, 27–9, 36
case summary, 72–3
definition of island, 6, 15–16, 18, 243, 254, 257–8
dependent archipelagos, 156–7
historic bays, 176–7
historic waters, 56–7, 172, 173–4
impact, 37
land reclamation, 34, 35, 36, 246
significance, 2, 3–4, 12
state practice and, 16–17
straight baselines, 169
South Georgia, 93–4, 182–3
South Korea:
archipelagic baselines and, 149, 167
continental shelf, 183
island territories, 77
maritime disputes, 17, 67
Svalbard and, 99
United States and, 167
South Pacific Forum, 23
South Sandwich islands, 93–4, 182–3
Soviet Union, 99, 129
Spain:
Canary Islands, 159–60
colonialism, 69, 98
Galapagos Islands and, 158
island territories, 58
Philippines and, 108–9
special regimes, 98–9
Sri Lanka, 61, 177, 181, 223, 224
state practice:
archipelagic sea lanes: designation, 138–40
archipelagic states, 126–30
artificial islands, 22–3, 29–33
bays, 175–6, 177
continental shelf, 188–9
definition of islands, 16–18
dependent archipelagos, 154–60, 161
historic waters, 173
land reclamation, 33–4
maritime boundaries, 204–13, 248
state responsibility, 256–7
statehood:
independence, 85–7
loss, 218
Montevideo criteria, 40–2, 258
recognition, 42–3
self-determination, 76
size and, 41–2, 244
status
see also individual countries
categories, 76–7
constituent units of states, 87–8
current status, 85–99
free association, 84–5, 88–90
independent states, 85–7
integration, 90–1
international system, 77–9
international trustee system, 79–81
non-self-governing territories, 81–99
overview, 76–100
sea levels and, 243–5, 259
special regimes, 98–9
sui generis categories, 96–7
Sudan, 176
Suriname, 194
sustainable development, 234, 235
Svalbard (Spitsbergen), 98–9, 101, 142, 158–9, 206–7, 215
Sweden, 158, 207–8, 215
Symmons, CR, 2, 177

Taiwan, 4, 30, 39, 42, 72, 73, 97
territorial sea:
archipelagic states, 124
artificial islands, 26–7
boundary delimitation, 190, 191
entitlements, 178–80
UNCLOS Article 121, 11
territoriality:
boundary treaties and awards, 63
current disputes, 39–40, 65–73
Aegean Sea/Mediterranean Sea, 65–6, 249
Cyprus, 67
Dokdo/Takeshima, 67–8
Falklands, 68–9
Hans Island (Tartupaluk), 69–70
Kuril Islands, 70–1
Mattthew and Hunter Islands, 71–2
Senkaku/Diaoyu Islands, 72
South China Sea Islands *see South China Sea*
current law, 54–65
annexation, 60
cession, 60–1
contiguity, 58–9
critical date, 62–3
discovery, 57

distinctive territorial features, 64–5
effective control, 55–6
effectivités, 55–6
historic title, 56–7
historical consolidation, 63
intertemporal law, 62
subsequent conduct, 63–4
uti possidetis, 59
historical cases, 44–8
Clipperton Island, 45–6
Eastern Greenland, 1, 46–7, 51, 55, 58, 64–5, 232
Island of Palmas, 44–5
Minquiers and Ecrehos, 47–8
international law, 40–3
modern cases, 48–54
Eritrea/Yemen Arbitral Award, 49–50
Land, Island and Maritime Frontier, 48–9, 176
Nicaragua v Columbia, 53–4
Nicaragua v Honduras, 51–2
Pedra Branca/Pulau Betu Putch, 52–3
Pulau Litigan and Pulau Sipadan, 50–1
Qatar v Bahrain, 50
overview, 38–75
sea levels and, 243–5, 259
size and, 41–2, 244
Thailand, 149, 167
Timor Leste:
baselines, 122, 128–9, 245
boundaries, 123, 195
independence, 85, 227
Indonesian occupation, 39, 41
status, 86, 113, 266
Tokelau, 23, 76, 87–8, 92, 221, 246, 259, 267
Tonga, 23, 111, 235, 237
Trinidad and Tobago, 10, 118, 132, 195, 200, 235, 267
Truman Proclamation (1945), 180, 188–9
Trümpler, K, 150
trust territories, 79–81, 95, 226, 262–7
Turkey, 65–6, 67, 87
Turks and Caicos, 91, 220, 267
Tuvalu, 41, 86, 118, 124, 127, 132, 141, 220, 235, 237, 263

Ukraine, 129, 192, 201–2
Ulfstein, G, 98–9
UNCLOS I
see also LOSC
archipelagic states, 104–5, 107
artificial islands, 22
baselines, 164, 165–6
maritime boundaries, 189
UNCLOS II
see also LOSC
archipelagic states, 105
UNCLOS III
see also LOSC
archipelagic states, 106, 110–12, 140
artificial islands, 23, 23–5
baselines, 166
navigation rights, 130
uninhabited islands, 46, 51, 70, 71, 72, 77, 82, 94, 98, 182, 185–6, 199, 211, 232
United Arab Emirates, 32
United Kingdom:
bays, 175, 177
boundaries, 41, 208–9
Anglo-French Arbitration, 196, 200, 214
Caribbean, 209
Chagos Archipelago *see* Chagos Archipelago
Channel Islands and, 96–7
Cod Wars, 184
colonialism, 86
Dominican Republic and, 128
exclusive economic zones, 183–4
Falklands Islands *see* Falklands Islands
Fisheries Case, 164–6
Galapagos Islands and, 158
human rights: territorial scope, 220, 222
internal waters, 178
island territories, 51, 58, 77
categories, 93–4
cession, 61
League of Nations mandates, 78
status, 102
islands, 8, 17
Isle of Wight, 77
LOSC negotiations, 105, 107
maritime disputes, 103, 104
Minquiers and Ecrehos, 1, 12, 47–8, 56, 58, 62, 97
New Hebrides, 71, 86, 145, 265
Philippines and, 110
state practice, 177
status, 79, 122
territorial sea, 180
United Nations:
archipelagic baselines, 147–8
Chagos Archipelago and, 66, 228, 229
decolonisation and, 76, 100, 230
East Timor and, 86
Global Compact for Migration, 250

human rights, 217–22, 237–8
International Trusteeship System, 79–81, 95
New Caledonia and, 230
non-self governing territories: list, 91–2
Office for Ocean Affairs and the Law of the Sea, 166–7, 181
self-determination, 76, 82–3, 90, 95, 218, 225–6, 259
small island developing states, 234–7
Special Committee on Decolonization, 76
state centrism, 113
statehood and, 76
status of islands, 79–85
sustainable development and, 234, 235
territorial annexation and, 60
territorial disputes and, 73
UNGA Resolution 1541, 83, 87, 90
United Nations Framework Convention on Climate Change (UNFCC, 1992), 239
United States:
archipelagic states and, 128
baselines, 149, 160–1
Indonesia, 138
LOSC negotiations, 107
Philippines and, 61, 108–9, 110, 129
sea lanes, 139
baselines and, 149, 160–1, 167
bays and, 176, 177–8
boundaries: Caribbean, 209
Chagos Archipelago and, 228
Chile and, 155
China and, 156, 167
colonialism, 38
Faroe Islands and, 157
Hawaii *see* Hawaii
historic waters and, 171–2
human rights and, 224
Island of Palmas, 44–5, 55, 61, 62
island territories, 3, 44–5, 76, 87, 88, 89
acquisition, 61
categories, 94–6
League of Nations mandates, 78
LOSC negotiations, 105, 107
maritime disputes, 103
Myanmar and, 158
Northwest Passage, 155
Universal Declaration of Human Rights (1948), 217, 237
US Virgin Islands, 91, 92, 94, 209, 267
uti possidetis, 59

Vanuatu, 43, 71–2, 86, 102, 115, 118, 124, 132, 177, 235, 237, 265
Vatican, 41, 244, 258
Venezuela, 17
Versailles Treaty (1919), 78, 256
Vienna Convention on the Law of Treaties, 219, 248, 249
Vietnam, 160
South China Sea Islands *see South China Sea*

Ward, S, 29
Watts, A, 84–5
Westerman, GS, 149, 170
Wight, Isle of, 77
WTO, 260

Yemen: ***Eritrea/Yemen Arbitral Award***, 49–50, 56, 168, 193, 198–9
Young, MA, 253, 255, 257

www.ingramcontent.com/pod-product-compliance
Ingram Content Group UK Ltd.
Pitfield, Milton Keynes, MK11 3LW, UK
UKHW020905190926
475560UK00010B/284

9 781509 955428